BAR INTERNATIONAL S

An Introduction to Gender Archaeology

ISABELLE ALGRAIN AND LAURA MARY

BAR
PUBLISHING

Published in 2025 by
BAR Publishing, Oxford, UK

BAR International Series 3247

An Introduction to Gender Archaeology

ISBN 978 1 4073 6332 5 paperback
ISBN 978 1 4073 6333 2 e-format

DOI https://doi.org/10.30861/9781407363325

A catalogue record for this book is available from the British Library

Originally published in French: © Isabelle Algrain & Laura Mary. 2024. *Introduction à l'archéologie du genre*. Éditions Fedora, Collection Simple & Précis: Talence. ISBN: 979-10-96137-20-6

COVER IMAGE: *Hydria attributed to the Class of Hamburg 1917.477. The Metropolitan Museum of Art, New York, inv. 06.1021.77. Rogers Fund, 1906. Ca. 510-500 BC (www.metmuseum.org); and archaeological excavations southeast of Borg Church at the ruins of Borgholm Castle. Source: Excavated memories From Skedemosse to Sandby Borg. Editors Kjell-Håkan Arnell & Ludvig Papmehl-Dufay, text by Stibéus. Bernving, Allan – Kalmar County Museum, Sweden – Public Domain.*

BACK COVER IMAGE: *Ulf Erik Hagberg and possibly Margareta Beskow are conducting archaeological surveys in Bredsättra parish, 1970. Bernving, Allan - Kalmar County Museum, Sweden - Public Domain.*

BAR
PUBLISHING

BAR titles are available from:

BAR Publishing
122 Banbury Rd, Oxford, OX2 7BP, UK
info@barpublishing.com
www.barpublishing.com

Of Related Interest

Gender Locales and Local Genders in Archaeology
Edited by Tove Hjørungdal
BAR International Series **1425** | 2005

From the Ground Up: Beyond Gender Theory in Archaeology
Proceedings of the Fifth Gender and Archaeology Conference, University of Wisconsin-Milwaukee, October 1998
Edited by Nancy L. Wicker and Bettina Arnold
BAR International Series **812** | 1999

The Future is Indigenous
Stories from the new Native North America Hall at the Field Museum
Edited by Alaka Wali and Tom Skwerski
BAR International Series **3194** | 2024

Blame it on the Gender
Identities and transgressions in Antiquity
Edited by Maria Cristina de la Escosura Balbás, Elena Duce Pastor, Patricia González Gutiérrez, María del Mar Rodríguez Alcocer and David Serrano Lozano
BAR International Series **3005** | 2020

The Archaeology of Hassanamesit Woods
The Sarah Burnee/Sarah Boston Farmstead
Edited by Stephen Mrozowski and Heather Law Pezzarossi
BAR International Series **3202** | 2024

La desigualdad de género en la Prehistoria ibérica
Una aproximación multi-variable
Marta Cintas-Peña
BAR International Series **2990** | 2020

A Consideration of Gender Roles and Relations in the Aegean Bronze Age Interpreted from Gestures and Proxemics in Art
Susan E. Poole
BAR International Series **2980** | 2020

Genre et hiérarchisation dans le monde nord-alpin, aux âges du Bronze et du Fer
Caroline Trémeaud
BAR International Series **2912** | 2018

Roles for Men and Women in Roman Epigraphic Culture and Beyond
Gender, social identity and cultural practice in private Latin inscriptions and the literary record
Peter Keegan
BAR International Series **2626** | 2014

Landscapes of Gender, Age and Cosmology
Burial Perceptions in Viking Age Iceland
Ruth Ann Maher
BAR International Series **2529** | 2013

The Archaeology of Gender, Love and Sexuality in Pompeii
Lourdes Conde Feitosa
BAR International Series **2533** | 2013

The Gendered Landscape
A discussion on gender, status and power in the Norwegian Viking Age landscape
Marianne Moen
BAR International Series **2207** | 2011

Gender Identities in Italy in the First Millennium BC
Edited by Edward Herring and Kathryn Lomas
BAR International Series **1983** | 2009

Aspects of Gender Identity and Craft Production in the European Migration Period
Iron Weaving Beaters and Associated Textile Making Tools from England, Norway and Alamannia
Sue Harrington
BAR International Series **1797** | 2008

Engendering Northern Plains Paleoindian Archaeology
Decision-making and gender roles in subsistence and settlement strategies
Caroline R. Hudecek-Cuffe
BAR International Series **699** | 1998

This book is dedicated to all those
who were once told
that their research did not matter.

Contents

Part Two – Interpreting the past through a gender lens

Part Three – The place of women and minorities in the profession

List of Figures

List of Tables

Foreword

This book provides an English translation of an essential volume published in 2024, by Belgian scholars Isabelle Algrain and Laura Mary. An important addition to anglophone literature, I am delighted to recommend this work to the reader at a significant juncture, twenty-five years after Marie-Louise Stig Sørensen's *Gender Archaeology*. The current volume joins a substantial and growing literature across Europe and will become the go-to textbook for its generation, with clear contemporary definitions of gender, a global history of gender archaeology and the move to intersectionality, how gender informs archaeological method, and the place of women and minorities in the global profession.

As co-founder of British Women Archaeologists in 2008 – a volunteer lobby group working to document the female experience of British archaeology in the absence of a sector equality agenda since the late 1990s – I have long admired and supported the work of our sister group in Belgium and France, Paye Ta Truelle. Established in 2017, Paye Ta Truelle has been working creatively to raise consciousness about the specific working conditions of women in French archaeology in the post-MeToo age. Over the last decade, sessions at the European Association of Archaeologists revealed that the experience of women archaeologists, as documented by the BWA in Britain, were mirrored across Europe and in urgent need of collaborative work.

My own interest in gender archaeology was inspired by the 1990s teaching of Marga Díaz-Andreu. As I started postgraduate study in 1998, Sara Champion recorded that there were just two women professors in UK archaeology. In a TAG session in 2008, an all-male panel stated that young archaeologists were no longer political, to which a young man shouted, 'Where are the women?'. I've spent my career working to answer that question, uncovering how a new discipline, with good women's involvement in the 1930s and 1940s, became so male-dominated by the time I entered; how self-proclaimed 'objective' scholars could so entirely write women out of the past. In my youth, gender archaeology was a fringe session at conferences. It is now mainstream. This volume marks the completion of that transition.

This book also documents the scale of additional labour that has rested with my generation of women archaeologists, with the generation before us, and yet still with young women today. Women scholars and fieldworkers must not only provide period or field specialism but must also create volunteer structures outside of institutional management to support women and minority archaeologists through workplace discrimination, harassment, and assault. We must also, in our evenings and weekends, analyse sector data and lobby bullish institutions who fail at instituting basic equality legislation. Archaeology is political. Additionally so for women. Yet more so for women of colour, working-class women, disabled women, young women and parents. Until we understand this basic principle, our sector will not progress.

This volume neatly pulls together where we are now. A statement of a new generation still having to work on four fronts: building method for the integration of women in past societies, from which they have previously been excluded or wildly stereotyped; understanding how gender works in contemporary society and how it was used to exclude women from the 20th century discipline; supporting and informing women and minority archaeologists in the present; and rewriting disciplinary histories to reintegrate those pioneering past women archaeologists so deliberately left out of our textbooks. Part of this too is recognising the action of previous generations, documenting and working across generations of activism, adapting as we go. We are not the first generation to be active and we will not be the last.

This work is particularly important in a political present in which gender studies programmes were closed down in Hungary in 2018, in which Afghan women have been increasingly stripped of their human rights under Taliban rule since 2021, as Danish politicians condemned academics researching gender in 2021, with attacks on scholars studying gendered children's play in Italy in 2024, the US Trump administration going yet further in 2025 – withdrawing scientific funding for any research focused on women, gender, or race whilst also denying women their reproductive rights amidst a popular 'trad wife' movement, as the UK moved to strip trans women of their human right to self-identify. In a climate such as this, studying gender archaeology is political. This is why we must do it even harder.

Isabelle Algrain and Laura Mary provide us with a contemporary call to arms in their important statement-of-a-generation. They record where we are to date on understanding gender as both social artefact and biological phenomenon, on the history of gender archaeology as a sub-discipline, on contemporary intersectional practice, on gender and archaeological method, and on the critical intersectional basis of our activism. Written in clear and accessible style, it is a great entry point for those still catching up on the revolution in archaeology since the 1980s. I hope you will enjoy reading it as much as I did.

Rachel Pope

Co-chair of AGE – Archaeology and Gender in Europe

Preface to the French edition

'The advent of gender studies arguably has marked one of the most significant developments in the last 50 years in archaeological practice and theory[1].'

'Gender archaeology has finally become a well-established part of the discipline, but still a sense of marginality lingers[2].'

While writing this book, we were immediately confronted with a paradox. Although quotations similar to the above appear regularly in books, articles and reviews on the subject to emphasise the significant impact of gender studies in archaeology over the last 50 years, the 'feeling of marginality' is still prevalent. Attitudes towards this subject, which is rarely taught in our universities, range from interest and ignorance to mistrust and rejection. Rose-Marie Lagrave's 1990 analysis of the reception of gender studies in general can also be applied to gender archaeology in particular: 'The institutional integration that has characterised feminist studies as a whole has diverted their subversive character in favour of their marginal and devalued inclusion in the scientific field'.

An increasing number of studies, special journal issues, symposiums, documentaries, popular science magazines, master's theses and doctoral dissertations are now addressing this issue in the French-speaking world. The aim of this book is to dispel the 'feeling of marginality' and demonstrate the importance of considering gender in archaeological research. It offers a didactic overview of gender archaeology with the aim of making it accessible to a wide audience of researchers and students, including archaeologists, anthropologists, and those in related fields.

Although this book is titled An Introduction to Gender Archaeology, it does not propose a particular methodology, but rather explores the history of the discipline through case studies and examples from various regions and periods. Although gender archaeology is based on unique questions, we attempt to answer them using traditional archaeological methods such as excavations and the analysis of material culture, as well as interdisciplinary approaches such as anthropology, sociology, and feminist theory. Therefore, there is no miracle method or one-size-fits-all approach to conducting gender archaeological research. This book covers a period of more than 40 years and explores a variety of research themes, ranging from physical anthropology and discrimination within the profession to interpretations of remains. Clearly, our presentation can only be brief. Nevertheless, we hope that it will demonstrate how studying gender can provide new insights into past societies and cultures, as well as our own profession.

In the introduction, we will define the terms 'gender' and 'sex', and trace their history and transformation. These are key notions for understanding gender archaeology. Gender is a fundamental aspect of our identity and influences many areas of our lives. Although gender is often seen as binary, with individuals classified as male or female, it is in fact a much more fluid and dynamic concept that can vary according to culture and time. The social, cultural and historical constructions of gender are shaped by a variety of factors, including biology, psychology, and social norms and expectations. Another important aspect of gender studies that archaeology must take into account is intersectionality, which has become increasingly important in recent years. This concept recognises the interconnected nature of social categories such as race, gender, age, class and sexuality, and how they interact to shape individual experiences. Intersectionality recognises that individuals are not simply defined by one category, but by the intersection of many. Understanding the interconnected nature of these categories is essential to gaining a comprehensive understanding of the complexities of gender. Finally, this introduction will define gender archaeology.

The first part will examine the influence of feminism on the development of gender archaeology, focusing particularly on how it has challenged traditional interpretations of the past. Emerging in the 1980s, the archaeology of gender aimed to emphasise the significance of women's roles in human societies throughout history. Research in this field aims to demonstrate how gender has been constructed and performed differently in various societies and cultures, and the influence this has had on social, political, and economic relations. We will also see that gender archaeology has evolved differently in various countries, reflecting their unique cultural and historical contexts. Finally, gender archaeology shares common concerns with other fields of research, such as the study of social structures and power relations, which form the basis of decolonial archaeology and Indigenous archaeology. Archaeology has been addressing issues of race and racism for several decades. It is also beginning to consider questions of sexuality and gender identity, particularly through the fields of queer archaeology and the archaeology of sexuality. These different fields of research aim to gain a more complete understanding of the past and challenge traditional narratives that have often excluded women and marginalised groups.

[1] Nicholas 2009, 150.
[2] Sørensen 2000, 3.

The second part of the book delves into the heart of gender studies in archaeology, beginning with funerary contexts. More specifically, we will explore the methods used to determine the sex of individuals, as well as the insights that sex estimation can provide into gender. The objects that accompany the deceased provide the most obvious starting point for addressing gender-related issues, and one chapter will present a number of case studies demonstrating the contributions of gender archaeology to the analysis of funerary offerings. We will then examine various themes that demonstrate the 'performativity' of gender, i.e. how women's and men's identities are constructed through material culture. We will also consider the gendered division of labour in ancient societies before examining interpretations of images produced by these societies. Finally, we will consider how our contemporary understanding of gender influences our interpretation of archaeological remains, and how we can present a more nuanced and inclusive understanding of gender in museums.

In the third part, we will examine the sexism, racism, classism, LGBT+phobia and ableism experienced by archaeologists in their professional lives. These issues must be acknowledged as they influence not only our approach to and interpretation of archaeological sites and artefacts, but also the relationships between archaeologists. As Rachel Pope points out, 'a patriarchal discipline can only produce a patriarchal past[3]'. The present and the past are inextricably linked, which is why we have detailed the research being conducted on these subjects. It is crucial that archaeologists are aware of these forms of discrimination and prejudice, and actively promote diversity, equity, and inclusion in their research and professional practice. This may involve amplifying diverse perspectives, creating safe and inclusive working environments, or providing greater representation and opportunities for marginalised groups within the profession.

This book would never have been published without the advice, participation and support of many people. It exists thanks to the support of Pierre Dejarnac, our editor at Éditions Fedora. We would like to thank him sincerely for his enthusiasm, trust and wise advice. We would also like to express our warmest thanks to Béline Pasquini and Ségolène Vandevelde, our colleagues, comrades-in-arms and, above all, our friends. The three years of research and writing that culminated in the publication of this book were characterised by our passionate and enlightening exchanges. The book would not be what it is today without their rigorous proofreading, pertinent suggestions and kind encouragement. We would also like to thank Benoît Fourneau for his unwavering support and for proofreading the entire book, not to mention his ruthless slaying of overly long sentences and superfluous commas. We would also like to thank Alexandra Boucherie for her advice and pertinent remarks on identifying the sex of individuals in funerary archaeology, as well as Caroline Trémeaud. Finally, we would like to thank our respective parents, our first proofreaders and lifelong supporters.

[3] Pope 2021.

Preface to the English edition

Translating a book is never straightforward, especially when it involves handling delicate concepts such as those at the heart of gender studies. This book was originally written for a French-speaking audience that, until recently, had limited exposure to gender archaeology as a formalised field of study. In most Francophone European countries, gender archaeology only began to gain traction in the 2010s and remains unevenly integrated into academic curricula and research agendas.

Consequently, this volume was conceived as an accessible, comprehensive introduction to gender archaeology for students, early-career researchers and anyone with an interest in the subject. It is intended to serve as an introduction to the discipline, which is still largely absent from university teaching in the French-speaking world. As this book was published in French in January 2024 and is a translation, the bibliography is not comprehensive for the past two years, except for a few selected titles.

As it was written in French for a Francophone audience, the book is also deeply informed by Francophone intellectual traditions, particularly in sociology, anthropology and feminist theory. Readers familiar with Anglo-American approaches may notice that some of the theoretical underpinnings diverge from those commonly encountered in the United Kingdom or United States. In particular, our definition of gender is strongly influenced by French materialist feminism, a tradition that views gender as a power relationship – a system of domination structured around two opposing social groups: women and men. This conceptual framework reflects a specific intellectual lineage that continues to shape feminist and critical thinking in many Francophone contexts. Nevertheless, we believe that the themes, methods and case studies presented here remain relevant and accessible regardless of national or disciplinary boundaries.

Ultimately, we hope that this English edition will provide students, professors and researchers, wherever they are based, with a valuable introduction to gender archaeology. We hope it will encourage new reflections, critical perspectives and conversations across linguistic and academic divides.

We are deeply grateful to our editor at BAR Publishing, Jacqueline Senior, for her support in bringing this translation to fruition and for helping to make this work accessible to a wider international audience.

Introduction

8 September 2017. The scientific journal *American Journal of Biological Anthropology* publishes an article entitled 'A female Viking warrior confirmed by genomics[4]'. The title is catchy, even provocative. The article reveals that the skeleton buried in Birka's tomb Bj 581 is in fact the skeleton of a woman. The sex was determined by DNA analysis. Since the discovery of this tomb in 1878, archaeologists have believed it to be the final resting place of a Viking chieftain. 'He' had all the appearances of one, buried with a sword, an axe, a spear, piercing arrows, a combat knife, two shields, two horses (a mare and a stallion) and a strategy game.

In the days that followed, the press picked up on the discovery. The magazine *Science* headlined 'DNA proves fearsome Viking warrior was a woman[5]', comparing the deceased to 'a figure from Richard Wagner's *Ride of the Valkyries*' and suggesting that the discovery proved 'a surprising degree of gender balance in the Vikings' violent social order'. *The Guardian* seems more cautious in its headline, asking: 'Does new DNA evidence prove that there were female viking warlords?' [6]; the photograph that follows the headline shows actress Katheryn Winnick as Lagertha in the series *Vikings*. A few days later, the newspaper emphasised the androcentric nature of archaeology with a new article entitled 'How the female Viking warrior was written out of history[7]'. *The New York Times* also presented the discovery with the following question: 'A female Viking warrior? Tomb study yields clues[8]', but is more circumspect in its presentation of the results. *The Washington Post* takes the prize for sensationalism with its headline 'Wonder Woman lived: Viking warrior skeleton identified as female, 128 years after its discovery[9]'.

Can a single grave call into question 150 years of research into the role of women in society? Can it prove, as the newspapers say, 'a surprising degree of gender balance in the Vikings' violent social order'? Doesn't this kind of announcement tell us more about our own claims about the place of women in our societies than about the women of the past? As we shall see in this book, gender issues are more complex than sensationalist newspaper headlines would have us believe.

1. What is gender?

Before we explore further the links between gender and archaeology, we first need to define what we mean by 'gender', in order to differentiate it from 'sex'. Sociologists Laure Bereni, Sébastien Chauvin, Alexandre Jaunait and Anne Revillard define gender as '**a system of hierarchical bicategorisation between the sexes (male/female) and between the values and representations associated with them (masculine/feminine)**[10]'. This definition is complemented by four analytical dimensions that are important for understanding gender as a concept. We detail these four dimensions in the following lines, following their chronological order of appearance in gender studies.

1.1. Gender is a social construct

The famous quote from Simone de Beauvoir's book, *The Second Sex*, could sum up the idea that gender is socially constructed. It takes on its full meaning when quoted in its entirety: 'One is not born, but rather becomes, a woman. No biological, psychological, or economic destiny defines the figure that the human female acquires in society; it is civilization as a whole that develops this product, intermediate between female and eunuch, which one calls feminine[11]'. This idea is opposed to that of essentialist theories, for which the immutable and universal characteristics of the feminine and masculine are rooted in the biological difference between the sexes.

Gender, far from being universal and unchanging, varies in time and space. The social perception of colours and clothing in the Western world provide particularly enlightening examples of this phenomenon. Today, certain items, such as pink clothes and high heels, clearly seem to belong to the feminine world. But these associations have not always been obvious. Since Antiquity, red and pink have often been symbolically associated with power and violence. They have therefore often been associated with men, particularly from the upper classes, even if this association tended to decline from the 16th century onwards[12]. From the mid-19th century onwards, the colour blue, through the wearing of sailor suits, gradually became associated with little boys, and it was not until the 1950s that the association pink/girls and blue/boys really took hold[13]. Similarly, the heeled shoe was not a gender symbol but a class symbol before the French Revolution, since it was worn by an aristocracy wishing to rise above the plebs.

[4] Hedenstierna-Jonsson *et al.* 2017.
[5] Price 2017.
[6] Cocozza 2017.
[7] Norton 2017.
[8] Anderson 2017.
[9] Nutt 2017.

[10] Bereni *et al.* 2020, 5–8, 8 for the quote ('un système de bicatégorisation hiérarchisé entre les sexes (hommes/femmes) et entre les valeurs et représentations qui leur sont associées (masculin/féminin)'). All foreign language quotations have been translated into English; the original can be found in the footnotes.
[11] De Beauvoir 1949, 13 ('On ne naît pas femme, on le devient. Aucun destin biologique, psychique, économique ne définit la figure que revêt au sein de la société la femelle humaine ; c'est l'ensemble de la civilisation qui élabore ce produit intermédiaire entre le mâle et le castrat qu'on qualifie de féminin').
[12] Beauvalet-Boutouyrie & Berthiaud 2015, 202; Bereni *et al.* 2020, 120.
[13] Beauvalet-Boutouyrie & Berthiaud 2015, 229; Paoletti 2012, 89.

When the heeled shoe reappeared at the end of the 19th century, it became a feminine attribute[14]. The expression of gender can therefore vary greatly over time.

Similarly, the variability of gender among certain populations such as the Inuit is expressed by the idea that sex and gender are not necessarily linked. An individual can be male and have a female gender identity, as Françoise Héritier tells us:

> 'Among the Inuit, identity and gender are not a function of anatomical sex but of the gender of the reincarnated name-soul. Nevertheless, when the time comes, the individual must engage in the activities and aptitudes of his or her apparent sex (tasks and reproduction), even though his or her identity and gender will always be a function of his or her soul-name. A boy can be raised and considered as a girl until puberty because of his feminine soul-name, fulfil his role as a male reproducer in adulthood and then carry out masculine tasks within the family group, while retaining his soul-name, i.e. his feminine identity, throughout his life[15]'.

In concrete terms, this means that interpersonal relationships are more important than a child's biological sex in the construction of his or her social identity[16].

More generally, these examples show us that being a man or a woman was not the same in Antiquity, in the Middle Ages or today, in Asia, Europe or other parts of the world.

1.2. Gender is a relational process

A common mistake is to link gender studies exclusively to the study of women. However, 'the characteristics associated with each sex are socially constructed in a relationship of opposition. It is therefore impossible to study women and the feminine without linking the analysis to men and the masculine[17]'. As we shall see, the introduction of gender into the various branches of the humanities and social sciences has made it possible to go beyond the first feminist approaches and theories, which felt the need, in archaeology, history and sociology alike, to re-establish a balance and compensate for a certain 'invisibility' of women.

> **Feminism**: Elsa Dorlin defines feminism as 'the tradition of thought, and consequently the historical movements, which, at least since the 17th century, have posited the equality of men and women according to various demonstrative logics, hunting down prejudices relating to the inferiority of women or denouncing the iniquity of their condition[18]'.

Studying a society, an archaeological context or an object through the prism of gender is a complex task that is not limited to highlighting the women of the past. Gender helps to explore the relationships between individuals or groups of individuals, the relationships of domination exercised by one group over another, the strategies of expression of subaltern groups, the way in which an object can be used to assert an identity, and the organisation and gendered division of labour and tasks. Since the 1990s, following the work of Raewyn Connell, there has been a growing body of work on masculinities, contributing to a renewal of research[19].

1.3. Gender is a power relationship

In the human species there is a biological binarity, i.e. males and females with clearly marked anatomical differences. Françoise Héritier has clearly shown that the biological difference between women and men serves as the basis for conceptualising the difference between the feminine and the masculine, and that this difference is always thought of in hierarchical terms[20]. The value placed on the difference between the sexes, and therefore on each sex, is eminently social and not biological. At the root of this power relationship between the masculine and the feminine, she argues, is the 'differential valence of the sexes' (*valence différentielle des sexes*), which constitutes one of the major social invariants in addition to those identified by Claude Lévi-Strauss (the incest taboo, the institution of a legal or recognised form of stable union and the gendered division of tasks)[21]:

> 'The differential valence of the sexes reflects the different place that is universally given to the two sexes on a table of values, and signals the dominance of the masculine principle over the feminine principle. The male/female relationship is constructed on the same

---

[14] Persson 2015.

[15] Héritier 1996, 21–22 ('Chez les Inuits, l'identité et le genre ne sont pas fonction du sexe anatomique mais du genre de l'âme-nom réincarnée. Néanmoins, l'individu doit s'inscrire dans les activités et aptitudes qui sont celles de son sexe apparent (tâches et reproduction) le moment venu, même si son identité et son genre seront toujours fonction de son âme-nom. Un garçon peut être, de par son âme-nom féminine, élevé et considéré comme une fille jusqu'à la puberté, remplir son rôle d'homme reproducteur à l'âge adulte et se livrer dès lors à des tâches masculines au sein du groupe familial, tout en conservant sa vie durant, son âme-nom, c'est-à-dire son identité féminine').

[16] Walley 2020, 25.

[17] Bereni *et al.* 2020, 6 ('les caractéristiques associées à chaque sexe sont socialement construites dans une relation d'opposition. Dès lors, on ne peut étudier ce qui relève des femmes et du féminin sans articuler l'analyse avec les hommes et le masculin').

[18] Dorlin 2008, 9 ('Tradition de pensée, et par voie de conséquence les mouvements historiques, qui, au moins depuis le XVIIe s., ont posé selon des logiques démonstratives diverses l'égalité des hommes et des femmes, traquant les préjugés relatifs à l'infériorité des femmes ou dénonçant l'iniquité de leur condition.').

[19] On masculinities, see Connell 2014 (1995).

[20] Héritier 1996.

[21] Structuralism has been criticised by feminists, in particular by Rubin 1998 (1975), 5 because, while the theory of invariant structures clearly shows the process of subordination and the mechanisms presiding over the production of gendered individuals, it fails to take into account the social and political dimension of gendered division, which is embodied in compulsory heterosexuality (see Dorlin 2008, 58).

> model as the parent/child relationship, the elder/cadet relationship and, more generally, the anterior/posterior relationship, with anteriority signifying superiority[22]'.

The idea of an asymmetrical and hierarchical relationship between women and men has been theorised since the 1970s, notably by French materialist feminists. Christine Delphy, Nicole-Claude Mathieu and Colette Guillaumin articulate this power relationship around the notion of 'patriarchy', which Pierre Bourdieu studied under the name of 'male domination[23]' and which, for Delphy, constitutes the 'main enemy' that needs to be dismantled[24]. In their view, patriarchy is the system by which men appropriate women's productive work (economy and domestic production) and reproductive work (their body).

Gender is thus a 'social, cultural and political construction [...] of hierarchical norms of femininity, masculinity and heterosexuality[25]'. Norms specify what is authorised, tolerated or prohibited according to the sex to which an individual belongs, and are materialised both in appearance, behaviour, practices and objects, and in social relations between women and men. For example, it is 'normal' for a boy to play football and a girl to dance, for a woman to have long hair and a man short hair, for a woman to wear a skirt and a man trousers, for a woman to study literature and a man mathematics. All this has very little to do with biology and everything to do with learning 'feminine' and 'masculine' behaviour.

As well as imposing behaviours that are specific to each sex, gender also imposes a hierarchy of norms, the most important of which is heteronormativity. This concept, popularised in particular by Adrienne Rich's work on compulsory heterosexuality, highlights the existence of a normative dimension in terms of sex, gender, sexual orientation and gender roles[26]. Behaviour that deviates from the norm is seen as a social transgression.

1.4. Gender is interwoven with other relations of power

Intersectionality was defined and popularised by Kimberlé Crenshaw in a 1989 article on the dual oppression of African-American women as women *and* as Black people[27]. According to Sirma Bilge and Patricia Hill Collins:

> 'Intersectionality examines the way in which interlocking relations of power influence social relations in different societies, as well as the experience of individuals in everyday life. As an analytical tool, intersectionality considers the categories of race, class, gender, sexuality, nationality, ability, ethnicity and age – among others – to be interdependent and shaped by each other. Intersectionality is a way of understanding and explaining the complexity of the world, of people and of human experience[28].'

In other words, this concept makes it possible to study the interweaving of different power relationships by considering that the categories 'women' and 'men' are not homogenous. For example, patriarchal oppression will be experienced differently by a White or racialised woman (i.e. a victim of racist discrimination), by a heterosexual or lesbian woman, by a cisgender or transgender woman, by a manager or a cleaner. Relationships of power are therefore interwoven to produce specific relationships of domination.

2. Sex or gender?

Once the contours of the concept of gender have been defined, the question arises of the relationship between gender and sex. Early definitions of gender put forward the idea of a 'social sex' including all the non-biological differences between women and men, as opposed to a strictly biological sex. But what is really the case? What are the links between sex and gender? Is sex strictly linked to biology or is it also constructed? The delimitation of these two concepts is all the more important given that, in many human societies, they have been and/or still are used indiscriminately. Before the concept of gender was created, they were mostly considered to be one and the same thing: sex, determined solely by biology. This representation of the sex/gender system[29] explains why we used to attribute a biological origin to socially and culturally constructed behaviours. The idea that gender roles are intrinsically linked to biology is not new. The biological destiny of women and men has been the subject of 'research' since Antiquity. Philosophers such as Aristotle and doctors such as Galen wrote extensively on the subject and had a lasting influence on the way the West conceived of the sexes and their differences. In order to gain a better understanding of these concepts, we will briefly retrace the theoretical

[22] Héritier 1996, 127 ('La valence différentielle des sexes traduit la place différente qui est faite universellement aux deux sexes sur une table des valeurs, et signe la dominance du principe masculin sur le principe féminin. Le rapport homme/femme est construit sur le même modèle que le rapport parents/enfants, que le rapport aîné/cadet, et plus généralement, que le rapport antérieur/postérieur, l'antériorité signifiant la supériorité').

[23] Bourdieu 1998.

[24] Delphy 1998; Mathieu 1991; Guillaumin 1992.

[25] Pavard *et al.* 2020, 7–8 ('construction sociale, culturelle et politique (…) des normes hiérarchisées de féminité, de masculinité et d'hétérosexualité').

[26] Rich 1980, 631–660.

[27] Crenshaw 1989; Crenshaw 1991.

[28] Bilge & Hill Collins 2023, 24 ('L'intersectionnalité examine la façon dont les rapports de pouvoir imbriqués influent sur les rapports sociaux dans diverses sociétés, ainsi que sur l'expérience des individu·e·s dans la vie quotidienne. En tant qu'instrument d'analyse, l'intersectionnalité considère que les catégories de race, de classe, de genre, de sexualité, de nationalité, de capacité, d'ethnicité et d'âge – entre autres – sont interdépendantes et façonnées les unes par les autres. L'intersectionnalité est une manière de comprendre et d'expliquer la complexité du monde, des personnes et des expériences humaines.').

[29] The sex/gender system is defined by Gayle Rubin as the system within which gender is produced in relation to biological sex and sexuality cf. Rubin 1998 (1975), 13–14: 'Every society […] has a sex/gender system – a set of arrangements by which the biological raw material of human sex and procreation is shaped by human, social intervention and satisfied in a conventional manner, no matter how bizarre some of the conventions may be'. On the basis of Judith Butler's work, we will consider the sex/gender system as the system that socially constructs not only gender, but also sex cf. Butler 2005 (1990).

development of 'sex' and 'gender', bearing in mind that it is important to avoid using the word gender 'as a synonym for sex or women[30]'.

2.1. History of 'sex' and 'gender'

Even before the term 'gender' appeared, Margaret Mead was one of the first researchers to separate sex from what she called 'temperament'. As an anthropologist, she travelled to New Guinea between 1931 and 1933 to study traditional cultures. In *Sex and temperament in three primitive societies* et *Coming of Age in Samoa*, she noted the existence of different temperaments depending on the groups studied (gentleness, sensitivity, aggressiveness)[31]. She concluded that these temperaments were the consequence of 'social conditioning', which varied from one society to another, and that they did not depend on biological sex[32]. Despite this, Mead did not question the hierarchy of the sexes or the gendered division of tasks, which were considered to be specific to each sex[33].

From the 1950s onwards, American psychology began to describe the discrepancies between anatomy (biological sex) and 'gender identity', a term coined by the psychiatrist Robert Stoller[34]. The term 'gender role' was coined by the psychologist and sexologist John Money as part of his work with other researchers on intersex variations and 'transexuality' (a term used at the time and which will be replaced by 'transidentity' in this book) in the 1950s and 1960s. These psychologists developed the concept of 'gender role' as a reference to an individual's social interactions and public behaviour, and 'gender identity' as a reference to the psychological construction of the self[35]. Far from seeking to explain the construction of difference between women and men or to denounce inequalities between the sexes, Stoller and Money considered gender as a psychological construction of the self, and used it in the very specific context of research and medical interventions on intersex and transgender people. Because of the 'success' of sex assignments performed on intersex children who needed to be given the 'right' sex – i.e. a functional sex that allows for 'natural' and expected sexual behaviour – they were convinced that sexual behaviour, and development towards male or female sex, is not innate but can be constructed through surgical intervention. The most extreme and high-profile case of Money's experiments is David Reimer, a Canadian born in 1965, who underwent vaginoplasty and was raised as a girl following a botched circumcision. Despite surgery and hormone treatments, Reimer struggled with his gender identity at puberty and, having learned the truth about his biological sex, decided to live as a man. The plasticity of biological sex put forward by Money turned out to be wrong; the use of the terms 'sex' and 'gender', on the other hand, has had a long life.

Drawing on the research of these psychologists, Ann Oakley in 1972 put forward an interpretation of sex and gender that was in turn taken up by feminists: while sex refers to the biological difference between women and men, gender refers to the social, cultural and psychological construction of female and male identities[36]. This interpretation allowed feminists to highlight the constructed and cultural nature of inequalities that have no basis in biology. Anthropology, sociology and history then took up this theme to explore the different ways in which the sex/gender relationship exists in human societies[37]. To oversimplify things, before gender was defined, the modern West assumed that the social roles of men and women were biologically inscribed in individuals. A woman brought up children and did domestic chores because she was biologically programmed to do so, just as a man was the breadwinner of his family and went off to war because he was biologically programmed to do so. The arrival of the notion of gender disrupted this cleverly constructed binarity.

However, feminists soon came up against a theoretical stumbling block: if gender is the social and constructed part of two sexes conceived as invariant, natural and immutable, does this not reinforce and naturalise the difference between women and men? In 1990, the idea emerged that sex is just as constructed as gender, thanks in particular to the work of Judith Butler[38]. In 1990, the historian Thomas Laqueur published *Making Sex*, which reinforced this idea of the construction and historicity of sex or, more precisely, of discourses on sex[39]. In his book, he proposed to retrace the evolution of the conceptualisation of biological sex in the West since Antiquity. He showed that the difference between the sexes and the idea of a distinct nature specific to each sex, as it is explained to us today, became established in the 18th century. Earlier conceptions would have favoured another explanation, a unisex model, according to which the female genitalia were in fact an imperfect and unfinished version of the male genitalia. This would imply that 'sexual difference is not inscribed in bodies but is socially instituted[40]'. While the notion of sex is indeed constructed and subject to historical evolution, the existence of this unisex model has been rightly called into question, particularly by specialists in Antiquity, the history of science and the philosopher Elsa Dorlin: it is clear to ancient authors that there are two biological sexes[41]. The whole point of Laqueur's approach

[30] Thébaud 2004, 62.
[31] Mead 1963.
[32] Bereni *et al.* 2020, 27.
[33] Delphy 2001, 244–245.
[34] Fausto-Sterling 2000, 46; Dorlin 2008, 33–37; Bereni *et al.* 2020, 27–28.
[35] *Ibid.*

[36] Oakley 1972.
[37] Sørensen 2000.
[38] Butler 2005 (1990).
[39] Laqueur 1992 (1990).
[40] Dorlin 2006, 21 ('la différence sexuelle n'est pas inscrite dans les corps mais qu'elle est socialement instituée').
[41] Critics have pointed out that the exclusive existence of this unisex model is far from being proven or demonstrable. For Antiquity in particular, the texts mobilised by Laqueur do not constitute the whole body of theories on biological sex and its division, and a competing model in which the two sexes were considered as distinct entities

was to demonstrate that the way in which we talk about the sexes and the way in which they are hierarchised is constructed.

From then on, gender as a system produces the sexes and posits them as antagonists:

> '[...] gender in turn creates anatomical sex in the sense that this hierarchical division of humanity into two transforms an anatomical difference that is itself devoid of social implications into a distinction relevant to social practice; [...] social practice alone transforms a physical fact that is itself devoid of meaning like all physical facts into a category of thought[42].'

The relationship between gender and sex is therefore not one of opposition, but of interdependence:

> 'Gender refers to the system that produces a hierarchical bipartition between men and women, and sex refers to the groups and categories produced and organised by this system. This rule of usage also makes it possible to assert the social dimension of the sexual division itself, breaking with conceptions that oppose 'gender' (social, acquired, variable) and 'sex' (biological, innate, invariant)[43]'.

This system implies a hierarchy defined by materialist feminists in the 1970s as 'patriarchy', 'oppression of women' or the French term '*sexage*'[44].

2.2. Biological variability of sex

The idea that sex is constructed, in the same way as gender, can be supported by medical research into determining the sex of individuals. Until very recently in history, it was only possible to determine the sex of an individual by examining their external genitalia: the individual was either male or female. In some cases, visual examination revealed an ambiguity, known as intersex variations, in the appearance of the genitals, which did not correspond to the prevailing norms. From the 19th century onwards, the development of research and surgery made it possible to extend the range of criteria used to determine an individual's sex: internal genitalia (for example, the prostate or the uterus), gonads (ovaries and testicles, i.e. the organs that produce gametes), chromosomes (XY for men, XX for women), hormones and even the organisation of the brain[45].

From a biological point of view, there is considerable variability[46]. For example, for the same individual, these last criteria can be discordant. Chromosomal sex defines male sex by the XY combination and female sex by the XX combination. The SRY (Sex-determining Region Y) protein gene on the Y chromosome is responsible for male gonadal sex (development of the testicles). The SRY gene can sometimes be non-functional, implying a female anatomical sex and a male chromosomal sex (XY). Faced with individuals with ambiguous organs, mixed gonads, non-standard sex chromosomes (e.g. X or XXY) or unexpected levels of androgens or oestrogens, research has shown that sex determination is much more complex than it first appeared, and that we cannot be satisfied with a strict male/female bicategorisation to understand how sex is expressed[47]. These phenomena have led Anne Fausto-Sterling to define sex not as a binary category, but as a continuum of sexual characteristics within which individuals are more likely to be male or female, depending on a combination of physical, chromosomal, gonadal and hormonal criteria. For the researcher, 'calling someone a man or a woman is a social decision[48]'. It is estimated that one to two people in a hundred are affected by intersex variations[49].

However, if this variability is identifiable in purely biological terms, its implicit or explicit recognition in society is not self-evident: sexual categorisation is far too deeply rooted in society for it to be easily discarded. The question then arises: what is the relevance of this notion of a 'continuum' if social structures are linked not to this notion but to that of the strict biological man/woman binarity? It is therefore useful for archaeologists to be aware of the debates that are stirring up specialists in these questions and to know that there is a great deal of variability between the sexes, while being aware of the limits of this theoretical approach[50]. In reality, most human societies have inferred the existence of two sexes from the biological data available to them, and it is on the basis of their conception of gender categorisation that we need to work.

2.3. Diversity of gender and genders

To complete the definition of gender, it is important to distinguish, on the one hand, between **gender** as an organisational and hierarchical system, in the singular, and, on the other hand, between **genders**, in the plural, linked to an individual identity characterisation, which could also be called 'gender identities'. Indeed, in

existed cf. King 1998; Dorlin 2006, 20–22. See also Park & Nye 1991; Dorlin 2002. Sellberg 2015 also criticises Laqueur's forced projection of queer onto social phenomena of the Renaissance that are nothing of the sort, and his downplaying of sources from that period that run counter to his unisex model.

42 Delphy 2001, 231 ('[...] le genre à son tour crée le sexe anatomique dans le sens que cette répartition hiérarchique de l'humanité en deux transforme en distinction pertinente pour la pratique sociale une différence anatomique en elle-même dépourvue d'implications sociales ; [...] la pratique sociale et elle seule transforme en catégorie de pensée un fait physique en lui-même dépourvu de sens comme tous les faits physiques.'): Christine Delphy highlights the economic dimension of women's oppression, with the appropriation by men of women's unpaid work, both productive and reproductive, in a domestic context.

43 Bereni *et al.* 2020, 8.

44 Bereni *et al.* 2020, 33–34. See below for an explanation on the French term '*sexage*'.

45 Löwy 2003; Bereni *et al.* 2020, 41–43.

46 Fausto-Sterling 2000, 30–54.

47 Kraus 2000.

48 Fausto-Sterling 2000, 3.

49 Wiels 2006; Bereni *et al.* 2020, 44–45.

50 Sørensen 2000.

Definitions

Cisgender person: refers to a person whose gender identity (female or male) corresponds to the sex assigned at birth.

Transgender person: refers to a person whose gender identity does not correspond to the sex assigned at birth.

Gender fluid: refers to a person whose gender is fluid and fluctuates between feminine and masculine.

Non-binary gender: refers to a person whose gender identity does not correspond to either feminine or masculine norms.

Queer: the term queer, both a political movement and a personal identification, refers to the deconstruction of dominant norms, particularly gender and sexuality, by minority identities.

The acronym LGBT, or LGBTQIA+ in one of its variants, refers to lesbian, gay, bisexual, transgender, queer, intersex and asexual people.

contemporary practice, the term has come to be used as an individual identity characteristic, covering a multiplicity of identities: cisgender, transgender, non-binary gender, genderfluid, etc. In this sense, it is opposed to sex, which continues to be defined in biological terms. These notions, which are widely used in queer archaeology, and which we will discuss in parts one and two, are essential in today's world, as they are the basis of claims and everyday definition of individuals in society.

Moreover, the definition given for gender at the beginning of this introduction is valid for contemporary Western and Westernised societies. To complicate matters, we need to realise, as we have already mentioned, that the sex/gender system varies in time and space. In practical terms, this means that the gender norms in force in ancient societies were probably different from those that underpin the current system. Today, this system seems universal and immutable, but numerous historical and ethnographic examples show us the variability of gender. Maria Lugones' work sheds light on the social mechanisms that, during colonisation, led to other gender systems being supplanted or even erased by the colonisers, creating this illusion of the universality and immutability of gender[51].

A number of societies, both modern and ancient, recognise genders other than the bicategorisation we know as feminine and masculine[52]. For example, the Zapotecs of Mexico have a third gender, where *muxe* are men who adopt behaviours associated with the female gender[53]; conversely, in Albania, sworn virgins (*burrnesha*) choose to dress and behave like men to compensate for the absence of a son in the family. In Indonesia, the Bugis recognise five genders: masculine, feminine, transcendent (*bissu*, who are intermediaries with the gods), men who take on the role of heterosexual women (*calabai*), women who take on the role of heterosexual men (*calalai*)[54]. These systems, in which gender is not limited to a strict binarity, are also known in ancient societies. For example, Byzantine authors mention a third gender in the person of eunuchs, a category that broadly includes people who cannot procreate, including monks and sometimes even nuns[55]. Furthermore, in addition to these societies where gender produces not a bicategorisation but a multicategorisation of sexes, genders and sexualities, we find more occasional occurrences of transidentity, non-binary gender or gender fluidity, which escape normative constraints, in societies where gender produces a priori a strict bicategorisation of sexes, genders and sexualities[56].

It is important to bear in mind the variability of sex/gender systems when studying ancient societies. Occasional transgressions of the norm or institutionalised – and socially accepted – differences involving a third gender, for example, are possible in societies of the past. This is all the more important for societies without writing, where archaeological study is the only source of information for reconstructing their social organisation.

3. Gender at the intersection of other power relations

The study of gender in ancient societies often requires taking into account other factors that may influence the way in which gender identities and gender roles are expressed, such as age, social class, (social) race, disability, etc. A brief overview of how these different power relations are articulated is therefore necessary for a better understanding of social relations as a whole. As we have already mentioned, gender is interwoven with power relations other than those linked to patriarchy. As early as the 19th century, there were analogies between the forms of domination highlighted by feminists campaigning for women's rights and other forms of oppression. In the United States, the struggle to obtain the right to vote ran parallel to the struggle to abolish slavery. In France, materialist feminists drew links between class struggles and struggles for women's emancipation.

In the 1980s, the American researcher Kimberlé Crenshaw theorised the concept of intersectionality, going beyond

[51] Lugones 2007.

[52] Journet 2014, 24.
[53] Stephen 2002.
[54] Graham 2001, 16–17.
[55] Ringrose 2003; Maillet 2020.
[56] Algrain 2021a; Algrain 2021b; Mary 2021.

the simple comparison based on the analogy of systems of oppression: we must avoid 'thinking of domination in the form of a simple sum of advantages or handicaps universally perceived as such'. The researcher draws on the contributions of Black feminism, a feminist political movement that emerged in the 1950s in the United States during the civil rights protests. Since then, this tool, originally designed to highlight the specific oppressions suffered by African-American women, both as women and as African-Americans, has been used to study the combined effects of different forms of oppression on groups of individuals[57].

In France, Danièle Kergoat uses the term 'consubstantiality' to define social relations: they 'do not exist independently of one another and cannot be defined without reference to one another[58]'. Consubstantiality makes it possible to account for the fact that each individual is constructed within relations of gender, class, race and other types of social relations, and that these relations are constantly evolving. Consubstantiality therefore concerns everyone and is not limited to certain groups situated at the intersection of different forms of domination and discrimination.

3.1. Gender and race

The first mention of the term 'race' in its modern sense appears in a text from 1684, in which the French philosopher and physician François Bernier divides humanity into four (or even five) major groups according to their size, skin colour, body hair and facial shape[59]. The paradigm shift was radical. While scholars since Antiquity had considered that 'race', linked to temperament, depended on cultural and environmental criteria (climate), and that temperament could be modified by changing latitude, Bernier naturalised race, making it a fixed and immutable criterion. This was the beginning of the scientific racism that culminated in the 19th and 20th centuries (see chapter 2), based on divisions constructed from the phenotype, but which in fact had no basis in biology, as Sarah Mazouz points out: 'There is no hierarchy between human groups that could be founded in nature and would be based on an origin manifested in particular by phenotypic differences[60]. [...] Races, as racists understand them, do not exist[61]'. However, this has not prevented many cultures from constructing racial hierarchies, in particular to justify colonisation and slavery, hierarchies that are still manifest today in the discrimination against racialised people[62].

Before the term 'intersectionality' was coined and popularised, there was already work drawing analogies between gender and race[63]. Although this approach, like the analogy between gender and class relations, has revealed similarities between different types of domination, it has sometimes tended to set women up as a homogeneous group and to erase specific relations of domination. For example, the research of the French materialist feminist Colette Guillaumin in *Sexe, race et pratique du pouvoir* led her to coin the neologism '*sexage*', based on the French terms '*servage*' (serfdom) and '*esclavage*' (slavery), to define the unpaid, open-ended appropriation of women's bodies under patriarchy. In the case of slavery, as in that of *sexage*, the production and reproduction work of the dominated groups is appropriated by the dominant group[64]. Guillaumin has also highlighted the constructed nature of 'sex' and 'race', which for her are semantic phenomena, 'showing how sexism and racism function according to the same process of differentiation and naturalisation of power relations[65]'.

In the United States, representatives of Black feminism renewed these approaches by showing the interweaving of relations of domination and the inappropriateness of a monolithic, universal category of 'woman'. In the 1960s and 1970s, they denounced White, bourgeois feminism, from which they felt excluded, and highlighted the fact that there was not one single feminism, but a plurality of feminist approaches and movements corresponding to the different situations and experiences of women. Angela Davis, bell hooks, Audre Lorde and others criticised the specific domination exercised over racialised women and highlighted the existence of other relations of domination, previously invisible[66]. In 1974, Audre Lorde and Barbara Smith founded the Combahee River Collective in Boston, named in homage to Harriet Tubman's action to free a group of 750 slaves at Combahee River (South Carolina) in 1863. In 1977, the collective published a declaration calling for the intersecting nature of different oppressions to be taken into account in the fight for equality, whether racial, gendered, heteronormative or classist. However, the proponents of Black feminism in the United States are not the only ones to have considered the specific oppressions suffered by racialised women. For example, Françoise Vergès highlighted in her work that, while women in mainland France in the 1970s were fighting to win the right to abortion, women on Réunion Island (an overseas French department) were organising to combat the gender, racial and class oppression they suffered, and which resulted in forced sterilisations and abortions[67].

[57] Boussahba *et al.* 2021.

[58] Bereni *et al.* 2020, 366; Kergoat 2000, 42 ('ils n'existent pas indépendamment les uns des autres et ne peuvent être définis sans références les uns aux autres').

[59] Dorlin 2006, 210–215.

[60] Mazouz 2020, 24 ('Il n'y a pas de hiérarchie entre les groupes humains, qui pourrait être fondée en nature et reposerait sur une origine manifestée notamment par des différences phénotypiques.').

[61] Mazouz 2020, 50 ('Les races, au sens où les racistes les entendent, n'existent pas.').

[62] The frequent analogies between sex and race found in 'scientific' texts in the late 18th and 19th centuries were used to explain the 'naturally inferior' position of women, racialised people, the poor and so on. See Stepan 1986.

[63] Dorlin 2008, 79–80.

[64] Bereni *et al.* 2020, 341–342.

[65] Guillaumin 2002; Dorlin 2006, 11 for the quote ('montrant comment sexisme et racisme fonctionnaient selon un même processus de différenciation et de naturalisation des rapports de pouvoir').

[66] Bereni *et al.* 2020, 339.

[67] Bereni *et al.* 2020, 351; Pavard *et al.* 2020, 300–303, 330–333; Vergès 2017. The same applies in the United States, where African-

When Kimberlé Crenshaw took up this subject in 1989 and 1991, she studied it through the prism of her own research in law [68]. She noted that 'in discrimination cases, American judges have refused to consider Black women as legitimately representative of one of the two groups of victims concerned (women and racial minorities), thus failing to qualify the discrimination of which they were victims[69]'. The interweaving of different types of domination is not simply an additional effect, but depends on factors specific to each era and each context. In fact, the intersection of different types of domination sometimes tends to attenuate one of them. In the case of slavery, for example, Céline Bessière notes that 'slavery and gender domination appear at first sight to be mutually reinforcing, but it can also *to some extent* be shown that slavery moderates the domination of enslaved men over enslaved women, or that gender *partially* mitigates the pressure of slavery on Black women[70]'.

3.2. Gender and class

In the 1970s, materialist feminists developed a model based on the analogy between social relations of gender, class and race, as these were the most politicised[71]. Drawing on the Marxist framework of analysis, French materialists saw women as a class dominated by patriarchy in the same way as the proletarian class was dominated and oppressed by the capitalist system and the bourgeois class. The only difference was that materialist feminists included bourgeois women in the class of women, unlike Marxist theories which radically opposed the proletarian and the bourgeois. They considered that all women were oppressed in the same way by patriarchy, which sets up 'husbands and wives as antagonistic classes (one deriving material profit from the exploitation of the other)[72]'. The work of Silvia Federici, an Italian researcher and advocate of Marxist feminism, demonstrated the gradual appropriation of women's labour and bodies. At the end of the 19th century, this appropriation led to the model of the full-time housewife who provides free labour for her husband. In this way, the housewife enabled the 'production' of a worker detached from any obligation to do domestic work, and the reproduction of the working-class body. According to Federici, capitalism is therefore inseparable from gender[73].

American women underwent forced sterilisations while abortion was prohibited for White women cf. Davis 1982 (1981), 255–278.

68 Crenshaw 1989; Crenshaw 1991; Dorlin 2008, 81–88.

69 Bereni *et al.* 2020, 347 ('dans des procès pour discrimination, des juges américains ont refusé de considérer des femmes noires comme légitimement représentatives de l'un des deux groupes de victimes concernées (les femmes et les minorités raciales), échouant ainsi à qualifier la discrimination dont elles étaient victimes').

70 Bessière 2003, 244–245 ('esclavage et domination de genre semblent à première vue se renforcer mutuellement, mais on peut aussi *dans une certaine mesure* montrer que l'esclavage tempère la domination des hommes sur les femmes esclaves, ou que le genre atténue *en partie* la pression de l'esclavage sur les femmes noires').

71 Bereni *et al.* 2020, 340–341.

72 Delphy 1998, 51 ('maris et femmes en classes antagoniques (les uns retirant un profit matériel de l'exploitation des autres)').

73 Federici 2014; Federici 2019.

3.3. Gender and sexuality

Sexuality is also one of the places where power relations are expressed, and this has been amply demonstrated by feminist and gender studies. Materialist feminists consider that the male class appropriates women's bodies – this is Colette Guillaumin's '*sexage*'. Following on from this work, Paola Tabet calls this appropriation of the work of production and reproduction 'a continuum of economic-sexual exchange[74]'. For Tabet, from courtship to prostitution and legal marriage, the division of reproductive and non-reproductive sexual labour is asymmetrical, turning women into a class forced to exchange sexual 'labour' for payment. Ownership of women's bodies, in particular through legal heterosexuality (marriage), and control over their sexuality, through access to contraception, abortion and a form of sex education, remain major issues today[75].

Elsa Dorlin also uses the intersection of gender, sexuality and race to explain the making of gendered and racialised bodies[76]. The notion of 'temperament', used since Antiquity in the Hippocratic-Galenic corpus with the theory of humours, opposed men, characterised by hot and dry, and women, characterised by cold and wet. On the basis of these ancient theories, doctors in the Early Modern Age turned men and women into two irreconcilable groups, according to their respective temperaments, which were supposedly rooted in nature. According to them, the very nature and temperament of women made them prudish and frigid, setting them up above all as wives and mothers. The existence of groups of women whose sexuality was outside the norm was therefore paradoxical according to these theories. The exclusion of prostitutes from the group of women was based on the theory of temperaments, since their hot and dry nature brought them closer to the temperament of men and explained their supposed sterility, thus excluding them from reproductive sexual work. Similarly, African women were said to have a hot temperament and an unbridled, even bestial sexuality, which also excluded them from the group of women and prevented them from reaping the social benefits of any reproductive sexual work.

When studying ancient societies, archaeologists need to understand the sexual norms in force in the society they are studying in order to gain a nuanced view of gender relations. For example, the sources on Archaic and Classical Athens show that sexuality was not considered in terms of the identity and gender of the partner. What mattered was the dominant/dominated relationship based on gender, age, socio-economic class and whether or not the person belonged to the group of citizens. A male citizen could therefore have sexual relations with his wife, a concubine, a slave or a younger lover, but never with another adult citizen[77].

74 Tabet 2001, 139 ('un continuum de l'échange économico-sexuel').

75 Dorlin 2008, 66.

76 Dorlin 2006.

77 Algrain 2022.

3.4. Gender and disability

The French word 'handicap' was first used in the horse-racing world in the 18th century, when it referred to the extra weight carried by the best horses in order to level the playing field between competitors[78]. It was not until the 1970s that the term became widely used to describe the physical damage caused to individuals and the resulting inequalities in treatment. Depending on the institution, the very definition of disability may differ, and in some cases remains open to debate[79]. The WHO defines disability as a 'result from the interaction between individuals with a health condition, such as cerebral palsy, Down syndrome and depression, with personal and environmental factors including negative attitudes, inaccessible transportation and public buildings, and limited social support[80]'. But while today disability is essentially defined from a medical perspective, this has not always been the case in the past. Perhaps this is why the definition of disability continues to have unclear contours. The social consequences of disability have often been a heavier burden on individuals than the physical limitations imposed on them in everyday life.

Disability studies emerged in the 1970s as a result of social movements led by people with disabilities, mainly in the United States and the United Kingdom. The work in this field shows that people with disabilities are systemically made inferior. In the case of women, stereotypes portray them as sexless, unable to reproduce and devoid of femininity. Similarly, disability calls into question the virility of men[81]. We shall see later, through the prism of archaeology, that the attitude of ancient populations towards physical ailments differed greatly from that of our contemporaries.

3.5. Gender and age groups

Age class is an important factor in categorising individuals in both ancient and modern societies. In some societies, it can be at least as important as gender. 'The Nigerian anthropologist Oyeronke Oyewumi shows how, in Yoruba society, seniority forms a principle of division of the social world that is at least as significant as gender, and that it is necessary to cross-reference with gender in order to understand this society in all its complexity[82]'. For example, Yoruba pronouns do not indicate gender but the age (younger or older) of the person being addressed[83].

Although age seems to be a given, the age group to which a person belongs can vary according to place and time. It depends largely on two factors: life expectancy and healthy life expectancy. Gender is obviously a factor in calculating an individual's relative 'old age'. For example, in Western societies, women age while men mature. The latter are less denigrated when the signs of age appear, such as grey hair: from a social point of view, 'old age comes earlier for women than for men[84]'. In the same way, the stigma of age taints love relationships between an older woman and a younger man, which are subject to a persistent taboo. As illustrated very recently in the book *Le jeune homme* by Nobel Prize winner Annie Ernaux, in which she recounts her love affair with a 25-year-old student at the age of 54, the discomfort aroused by relationships of this kind stems, among other things, from the impossibility of thinking about the sexuality of older women beyond the menopause – whereas this is not the case when the woman is the younger partner[85].

The question of age group also implies taking into consideration the group of children. Once again, leaving childhood is a variable factor in time and space, unrelated to the age of puberty. For example, in fifth-century Athens, it was normal for a 14-year-old girl to marry a 30-year-old man, reinforcing patriarchal domination through domination by age. In our modern societies, an age difference between (older) men and (younger) women still exists and often implies a difference in the capital accumulated at the time of marriage, an economic domination/dependence of wives in relation to their husbands that culminates in divorce, leaving the woman poorer than when she entered into the marriage[86]. Unrelated to actual age, social age is also important to consider, for example in a colonial context where colonised populations are considered to be 'grown-up children', which justifies the maintenance of domination and inequality of rights between colonists and the colonised[87].

4. Defining gender archaeology

4.1. Gender archaeology: a militant and subjective science?

Before we come to the definition of gender archaeoology, we need to clarify the criticisms levelled at gender studies.

> "'Feminist' research, 'gender research' or 'gender studies' are three expressions that refer to the same area of research, that of inequalities and power relations between men and women. The first formulation is the oldest, but it should be noted that the researchers who helped forge the concept of gender were precisely those who considered themselves feminists. It was feminist research that forged gender research or gender studies.

[78] 'Handicap', in *Dictionnaire de l'Académie française*, sur *Centre national de ressources textuelles et lexicales*, [Retrieved October 1, 2023, from https://www.cnrtl.fr/definition/academie9/handicap]; Delattre 2018.
[79] Husquin 2020, 12–13; Delattre 2021.
[80] World Health Organization, *Disability* [Retrieved November 7, 2024, from, https://www.who.int/health-topics/disability#tab=tab_1].
[81] Bereni *et al.* 2020, 363–364.
[82] Bereni *et al.* 2020, 340 ('L'anthropologue nigériane Oyeronke Oyewumi montre ainsi comment la séniorité, dans la société yoruba, forme un principe de division du monde social au moins aussi conséquent que le genre, et qu'il est nécessaire de croiser avec ce dernier pour comprendre cette société dans sa complexité.').
[83] Oyewumi 1997; Id. 1998.
[84] Beauvalet-Boutouyrie & Berthiaud 2015, 187 ('la vieillesse est plus précoce chez les femmes que chez les hommes').
[85] Sontag 1972; Froidevaux-Metterie 2021, 23, 345–364.
[86] Bessière & Gollac 2020.
[87] Bereni *et al.* 2020, 365.

These expressions should therefore be considered as equivalent to 'gender studies'[88].'

Because of their feminist roots, gender studies in general have often been accused of being militant and subjective. While it is true that the sociological research conducted in France in the 1970s and 1980s was often carried out by figures associated with the Mouvement de Libération des Femmes – MLF (Women's Liberation Movement), they were nonetheless critical researchers who applied the most rigorous methodologies. The same is true of gender archaeology. Although this is a cross-disciplinary theoretical approach, there is still a certain 'sense of marginality' among these researchers and a form of suspicion on the part of their peers. Yet social movements, such as the workers' movement or the anti-racist movement, have often contributed to the development of science, not just through their desire to understand and deconstruct social phenomena, but through the scientific treatment and method used, based on arguments and data that can be verified by peers[89].

Furthermore, sciences, including exact sciences, are not necessarily objective. On the contrary, the affirmation of the researcher's subjectivity lies at the heart of the post-processual archaeology approach and can be put forward in other disciplines. As Claude Gautier and Michelle Zancarini-Fournel point out in relation to the humanities and social sciences, which have been widely criticised and attacked in France in recent years, 'what we are inevitably affects what we do[90]'. We need to be aware that a researcher adopts a point of view from which he or she describes his or her subject of study, and that this point of view is never neutral: 'it would be naïve to believe that it is possible to cut ourselves off from the present in order to write a neutral and objective history of the past; that would be to want to detach ourselves from everything that makes us who we are: social and cultural affiliations, values, etc.[91]'. To this we can add Max Weber's remark: 'Nowhere is the interest of science more denied in the long run than where we refuse to see the unpleasant facts and the reality of life in all its harshness[92]'.

[88] ANEF (Association nationale des études féministes), 'Plaidoyer pour l'institutionnalisation des études sur le genre dans les orientations stratégiques de la recherche et de l'enseignement supérieur', October 2012, [Accessed 11 March 2022, https://m.centre-hubertine-auclert.fr/sites/default/files/fichiers/1-plaidoyer-anef-octobre-2012–19p.pdf]. ('Les recherches "féministes", "recherches sur le genre" ou "études de genre" sont trois expressions qui renvoient à une même aire de recherche, celle portant sur les inégalités et rapports de pouvoir entre hommes et femmes. La première formulation est la plus ancienne, mais il faut noter que les chercheuses qui ont contribué à forger le concept de genre sont précisément des chercheuses se considérant comme féministes. Ce sont les recherches féministes qui ont forgé les recherches sur le genre ou études de genre. Aussi, faut-il considérer ces expressions comme des équivalents.')

[89] Sebillote-Cuchet 2022, 9.

[90] Gautier & Zancarini-Fournel 2022, 10.

[91] Gautier & Zancarini-Fournel 2022, 140.

[92] Weber 1965, 130–131.

One of the best-known examples is the article by anthropologist Emily Martin, 'The Egg and the Sperm: How Science Has Constructed a Romance Based on Stereotypical Male-Female Roles[93]'. In this work, Martin analyses the metaphors used in biology teaching and argues that these metaphors reflect 'our cultural definitions of male and female'. For example, the words 'debris' and 'dying' associated with the egg are contrasted with the words 'remarkable', 'strong' and 'produce' associated with spermatozoa, resulting in a hierarchy of female and male biological processes. The spermatozoon is thus conceived as a knight who comes to the rescue of a damsel in distress and saves it from destruction. Martin also analyses the reversal of language used by biologists when they realised that the ovum was less passive than it appeared and was in fact capturing the spermatozoon on its surface. The egg then becomes 'dangerous', a veritable spider which 'captures and tethers' its 'victim', the spermatozoon. Stereotypes tend to influence researchers, whether consciously or not, and it is difficult, if not impossible, to claim total objectivity.

Feminist epistemologies have thus endeavoured to account for the biased and situated position of the sciences, both in exact sciences and humanities, especially when they put forward the idea of objectivity and neutrality inherent in the scientific approach. But no scientific approach is neutral: in the same way that the personal is political, science is also political, because no theory and no scientific approach is 'outside the social world'[94]. With regard to the work of the American philosopher Sandra G. Harding, who has taken an interest in this notion of scientific objectivity, Elsa Dorlin says:

> 'Harding bases scientific objectivity on a definition of democracy that is genuinely anti-sexist and anti-racist, considering that the routine functioning of science is based on a status quo maintained by an elite, on 'a matrix of privileges' based on class, gender and 'race'. *Those who are subject to this status quo, and want to shake it, are the most likely to produce highly objective points of view and knowledge*[95].'

As Céline Bessière and Sylvie Gollac point out more generally in relation to gender studies: 'Like all critical knowledge that sets out to describe relations of power, gender studies in the social sciences propose a vision of scientific objectivity based not on feigned neutrality, but on a reflexive process of taking into account the researcher's social and political position, while at the same time implementing objectivity criteria (making hypotheses and methods explicit, criticising sources, coherence of

[93] Martin 1991.

[94] Dorlin 2008, 24–31.

[95] Dorlin 2008, 29 (emphasis addes).

the demonstration, etc.)[96].' The critical approach and methodology developed in gender archaeology studies is therefore essential and must be clearly explained. Reappraisal and questioning of one's work is also an integral part of the approach, as it is impossible to escape a form of anachronism: research into the past remains a product of a given present and its political and social concerns[97].

4.2. Vocabulary

The term 'gender', whether in archaeology or other disciplines, has sometimes been used in different ways. Depending on who is using it, it can be used to mean anything from a system of domination, to an individual characteristic, to an equivalence with the word 'sex'. It is therefore important to define precisely what we are talking about each time we use one of these terms[98].

In archaeology, 'biological sex' is often difficult to determine since it depends on knowledge of the conformation of the genital organs, of the gonads in the more precise case of 'anatomical sex', or of the chromosomes and DNA in the case of 'genetic sex'. These elements are inaccessible to us in archaeology, except in the case of mummies or via DNA analysis. However, part of the population (around 1.7%) is intersex and cannot be categorised in a binary way, either by anatomy or genetics[99].

'Anthropological sex' is linked to the study of the skeleton. Various measurements on the long bones, skull, pelvic bones and inner ear can be used to define on a scale of 1 to 5 the probability of an individual belonging to the male sex, the female sex or an undetermined category. The poor state of preservation of bones is one of the obstacles to this identification. When measurements are reliable, the anthropological sex is the same as the biological sex[100].

Finally, 'archaeological sex' is a misnomer, as it does not refer to sex at all, but to the objects that archaeologists describe as 'feminine' or 'masculine'. It is the expression of the gender identity of the deceased, as expressed by the people who buried them. It is a social sex, assigned to an individual by society, which does not always correspond to his or her biological sex (e.g. two-spirit individuals in North America), but may also not reflect the way in which the deceased perceived him or herself (e.g. trans-identity).

The objects associated with an individual can therefore express both gender as an individual identity characteristic as perceived by society (*genders*) and gender as a power relationship manifested through material culture.

The term '*rapports sociaux de sexe*', widely used by French-speaking feminists before the word 'gender' spread, can help to distinguish between 'gender' and 'genders' in French. It reminds us that gender is not constructed individually but in relation to others. This expression is extremely difficult to translate into English. It uses the term '*rapports sociaux*' to refer to relationships that take place not at the interpersonal level but in the social fabric as a whole. '*Rapports sociaux de sexe*' are therefore synonymous with 'gender' as a system of domination.

In this book, we will use the term 'sex' only in reference to biology, with the adjective 'sexed' also referring to biology, while the adjective 'sexual' will be used in relation to sexuality. The word 'gender' will refer to the system of domination and, when it refers to an individual identity characteristic, we will make this clear.

Similarly, we will use the adjectives 'feminine' and 'masculine' in inverted commas when referring to objects or graves, as an object does not have a gender of its own. The idea of gendering objects stems from concepts that were already in vogue in the 19th century, but to be valid it needs to be based on an in-depth and exhaustive study of the raw data[101] – as is the case with some recent work in the French-speaking world – and not on the preconceptions of archaeologists.

4.3. Definition of gender archaeology

Gender archaeology is a discipline that contributes to the understanding of gender norms in past societies. It highlights the variations in these norms (particularly with regard to the construction of femininity and masculinity), both in different regions and in different social groups within the same society, as well as their evolution over time, through practices and objects. It also informs us about how gender influences material living conditions, ideological structures and participation in community life[102]. In this way, it aims to denaturalise the social and show how human societies unconsciously construct and maintain the domination of one group over another on the basis of an irrelevant biological criterion (the question to be asked is: why are sex and skin colour so important in the construction of our society, and not the fact of having or not having flat feet?). By denaturalising the social, it highlights the stereotypes projected onto the past by archaeologists. It also highlights the stereotypes of ancient societies themselves, stereotypes rooted in the belief that social norms and hierarchies are a product of nature.

96 Bessière & Gollac 2020, 271–272.
97 Cryle 2015.
98 The following definitions are based on those used by Trémeaud 2018, 7–8.
99 Fausto-Sterling 2000, 51–54; Blackless *et al.* 2000; Geller 2005, 601.
100 Boucherie 2020; Boucherie *et al.* 2021.
101 For such thorough studies, see Belard 2017a; Trémeaud 2018; Augereau 2021.
102 Sørensen 2000, 70–73.

As such, gender archaeology, in its interpretative dimension of the past, can be defined as an **archaeology that analyses social relations and the social construction of identities, by studying the way in which gender – as a hierarchical system that produces the bicategorisation of the sexes – produces a material culture in which both the values and the representations associated with the feminine and the masculine are embodied**.

Research into gender archaeology is based on rigorous methodologies and borrows theoretical tools from sociology, social anthropology, ethnology, women's studies and gender studies. We will have the opportunity to present many examples of this type of research in the second part of the book.

Where to start?

L. Bereni, S. Chauvin, A. Jaunait & A. Revillard, *Introduction aux études sur le genre*, 3rd ed., De Boeck Supérieur, 2020.

R. Gilchrist, *Gender and Archaeology. Contesting the Past*, Routledge, 1999.

M. Moen & U. Pedersen, *The Routledge Handbook of Gender Archaeology*, Routledge, 2024.

M.L.S. Sørensen, *Gender Archaeology*, Polity Press, 2000.

Part One

A history of the archaeology of gender and identities

1

Gender archaeology around the world: beginnings and development

'It is necessary to remember, though, the fact that gender archaeology has roots in the women's movement.[103]'

Afrofeminism, anarcho-feminism, cyberfeminism, differentialist feminism, ecofeminism, essentialist feminism, materialist feminism, Muslim feminism, queer feminism, radical feminism, reformist feminism, universalist feminism, transfeminism, etc. Feminist struggles are part of a long and complex history, made up of various currents of thought that sometimes clash and other times converge, of individual initiatives and collective mobilisations, of theories and practical applications, inside and outside academia, in the private and public spheres, across the globe. The aim here is not to give an exhaustive history, especially as it is not a linear history, but one made up of advances, setbacks, moments of inactivity and periods of intense demands.

Feminist thinking is based on the premise that 'women suffer a specific and systematic injustice as women, and that it is possible and necessary to redress this injustice[104]'. Feminist knowledge today comes from 'a multidisciplinary intellectual production, a critical reflection, which has continued to develop, diversify – and become institutionalised – over the last [fifty] years, within, since, or alongside, women's thought or the women's movement[105]'. The vast corpus of feminist critical tools enables us to tackle a wide range of issues, from the materiality of power relations to sexual violence, heterosexuality as a norm, masculinities and trans-identity.

In this chapter, we will briefly trace the major advances in feminism, particularly from what has been called the 'second wave' onwards[106]. We will concentrate on France, while showing the links that French feminisms have maintained with the United States, one of the cradles of gender archaeology. This introduction is necessary because the work of American and French feminist researchers has been extensively used in archaeologists' books and articles. We will then highlight the links between gender archaeology and feminism, particularly in terms of the theoretical borrowings made by archaeologists, while then tracing in detail the emergence of this new archaeological discipline in different geographical areas.

[103] Nelson 2006b, 15.

[104] Bereni *et al.* 2020, 18 ('les femmes subissent une injustice spécifique et systématique en tant que femmes, et qu'il est possible et nécessaire de redresser cette injustice').

[105] Dorlin 2008, 9–10 ('d'une production intellectuelle pluridisciplinaire, d'une réflexion critique, qui n'a cessé de se développer, de se diversifier – et de s'institutionnaliser – au cours des [cinquante] dernières années, au sein, depuis, ou à côté, de la pensée ou du mouvement des femmes').

[106] On the use of the term 'wave' to describe the different phases of feminist demands and its relevance, see Pavard 2017.

1.1. Feminisms from the second wave onwards

1.1.1. The beginnings

> 'The word feminism did not appear until 1872 in the unflattering writings of Alexandre Dumas *fils*, always on the lookout for scandal. At the time, it pejoratively referred to supporters of gender equality as 'effeminate' men, in the medical vocabulary of the time, before Hubertine Auclert turned the stigma on its head and used it to describe her own militant struggle[107].'

The struggle for women's emancipation has a long history[108]. What follows is a broad outline of some of the key moments that led to the institutionalisation of feminist and gender studies. At the time of the Enlightenment, the 'women's quarrel' (*querelle des femmes*) showed that the question of the equality of women and men was already being debated. However, it was after the French Revolution that the first real demands emerged. The first French feminist demands concerned women's right to vote, – a cause also championed by suffragettes in the United Kingdom. Obtaining this right was seen as a first step towards enabling women to be considered full citizens and thus opening the door to all the rights accorded to men[109]. This right would be at the heart of the demands of the first wave on every continent. Although it may seem paradoxical and essentialist today, the arguments put forward were based on 'the theory of the 'mother's right', which establishes maternal wisdom and tenderness as the foundation of civilisation[110]'. On the other side of the Atlantic, the fight for the right to vote in the United States was led in the 19th century by feminists who were also fighting against slavery. Obtaining this right only for Black men in 1869 (15th Amendment) led to a split among feminists. Moreover, the campaign to win the support of the racist southern states led to the marginalisation of African-American women in the movement[111]. The fight

[107] Pavard *et al.* 2020, 6 ('Le mot féminisme n'est apparu qu'en 1872 sous la plume peu flatteuse d'Alexandre Dumas fils, toujours à la recherche de scandales. Il désignait alors, péjorativement, les partisans de l'égalité des sexes comme des hommes "efféminés", selon le vocabulaire médical de l'époque, avant qu'Hubertine Auclert ne retourne le stigmate et s'en empare pour désigner son propre combat militant.').

[108] On this issue, see Rochefort 2018; Pavard *et al.* 2020; Froidevaux-Metterie 2021, 9–61.

[109] Rochefort 2018; Froidevaux-Metterie 2021, 13.

[110] Froidevaux-Metterie 2021, 14 ('la théorie du "droit de la mère" qui érige la sagesse et la tendresse maternelle en fondement de la civilisation').

[111] Rochefort 2018, 57–58. Women obtained the right to vote in the United States in 1920 (19th Amendment).

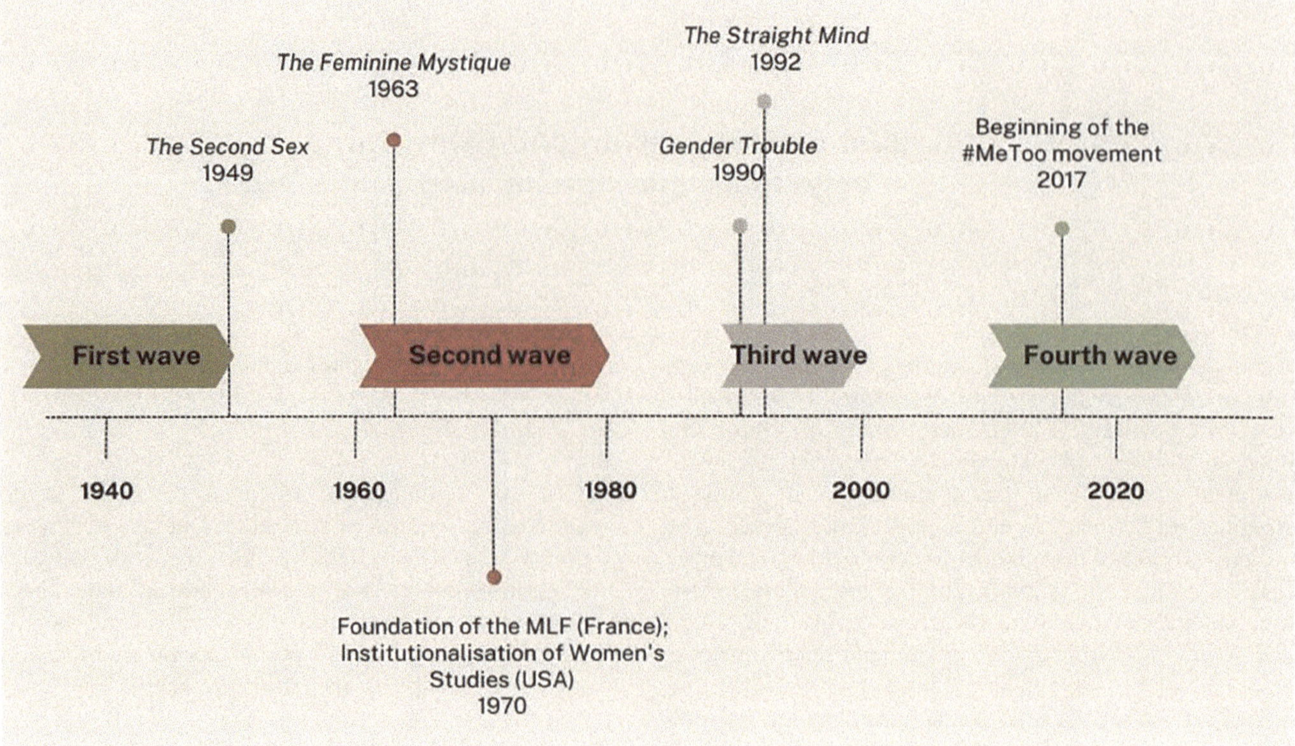

Figure 1.1. Chronological timeline showing the major stages in feminist studies.

for suffrage would not bear fruit until the first decades of the twentieth century.

The immediate post-war period saw a marked decline in women's emancipation (Figure 1.1). In France, the publication of Simone de Beauvoir's book *Le Deuxième Sexe* (*The Second Sex*) in 1949 marked a break with previous approaches. Beauvoir's originality lies partly in her critique of essentialism and the 'natural' functions attributed to women, arguments that were often used in the rhetoric of pre-war feminists and suffragists. She considers that 'the weight of male society that weighs on them[112]' is the main element in the oppression and prejudice that women suffer and have internalised. She blurred the boundary between the private and the public by tackling women's sexuality and contraception, controversial subjects that had previously had no place in public debate: what had been private now became political[113]. In the United States, the publication of Betty Friedan's book, *The Feminine Mystique*, in 1963, is often seen as a trigger for the second wave of American feminism[114]. Friedan was inspired in particular by *The Second Sex* and denounced the pressure exerted on educated middle-class women to conform to the image of the happy, smiling housewife extolled by advertisements and magazines, entirely focused on satisfying the needs of her husband and children, and forgetting herself in the process: freeing women from domestic assignment became one of the issues at stake in feminist struggles.

The link between feminist ideas and university research began in the 1970s in the United States, with the creation of women's studies. The opposition between women and men was seen as a mirror image of the opposition between nature and culture. The anthropologist Sherry B. Ortner tackled this issue in 1974 in an article entitled 'Is Female to Male as Nature is to Culture?[115]' According to her, in all societies, while men are associated with the notion of culture, women, by virtue of their maternity, are inextricably linked to nature. Gayle Rubin's work on the 'sex/gender system' also contributed to the development of women's studies and had a significant impact on queer theory in the 1990s[116]. This field of research, which has been taken up by various disciplines such as history, sociology and political science, is unique to the United States, particularly in comparison with France, where gender studies missed the turning point of institutionalisation at the time, despite some particularly fruitful analyses[117].

In the 1970s, the creation of the Mouvement de Libération des Femmes – MLF (Women's Liberation Movement) by second-wave French feminists took place against the backdrop of the struggles of May 1968 and an increase in the transnational circulation of ideas, particularly

[112] Pavard *et al.* 2020, 244 ('le poids de la société masculine qui pèse sur elles').
[113] Pfefferkorn 2016, 10. The slogan 'The personal is political' was used as part of the liberation movements of the 1960s and popularised by an essay by the American feminist Carol Hanisch (Hanisch 1970).
[114] Friedan 1963.
[115] Ortner 1974.
[116] Rubin 1998 (1975).
[117] Fassin 2004, 27–28.

with American feminists. The right to freely dispose of their bodies was the main demand of these women, who fought for access to contraception and the legalisation of abortion[118]. This period marked the birth of feminist studies in France, with leading researchers such as Christine Delphy and Monique Wittig, who belonged to the MLF, conducting research on the 'female condition'. However, gender studies were not yet institutionalised and many of these researchers worked outside of academia at first.

These materialist feminists developed original thinking based on Marxist theories of capitalist exploitation. Alongside capitalist exploitation, they identified the existence of material and intra-family exploitation, known as patriarchal exploitation, which is specific to women. Women provide free labour that is both productive and reproductive (childcare, education, domestic work, sewing, housework, help with the husband's work, etc.)[119]. Colette Guillaumin theorised this oppression as '*sexage*' in French, while Nicole-Claude Mathieu used the term '*rapports sociaux de sexe*' to refer to the antagonistic relationship between the sexes, which is rooted in the gendered division of labour[120]. In a manifesto published in 1970 in the protest newspaper *L'idiot international* and entitled 'Combat pour la libération de la femme', Monique Wittig wrote that 'in the family, the man is the bourgeois; the woman, the proletarian'. Materialist feminists see women as a social class that has always been oppressed. For them, 'women and men form two social categories held together by the relationship of oppression of the latter over the former[121]'. The work of the materialists was to have the greatest impact in the French-speaking world[122].

However, it would be wrong to regard French feminists as a homogeneous group. Within the MLF, for example, there are several tendencies, two of which have set the standard. On the one hand, the Revolutionary Feminists group (*Féministes révolutionnaires*) brought together materialist feminists. On the other, an antagonistic current emerged, represented in particular by Antoinette Fouque and the Psychoanalysis and Politics collective (*Psychanalyse et politique – PsychéPo*), made up of proponents of differentialist feminism. The latter wished to revalorise the specificity of women – expressed in particular through motherhood. However, these ideas were considered regressive by materialists. The work of differentialist feminists, in particular that of Luce Irigaray and Julia Kristeva, has been widely echoed in the United States, where they are known as the representatives of French feminism, although differentialism does not represent all French-speaking feminist theory, and growing resistance to these theories began to emerge in France in the late 1970s[123].

Materialist feminism vs. differentialist feminism

French materialist feminism emerged in the 1970s. It sought to understand the role of economic and material conditions in shaping women's experiences of oppression. Drawing on Marxist theory, it argues that women's subordination is not only the result of social relations between the sexes (gender), but also of class and economic factors. It insists on the need to take into account the material conditions of women's lives, such as their work, access to resources and economic power, in order to achieve gender equality. French materialist feminism has also criticised traditional feminist movements, such as differentialist feminism, for focusing on women's experiences in the private sphere, and has instead called for a broader analysis of the social and economic structures that perpetuate women's subordination.

In France, differentialist (or essentialist) feminism postulates that there is no need to separate sex and gender and that the 'nature' of women and men predestines them to defined roles in society. It aims to value so-called feminine qualities and gender roles, such as housework and childcare, without attempting to deconstruct the gendered division of labour that underpins these roles. Strongly rooted in the binarity of men and women and the idea of the complementarity of the sexes, it is opposed in this respect to currents such as materialist feminism, which has strongly criticised essentialists. For materialists, the origins of patriarchal oppression of women lie in the organisation of society and the norms that construct the sexes and the values associated with them.

The links between Anglophone and Francophone feminism are less tenuous than they might at first appear. Simone de Beauvoir was translated into English in the 1960s and American feminists immediately seized on her book and her theses. She was a particular inspiration to Kate Millet, who published *Sexual Politics* in 1970, in which she set out to demonstrate the political dimension of sexuality and to reveal the patriarchal domination at work in our societies[124]. The links between the two countries encouraged the translation of terms coined in the United States, such as 'sexism' (by analogy with the word racism)[125]. Christine Delphy's work has been disseminated internationally, influencing the field of sociology of the family in the UK[126].

118 Rochefort 2018, 83–85; Froidevaux-Metterie 2021, 17.
119 Delphy 1998 and 2001; Wittig 2018b (1980); Pavard *et al.* 2020, 271–284.
120 Mathieu 1973 and 1991; Guillaumin 1992.
121 Froidevaux-Metterie 2021, 37 ('les femmes et les hommes forment deux catégories sociales tenues ensemble par la relation d'oppression des seconds sur les premières').
122 See Tabet 2001, 139; Dorlin 2008, 66.
123 Rochefort 2018, 89–90; Froidevaux-Metterie 2021, 39–40.
124 Millett 1970.
125 Pavard *et al.* 2020, 272.
126 Pfefferkorn 2016, 30–31.

The greatest contribution to these exchanges was undoubtedly the concept of 'gender', used by American researchers from the 1970s onwards. At the same time, French-speaking researchers were working with the concepts of 'patriarchy', 'social sex', and French concepts such as '*sexage*' and, above all, from the 1980s onwards, '*rapports sociaux de sexe*' to designate the system of domination and oppression of men over women. The use of the latter concept, which is directly modelled on the '*rapports sociaux de classe*' (class relations) of Marxist studies, is particularly fruitful in French-speaking countries and in Romance languages[127]. While being, for some feminist theorists, a synonym for '*rapports sociaux de sexe*', gender 'also makes it possible to insist on the fact that men and women are the result of a social construction and that they are in no way reducible to the biological sexes[128]'. The expression '*rapports sociaux de sexe*' and other terms used in French have the advantage of showing that relations between women and men are socially constructed in terms of domination and subordination.

Theorised during the 1970s in the United States, the notion of 'gender' was already being used by Christine Delphy in 1976, although other French researchers were more reticent[129]. It seemed to gradually gain popularity in French-language research from 1988 onwards, following the translation in French of an article by the historian Joan W. Scott ('Gender: A Useful Category of Historical Analysis'), but it is especially since the beginning of the 21st century that the term has been used massively by researchers[130]. In this article, Scott defined gender as 'a constitutive element of social relationships based on perceived differences between the sexes, and gender is a primary way of signifying relationships of power[131]'. She emphasised the antagonistic and relational aspect of gender, and thus came close to the French feminists' definition of '*rapports sociaux de sexe*'.

1.1.2. From the third wave to #metoo

The so-called third wave of feminism began in the 1990s and differed from previous movements in its focus on diversity and the intersection of discrimination. By reappropriating the insult 'queer', activists launched a radical critique of gender and sexuality binarism[132]. This has led to the development of 'questions about gender identities and multiple sexual identities[133] ' and a deconstruction of the binary categories that confine women and men to stereotyped identities and sexualities. These issues, driven by the demands of LGBTQIA+ people, have not only made it possible to legitimise other forms of sexuality outside the heteronorm, but have also opened up the field of gender studies and seen the emergence of queer studies. For Judith Butler, gender naturalises a system of power, heterosexuality, and in order to deconstruct it and make it dysfunctional, it is necessary to blur and multiply gender identities. As Camille Froidevaux-Metterie points out, 'this is a crucial turning point that broadens the feminist field to include a diversity of discriminatory and oppressive configurations[134]'.

Judith Butler is an American philosopher. Her book *Gender Trouble: Feminism and the Subversion of Identity*, published in 1990, was translated into French in 2005 under the title *Trouble dans le genre*. Research in the fields of lesbian and gay studies, LGBT studies and queer theory still relies heavily on this classic work. In it, Butler challenged assumptions about the distinction often made between sex and gender, according to which sex is biological while gender is culturally constructed. She postulated that sex, gender and sexuality are all socially constructed, and put forward the idea of the **performative nature of gender**. 'Gender is not innate, it is achieved through norms and everyday injunctions[135]'; it is underpinned by learned and repeated acts and discourses: to show one's gender is to perform. Butler used the example of drag performance because, in her view, it has the power to disrupt gender norms[136]'. The philosopher also questioned the homogeneity of the 'female' subject and the need to take account of the other power relations that impact on them (class, race, ethnicity, etc.). These different currents of thought have made it possible to question the centrality of heterosexual norms in feminist research and to pave the way for questions about trans-identity, fluid and non-binary genders and postcolonial studies.

To understand the American genesis of gender studies, and especially queer studies, we need to look at Monique Wittig, a French materialist feminist. As early as the 1970s, a group of homosexual women from the MLF, including Wittig, were already highlighting the issue of the double oppression of lesbians, on the one hand because they are women and on the other because they are lesbians[137]. Among them, Wittig criticised the feminine universalism advocated by the MLF, which made invisible minority groups such as lesbians. Following a growing rift with the feminists of the MLF, of which she was one of the initiators, Wittig decided to settle permanently in the United States in 1976. In her feminist writings, she took the view that 'lesbians, removed from the relationship of domination with a man, are not concerned by a category

[127] Pfefferkorn 2016, 19, 97.

[128] Pfefferkorn 2016, 20 ('aussi d'insister sur le fait que les hommes et les femmes résultent d'une fabrication sociale et qu'ils ne sont en aucun cas réductibles aux sexes biologiques').

[129] Fassin 2004; Pfefferkorn 2016, 88.

[130] Scott 1986. Concept questioned by the author in Scott 2010. On the emergence of 'gender' in research, see Pavard *et al.* 2020, 395–404; Froidevaux-Metterie 2021, 17; Pfefferkorn 2016.

[131] Scott 1988, 141.

[132] Dorlin 2008, 109–110.

[133] Pavard *et al.* 2020, 388 ('questionnements sur les identités de genre et les identités sexuelles multiples').

[134] Froidevaux-Metterie 2021, 18 ('c'est un tournant crucial qui élargit le champ féministe à une diversité de configurations discriminantes et oppressives').

[135] Pavard *et al.* 2020, 397 ('Le genre n'est pas inné, il se réalise à travers les normes et les injonctions quotidiennes.').

[136] Sellberg 2015, 254.

[137] Dorlin 2008, 73–74; Pavard *et al.* 2020, 324.

constructed in the discourses of heterosexuality[138]'. She therefore concluded that lesbians are not women 'because what makes a woman is a particular social relationship to a man, [...] a relationship that lesbians escape by refusing to become or remain heterosexual[139]'. This phrase, 'lesbians are not women', from her major work 'La pensée straight[140]' ('The Straight Mind'), swept aside the feminist movement's preconception that women were a homogenous, unified group and led it to see heterosexuality as the major problem facing women. For her, heterosexuality is 'a political regime, a regime of domination[141]'. Wittig also criticised essentialist feminism, seeing it as belonging to the 'straight mind', to conformity, to the oppressive heterosexist mentality in which heterosexuality is considered mandatory.

If Wittig found fertile ground for a lasting presence in the United States, it was because she was not the only representative there of a radical feminism that criticised compulsory heterosexuality. Leading figures such as Adrienne Rich and Gayle Rubin saw political lesbianism as a way for women to break free[142]. A key figure in the United States, Wittig and her work exerted a major influence on American feminism and contributed to the emergence of queer theories in the 1990s, although she remained little known in France until recently. Published in 1992 in the United States, *The Straight Mind*, a collection of her articles, was not translated into French until ten years later. Yet, *La pensée straight* is one of the important theoretical foundations used by Judith Butler in her essay *Gender Trouble*[143].

In France, queer theories began to find an echo in the late 1990s, thanks in particular to the impetus of sociologist and queer theorist Sam Bourcier. It was during this same period that the term 'heteronormativity', used since 1993 by Michael Warner[144], began to spread. Current definitions agree on several points

> 'Heteronormativity describes the institutionalization and naturalization of dimorphic, deterministic beliefs about socio-sexual lives. Firstly, sex, gender, and sexuality are only understandable in terms of binary oppositions (i.e. male/female, man/woman, masculine/feminine, hetero-/homosexual). Divvying the world up into dualisms, universal in their applicability and hierarchical in their valuation of terms, is pervasive and longstanding in Western philosophical thought. Second, biology is social destiny with regard to behavior and identity. [...] Hence, sex is equal to gender is equal to sexuality. [Heteronormativity] also explains how the division of labor is presented as a natural state of human affairs. Third, heterosexuality is ideal and ancestral to our species as are monogamy and the nuclear family. Finally, the misogyny that undergirds patriarchy and homophobia dictate the valuation of masculinity, and those individuals who fall between the cracks of division (or dimorphism) are erased or deemed deviant[145].'

The term thus crystallises the many demands of feminists and LGBTQIA+ movements by highlighting several discriminatory dimensions of gender relations.

Alongside questions of identity and recognition of other forms of sexuality, the other area of demand concerns intersectionality and the place of racialised women in the dominant White discourse. Intersectionality, theorised by Kimberlé Crenshaw and whose genesis we outlined in the introduction, envisages the interweaving of multiple oppressions. According to Crenshaw, racism and sexism create social inequalities and involve both massive discrimination and a social reproduction of the subaltern condition[146]. Gayatri Chakravorty Spivak, in her 1988 essay *Can the Subaltern Speak?* argues that subalterns, and subaltern women in particular, have no space where their voices can be heard and no access to social mobility. It opened up the field of subaltern studies and postcolonial studies, and articulated questions of gender and class. Spivak highlighted the specificity of subaltern women in the Third World, whose situation is the most problematic, using the example of India, where they were instrumentalised by British power. Spivak used *sati* (the ritual suicide of widows) to demonstrate how Western discourse, particularly colonial discourse, had often distorted and misunderstood the practices of colonised peoples. She argued that the British colonial authorities had seen *sati* as a symbol of the oppression of Indian women and had used it to justify their intervention in Indian society. However, Spivak stressed that the British discourse on *sati* was a form of control and power, rather than a genuine concern for women's rights. By focusing on *sati*, the colonisers presented themselves as enlightened and civilised, while silencing the voices and perspectives of Indian women[147].

In the 2010s, and especially in the wake of the #metoo movement, new feminist movements have been springing up all over the world, with their main demand being the recognition of sexist and sexual violence against women, while in most countries the legal mechanisms put in place to combat such violence are largely unsatisfactory. This redeployment of feminist action and struggle is taking the form of militant action, whether in the form of demonstrations or happenings, collage actions

[138] Pavard *et al.* 2020, 328 ('les lesbiennes, extraites du rapport de domination avec un homme, ne sont pas concernées par une catégorie construite dans les discours de l'hétérosexualité').

[139] Wittig 2018b (1980), 64–65 ('car ce qui fait une femme, c'est une relation sociale particulière à un homme, (...) relation à laquelle les lesbiennes échappent en refusant de devenir ou de rester hétérosexuelles').

[140] The article was first presented as a conference paper in 1978 in New York before being published in France: Wittig 2018a (1980).

[141] *Libération*, 17 June 1999, interview ('un régime politique, un régime de domination').

[142] Rich 1980; Rubin 1998 (1975); Froidevaux-Metterie 2021, 40–41.

[143] Published in English in 1990 and translated into French in 2005. It is through this essay by Judith Butler that Wittig was rediscovered in France.

[144] Warner 1993.

[145] Geller 2017b, 70–71.

[146] Pavard *et al.* 2020, 442.

[147] Spivak 2020 (1988).

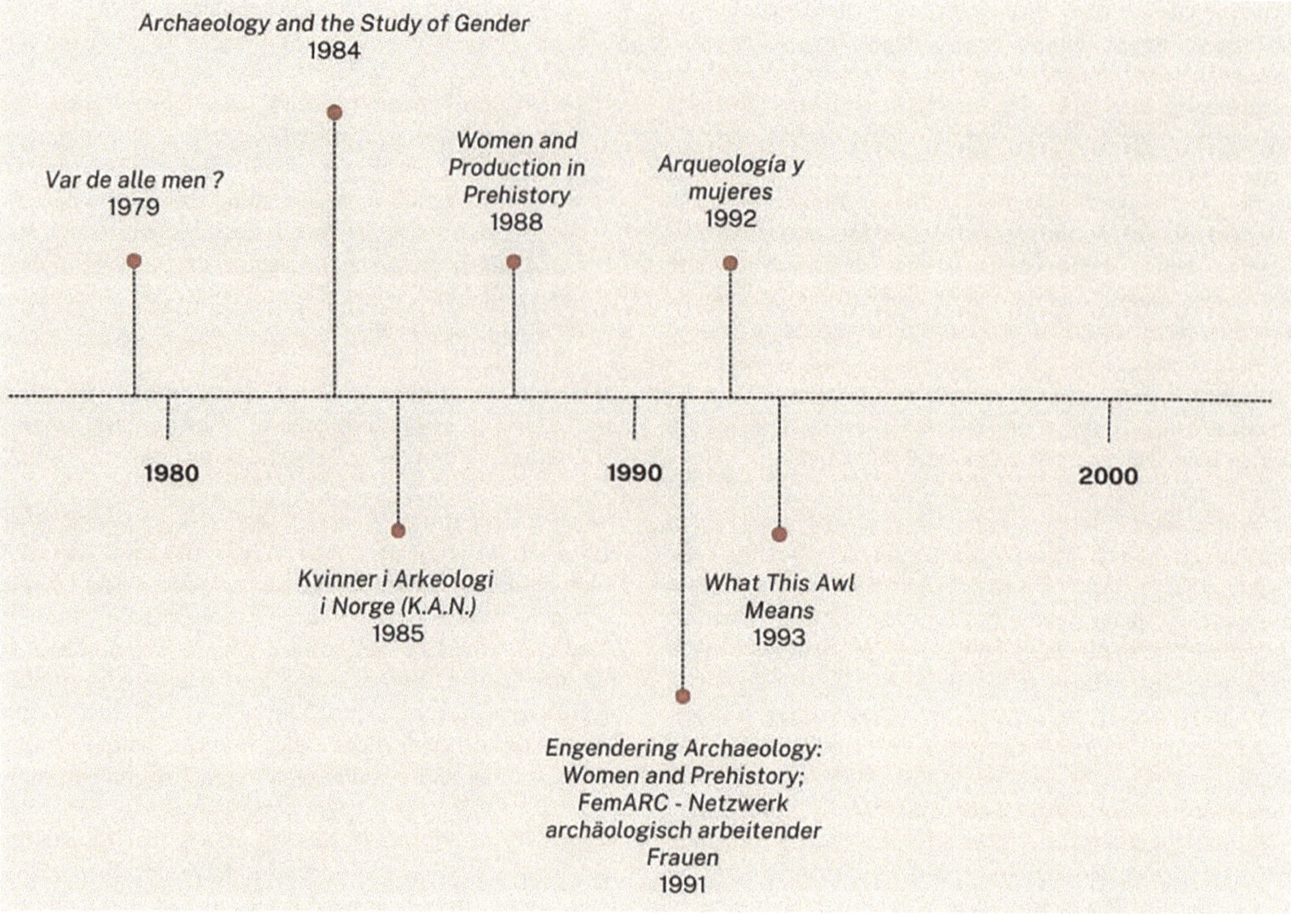

Figure 1.2. Timeline showing some of the most significant publications in the early days of the archaeology of gender.

denouncing feminicide or the creation of social media accounts dedicated to harassment in different professions, for example[148]. The massive sharing of testimonies leads to increased awareness, debate and policy change around sexual misconduct, advocating greater responsibility and cultural change to create safer and more inclusive environments for all.

This very brief history of feminism, which is largely centred on France, provides only a glimpse of the themes that were put forward by activists on the one hand and researchers on the other, and which made a major contribution to the progress of various academic fields, such as sociology, anthropology and history. We will see, however, that while these themes infiltrated American and Norwegian archaeology very early on, they were neglected for a very long time in French-speaking European archaeology.

1.2. Gender archaeology: development and institutionalisation

The birth of gender archaeology is linked to the theoretical developments of the feminist movements that took off in the mid-1960s, during which the struggles centred on sexuality, reproductive rights, work and the family[149]. In historiography, gender archaeology is linked to these feminist struggles, but it was research in history and social anthropology that mainly inspired the first gender archaeologists, in the United States and Norway, and initiated the contestation of male domination, gender norms and sexist prejudices within the discipline[150] (Figure 1.2).

From the 1980s onwards, gender archaeology met with uneven success across the globe. It is well established in some countries (including Australia, Brazil, Egypt, Germany, the United Kingdom, Norway, Spain and the United States), but has only been developing for a few years in others (Belgium, France and Greece), and is awaiting development elsewhere (e.g. China, Denmark, Portugal, Romania and Russia). The reasons for these disparities are not always very clear. The language barrier, a lack of interest in theoretical research within the discipline and a general anti-feminist climate are sometimes cited[151].

The context in which gender emerged as a field of research differs from one country to another. In Norway, for

[148] For example *Las Tesis* in Chile cf. Raynal 2021.

[149] Sørensen 2000, 17–18.

[150] Nelson 2006b, 2–3, 10–11. More recently, see Díaz-Andreu & Pope 2024.

[151] Augereau 2021; Coudart 1998; Mary 2020a et b.

example, gender archaeology emerged as a direct result of second-wave feminist demands, while in Spain its roots lie in both feminist and Marxist criticism. In the United States, feminist researchers such as Nancy Hartsock, Sandra Harding, Donna Haraway, Judith Butler and Simone de Beauvoir have had a major impact on gender archaeologists such as Margaret Conkey, Janet D. Spector and Alison Wylie, while in France Simone de Beauvoir's writings had no influence on archaeological studies, or at least not until the 2010s. The approaches, subjects and forms that this field of research can take are also very diverse[152]. The UK is the only country in Europe to have really taken up queer issues, work on care is more common in Spain, and Australian women are more interested in the place of women in the profession. Internationally, the reception of these various works also varies, depending on whether they are written in English or not, and whether they come from the United States or the rest of the world[153]. Norwegian archaeologists were the first to produce studies on gender, but for a time the use of their national language limited the reception of their work within the international academic sphere, an obstacle that never confronted American archaeologists. The same is true of Germany, where research into gender archaeology has been rich and very active since the early 1990s, but relatively little read and cited outside the country's borders.

The first articles to combine archaeology and feminism were mainly criticisms of working conditions and male domination within the profession, reflections on the lack of female representation in museums and a **critique of the androcentrism** that permeates publications' interpretations of the past[154]. The questioning of the division of domestic tasks is therefore echoed in archaeology, with publications devoted, in whole or in part, to highlighting the gendered division of tasks that is manifested both in the past, in interpretations of the past (sometimes in a caricatured way) and on the excavation site. The issues of women's access to the archaeological profession, the very large number of men occupying academic posts in a section that is nonetheless highly feminised on the student body side, and vertical segregation are also heirs to the feminist movements of the 1970s.

The observation, sometimes a little caricatured, of most of these studies was the same: 'The absence of women, whether in the profession, in representations or in interpretation, was [...] the consistent theme, and the emphasis was therefore upon gaining visibility[155]'. Early research therefore set out to rectify this absence and **make women visible**, so that they were no longer seen as passive subjects but as actively involved in the making of history. This process of making women visible has focused on four main areas of research[156]:

> **Androcentric biases**
>
> Androcentric biases lead to men's activities being over-valued and women's being under-valued or ignored. For example, men's work is seen as art, while women's is seen as craft, or women's work is always seen as less arduous than that of men.

1. The visibility of women in interpretations of the past
2. Valuing the role of women in the history of the discipline
3. Issues of equality and equity in archaeology
4. The visibility of women in museums

1.2.1. In the United States

Participating in what the historian Françoise Thébaud has called a 'compensatory' dimension in the face of publications presenting the masculine as a neutral universal, women researchers in the United States have committed themselves, as we shall see, to the rehabilitation of women in history and archaeology[157]. The first archaeologists to question the androcentrism of research insisted on the invisibility of women in interpretations of the past. However, the main problem with these interpretations was not the invisibility of women, but the stereotyped gender roles attributed to both men and women in the past, which were considered universal and unchanging. By simply applying the gender roles of the 19th and early 20th centuries to ancient societies, the fact that these roles may have been different or may have changed over time became and remained an unthought of research issue. It was by making visible the role of prehistoric women that the pioneers of gender archaeology tackled this problem.

As early as 1975, the anthropologist Sally Slocum presented the women of prehistoric societies as active people in her essay *Woman the Gatherer: Male Bias in Anthropology*, in which she criticised the universalist use and supposed neutrality of the word 'man' to designate human beings. This supposedly neutral term implies that men are designated as the main actors in human evolution, while women are relegated to the background[158]. In 1970, when a group of French feminists took part in an action under the Arc de Triomphe in Paris to lay a wreath of flowers in tribute to a woman who was 'even more unknown than the Unknown Soldier: his wife', one of the placards they held up reminded them that 'one man in two is a woman'. In this way, feminists aimed to overturn the male universalism that resulted in the erasure of women. In the 1950s and 1960s, for example, the hypothesis emerged that Man the Hunter, and he alone, was the key to the success and evolution of human societies. Slocum, like other researchers of her

152 Dommasnes 2018, 2975; Dommasnes & Wicker 2010, 12–14.
153 Whitehouse 2006, 735.
154 These include Kenyon 1969; Fonnesbeck-Sandberg *et al.* 1972; Gimbutas 1974; Thålin Bergman 1975.
155 Sørensen 2000, 17.
156 Sørensen 2000, 26.

157 Thébaud 2007 (1998).
158 Slocum 1975.

time[159], opposed these theories, and therefore focused on the role of women as gatherers – as opposed to male hunters – and on the active role they played in providing food.

This innovative research and the contribution of the social sciences certainly enriched the writing of the article that is often considered to be the birth certificate of gender archaeology, as it was the most widely distributed and read outside the restricted circle of gender archaeologists in the 1980s: 'Archaeology and the Study of Gender' by Margaret Conkey and Janet D. Spector, published in 1984[160]. In their introduction, Conkey and Spector stated that 'archaeology has substantiated a set of culture-specific beliefs about the meaning of masculine and feminine, about the capabilities of men and women, about their power relations, and about their appropriate roles in society[161]'. Drawing explicitly on a feminist perspective, the two researchers went on to highlight a large number of errors made by archaeologists in their interpretations of the past. They introduced the idea that archaeological interpretations are often based on the norms of the present, and that archaeology thus serves to construct a kind of 'gender mythology'. Finally, they called for a framework to be put in place and methodological tools to be developed in order to properly address the question of gender in archaeology. During the 1980s, however, the impact of this seminal article remained moderate.

The *Women and Production in Prehistory* conference was organised by Margaret Conkey and Joan Gero in 1988 in response to the slow progress of the ideas put forward by Conkey and Spector four years earlier. The same was true of the 22nd conference of the Chacmool Archaeology Association (an association of archaeology students at the University of Calgary) in 1989[162]. The proceedings of the 1988 conference were published under the title *Engendering Archaeology: Women and Prehistory*[163]. This was the first collective work to address the question of gender in prehistory. It included a series of European case studies and was therefore very well received in Europe[164]. In 1993, Janet Spector laid the foundations for what was to become feminist intersectional criticism in archaeology.

> 'I began writing this book about Little Rapids with several goals in mind. First, I wanted to communicate in an easily accessible way what we had learned about the Wahpeton community during a turbulent period of its history. Second, I wanted to highlight women's activities and the relation between men and women, topics typically ignored in archaeological writings. Third, I wanted to incorporate Dakota voices, visions and perspectives into the story[165].'

Conkey and Spector

Margaret Conkey (1943-): Margaret Conkey is an American archaeologist and Emeritus Professor of Anthropology at the University of California, Berkeley. A specialist in the question of gender and Palaeolithic art in the French Pyrenees, Conkey is co-author of one of the founding articles on gender archaeology, 'Archaeology and the Study of Gender' (1984), and co-editor of one of the first books to address the question of gender in prehistory, *Engendering Archaeology. Women in Prehistory*.

Janet D. Spector (1944–2011): Janet D. Spector is an American archaeologist known for her contributions to gender archaeology and ethnoarchaeology. She is notably the co-author of the famous article 'Archaeology and the Study of Gender[166]' and the author of the book *What This Awl Means: Feminist Archaeology at a Wahpeton Dakota Village*[167]. For 25 years she was a professor of anthropology at the University of Minnesota, where she helped to set up the university's gender studies section.

These writings were quickly followed by others, including a *Handbook of Gender in Archaeology*[168], which provided an exhaustive overview of the subject from a thematic, chronological and geographical perspective, and a special issue of the *Journal of Archaeological Method and Theory* devoted to feminist archaeology, which included articles by Margaret Conkey, Ericka Engelstad, Joan Gero, Stephanie Moser and Alison Wylie. Today, most publications in gender archaeology still come from the United States. Between 2001 and 2010, 97 articles (out of a sample of 3,525 articles published in archaeology worldwide, i.e. just over 2%) dealt with a subject related to gender archaeology. 70% of these came from the United States, 12% from the United Kingdom, 5% from Canada and 2% from Norway[169].

1.2.2. In Europe

Three recent articles and a book provide a relatively comprehensive overview of research into gender archaeology in Europe[170]. Ruth D. Whitehouse presents an overview by theme: the place of women archaeologists within the profession and in the history of the discipline, theoretical approaches, funerary studies, gendered roles in subsistence activities, gendered use

[159] Friedl 1975; Zihlman 1978; Dahlberg 1983a. It should be pointed out that the theses presented at the *Man the Hunter* conference in 1966 (Lee & DeVore 1968), while highlighting hunting as the driving force behind the development of humanity, also showed the importance of gathering and collecting foodstuffs, which contributed to 70% of the diet of hunter-gatherer groups.
[160] Nelson 2006b, 5.
[161] Conkey & Spector 1984, 1.
[162] Wylie 1997, 88–89.
[163] Gero & Conkey 1991.
[164] Whitehouse 2006, 734.
[165] Spector 1998, 361.
[166] Conkey & Spector 1984.
[167] Spector 1993.
[168] Nelson 2006.
[169] Alberti & Danielsson 2018, 2994.
[170] Whitehouse 2006; Dommasnes *et al.* 2010; Dommasnes & Montón-Subias 2012; Dommasnes 2018. See also Díaz-Andreu & Pope 2024.

of space, iconography[171]. The other three publications adopt a more traditional country-by-country structure. At the European level, the annual conferences of the Theoretical Archaeology Group in the UK are regular venues for discussing gender issues in archaeology[172]. Archaeologists working on subjects related to gender archaeology are also brought together in the Archaeology and Gender in Europe (AGE) group[173]. Founded in 2008 within the European Association of Archaeologists (EAA), the aim of this working group is to provide a meeting place and a forum for discussion on issues relating to gender. The group emerged in the wake of the session on *Gender, identity and materiality* organised by Spanish, Norwegian, American and Swedish researchers Margarita Sánchez Romero, Sandra Montón Subías, Liv Helga Dommasnes, Nancy L. Wicker and Tove Hjørungdal at the EAA's annual conference in 2008. The AGE's first action dates from 2009. The Gender and Archaeology in Europe round table brought together several researchers from Norway, Sweden, Germany, Spain, the UK, Romania and Russia. Since then, sessions and congresses have been regularly organised and published by members of the group[174].

In Europe, gender archaeology first appeared in Norway in the 1970s, in connection with the feminist demands of the second wave. The handful of researchers interested in the subject at the time were influenced by the writings of Simone de Beauvoir, Nancy Hartsock and Sandra Harding[175]. Attention focused firstly on the place of women within the profession, and secondly on the representation of women in interpretations of the past[176]. Gro Mandt's *Konferanse om kvinneforskning* (Conference on women's studies) was the first article to address the issue of gender[177]. It defined the foundations of gender archaeology and outlined the themes that should be developed in the near future[178]. The *Var de alle menn?* conference (Were they all men?) organised by Reidar Bertelsen, Arnvid Lillehammer and Jenny-Rita Næss in 1979, the proceedings of which were not published in English until 1987, is nevertheless regularly cited as the starting point for reflection on gender in the country. The creation of the organisation and journal *Kvinner i Arkeologi i Norge* (Women in archaeology in Norway) in 1985 also helped to develop this field of research, both nationally, through articles, conferences and round tables in Norwegian, and internationally, with articles published in English from the early 1990s[179].

In the UK, gender archaeology developed alongside post-processualist approaches and feminist criticism. It was also strongly influenced by articles published by American women researchers in the 1980s and early 1990s (Conkey, Spector, Gero, Wylie). Gender issues were discussed at conferences organised by the Theoretical Archaeology Group at Durham University in the early 1980s, but the first publication on the subject dates from 1988[180]. It was written by several students at Cambridge University, including Roberta Gilchrist, who went on to publish the reference work *Gender and Archaeology: Contesting the Past* around ten years later[181]. The first monograph, on women in prehistory, was published in 1989[182]. Since then, there has been a proliferation of articles, congresses, symposia, dissertations and doctoral theses. In 2008, the British Women Archaeologists network was founded. The UK is also one of the few countries in Europe to have developed the field of queer archaeology[183].

In Germany, the first research into gender archaeology date back to 1988, when the first seminar on the subject was organised in Tübingen[184]. As in England, it was the students who took up the theme. In 1989, a lecture on prehistoric women was given at the first national meeting of students of prehistory and protohistory in Kiel. In 1991, a second seminar entitled *Feminismus und Archäologie* (Feminism and archaeology) was held in Tübingen. It was quickly followed by a first article entitled *Feminismus und Archäologie?*[185] In the same year, the organisation Netzwerk archäologisch arbeitender Frauen - FemArc (Network of women working in archaeology) was founded[186]. From then on, German research into gender archaeology was conducted within the framework of, or with the support of, this organisation. FemArc remains very active, sending out regular newsletters and organising conferences, symposia and exhibitions. The group also publishes a series of monographs entitled Frauen - Forschung - Archäologie (Women - Research - Archaeology).

Liv Helga Dommasnes

Emeritus professor at the University of Bergen in Norway, Liv Helga Dommasnes was the first person to write a thesis in gender archaeology in Scandinavia. *Yngre jernalder i Sogn, forsøk på sosial rekonstruksjon* (The Late Iron Age at Sogn. Attempts at social reconstruction) is an unpublished study of the gendered division of labour during the Late Iron Age (600–1050 AD) in Norway. Dommasnes is the author and editor of numerous articles and books on gender and feminism in archaeology.

[171] Whitehouse 2006.
[172] Dommasnes 2018, 2976.
[173] Palincas 2021.
[174] Among others, see Dommasnes *et al.* 2010; Matić & Jensen 2017; Coltofean-Arizancu *et al.* 2021.
[175] Dommasnes 2018, 2970.
[176] Sørensen 2013, 400.
[177] Mandt 1976.
[178] Sørensen 2013, 399.
[179] Dommasnes & Montón-Subías 2012, 370–371.
[180] Arnold *et al.* 1988, quoted by Dommasnes 2018, 2970.
[181] Gilchrist 1999.
[182] Ehrenberg 1989, quoted by Dommasnes & Montón-Subías 2012, 371–372.
[183] Dommasnes 2018, 2970; Montón-Subías 2018, 2980.
[184] Dommasnes 2018, 2970–71; Dommasnes & Montón-Subías 2012, 372; Mertens & Koch 2005, 29.
[185] Kästner & Karlisch 1991.
[186] Moraw 2021.

German publications on the subject also include a series of collective works published by the University of Trier from 2002 onwards. The series, entitled IPHIS - Gender Studies in den Altertumswissenschaften, includes many contributions relating to the study of ancient texts, but some also look at the material culture and iconography of the classical world.

In Spain, gender archaeology also emerged in the 1980s, on the initiative of a handful of archaeology students at the University of Barcelona who had reappropriated the tools developed by second-wave feminists and Marxist critics[187]. The writings of Norwegian and American archaeologists also provided food for thought[188]. Their first article was published in 1989 and focused on the place of women in prehistory and Greek antiquity[189]. The first series of conferences on women in archaeology, *Arqueologiá y Mujeres*, dates back to 1992. The topics covered ranged from the androcentrism of interpretations to the discrimination faced by women in professional practice, not to mention sexist stereotypes in museums[190]. According to Díaz-Andreu and Montón-Subías, this session 'had a decisive impact on many of the women in the audience[191]'. In 1999, the first book in Spanish on feminism and archaeology was published[192]. Since then, the popularity of gender archaeology in Spain has not waned. Questions relating to gender and feminism are the subject of numerous debates, courses, conferences, exhibitions, articles, books, dissertations and doctoral theses[193]. Events are also organised in partnership with Spanish-speaking feminist archaeologists on the other side of the Atlantic (forums for debate, joint publications, etc.)[194].

In the rest of Europe, the situation varies from country to country. In Sweden, gender studies in archaeology emerged a few years after the first Norwegian initiatives and followed a similar development, leading to an increase in the number of dissertations and doctoral theses on the subject[195]. It took a little longer to get off the ground in Greece. The first monograph on the subject was published in the early 1990s[196], but it was not until 2005 that the first colloquium on the question of gender in Aegean prehistory was organised at the University of Crete[197]. In Denmark, Marie-Louise Stig Sørensen noted in 2013 that 'apart from works by Danish archaeologists working abroad [of which she is one] there has been very little interest in explicit gender research within Danish archaeology since the 1970s[198]'. The situation is similar in Portugal[199] and the countries of Eastern Europe, where gender archaeology is essentially the work of a handful of researchers[200]. In Romania, for example, Nona Palincas was the only archaeologist working on these issues in the 2010s. The same is true of Russia, where Natalia Berseneva is the exception[201].

1.2.3. French-speaking countries in Europe: France, Belgium and Switzerland

In 2012, Margarita Díaz-Andreu and Sandra Montón-Subías noted that 'in France, feminism and archaeology seem to have gone separate ways, and gender archaeology stirs little enthusiasm[202]'. The same year, Jean-Paul Demoule also noted that 'Gender Archaeology [...] has not really taken off in France[203]'. The same observation applies to French-speaking Belgium and Switzerland. Gender archaeology is struggling to develop in these three countries. Although a few occasional works were published between 2000 and 2012, the first one-day conference entitled *Genre et archéologie : le corps et ses identités* (Gender and archaeology: the body and its identities), organised by Sandra Péré-Noguès, Adeline Grand-Clément and Sophie Brouquet-Cassagne, dates from 2013[204]. The subject only really began to emerge after 2014, thanks to the theses of two young researchers. Chloé Belard's research on graves in Champagne during the Iron Age and Caroline Trémeaud's on Celtic graves in the northern Alps during the Bronze and Iron Ages were the first to clearly assert the use of gender as a theoretical and interpretative tool for material remains from the past[205]. Belard and Trémeaud have also published numerous articles on their respective subjects, in both French and English[206]. Gender archaeology finally took off timidly in France and French-speaking Belgium in the second half of the 2010s. A second one-day conference (*Approches genrées des populations du passé : Archéologie - Bioanthropologie - Histoire*) was organised in France in June 2017 by Luana Batista Goulart and Isabelle Séguy. Belgium followed in October 2019 with *Genre et archéologie, rapports sociaux de sexe dans les sociétés anciennes*, organised by Isabelle Algrain. In 2020, this study day gave rise to the first French-language collective work on gender issues in archaeology, *Archéologie du genre. Construction sociale des identités et culture matérielle*, which included around ten articles on the issue of gender from a theoretical point of view, the place of women and minorities within the profession, and case studies[207]. The French-language equivalent of *Were They All Men?* appeared in June 2021 in the form of the session *Où sont les femmes? Archéologie*

[187] Dommasnes & Montón-Subías 2012, 372–376.
[188] Montón-Subías 2018, 2980.
[189] Sanahuja & Picazo 1989, quoted by Dommasnes & Montón-Subías 2012, 372; Díaz-Andreu & Montón Subías 2013.
[190] Montón-Subías 2018, 2981.
[191] Diaz-Andreu & Montón-Subías 2013, 440.
[192] Colomer *et al.* 1999.
[193] Diaz-Andreu & Montón-Subías 2013, 440–441; Dommasnes & Montón-Subías 2012, 376; Dommasnes & Wicker 2010, 15. See also the collaborative project *Past Women*.
[194] Montón-Subías 2018, 2985.
[195] Dommasnes & Montón-Subías 2012, 371.
[196] Kokkinidou & Nikolaidou 1993.
[197] Hitchcock & Nikolaidou 2013, 503.
[198] Sørensen 2013, 407.
[199] Abrunhosa & Valdez-Tullet 2021; Diaz-Andreu & Montón-Subías 2013, 439.
[200] Dommasnes 2018, 2971.
[201] Palincas 2021, 108.
[202] Diaz-Andreu & Montón-Subías 2013, 439.
[203] Demoule 2012, 2 ('la *Gender Archaeology* [...] n'a pas vraiment décollé en France').
[204] Audouze 2006; Coudart 1998; Mathieu 2010; Péré-Noguès 2011; quoted by Demoule 2012, 2.
[205] Belard 2017a; Trémeaud 2018.
[206] For example Belard 2012, 2015, 2017b and 2020; Trémeaud 2015a, 2015b, 2015c, 2017, 2019, 2021.
[207] Algrain 2020.

du genre dans la Préhistoire et la Protohistoire : La France à l'écart des gender studies? organised by Anne Augereau, Sophie Archambault de Beaune and Caroline Trémeaud as part of the 29e Congrès préhistorique de France[208]. The session featured twenty papers on subjects ranging from the question of gender in prehistory to the place of women archaeologists, past and present, within this field of research.

Gender archaeology is also developing in the French-speaking world thanks to the Paye ta Truelle collective. Created in January 2017 by archaeologist and feminist activist Laura Mary, Paye ta Truelle is a group made up of Belgian and French feminist archaeologists fighting for equality and diversity in archaeology. They promote French-language research into gender archaeology, as well as raise awareness of the issue of discrimination within the profession. The actions undertaken by this collective are varied and take the form of testimonies on discrimination shared on social networks[209], videos[210], podcasts[211], articles[212], book reviews[213], organisation of or participation in conferences, seminars, courses, round tables and colloquia in both French and English, in France, Belgium, Switzerland, Quebec, the United States and England[214].

In October 2020, in partnership with the Belgian feminist association Université des femmes, Paye ta Truelle organised the first French-language one-day conference on feminist archaeology, entitled *Féminismes et archéologie. Égalité, diversité et convergence des luttes : pour une archéologie de la subversion.* With the Archéo-Éthique association, Paye ta Truelle was behind Archéo-Sexisme, the first exhibition on discrimination in archaeology, as well as the 'Chantier Éthique' charter and vade-mecum, covering 37 archaeological operations between 2019 and 2022. The majority of these are in France, but excavations in Belgium, England, Cyprus, Oman, Italy and Alaska have also signed up. In 2021, Paye ta Truelle, in collaboration with the Archaeology of Gender in Europe group, launched the first survey to determine the extent of various forms of harassment and assault in European archaeological communities (Harcèlement et agressions en archéologie/Harassment, Assault, Bullying and Intimidation in Archaeology)[215].

Antiquipop

Antiquipop is a collective project that 'identifies and decodes references to Antiquity in contemporary popular culture'[216]. Edited by Fabien Bièvre-Perrin, the project's scientific notebook compiles a series of articles analysing references to Antiquity in contemporary art, cinema, video games, literature, fashion, music, advertising and series. Some of these analyses were carried out through the prism of gender, masculinities and queer theory. Anaïs Tillier, for example, examined the figure of Helen of Troy in cinema and television from a feminist perspective[217].

Over the last few years, gender archaeology has met with some success among students and young researchers, as evidenced by the growing number of master's theses and doctoral dissertations on the subject. Aparca, a very active student association in Toulouse, has organised conferences, café-debates, meetings and the hosting of the Archéo-Sexisme exhibition as part of its *Sex, Gender and Archaeology* festival in 2019 and 2020[218]. Alter Ego Rennes, a student association at the University of Rennes 2, initiated a series of events entitled 'RenCONTRER le sexisme en archéologie' to coincide with the hosting of the Archéo-Sexisme exhibition to their university and the creation of the 'Portraits of women archaeologists and activists' exhibition. Issue 5 of the journal *Frontière-s*, entitled *Aux frontières des genres*, edited by Loubna Ayeb and Élise Pampanay, was devoted entirely to the issue of gender in ancient and medieval cultures[219]. Even if it is not strictly devoted to gender archaeology, the annual organisation of the Virtual Conference for Women Archaeologists and Paleontologists[220] by a group of female doctoral students in archaeology and palaeontology from various French universities since 2021, as well as the creation of the Association for early-career Women Archaeologists and Paleontologists in January 2022, also demonstrate this desire to recognise the work carried out by women, particularly young female researchers, within the discipline. A round-table discussion on the place of women in archaeology and palaeontology closed the first day of the conference in 2021 and the second day in 2023. However, exploration of this field of research remains limited for the time being[221].

[208] Published online in 2023: https://www.prehistoire.org/515_p_58172/cpf29_sessoin_augereau.html.
[209] See Paye ta Truelle tumblr [https://payetatruelle.tumblr.com].
[210] *Les erreurs sexistes de l'archéologie*, produced in partnership with the YouTube channel 'C'est une autre histoire' created by Manon Bril/Champier.
[211] For example 'Archéologie du genre avec Isabelle Algrain' (*Paroles d'Histoire*, episode 178); 'Rendez-vous avec Matilda - #4 Laura Mary' (*The Meta News*); 'Paye ta Truelle' (*Histoire de Savoir*); I. Algrain and L. Mary, 'Les femmes archéologues au tournant du xxe siècle : petites mains ou *Men-Women* ?', podcast produced for the symposium 'Le genre des célibats', October 1–2 2021, [Accessed 2 September 2022, https://legenredescelibats.wordpress.com/2021/08/30/isabelle-algrain-laura-mary/].
[212] Algrain 2020, 2021a and 2021b; Mary 2020a, 2020b and 2021; Mary *et al.* 2019; Vandevelde, 2020.
[213] Denis & Mary 2021; Mary & Rocca 2021.
[214] See the Paye ta Truelle collective website [https://payetatruelle.wixsite.com/projet].
[215] Coltofean-Arizancu *et al.* 2023.

[216] See the Antiquipop website [https://antiquipop.hypotheses.org/].
[217] Tillier 2021.
[218] Site de l'association Aparea [https://blogs.univ-tlse2.fr/aparea/].
[219] Ayeb & Pampanay 2021.
[220] Site de la *Virtual Conference for Women Archaeologists and Paleontologists* [Accessed 12 February 2022, https://womenpaleoarch.sciencesconf.org/].
[221] Par exemple Augereau 2019 et 2021 ; Algrain 2020a, 2021b, 2022 et 2023 ; Belard 2012, 2015, 2017a, 2017b et 2020 ; Mary 2020a, 2020b et 2021 ; Trémeaud 2015a, 2015b, 2017, 2018 et 2019s.

1.2.4. And the rest of the world?

In Africa, research into gender archaeology has mainly been carried out by archaeologists from outside the continent, and mainly in Egypt and South Africa[222]. Due to political instability and a lack of funding in many states, very little archaeological research from a gender perspective has been carried out in West, Central and North Africa[223].

In China, South Korea, Japan, Thailand and the Philippines, gender archaeology has been developing slowly since 2000. Elisabeth Bacus explains this delay by the low number of women archaeologists in these regions[224]. Katheryn M. Linduff and Yan Sun share this view of China[225]. Moreover, Marxist archaeology is still predominant in China, and this contributes to marginalising or ignoring gender studies. Gender studies did not develop in Chinese archaeology until the 2000s, thanks to the support of two American researchers, Sarah M. Nelson and Katheryn M. Linduff[226]. In Afghanistan, Pakistan, Nepal, Bangladesh, India and Sri Lanka, research remains rare. In the Near East, gender studies are more numerous but remain a minority in relation to overall archaeological production. The vast majority of studies have focused on Catalhöyük and the Mesopotamian city-states of the fourth and third millennia[227].

In South America, gender studies in archaeology are still mostly in their infancy[228], with the exception of Brazil. The article by Camila Jácome and Laura Furquim provides a good overview of the development of this field of research in Brazil[229]. Gender studies are developing within Brazilian archaeology in connection with second-wave feminist movements, anthropologist Margaret Mead's research on Indigenous societies in North America and the numerous archaeological studies published on the African diaspora. Tânia Lima was one of the first archaeologists to apply feminist criticism to the interpretation of material remains[230]. Since the 2010s, queer issues have also been incorporated into archaeological thinking. The first publication on feminist archaeology dates from 2017[231]. Peru and Colombia have also stood out in recent years thanks to the work of a number of young female researchers. In Peru, scientific production in gender archaeology remains limited and focuses mainly on the place of women and minorities within the discipline. The first articles date from the second half of the 2010s and are inspired by the work of American archaeologists such as Conkey, Gero and Wylie[232]. The work of Carito Tavera Medina and Lady Santana Quispe, in particular the organisation of the conference and the publication of the book *Mujeres del Pasado y del Presente. Una visión desde la arquelogía peruana*[233], the #MeTooArquelogía survey, and the creation of the Red de Mujeres en Arquelogía Peruana collective, have become benchmarks in Peru. In Colombia, the members of the GEFA – Género Feminismo y Arquelogía collective, set up in 2017, are pursuing work similar to that of their Peruvian colleagues[234].

In Australia, the gender issue emerged in the early 1990s. The first *Women in Archaeology Conference* was organised by Hilary du Cros and Laurajane Smith in 1991. Margaret Conkey, Joan Gero and Alison Wylie were the keynote speakers and encouraged the recognition of gender archaeology as a field of research within Australian archaeology. The conference was a huge success, leading to the publication of three monographs and the organisation of five other conferences on the subject[235]. The first session on gender at the Australian Archaeological Association's annual conference was held in 1998[236]. Organised by Cherrie de Leuien and Robert Pilgrim, it was entitled *Power and Gender in Archaeology*[237]. Since the 1990s, studies in gender archaeology have focused mainly on the place of women within the profession, and less on questions of gender or sexuality within interpretations of the past[238]. For example, Stephanie Moser is working on the question of gendered stereotypes within the profession (see chapter 10). Links have also been forged with Indigenous archaeology. However, Cherrie De Leieun stated in 2018 that 'despite its promising development, particularly in the 1990s, the future of an archaeology of gender (and especially of feminist archaeology) in Australia is uncertain[239]', blaming the lack of interest in feminist issues and the low rate of specialists in this field managing to obtain an academic post.

[222] For example Kent 1998; Matić 2021; Wadley 1998.
[223] Lyons 2007, 1.
[224] Bacus 2006, 637.
[225] Linduff & Sun 2004, 2.
[226] Linduff & Sun 2004, 4.
[227] Sinopoli 2006, 668, 675 et 677.
[228] Ebert & Patterson 2007.
[229] Jácome & Furquim 2018.
[230] Lamia 1995 and 2003.
[231] Ribeiro *et al.* 2017.
[232] Santana 2019; Tavera & Santana 2021; Tavera 2019; Torres & Moncayo 2018.
[233] Tavera & Santana 2022.
[234] Medellín *et al.* 2021.
[235] De Leieun 2018, 2962 ; Smith & O'Donnell 2006, 694.
[236] De Leieun 2018, 2962.
[237] Smith & O'Donnell 2006, 696.
[238] De Leieun 2018, 2963.
[239] De Leieun 2018, 2966.

Where to start ?

I. Algrain (ed.), *Archéologie du genre. Construction sociale des identités et culture matérielle*, Université des femmes, 2020.

L. Coltofean-Arizancu, B. Gaydarska & U. Matić, *Gender Stereotypes in Archaeology. A Short Reflection in Image and Text*, Sidestone Press, 2021.

L.H. Dommasnes, 'Gender, Feminist, and Queer Archaeologies: European Perspective', *in* C. Smith, *Encyclopedia of Global Archaeology*, Springer, 2018, 2968–2980.

S.M. Nelson (ed.), *Handbook of Gender in Archaeology*, AltaMira Press, 2006.

A. Wylie, 'Doing Archaeology as a Feminist: Introduction', *in Journal of Archaeological Method and Theory* 14, 2007, 209–216.

2

Race, racism and archaeology

'As archaeologists, we may recognize the open-ended potential for abuse through the control and subsequent distortion of historical and archaeological interpretations. [...] We stop short of questioning our own position as guardians of the past [...]. It is as if we are unaware that the social and political context within which we operate has any influence on our interpretations and representations of the past[240].'

The study of the past has often been used to justify and perpetuate various forms of discrimination based on race and gender. For example, the history of archaeology is marked by a lack of diversity, with the field dominated by White male scholars. As we will see in the second part of the book, this has led to biases in the interpretation of archaeological data, with many researchers overlooking or downplaying the contributions and perspectives of women and people of colour in the past

Furthermore, archaeological research has often been used to promote sexist and racist ideas about the roles and abilities of women and racialised people. For example, archaeological studies have sometimes been used to justify the subjugation and exploitation of non-White peoples, with researchers using archaeological data to assert that certain ethnic groups were less advanced or civilised than others. Research into decolonial and Indigenous archaeology thus makes it possible to question the links between power, gender, race and class. The issue of decolonisation is also of major interest in helping us to think through the different sex/gender systems that existed before colonisation and were erased by it.

In recent years, under the influence of feminist studies, gender studies and critical race theory, archaeologists have become more aware of the need to integrate diverse perspectives into their research and to challenge discriminatory beliefs and practices in the field. This has led them to focus more on studying the contributions and experiences of women and racialised people in the past, as well as placing greater emphasis on exploring the ways in which archaeology can be used to promote social justice and equality in the present.

2.1. Archaeology and racism

Archaeology and racism are intimately linked. From the very beginnings of the discipline in the 19th century, archaeology has been used throughout the world to establish the legitimacy of European nation-states by creating a '*roman national*[241]' (a national fiction) and to justify colonialism, neo-colonialism, slavery, imperialism, xenophobic nationalism and ethnocentrism, leading to the forced displacement of Indigenous populations from their territories, the plundering of their heritage, the devaluation of their knowledge, and the marginalisation and oppression of minorities.

In the course of the 19th century, a so-called 'scientific racism' emerged. It postulated a link between physical characteristics, such as skin and hair colour or cranial measurements, and the mental capacities of individuals – always to the advantage of White populations. Populations were also hierarchised according to their proximity to White populations, and there was a tendency to try and prove that 'advanced' civilisations were White, as in the case of Pharaonic Egypt[242]. Thus, the grouping of populations under the term 'race' was determined culturally rather than biologically.

Egyptology is one of the sciences that has been used to validate these pseudo-scientific theories. On the basis of cranial measurements that took no account of sexual dimorphism or the size of individuals, Egyptologists at the end of the 19th century considered that two 'races' lived in the Nagada region, the cradle of Egyptian civilisation: a 'dynastic race' from the East came to settle in the region, among a 'negroid' population, and thus enabled the development of the first dynasties[243]. As Uroš Matić pointed out, 'the idea of a 'dynastic race' is the culmination of racist and colonial attitudes as at that time it was not imaginable that non-White populations could produce high culture[244]'. The alleged whiteness of the ancient Egyptians also reinforced the idea that no non-White population could be the source of a 'civilised' culture.

During the 19th and early 20th centuries, archaeologists also began collecting material remains and human remains belonging to colonised populations on a massive scale, on the assumption that many of these populations were on the verge of extinction. This research led to the production of classifications, typologies and exhibitions that theorised the inferiority of these peoples and, by extension, the justification for their domination by Western countries. Today, racism continues to permeate methods and theories used in archaeological research, relations between archaeologists and local populations, and relations between archaeologists themselves.

240 Franklin 1997a, 36.
241 For example Arnold 1990 and 2005; Chapoutot 2008; Demoule 2020.
242 Matić 2020, 8, 15, 18–21; Siapkas 2014, 68.
243 Matić 2020, 16–18.
244 Matić 2020, 18.

Definitions

Colonialism: ideology justifying the political domination and economic exploitation of territories annexed by a state.

Neo-colonialism: term used to describe the political and economic control that a former colonial state continues to exercise over its former colonies.

Imperialism: domination by one country over another or several other countries. Imperialism is often justified by ethnocentric arguments. For example, 'superior' European countries have a duty to 'civilise' 'savage' and 'inferior' non-European populations.

Ethnocentrism: the tendency to focus on the norms and values of one's own society when analysing other societies.

In 2006, Sonya Atalay, an Indigenous archaeologist specialising in the repatriation of material remains from Native American populations, emphasised that 'archaeology is much more than simply a tool for understanding the past: archaeological practice and the knowledge it produces are part of the history and heritage of living people and have complex contemporary implications and relevance for those people in daily life[245]'. She added that this was particularly true of Indigenous and colonised populations, because Western researchers, the majority of whom were White middle-class and affluent men, held and still hold the political, social and economic power to study, interpret, write and teach about these populations' pasts, and to create knowledge for consumption by the Western public and academics. Margaret Bruchac noted that although Indigenous people have long been used as informants, Western researchers have in practice exercised control over their property. The concerns of these populations have also been relegated to the background[246]. In 2020, Lynn Gamble and her colleagues – editors of the four journals of the Society for American Archaeology – acknowledged that the lives and stories of racialised people, both past and present, have been neglected in their various publications: 'We have not done enough to create room for their voices and viewpoints in our publications[247]'. Laura Heath-Stout's research into 21 archaeological journals in the United States between 2007 and 2016 came to the same conclusion[248]. Yannis Hammilakis also pointed out that almost all the editors and contributors to general and theoretical textbooks in archaeology come from British and American universities, and occasionally from Australia[251]. For Atalay, starting by acknowledging the colonial heritage in archaeological interpretations is the first step towards decolonising the discipline.

Pseudo-archaeology

Pseudo-archaeology refers to a set of non-scientific approaches to the material remains of the past: the pyramids of Giza, said to have been built by Atlanteans, or the Nazca lines, said to have been made by extraterrestrials, are two examples. Pseudo-archaeology is fuelled in particular by racism, with its adherents fond of denigrating or denying the intelligence and skills of Indigenous (non-White) populations in the construction of these monuments. It is very popular with white supremacists, who often accuse archaeologists of 'hiding the truth' about these theories. In France, the Association de lutte contre la désinformation dans les domaines de l'Archéologie, de l'Histoire de l'Art et de l'Histoire (ALDHHAA) aims to take action 'against disinformation and the rewriting of historical facts (at the expense of scientific consensus), in particular for the benefit of political and/or nationalist ideologies, the manipulation of discourse, sectarian or conspiracy theories[249]' through conferences, workshops and events aimed at a variety of audiences outside the heritage world[250].

2.2. Decolonising archaeology?

> 'As archaeologists, we must question how racism conditions our discipline and, in so doing, how an unreflective archaeology is fed right back into a racist society without challenging[252].'

Archaeological research is by no means neutral or objective[253]. Decolonial approaches have emerged as a means of combating the predominance of racist discourse and improving knowledge of minorities in archaeology. Decolonising has political and practical effects: it changes the power relations between scientists and research themes, while increasing the volume and accuracy of the data

245 Atalay 2006, 283.
246 Bruchac 2014, 2069.
247 Gamble *et al.* 2020, vi.
248 Heath-Stout 2020a.

249 Interview of Faustine Boulay, founder of ALDHHAA, by Ch. Asselin on Digimind (May 21, 2021), [Accessed 20 October 2021, https://blog.digimind.com/fr/tendances/fake-news-histoire-art-archeologie] ('contre la désinformation et la réécriture des faits historiques (aux dépens des consensus scientifiques) notamment aux profits d'idéologies politiques et/ou nationalistes, de manipulations des discours, de théories sectaires ou complotistes').
250 For further information on this subject, see also the work of Canadian researcher Stephanie Halmhofer, which she presents on her blog [Accessed 20 October 2021, https://bonesstonesandbooks.com/].
251 Hammilakis 2012, 70. This is a problem we also had to face when writing this chapter, as most of the references come from researchers from the English-speaking world and/or who write in English.
252 Franklin 1997a, 40.
253 Brown 2019, 189.

available on the populations studied[254]. This approach to archaeology has been influenced by feminism, gender and queer studies, as well as critical race theory, which looks at the relationship between race, power and politics, and the field of post-colonial research in political science, in particular the work of Edward Saïd on orientalism, i.e. the – often false – construction of the East in Western thought and discourse, and that of Gayatri Chakravorty Spivak, who questions the possibility of subalterns speaking out[255]. This line of thought first emerged in the United States in the early 1990s, in connection with the claims and demonstrations by Native Americans concerning their heritage.

For a long time, archaeologists claimed almost exclusive ownership of the material remains they unearthed[256]. From the 1990s onwards, some of them, together with researchers from other disciplines and activists, organised conferences and debates on the issues of reburial of human remains and repatriation of material remains. Articles exposing the links between archaeology, colonialism and racism were published, and regulations were introduced to govern archaeological practice. In the United States, the Society for American Archaeology adopted a code of ethics in 1991 that included a passage on the importance of collaboration with Indigenous populations and the reburial of human remains[257].

This anti-racist approach to archaeology now applies just as much to Indigenous populations, ethnic minorities and groups from the various diasporas, as it does to people whose histories have been misrepresented by archaeologists[258]. Indigenous archaeology, Black feminist archaeology and the archaeology of the African diaspora are all part of this theoretical and political movement.

The general aim of the decolonial movement is to systematise ethical questioning in archaeology by uncovering 'new intersections among past and present identities and cultures[259]'. This can take many forms: a reflexive approach to research practices, the creation of excavation projects in collaboration with Indigenous communities, the repatriation and reburial of human remains, the development of codes of ethics to protect these remains in conjunction with the populations concerned, the establishment of scholarships and training opportunities for Indigenous people and ethnic minorities in order to increase their numbers in archaeology, the management of archaeological collections in partnership with Indigenous and Afro-descendant populations, the restoration of heritage sites, the correction and design of more historically and culturally accurate museum representations, and so on. In so doing, 'archaeologists can redistribute control [over material remains]. [...] Change should be spurred on by responsibility, rather than guilt.[260]'.

NAGPRA

In 1971, Maria Pearson, a Dakota activist, fought for the reburial of the remains of a Native American woman found in a colonial cemetery in Iowa. At the time, she pointed out the difference in treatment between the majority of the human bones, which belonged to White settlers and were immediately reburied, and those of this Native woman, which had been sent to a laboratory for study. As a result of her struggle, the body was finally reburied[261]. This case served as a catalyst for the enactment in 1990 of the Native American Graves Protection and Repatriation Act (NAGPRA), a federal law on the reburial of Indigenous human remains.

> 'The practice of decolonization is a way for us to think about the political implications of our work as archaeologists, to transform our scholarship so that it benefits those whose heritage we study, and to situate ourselves as individuals within a disciplinary framework[262].'

The issue of decolonisation is all the more important in that it can help us to think about the different sex/gender systems that existed before colonisation and were erased by it. This is the case in North American societies, to take just one example, where gender fluidity, non-binarity and/or a third gender could frequently be found. The imposition of the Western sex/gender system, conceived by the colonists as natural and moral, and the erasure of Indigenous systems and their 'transgressions', considered perverse, thus blurred the norms in force before colonisation[263]. Many studies of gender in North American cultures have often presupposed the existence of a rigid binary system before interpreting material culture and archaeological remains. A decolonial archaeology can therefore only be conceived by denaturalising a sex/gender system imposed on ancient societies and re-evaluating our way of conceiving sex, gender and identities in the light of the richness and diversity of human societies[264].

2.3. Indigenous archaeologies

George Nicholas first defined Indigenous archaeology in 1997 as 'archaeology done with, for and by Indigenous people[265]'. In *Power to the (indigenous) past and present!*, Hans Martin Wobst expands on this definition, stating that Indigenous archaeology is 'decolonized archaeology that helps Indigenous people obtain control over their material patrimony and where non-Indigenous people can learn to

254 Bruchac 2014, 2069.
255 Spivak 2020 (1988).
256 Atalay 2006, 289; Bruchac 2014, 2072.
257 Atalay 2006, 289.
258 Bruchac 2014, 2069.
259 Bruchac 2014, 2070.
260 Fitzpatrick 2021, 15.

261 Atalay 2006, 288.
262 Gonzalez *et al.* 2006, 388–389.
263 Lugones 2007; Algrain 2021a.
264 For example Walley 2018; Walley 2020.
265 Nicholas & Andrew 1997, 3, quoted by Martinez 2014, 3773.

use non-colonizing, non-statistic, non-capitalist ways of interacting with artifacts[266]'. For Sonya Atalay, Indigenous archaeology is not only an archaeology 'with, for and by' Indigenous populations, but also has repercussions outside these populations. For her, 'one need not be an Indigenous person to engage in the practice of Indigenous archaeology - it does not include such essentialist qualities[267]'. This view is shared by Peter Ucko, Dorothy Lippert, Anne Agbe-Davies and Chip Colwell-Chanthaphonh and her colleagues[268]. Finally, these researchers note that this archaeology is both theoretical and practical, and takes into account 'the rich diversity of practices, discussions, and viewpoints that are developing under the banner of Indigenous archaeology[269]', through collaborative projects and the development of new ways of interpreting the material remains of the past.

> 'While Indigenous peoples have long served as laborers at archaeological sites, for more than a century they have been excluded from participating in the full choice of research activities[270].'

Indigenous archaeology developed in conjunction with post-processual archaeology and Marxist and feminist thought, first in the United States, where the focus was on Native American populations who were absent from both interpretation and the profession, then in Canada, Australia and the rest of the world. The term 'Indigenous' now encompasses the Sami of northern Europe (Sweden, Norway, Finland, Lapland), the First Peoples of Canada, the First Nations of the United States, traditional Amazonian communities[271], the Aboriginal populations of Australia, the Maori of New Zealand, the Kanak of New Caledonia[272], the Khoïsan of southern Africa, the Pygmies of central Africa, the Hadza and Dorobo of East Africa, among many others[273].

> 'Archaeologists might take a more reflexive approach and contextualize the present situation by tracing archaeologists' (and physical anthropologists') current position of power to both colonization and the historical reality of the egregious acts that led to the collections held by museums, universities, and historical societies internationally[274].'

This archaeology encompasses a multitude of practices and approaches, ranging from the study of material remains to non-material aspects such as folklore, oral history and music[275]. It includes the active participation or consultation of Indigenous peoples in the research process. It also campaigns for people from these populations to have greater access to archaeological studies and to their heritage. Its practitioners are involved in struggles such as the repatriation of material remains, the reburial of human remains and the promotion of the history of Indigenous peoples. To better reflect the diversity of the populations involved and the research being carried out, the term 'Indigenous archaeologies' is also used in the plural.

2.3.1. United States

In the United States, American First Nations have been fighting for their heritage since the 1970s. The first legislation governing Indigenous heritage dates back to the 1990s. The 1990 federal Native American Graves Protection and Repatriation Act stipulates that museums must work with Indigenous peoples to repatriate material remains. The 1992 amendments to the National Historic Preservation Act also established the creation of offices for the protection of Native history.

Much archaeological work in the United States involves the recording and interpretation of Indigenous remains, sacred sites or burial grounds. Paulette Steeves notes that 'over the last century, millions of American Indian, First Nations, and Native Hawaiian cultural items and thousands of human remains were obtained by museums, governmental institutions, and private collections [276]'. She writes that prior to the 1990s, the majority of archaeologists in the United States did not communicate with Indigenous populations about their heritage and sites. Dorothy Lippert also mentions that 'prior to the passage of repatriation laws efforts to reconnect artifacts with the descendants of their creators was at the discretion of individual scientists[277]'. Steeves reports:

> 'What I witnessed as a CRM archaeologist was disturbing and heartbreaking to say the least. Although a few firms strove to carry out ethical practices through field work, many others blatantly disregarded professional standards for ethical practices in fieldwork. Native american monitors were only present on one site I worked on, a site in California, and their presence did not stop the massive site destruction that took place[278].'

The problem is that training in ethical practices and heritage laws is rare in the United States. Moreover, these laws continue to be seen as restrictive by archaeologists in the field[279].

Sonya Atalay, Dorothy Lippert and Joe Watkins are among the most active researchers defending Indigenous rights in archaeology. For example, Joe Watkins examined the relationship between archaeologists and

[266] Wobst 2005, 29, quoted by Martinez 2014, 3773.
[267] Atalay 2006, 293–294.
[268] Ucko 1987; Lippert 2006; Agbe-Davies 2010; Colwell-Chanthaphonh *et al.* 2010.
[269] Colwell-Chanthaphonh *et al.* 2010, 230.
[270] Colwell-Chanthaphonh *et al.* 2010, 230.
[271] Rostain 2011.
[272] Sand 2017 and 2020; Sand *et al.* 2011.
[273] The populations in this non-exhaustive list are cited by Chirikure 2014, 3886; Rostain 2011; Dotte-Sarout *et al.* 2020.
[274] Atalay 2006, 282.
[275] Colwell-Chanthaphonh *et al.* 2010.

[276] Steeves 2015, 123.
[277] Lippert 2006, 431–432.
[278] Steeves 2015, 127.
[279] Steeves 2015, 129–130.

Indigenous populations in the United States and offers ethical guidelines for improving both interpretation and practice within the profession[280]. The special issue on decolonisation in archaeology, edited by Sonya Atalay, also provided a good overview of archaeological research on Native American populations. Atalay's introductory article looked in particular at the theories and methods associated with this practice, and how these help to convey a more nuanced and complex vision of the past[281]. Dorothy Lippert examined the case of museum collections and the role of archaeologists in the control exercised over material remains belonging to Indigenous communities[282]. She gave the example of the objects belonging to the Caddo people in Oklahoma: for archaeologists, they were simply material remains stored in museum reserves, but for Lyman Kinoute, a member of the Caddo community, they were clear evidence of the long history of his people, to which they have not had access for hundreds of years[283].

2.3.2. Canada

In Canada, archaeology has traditionally played the role of an instrument of the colonial state, contributing to the erasure of the past and present of Indigenous populations through 'removing Indigenous material culture and ancestors from Indigenous lands without permission, interpreting Indigenous histories without Indigenous input under the guise of objectivity, and failing to share research results with Indigenous communities[284]'. Kelvin and Hodgetts gave the example of the division between prehistoric and historical archaeology in Canada, where the former focuses on Indigenous populations and the latter on the establishment of colonial sites by Europeans, creating the illusion that Indigenous populations disappeared after the arrival of the colonists and had no history from that date onwards[285]. There is no Canadian equivalent to the Native American Graves Protection and Repatriation Act: regulations concerning heritage and archaeological excavations vary from province to province[286]. In 2011, the draft technical bulletin for Ontario archaeologists issued by the Ministry of Culture and Tourism listed the standards and guidelines for encouraging the participation of Indigenous communities in the archaeological process. The first point in the text stated that 'you *must* solicit the participation of Indigenous communities' at various levels of archaeological work, from the development of research questions to the communication of excavation results.

2.3.3. Australia

As in the United States and Canada, Australian archaeology is marked by colonisation. The field of prehistoric research was once again used to draw a line between 'prehistoric' and 'primitive' Indigenous populations and populations of European settlers, known as 'the first Australians'[287]. The first demonstrations by Indigenous peoples calling for the repatriation of cult objects and the reburial of human bones date back to the 1970s, but it was not until the 1980s that the issue reached the archaeological sphere[288]. For example, Peter Ucko worked as Principal of the Australian Institute of Aboriginal Studies in Canberra between 1972 and 1981. During this time, he introduced a number of measures to encourage the involvement of Indigenous Australian communities in their heritage[289]. For some archaeologists, 'working closely with Aboriginal communities forced them to confront colonial legacies of the discipline and acknowledge Aboriginal people as the rightful owners of the cultural heritage that is the archaeological signature of the continent[290]'. In 2011, the Australian Indigenous Archaeologists Association, the first organisation to defend Aboriginal heritage, was created within the archaeological profession itself[291]. The association's missions include establishing ethical methods for the excavation, treatment, study and conservation of Aboriginal material remains, establishing procedures and codes of ethics, and promoting the history of the Aboriginal and Torres Strait Islander populations. Research by Aboriginal people and archaeologists and by Aboriginal archaeologists is currently underway in many parts of Australia[292].

2.4. From African archaeology to the archaeology of the African diaspora

Racism is particularly prevalent in the history of African archaeology. In terms of the interpretation of remains, the example of Great Zimbabwe (11th–15th centuries AD) is particularly illuminating. In 1928, the British Academy invited Gertrude Caton Thompson to study the ruins of this site in south-east Zimbabwe, near Lake Mutirikwe. The site comprises three sets of very imposing stone structures and several buildings. A debate raged at the time as to whether the site was the work of African populations or another civilisation. Gertrude Caton Thompson assembled an all-female expedition (including Kathleen Kenyon) for the dig. On the basis of the ceramics, which were similar to those used by twentieth-century villagers, and thanks to a meticulous study of the various structures, she concluded that Great Zimbabwe had been built by the Indigenous populations. This conclusion was not well received by the scientific community, which until then had largely considered that only non-African populations could have been responsible for such monuments. In 1970, the archaeologist Peter Garlake was exiled by the White

[280] Watkins 2000.
[281] Atalay 2006. See also Atalay 2008, 2012 and 2019.
[282] Lippert 2006. See also Lippert 2008.
[283] Lippert 2006, 438.
[284] Kelvin & Hodgetts 2020, 5.
[285] Kelvin & Hodgetts 2020, 6.
[286] Ferris 2003, 162.
[287] Wilson 2018, 3787–3788; Smith & Jackson 2006, 313; Smith *et al.* 2019, 539.
[288] Smith & Jackson 2006; Wilson 2018, 3789.
[289] Ucko 1987.
[290] Smith *et al.* 2019, 539.
[291] Wilson 2018, 3789.
[292] Smith *et al.* 2019, 539.

government of Rhodesia[293], then ruled by the British, for arguing that the monuments of Great Zimbabwe had not been built by Arabs or Phoenicians, but by the ancestors of the local population, the Shonas. It was unthinkable to the whites that the local populations of Africa, considered primitive, could have built these stone structures, some of which were 11 m high and 250 m in perimeter. Modern archaeologists now agree that the buildings on the site can be attributed to the Shonas[294]. This example shows that the decolonisation of African archaeology is far from being an empty and pointless claim.

Charles E. Oser enthusiastically points out that 'the archaeology of the post-Columbian African diaspora has the potential to become one of the most important kinds of archaeology in the world[295]'. Initially, this field of research was called 'African archaeology' (or 'African-American archaeology' in the United States) and envisaged 'Africa' as a monolithic block. It really took off in the 1960s in the United States, in connection with the civil rights movement[296]. In the early 1960s, Charles Fairbanks directed what was to become one of the first archaeological studies of African-American populations at the Kingsley plantation in Florida[297]. At the end of the 1990s, the perspective was broadened to include the various ethnic communities of the diaspora around the world, from Northern Ireland to Australia, via Peru, South Africa, Martinique and Canada[298]. Several recent books take stock of recent developments in research themes related to the archaeology of the African diaspora[299].

This archaeology covers a wide range of subjects, from the material aspects of slavery to the study of racism, in all African territories and colonial sites occupied by Africans and their descendants[300]. In the United States, the study of 17th- and 18th-century plantations, as well as the relationships between these plantations and the properties of slave owners in the Caribbean, is the most common subject of research[301]. For example, Maria Franklin analysed the eating habits of the occupants of the Rich Neck plantation in Williamsburg (Virginia) to understand the cultural differences and social relationships forged between slaves of different origins attached to the same plantation[302]. The links between the material culture of sites occupied by enslaved or free African-Americans, religious practices and spirituality are another major research issue in the United States[303].

Critical Race Theory

Critical Race Theory is a method that analyses and questions the predominant role played by the law in the construction of racial differences and the perpetuation of racism in American society (mixed unions between Black and White people, for example, were banned in the United States until 1967). This method is supported by researchers and activists who reject the concept of biological race, and adopt the concept of race as being socially constructed and having profound material consequences for the victims of racist oppression[304].

Studies on Maroon communities, clandestine societies founded and made up of escaped former slaves, emerged in the early 2000s. Mark Leone, Cheryl Janifer LaRoche and Jennifer Babiarz point out that 'resistance is a phenomenon that cannot be separated from slavery or oppression[305]'. Between 1672 and 1864, more than fifty Maroon colonies existed in America. They have been excavated in Brazil, Suriname, Jamaica, Colombia, the Dominican Republic, Cuba and Barbados. The study of these sites has led to a more complete and nuanced understanding of the responses of Black communities to slavery[306]. Moreover, 'the identification and study of sites from everyday life such as cemeteries, churches, enslaved quarters, freedmen's communities, and schools broadened popular and academic knowledge of the Black past by revealing how slavery was intertwined with the founding of the nation and more broadly the rise of the modern world[307]'.

> 'It is imperative that archaeologists stay actively engaged in what is happening in society because their work is political even if they do not see it[308].'

The archaeology of the African diaspora therefore also covers themes such as the deconstruction of the concept of race as a biological reality and the consequences of racism for our contemporary societies[309]. It also looks at power relations and the links between race, class and gender[310]. It uses the tools and methods developed by gender studies, Afrofeminism and critical race theory[311].

For Ayana Omilade Flewellen and her colleagues, the archaeology of the African diaspora is 'more than just an archaeology of the African diaspora or archaeology

293 Whose territory corresponds to that of present-day Zimbabwe.
294 Chirikure 2020.
295 Oser 1998, 63.
296 Lee & Scott 2019, 85–86.
297 Franklin *et al.* 2020, 754.
298 Agbe-Davies 2010; Delpuech & Jacob 2014; Franklin *et al.* 2020; Leone *et al.* 2005; Oser 1998.
299 Delpuech & Jacob 2014; Lee & Scott 2019.
300 Leone *et al.* 2005, 576.
301 Lee & Scott 2019, 86.
302 Franklin 2001b.
303 Leon *et al.* 2005, 584–585.
304 Epperson 2004.
305 Leone *et al.* 2005, 577.
306 Leone *et al.* 2005, 578–579.
307 Lee & Scott 2019, 86.
308 Lee 2020, 22.
309 For example Epperson 2004; Flewellen *et al.* 2021; Franklin *et al.* 2020; Lee & Scott 2019.
310 Leone *et al.* 2005, 580; Flewellen *et al.* 2021, 228.
311 Epperson 2004; Franklin *et al.* 2020, 755.

conducted by people of African descent. It necessitates a methodological and theoretical reconceptualization of the manner in which archaeology is conducted[312]'. In particular, Terrence Epperson denounces the problems of authority, control over interpretations of the past and the processes of superficial integration of Black communities into archaeological excavations[313]. For example, on the archaeological site at the Levi Jordan plantation in Texas, dialogue between archaeologists and local people was established more with a view to obtaining validation of decisions already taken by White archaeologists, than to establishing genuine collaboration between archaeologists and the local Black community. Researchers in African diaspora archaeology are now striving to include Black communities more in the research process and to improve their representation in interpretations of the past and in the profession[314]. They are also involved in projects for the reburial of human remains, the recontextualisation of monuments and statues linked to the celebration of the colonial and slave-owning past, and the promotion of Black community history[315].

Nevertheless, Nedra Lee notes that archaeologists generally continue 'to ignore the voluminous scholarship detailing the history of race, the role of academic institutions in creating the concept of race, and the continued legacy of race in the lives of black people and other people of colour[316].'

In France, the collective work *Archéologie de l'esclavage colonial*, edited by André Delpuech and Jean-Paul Jacob, provided the first French-language overview of studies in this vast field of research. It was published following an international symposium organised in 2012 by the Inrap, the Comité pour l'histoire et la mémoire de l'esclavage (Committee for the History and Memory of Slavery), the French Ministry of Culture and Communication and the Musée du Quai Branly. With over twenty chapters, it covered a wide range of themes, from slave ships to marooning sites, from Brazil to Reunion Island, via Cuba, French Guiana and Louisiana. The first part was devoted to the challenges of this research[317]. In 2021, a travelling exhibition, also entitled 'Archaeology of Colonial Slavery', was designed by the Inrap. Accompanied by an educational pack produced by the Fondation pour la Mémoire de l'Esclavage, it looked at the value of archaeology in shedding light on the mechanisms of enslavement put in place by colonial states, and presented the daily lives of slaves and their strategies for resisting authority[318].

The New York African Burial Ground Project

The New York African Burial Ground Project (1992–2009), for example, was the first ethical bioarchaeology project in which scientific methods and respect for human rights were used together[319]. The New York African Burial Ground is one of the largest colonial-era cemeteries in the United States. More than 419 African-Americans, mostly slaves, were buried there during the 17th and 18th centuries. The excavations were carried out in close collaboration with New York's Black community. The memorial was inaugurated in 2007.

2.5. Black feminist archaeology

In 2001, Maria Franklin noted that Black feminist theories had not penetrated archaeology, despite the emergence of feminist criticism within the profession in the early 1980s. With her article 'Black feminist-inspired archaeology?', now considered to be the foundation of Black feminist archaeology, she attempted to demonstrate the potential of Black feminist thinking to nuance our interpretations of material remains[320]. She was also self-critical of the work she carried out on the Rich Neck slave quarter in Virginia, claiming that she neglected Black feminist analytical tools and therefore focused primarily on the Black male slaves living in the quarter, forgetting to include Black women and children in her interpretations of the site. For her, archaeologists are among the few researchers who have the opportunity to gather data on the lives of Black women who left no written record. Franklin also asserts the relevance of using Black feminist theories as part of a global rethink of the profession and its practitioners.

Laurie Wilkie, for example, analysed the objects belonging to Lucrecia Perryman in order to retrace the life of this Black widow and midwife who lived in Alabama in the nineteenth century[321]. *Engendering African American Archaeology: A Southern Perspective* edited by Jillian Galle and Amy Young was the first collective work to examine African American contexts from a feminist perspective[322]. Whitney Battle-Baptiste analysed the slave quarter attached to the home of President Andrew Jackson in Nashville, the home of the grandfather of researcher and civil rights activist W.E.B. Du Bois in Massachusetts, and the home of Lucy Foster in Andover, demonstrating how Black feminist tools can be used to highlight the lives of Black women during the period of slavery[323]. Morris and Sesma chose the same research angle[324]. Nedra Lee was interested in the work of free Black women in the whaling

[312] Flewellen *et al.* 2021, 228.
[313] Epperson 2004.
[314] Franklin *et al.* 2020, 755.
[315] Blakey 2020, 187; Carter 2018; Flewellen *et al.* 2021, 230; Lee & Scott 2019, 86.
[316] Lee 2020, 22.
[317] The conference papers are available online on the Inrap website [Accessed 11 March 2022, https://www.inrap.fr/archeologie-de-l-esclavage-colonial-8435].
[318] [Accessed 11 March 2022, https://enseignants.inrap.fr/activite-pedagogique/archeologie-de-lesclavage-colonial-140].
[319] Blakey 2014; Blakey 2020; LaRoche & Blakey 1997.
[320] Franklin 2001.
[321] Wilkie 2003.
[322] Galle & Young 2004.
[323] Battle-Baptiste 2011.
[324] Morris 2017; Sesma 2016.

industry on the island of Nantucket, Massachusetts[325]. On 25 June 2021, one of the sessions of the *Archaeology in the Time of Black Lives Matter* seminar was devoted to Black feminist archaeology[326].

Since 2001, however, archaeological research from a Black feminist perspective has been rare. Kathleen Sterling, for example, was the first to apply feminist thinking to research into European prehistory[327]. For her, this reflection necessarily includes 'a critique of the practice and pedagogy of prehistoric archaeology; critiques of interpretation, particularly unexamined assumptions about race and gender in the past; and building an interpretive framework and an engaged pedagogy for prehistory that takes the entangled nature of identity seriously and resists naturalizing our current ideas of race and gender[328]'.

> 'There are so few Blacks in archaeology and anthropology and fewer Black women, that Black feminist approaches have made little traction. [...] In applying Black feminist theory to the practice of prehistory, my concerns are primarily how we produce knowledge and to what ends; how knowledge production of prehistory is impacted by racism, sexism, and other forms of oppression[329].'

2.6. Archaeology and the Black Lives Matter (BLM) movement

In *'Power To The People': Sociopolitics and the Archaeology of Black America*, published in 1997, Maria Franklin, who had just defended her doctoral thesis at UC Berkeley and is now a professor at the University of Texas, encouraged her peers to think more about how our research affects African-Americans today and to question their social responsibilities. She denounced 'the overwhelming number of whites excavating African-American sites, and the relatively weak efforts to involve Black Americans through outreach[330]'. For her, diversifying our perspectives is crucial, as is educating the public and establishing a dialogue with Afro-descendant communities. She will have to wait more than a decade before her words find an echo in archaeology.

> 'Is archaeology ready for the changes that BLM has instigated ? The discipline's history suggests that it may be[331].'

The Black Lives Matter political movement was launched in 2013 in the African-American community in the United States. The movement fights against the racism faced by Black people, particularly through racist profiling and police violence. It went global in the summer of 2020, following the death of George Floyd, a Black American man who was killed when stopped by several police officers. One of them, a White police officer named Derek Chauvin, was found guilty of second-degree murder without premeditation on 25 June 2021. These protests, coupled with the Covid-19 health crisis, brought racial inequalities in the United States into sharp relief.

The archaeology sector, which until now has been rather reluctant to tackle the problems associated with anti-Black racism within its own discipline, is finally joining the movement[332], on an ad hoc basis until 2019 and more actively from 2020 onwards. The Society of Black Archaeologists, founded in 2011, is behind the majority of these events, training courses and articles. For example, archaeologists Gayoung Park, Li-Ying Wang and Ben Marwick analysed the content and keywords of 68,176 abstracts sent to Society for American Archaeology conferences over a period of 41 years[333]. They found that the number of proposals for papers relating to racism increased from 2015 onwards, but that overall they remained rather rare. The majority of these related to the experiences of African-Americans. None of them concerned Indigenous populations or anti-Asian racism.

In 2016, Kelley Deetz organised a conference at the Society for Historical Archaeology entitled *Historic Black Lives Matter: Archaeology as Activism in the 21st Century*, which addressed the issue of protecting archaeological sites of the African diaspora. The issue also came to the fore in 2019 with a session entitled *Black Lives Matter: The Fight Against Intersectional Operations of Oppression within Historical Archaeology*[334]. In 2020, the anthropology webzine *Sapiens* proposed a series of nine webinars devoted to racism in archaeology entitled *From the Margins to the Mainstream: Black and Indigenous Futures in Archaeology*[335]. On 25 June 2020, the *Archaeology in the Time of Black Lives Matter seminar*, organised by the Society of Black Archaeologists (SBA), the North American Theoretical Archaeology Group (TAG) and the Columbia Center for Archaeology, went online[336]. It was attended by 1,700 people. The aim of the seminar was to examine the role that archaeology can play within this vast political movement to combat racism. The discussions ranged from individual questioning to the collective improvement of teaching, research and mediation practices in universities, public and private services, museums and heritage organisations. The conference and the various workshops were live-tweeted by archaeologist Laura Heath-Stout on the Society of Black Archaeologists Twitter account, which increased the scope of the discussions. All the recommendations for combating racism in archaeology are now compiled in the 'resources' tab on the SBA website[337].

325 Lee 2019.
326 Flewellen *et al.* 2021, 225–226.
327 Sterling 2015.
328 Sterling 2015, 94.
329 Sterling 2015, 102.
330 Franklin 1997a, 40.
331 Franklin *et al.* 2020, 754.
332 Flewellen *et al.* 2021, 227; Franklin *et al.* 2020, 754.
333 Park *et al.* 2020.
334 Franklin *et al.* 2020, 756.
335 Park *et al.* 2020.
336 Flewellen *et al.* 2021, 225; Franklin *et al.* 2020, 759.
337 Website of the Society of Black Archaeologists, Resources [Accessed 15 March 2022, https://www.societyofblackarchaeologists.com/resources].

Where to start?

S. Atalay, 'Multivocality and Indigenous Archaeologies', *in* J. Habu, C. Fawcett, J.M. Matsunaga (eds.), *Evaluating Multiple Narratives. Beyond Nationalist, Colonialist, Imperialist Archaeologies*, Springer, 2008, 29–44.

S. Atalay, 'Can Archaeology Help Decolonize the Way Institutions Think? How Community-Based Research Is Transforming the Archaeology Training Toolbox and Helping to Transform Institutions', *in Archaeologies* 15/3, 2019, 514–535.

W. Battle-Baptiste, *Black Feminist Archaeology*, Routledge, 2011.

N. Lee et J. N. Scott, 'Introduction: New Directions in Africa Diaspora Archaeology', *in Transforming Anthropology* 27/2, 2019, 85–90.

K. Sterling, 'Black Feminist Theory in Prehistory', *in Archaeologies: Journal of the World Archaeological Congress*, 2015, 93–120.

3

Developments and convergences in gender archaeology

Theoretical developments in gender archaeology have led to a series of specific questions being asked about societies of the past, in particular questions relating to masculinities and sexualities. The construction of masculinities has a significant impact on the way in which individuals and societies perceive and apply gender norms. The study of masculinities provides insight into how men and boys understand and adopt their gender identities, and how these identities intersect with other social identities such as race, class and sexuality. Sexualities, interconnected with the notion of gender, have also been widely studied in academic research. In the historical sciences, these studies give us an insight into how sexual attitudes and behaviour have evolved over time, and in particular account for the diversity of sex/gender systems.

This chapter will also allow us to discuss the convergences between gender archaeology and anarchist archaeology. The latter seeks to apply anarchist principles to the practice of the discipline by emphasising decentralisation, mutual aid and direct action, as well as the rejection of hierarchical structures and authority. In this way, an anarchist approach can support the aims of gender archaeology by, for example, enabling greater participation and collaboration with and between marginalised groups.

3.1. Masculinities

In archaeology, the question of masculinities developed at the end of the 1990s as a result of research into gender archaeology and feminist archaeology on the interpretation of 'gendered' material remains[338]. It is largely based on the research of sociologists such as Raewyn Connell, Tim Carrigan, John Lee and Michael Kimmel[339]. More generally, it is similar to research into men and masculinities (men's studies). However, there is no 'archaeology of masculinities' that is as clearly detached from gender archaeology as men's studies is from gender studies. For Benjamin Alberti, there is no need to differentiate between research on masculinities and that undertaken as part of gender archaeology, since the methodological tools and thinking that would enable the development of critical studies on men of the past and masculinities have already been put in place by researchers in gender archaeology[340]. This point of view is also shared by other authors, including L. Skogstrand, who states that:

> '[...] there is a need to explicitly study men and masculinities within archaeology and that it should be done within the already established feminist inspired gender archaeology[341].'

Defining masculinities is no easy task. Although gender archaeology makes it possible to demonstrate the essentialist nature of most interpretations, Eleanor Scott notes that, ironically, criticisms of androcentrism in archaeology have not led to the definition and theorisation of masculinities per se[342]. Many researchers in archaeology, and not only in gender archaeology, often choose not to define precisely what is meant by this term[343]. Alberti deplores this lack of a clear definition because 'any interpretation of past societies implies an understanding of what the term 'masculinity' means[344]'.

In studies of the past, masculinity is frequently used as a descriptive term: it is defined by a series of attributes, qualities, behaviours and expectations that are immutable and therefore unchanging in time and space. This use is particularly damaging because it leads to an essentialization of the notion of masculinity, and more broadly of the category 'man'.

> 'Studying men and masculinities in archaeology is a sticky proposition. [...] Feminist and gender archaeologies continue to reveal how "women" have been an invisible category in archaeological interpretation and history. "Men", in contrast, have always been visible, but their gender has been "unmarked". Their presence has been assumed – but assumed on the basis of a "neutral" body, unmarked by gender, race, or any other category of identity[345].'

Men are presented as a homogenous dominant group that varies little or not at all over time and space. The archetypes of the warrior, the hunter, the farmer or the active, dominant, robust, courageous, aggressive and violent leader inherited from the gendered stereotypes of the 19th century are difficult to challenge[346]. Focusing in particular on prehistoric societies, Lisbeth Skogstrand points out:

> '[...] how gender may structure action, space or development or how masculinity may differentiate between different groups of men are not a part of the

[338] Bertelsen *et al.* 1987; Conkey & Spector 1984; Gero 1985. For example, Treherne 1995.
[339] Connell 2014 (1995); Carrigan *et al.* 1985; Kimmel 1987. On this issue, see Le Talec 2016.
[340] Alberti 2006, 402–404. See also Meskell 1999, 84; Skogstrand 2011, 57.
[341] Skogstrand 2011, 57.
[342] Joyce 2005, 150; Scott 1997, 8.
[343] Alberti 2006, 404–406.
[344] Alberti 2006, 405.
[345] Alberti 2006, 401.
[346] Gilchrist 1999, 64; Skogstrand 2010, 65.

understanding of prehistoric men. The fact that men are representing the entire prehistoric society is not simply because women are ignored; it is mainly because men are not gendered[347].'

For this reason, and based on the work of sociologist Raewyn Connell, Alberti encourages us to think of masculinity not as a set of fixed traits, but as plural, variable, often contradictory and in tension, socially constructed tendencies and possibilities: *masculinities* in the plural form[348]. In fact, Connell insists on the fact that an individual's masculinity is constructed in opposition to the other (woman, Black man, poor man, etc.) and she defines four types of masculinities. **Hegemonic masculinity** corresponds to the most recognised and ideal way of being a man, at a given time and in a given place. This concept refers to the way in which a particular group of men occupies certain positions of power and wealth, and legitimises and reproduces the social relations that enable it to establish its dominance over both women and other men. The categories of masculinity depreciated by hegemonic masculinity are the **complicit masculinities** who adhere to the ideology conveyed by hegemonic masculinity but do not fully embody it (men who help with household chores but enjoy all the benefits of patriarchy, for example), **subordinated masculinities**, which are devalued forms of masculinity (such as homosexuals and men with disabilities) and **marginalised masculinities**, made up of racialised men or men from other social classes who can individually attain positions of power but who cannot share this power with their entire group[349].

Studies of masculinities in archaeology can be divided into two main categories[350]: on the one hand, studies of the way in which a dominant form of masculinity (hegemonic masculinity) is socially and symbolically constructed in a given context and at a given period[351]; on the other, theoretical research that looks more broadly at the concept of masculinities, with studies that question the category of 'men', criticise the limits of gender binarity or demonstrate the existence of multiple masculinities within past societies[352].

> 'To avoid androcentrism, and to obtain knowledge of the gendered men in prehistory we need to critically explore how masculinities may have structured society, affected power and individual actions and identities, and even question the concept of masculinity itself and challenge any a priori binary understandings of gender[353].'

Although relatively few in number, this research has successfully demonstrated the complexity of the hitherto taken-for-granted categories of 'man' and 'masculinity'. Examples of this type of research will be presented below (see chapters 6 and 8).

3.2. Archaeology of sexualities and queer archaeology

> 'For centuries, archaeologists have encountered sexually explicit materials from past cultures, but their sexual content has been either minimized or treated lasciviously[354].'

Interest in the study of sexuality in archaeology really took off in the late 1990s and early 2000s, in the wake of research into gender archaeology and feminist archaeology. This work is more broadly linked to the interdisciplinary field of queer studies. It is also heir to the research carried out in sexology since the late 1800s, in the sense that it considers sexuality to play an essential role in the construction of identities. Finally, they owe a great deal to the work of Judith Butler, who has been challenging the binarity of the sex/gender system and considers gender as a learned, repeated and reproduced social performance[355].

The major difference between these studies and earlier archaeological research into sexuality is that they 'focus on the cultural and historical specificity of sexuality rather than to interpret archaeological finds as evidence of universal principles of human sexual behavior[356]'. In other words, the archaeology of sexuality makes it possible to look directly at the question of sexuality in past societies, which until now has been considered in a stereotyped way[357].

Queer archaeology also questions the heteronormativity of archaeological interpretation more broadly. In particular, it criticises the conventional divisions between sex, gender and sexuality, and explores the way in which these three categories construct each other. It also does not immediately accept the universality of heterosexuality, marriage and the nuclear family. It addresses issues of gender fluidity and ambiguity, acknowledging that differences in gender and sexuality were not always discriminated against in past societies. Finally, it points out that categories such as 'heterosexual', 'homosexual', 'transgender' or 'transvestite' are recent and cannot therefore be used as universal, timeless categories. Queer archaeology also highlights the fact that:

> 'More commonly, archaeological interpretations relied on latent sexual narratives that portrayed people in the past as monogamous heterosexual couples whose sex lives were oriented entirely toward reproduction[358].'

347 Skogstrand 2010, 65–66.
348 Alberti 2006, 406.
349 Connell 2014 (1995), 72–80.
350 Montón-Subías & Meyer 2018, 4.
351 For example Alberti 1997; Osborne 1998; Joyce 2000; Skogstrand 2010; Peled 2016; Skogstrand 2016.
352 For example Yates 1993; Knapp 1998a and b; Caesar 1999; Meskell 1999; Alberti 2006; Joyce 2007; Skogstrand 2010; Skogstrand 2017; Hayeur-Smith *et al.* 2019; Augereau 2021.
353 Skogstrand 2010, 67.
354 Voss 2006, 365.
355 Voss 2000a; Geller 2009; Aimers & Rutecki 2016; Springate 2020.
356 Voss 2008, 319.
357 Voss 2006, 366.
358 Voss 2008, 318.

Several books have addressed this question[359]. The collective volume *The Archaeologies of Sexuality* aimed to show that the study of sexuality in archaeology was possible, in the same way as the political or religious organisation of a given society, gender or social status. In the introduction, Robert Schmidt and Barbara Voss asked:

> 'Can sexuality be studied historically, and if so, does sexuality leave any material traces? How can we use potsherds, soil strains, animal bones, collapsed walls, or other archaeological datas to study sexual identities, sexual activities, and sexual relationships[360]?'

The book set out to explore the broader question of what is covered by the term 'sexuality' and took stock of the issue in archaeology. It also offered methods and avenues for theoretical reflection based on research carried out in social and physical anthropology, history, art history and geography. The cases studied ranged from medieval England to European prehistory, via the Maya and New Kingdom Egypt.

The *Queer Archaeology* dossier edited by Thomas Dowson in the journal *World Archaeologies* pursued a similar aim, even though according to Barbara L. Voss 'queer archaeology is not always about sexuality, and research on sexuality in archaeology is not always linked to queer theory[361]'. In the introduction, Thomas Dowson stated:

> 'Queer theory actively and explicitly challenges the heteronormativity of scientific practice. [...] "Queer" began as a challenge to essentialist constructions of a 'gay' identity. [...] Queer is by definition whatever is at odds with the normal, the legitimate, the dominant [...]. Queer theory is not like a theory in the scientific use of the word in that it does not provide a system of ideas used to explain something, as in Marxist theory or Einstein's theory of relativity. [...] It is a way of producing reflection, a way of taking a stand vis-a-vis the authoritative standard[362].'

The aim of this volume was therefore to challenge heterosexuality as a norm within archaeological interpretation. With this in mind, the research carried out was not limited exclusively to homosexuals and lesbians, but took into account all those marginalised because of their gender identity and sexual orientation. The volume also looked at the discrimination experienced by homosexuals within the profession.

> 'Queering archaeology [...] is not a manifesto for promoting homosexuality. Queer theory forces us to explore practices that openly exist in our cultures today, that have existed for a long time in all cultures, but are today branded as deviant or excluded altogether[363].'

[359] For example Taylor 1998.
[360] Schmidt & Voss 2000, 1.
[361] Voss 2008, 328.
[362] Dowson 2000,
[363] Dowson 2000, 165.

Since the 2000s, there has been a growing body of work on the archaeology of sexuality. The Queer Archaeology website provides a regularly updated bibliography of publications on the subject[364]. Notable productions include *Que(e)ring Archaeology*[365], the formation in 2014 of the Queer Archaeology Interest Group, which organises and supports annual conferences held within the framework of the Society of American Archaeology[366], and the special issue of the *SAA Archaeological Record* devoted in 2016 to queer archaeology[367].

According to Barbara Voss, this research can be divided into five main categories[368]: fertility management, homosexuality and transidentity, architecture and spaces, prostitution, and sexual and erotic representations. This last category is the one in which the most work has been produced, particularly in relation to Palaeolithic, Mesolithic and Neolithic figurines and representations unearthed on European sites. There are fewer articles on homosexuality, transidentity, non-binarity or other gender minorities and sexual orientations[369]. Some of this research takes intersectionality into account and looks at other subjects such as sexual violence. For example, Whitney Battle-Baptiste addressed the issue of sexual assault and rape of enslaved and free Black women in the United States[370]. Chelsea Blackmore encouraged the development of queer archaeology beyond sexuality and the use of queer theory to consider all aspects of Mayan identity formation[371].

The archaeology of sexuality is ultimately a recent field of research, but it has shown that 'human sexuality is much more varied across cultures and over time than was previously imagined[372]'. We will return to this point in the second part of this book (see chapter 6).

3.3. Anarchist archaeology

In An Introduction to Anarchism in Archaeology, Lewis Borck and Matthew Sanger state that 'as a non-dogmatic philosophy, anarchism is difficult to circumscribe and define[373]'. There are many different ways of being an anarchist, and many different approaches to anarchism. Despite this, these approaches are united on a number of points. For Borck and Sanger, anarchism is deeply linked to an interest in self-governance, equal rights and voluntary power relations marked by reciprocity and free collaboration.

[364] See the *Queer Archaeology* website [Accessed 15 March 2022 https://queerarchaeology.com/resources/information-about-queer-archaeology/].
[365] First conference on the subject, held at the University of Calgary in the United States in 2004, the proceedings of which were published in 2009 cf. Terendy *et al.* 2009.
[366] Blackmore & Rutecki 2014.
[367] Rutecki & Blackmore 2016.
[368] Voss 2006, 383–384.
[369] For example Algrain 2021; Eger 2007; Hollimon 2000, 2006 and 2009; Mary 2021; Matic 2012 and 2016; Moral 2016; Power 2020; Tjahjadi 2020; Walley 2019; Weismantel 2013.
[370] Battle-Baptiste 2011.
[371] Blackmore 2011.
[372] Voss 2006, 390.
[373] Borck & Sanger 2017, 10.

James Flexner and Edward Gonzalez-Tennant also agree that 'a deep and abiding scepticism of and resistance to authority and orthodoxy' and 'a quest to redefine social and ecological relationships on more egalitarian terms, including with non-humans' are the foundations of anarchist thought[374]. Today, anarchist theories also incorporate feminist, queer and anti-racist perspectives[375].

Anarchism has met with some success in North America in the humanities and social sciences. The work of James C. Scott and David Graeber in particular have played a leading role in popularising and integrating anarchist theories into anthropology[376]. However, these theories were slow to percolate through to archaeology, despite the 'long-standing archaeological engagement with "egalitarian", "heterarchical", "horizontally-organised", "middle-range", or "acephalous" societies[377]'. The first explicit attempt to apply these theories to the interpretation of material remains dates from 2012[378]. In 2016, the anarchist archaeology collective called The Black Trowel also published online the *Foundations of an Anarchist Archaeology: A Community Manifesto.* This was followed in 2017 by a second manifesto entitled *An Anarchist Archaeology for the Anthropocene*, published in the special issue *Anarchy and Archaeology* of the *SAA Archaeological record.* Since Angelbeck and Grier's publication in 2012, there has been a proliferation of work, but research claiming to be distinctly anarchist remains few and far between[379]. It is sometimes referred to as 'punk archaeology'[380]. Anarchist archaeologists also point out that it is not necessary for a person or a study to identify itself as an anarchist in order to contribute to anarchist thinking[381]. In 2022, a session (#225) at the annual congress of the European Association of Archaeologists was devoted to the new theories and practical perspectives of anarchist archaeology. Broadly speaking, this research can be divided into two groups: those concerned with the study of past societies[382] and those concerned with the practice of the discipline itself[383].

> 'Simply, we offer an anarchist archaeology as an alternate way to think about the past and to consider our methods and practices in the present. An anarchist approach reminds us to consider relations of power and to question whether those relationships are authoritarian or coercive, whether in past societies we study, among archaeologists as teams in practice, among archaeologists and descendant communities concerning heritage, or in the relationships between archaeology and contemporary nation-states[384].'

Protests by the Lil'wat community

In February 1991, the Lil'wat community organised to protect sites they considered sacred. Located along Lake Lillooet, these sites are decorated with multiple pictograms and include culturally modified trees as well as burials of people who died of smallpox and stillborn babies. An archaeological survey of the area carried out prior to logging identified seven sites. The authors of the report later admitted that the Lil'wat had informed them of the presence of the burials. They recommended that developers avoid the area. Despite opposition from the Lil'wat, the work went ahead. Within the first few days, the workers damaged one of the pictograms. In response to this damage, the Lil'wat blocked the access road to the site. The demonstrators were arrested by the police. Johnny Jones, an Indigenous archaeologist who had also taken part in the demonstrations, escaped arrest. He remained on site to observe the work, then returned to block the site wearing the insignia and emblems of his community. Following these actions, the work was finally stopped. Since 2008, Johnny Jones, Bill Angelbeck and members of the Lil'wat community have been working together on a number of prospecting and excavation projects. Some of these projects are financially supported by the Lil'wat community. Lil'wat people have also been included as members of the excavation teams, both as assistants and volunteers.

As far as the study of past societies is concerned, anarchist theories are particularly useful for studying so-called transitional or intermediate periods. For anarchist archaeologists, these periods of 'cultural disorganization, collapse, and disintegration are instead seen as points of potential societal growth and freedom[385]'. In general, anarchist archaeologists are not satisfied with the 'linear narrative building that places capital and the state as inevitable endpoints of cultural evolution[386]'. They also reject the more or less implicit notion that 'certain societies should be seen as inferior or as having failed because they lack hierarchical social organisation[387]'. Anarchist archaeologists are also interested in resistance movements within hierarchical societies[388]; Maroon communities and pirate colonies[389], as well as resistance groups on the Ethiopian-Sudanese border[390], have recently been studied.

[374] Flexner & Gonzalez-Tennant 2018, 213.
[375] Rathbone 2017, 10.
[376] Flexner & Gonzalez-Tennant 2018, 214.
[377] Flexner & Gonzalez-Tennant 2018, 214.
[378] Angelbeck & Grier 2012, quoted by Rathbone 2017, 293
[379] Flexner & Gonzalez-Tennant 2018, 215.
[380] Morgan 2015.
[381] The Black Trowel Collective 2016.
[382] For example Flexner 2014; Wengrow & Graeber 2015 and 2021.
[383] For example Angelbeck & Jones 2018; Eddisford & Morgan 2018; Gonzalez-Tennant 2018; Morgan 2015.
[384] *The Black Trowel Collective* 2016.

[385] Borck et Sanger 2017, 11.
[386] Flexner & Gonzalez-Tennant 2018, 214.
[387] Flexner & Gonzalez-Tennant 2018, 214.
[388] Flexner & Gonzalez-Tennant 2018, 215.
[389] Rathbone 2017, 299.
[390] Gonzalez-Ruibal 2014, cité par Angelbeck *et al.* 2018, 4.

Within the practice of the discipline, anarchist critique takes various forms, from questioning the hierarchical organisation of excavation sites to introducing new pedagogies in the classroom[391], transforming publication procedures and integrating local and Indigenous communities into the research process.

> 'Anarchist theory can provide a new philosophical grounding by which archaeologists can reframe their engagements with the past, with students, descendant peoples, the engaged public, and each other in ways that will redistribute authority and empower individuals and communities often relegated to the margins of our discipline[392].'

Anarchist archaeologists' campaign for the development of more transparent, collaborative, egalitarian and reflexive projects. In this sense, they join the movement launched by feminist, queer, Indigenous and African diaspora archaeologists. They are focusing in particular on free access to information, the democratisation of decision-making procedures and greater equality in representations[393].

> 'Most archaeological fieldwork remains deeply hierarchical with rigid, top-down structures of authority and varying degrees of alienation of labour in academic and professional settings. [...] Research strategies in archaeology that rely heavily on the unskilled labour of students, community members, or workmen may be fatally flawed to engender a truly emancipatory archaeology[394].'

One of the aims of anarchist archaeologists is to dismantle the divisions between archaeologists and amateurs, and between archaeologists as producers and holders of knowledge and the public as passive consumers of that knowledge. They are also setting up collaborative projects with local or Indigenous communities. For example, Bill Angelbeck and Johnny Jones are developing a collaboration between archaeologists and persons from the Lil'wat community in Canada[395].

Where to start?

B. Alberti, 'Archaeology, Men, and Masculinities', *in* S. M. Nelson (ed.), *Handbook of Gender in Archaeology*, AltamiraPress, 2006, 401–434.

T.A. Dowson (ed.), *World Archaeology* 32/2 'Queer Archaeologies', 2000.

J.L. Flexner & E. Gonzalez-Tennant, 'Anarchy and Archaeology. Introduction', *in Journal of Contemporary Archaeology* 5/2, 2018, 213–302.

M. Springate, 'Intersectionality, Queer Archaeology, and Sexual Effects', *in* Ch. E. Oser, A. Zarankin, P. Funari, S. Lawrence & J. Symonds, *The Routledge Handbook of Global Historical Archaeology*, Routledge, 2020.

B.L. Voss, 'Feminisms, Queer Theories, and the Archaeological Study of Past Sexualities', *in World Archaeology* 32/2, 2000, 180–192.

[391] Eddisford & Morgan 2018; Gonzalez-Tennant 2018.
[392] Rathbone 2017, 13.
[393] Angelbeck *et al.* 2018; Flexner & Gonzalez-Tennant 2018; Rathbone 2017.
[394] Eddisford & Morgan 2018, 245–246.
[395] Angelbeck & Jones 2018.

Part Two

Interpreting the past through a gender lens

Preamble

'Anything written by men about women must be suspect, because they are both judge and jury[396].'

Poullain de la Barre, *De l'égalité des deux sexes*, 1673.

The fragmentary nature of the information offered by archaeology, even when weighted by texts and other types of documents, is such that we will never be able to reconstruct with certainty the lives of the women and men of ancient societies. This is all the more true given that these societies are so far removed from us in time, and that the artefacts found are only a fraction of the objects they used. Archaeologists are therefore reduced to proposing interpretations. But even when they are drawn up with the utmost scientific rigour, these interpretations often reflect the prejudices and stereotypes that permeate those who formulate them.

At the time of the birth of archaeology and its gradual professionalisation in the 19th century, the status of women was severely restricted. Despite numerous demands since the French Revolution for women to be granted the right to vote and the status of full citizens, despite their struggles for the right to divorce and, in some circles, for free love, despite their repeated demands for access to education and better working conditions for women workers, women were constantly referred to their so-called nature and summoned to embrace their domestic vocation. In a society that left little room for women and ignored their voices, it was inevitable that the discipline of archaeology, dominated by White cisgender men, should itself be dominated by interpretations that proposed a limited and stereotyped role for women in ancient societies.

In addition, the idea of a gentle, sensitive female nature was reinforced in the collective imagination by medical texts that sought to demonstrate the inferiority of women using pseudo-scientific arguments. As a result of these widespread prejudices, internalised by the women themselves, the interpretations of archaeological remains developed on a sexist basis: scholars focused solely on the male point of view (scientific androcentrism); the binary way of thinking created oppositions such as feminine/masculine, private/public and presided over the hierarchisation of the sexes[397]. Unaware of the diversity of ancient societies and their relationship to material culture, early archaeologists sometimes conveyed simplistic ideas about the 'gender' of objects. Jewellery, the quintessential feminine object in the 19th century, always indicated a woman's grave. Weapons, on the other hand, undoubtedly indicated a man's grave. These ideas have had such an impact on our collective imagination that we still find it hard to shake them off today.

The aim of gender archaeology is to enrich our understanding of how gender has influenced the social, economic, political and cultural practices and power dynamics of ancient societies, based on the study of material culture. It also explores how these practices have changed over time. Women, and then marginalised groups, have been the starting point for this research, but they are not the only focus. As Pauline Schmitt Pantel has rightly pointed out:

> 'The aim of gaining a better understanding of the place of women in primitive or archaic societies [...] is not to 'rehabilitate' women or to replace the description of male power with that of omnipresent female power. It simply requires us to analyse all the roles assumed by the sexes in every society, to study how these roles are articulated in each culture, and to draw all the consequences for the overall interpretation of the social system[398].'

How can a social fact – gender – be studied on the basis of material culture? Anne Augereau has listed the various dimensions of gender, their material expression and the remains on which they can be studied in Table 1. In the following pages, we will look at many of the themes presented in this table by means of cases studied by archaeologists.

[396] 'Tout ce qui a été écrit par les hommes sur les femmes doit être suspect, car ils sont à la fois juge et partie.'

[397] Maceira-Ochoa 2017.

[398] Schmitt Pantel 2009, 25 ('Le souci de mieux comprendre la place des femmes dans des sociétés primitives ou archaïques [...] n'a pas pour but une quelconque "réhabilitation" des femmes et la substitution de la description d'un pouvoir féminin omniprésent à celle du pouvoir masculin. Il exige seulement de prendre en charge dans toute société l'analyse de l'ensemble des rôles assumés par les deux sexes, d'étudier l'articulation, propre à chaque culture, de ces rôles, et d'en tirer toutes les conséquences pour l'interprétation globale du système social.').

Table 1. Materiality of gender and archaeological correspondences (after Augereau 2021, 56–57).

Gender dimension	Material expression	Archaeologically perceptible in:
Identities	Elements of costume (fabrics, clothing, attachments, ornaments, accessories, etc.)	Funerary environment: gender and age distribution of items worn by the deceased
	Body canons	Iconography: figurines, statuettes, rock art, etc.
	Gender attributes	Funerary environment: distribution according to sex and age of items associated with the deceased
Gender roles	Division of labour in craft, subsistence and maintenance activities	• Identification of different productions according to the skills or raw materials used • Funerary environment: distribution of tools, utensils, etc. according to sex and age • Human bone material: bone pathologies, bone markers, trauma and injuries • Spatial distribution of activities
Gender acquisition and construction	Craft apprenticeships	Burial environment: distribution of tools, utensils, etc. according to sex and age
	Learning about subsistence activities	Identification of different technical levels for the same production
Gender inequality	in the organisation and use of space	Spatial analysis of the distribution of archaeological structures, artefacts and ecofacts; function and use of spaces; comparative architecture
	in food and commensality, in health and origins	Human bone material: stress markers, stable isotope analysis, palaeogenetic analysis
	in funeral treatment	Treatment of the dead according to age and sex at all stages of the funeral process: access to the burial site, preparation of the bodies, location and layout of funeral structures, positioning of the bodies, storage of funerary offerings, etc.
Power and gender	Social elites and regalia	• Funerary environment: distribution of objects according to gender and age and to a value index (rarity, origin of raw materials, complexity of manufacture or acquisition...) • Comparative funerary architecture

4

Funerary archaeology (I): the gendered body

Identifying the sex of human remains in archaeological contexts can provide valuable information about the social, cultural and biological characteristics of past populations. Sex determination is a crucial aspect of bioarchaeology, the study of human biology in archaeological contexts. It is often necessary to establish the sex of an individual in order to examine questions of demography and biological variability. In this process, biological, morphological and/or genetic indicators are used to make inferences about the sex of an individual.

In bioarchaeology, sex and gender are concepts that are often confused. Sex refers to an individual's biological characteristics, such as chromosomes, hormones and anatomy. Gender, on the other hand, refers to the social and cultural roles, behaviours and expectations associated with being a man or a woman. In some cultures, gender roles and expectations were very rigidly defined, while in others they were more fluid. Bioarchaeologists can use a variety of indicators to understand the relationship between sex and gender in a given population. For example, the examination of funerary objects and tomb architecture, combined with skeletal morphology, can provide information about cultural gender roles.

The skeleton also preserves traces of gendered and non-gendered practices relating to body modifications and diet. These traces provide valuable insights into the social and gender hierarchies of ancient societies. This chapter will look at what the skeleton can tell us about sex, gender and social class, and how we can access it.

4.1. Identifying sex, identifying gender

Funerary archaeology gives archaeologists direct access to individuals and is the easiest gateway for studying gender and other types of social relationships on the basis of funerary arrangements (type of burial, architecture, structure, etc.), funerary treatment (e.g. cremation versus inhumation) and offerings deposited in the grave. The funerary context thus provides us with information on both gender and, thanks to the study of the skeleton, on the sex, age, stature, state of health, origin, diet and family ties of the individuals[399]. Determining the sex of individuals is essential because, as we shall see, without a biological sex, archaeologists have to rely on objects to sex individuals found in funerary contexts, which poses a methodological problem[400]. However, in the case of analyses carried out on skeletons, it would be better to speak of 'estimating' the sex of individuals rather than 'determining' it, because of

Table 2. Standard three-point scale for skeletal sex analysis (after Wesp 2017, 104, table 5.1).

Three-point scale		
Female	**Indeterminate/Ambiguous**	**Male**
1 or F	2 or ?	3 or M

Table 3. Standard five-point scale for skeletal sex analysis (after Wesp 2017, 104, table 5.1).

Five-point scale				
Female	**Probable female**	**Indeterminate/ Ambiguous**	**Probable male**	**Male**
1 or F	2 or F?	3 or ?	4 or M?	M

the degree of ambiguity that remains in the identification process. The estimate is made by means of what are known as a posteriori probabilities of belonging to one sex or the other. Ideally, the result should be given in numerical form to support the analysis, which limits the dichotomous view of men and women[401] (Tables 2 and 3).

In archaeology, although DNA analysis is used in some cases, the sex of individuals is estimated mainly on the basis of the morphological and/or metric characteristics visible on the skeletons. This anthropological sex, determined from the bones, is based on the sexual dimorphism that exists in our species. In order to develop estimation methods, anthropologists observe bone variations between the sexes directly on the skeleton, or on the basis of X-rays, in reference groups[402]. The sex of individuals in these reference groups is known from civil status registers, cemeteries or medical data (body donation programmes, for example). The history of the study of the human skeleton and sexual dimorphism has not been spared from stereotypes, both sexist and racist. For example, the features associated with women's skeletons were often used by scholars in the 18th and subsequent centuries to justify their role as mothers attached to the domestic sphere (emphasis on reproductive capacity when the pelvis is mentioned) or their secondary place in society (emphasis on lower intelligence when the cranium is mentioned). These particularities, among which cranial measurements, were also evoked to justify a so-called hierarchy of 'races', whether with regard to non-European populations, enslaved people or even Jews during the Second World War[403].

[399] Boucherie 2020.
[400] Wesp 2017, 99–103.
[401] Wesp 2017, 105.
[402] Sofaer 2006, 90–91; Kranzbühler 2019.
[403] On this issue, see Schiebinger 1986; Geller 2017b, 24–40.

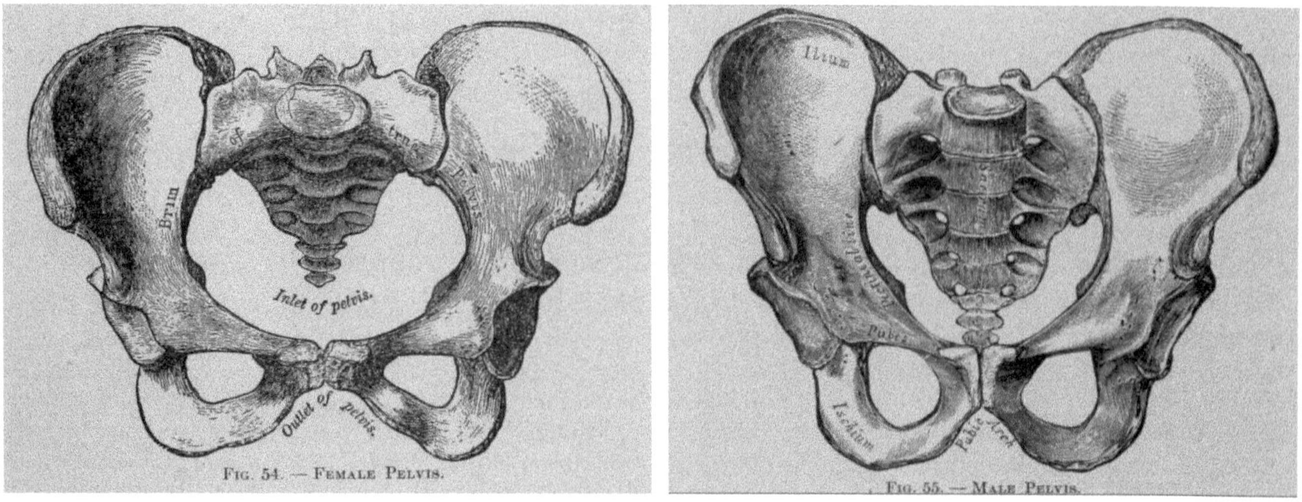

Figure 4.1. Female and male pelvis. Adapted from D.C. Kimber and C.E. Gray, *Anatomy and Physiology for Nurses*, The Macmillan Company, 1916, 75–76.

When preserved, coxal bones are among the most useful for determining the sex of the deceased, and the accuracy rate with this method reaches 96%: the morphological difference is clearly marked between women and men, with women having a wider pelvis, allowing the foetus to pass through in the event of potential childbirth[404] (Figure 4.1). It is necessary to explain why this estimation rate is 'only' 96%. Sexual dimorphism does not always show up clearly on bones, and anthropologists cannot always tell a female from a male. This is because sex is not assessed on the basis of a binary choice (female/male) but on a continuum, a spectrum ranging from female to male. Between the two lie individuals, men and women, who are average and may have similar statures and conformations, and therefore remain of undetermined sex[405]. The category 'indeterminate' therefore appears alongside the categories 'man' and 'woman' in the work of anthropologists (Tables 2 and 3). What is at issue here, according to Joanna R. Sofaer, is not so much the instability of the sexed categories as the inability of the bioarchaeologists to determine the sex in 100% of cases, which explains and reinforces the idea that it is necessary to present the result of the estimation in the form of a **probability**. The fact remains, however, that indeterminate and unsexed individuals did have a sex during their lifetime[406]. Similarly, the sex of infants (0–1 year) and immature individuals (<20 years) often cannot be determined on the basis of the skeleton, as sexual dimorphism is marked on the bones from the pubertal phase onwards[407].

On fragmentary coxal bones, *diagnose sexuelle probabiliste* (DSP), based on a set of morphometric measurements, is an effective tool[408]. In the absence of coxal bones, skull bones can also be used to estimate sex and, to a lesser extent, the long bones of the upper and lower limbs. Recently, other estimation methods have been proposed, in particular using the bones of the inner ear. This method is particularly valuable when the bones are fragmentary, and is a promising way of sexing the skeletons of immature individuals[409]. In these latter cases, DNA analysis is also a method used to estimate sex[410].

Sex is estimated for an individual at a precise moment in its life. However, bone morphology is influenced by other factors and age, for example, can affect the degree of sexual dimorphism by reducing it. Anthropologists therefore use the notion of plasticity to account for phenomena that can alter bones, whether these are intentional, such as cranial modifications (see point 1.2), or the result of repetitive activities (see point 1.3), disease or trauma. Bones also change over time, and a 'masculinisation' of the greater sciatic notch or cranial features has been noted in post-menopausal women. As Pamela Geller notes, the use of the term 'masculinisation' is problematic, as it perpetuates the stereotypes associated with the de-feminisation of post-menopausal women[411]. However, the skeleton can undergo changes during adulthood, and this fact needs to be taken into account.

The older the human remains, the greater the difficulties in estimating sex. It is difficult to know with any certainty whether sexual dimorphism was as marked in hominin species other than *sapiens*, or whether it became more pronounced in more recent periods. The criteria most often used to determine the sex of prehistoric skeletons are, for example, gracility or the conformation of the pelvis. However, in the absence of a sufficiently large sample, it remains difficult to determine whether the criterion of pelvic conformation is sufficiently discriminating. The aforementioned methods

404 Walrath 2017, 20; Geller 2017b, 43. See also Bruzek & Ferembach 1992; Bruzek 2002; Murail *et al.* 2005; Boucherie 2020, 45.
405 Bruzek 2002; Sofaer 2006, 92; Geller 2008, 121–122; Agarwal 2012, 324; Wesp 2017, 103.
406 Sofaer 2006, 94–97.
407 Sofaer 2006, 91.
408 Murail *et al.* 2005.
409 Boucherie 2020; Boucherie *et al.* 2021.
410 DNA studies and other types of biochemical analysis are also used to determine the ethnic origin of individuals, although not without methodological problems, particularly with regard to the definition of ethnicity and its social implications over the period studied. Matić 2020, 53–60 urges great caution in interpreting the results.
411 Geller 2017b, 79–80.

may not always give conclusive results on older populations due to less marked morphological differences in the skull or pelvis between men and women. A slender skeleton can just as easily be a woman of small stature as an adolescent male. In fact, in some cases, these criteria are barely perceptible: for example, the skeleton of the Neanderthal woman from La Quina has changed sex five times since its discovery in 1911[412]...

Moreover, as we mentioned in the introduction, biological sex, far from being divided binary into two categories, 'man' or 'woman', can present ambiguities: 'Far beyond a simple binarity, the biological processes of sex are characterised by an inherent complexity that does not preclude the existence of visible intersexuation at the genetic, gonadal and/or genital level[413]'. Archaeologists are increasingly questioning the binary division of the sexes under the influence of advances in sociology, particularly the work of Judith Butler and queer studies[414]. Archaeologists and palaeoanthropologists are also questioning the distinction between the information provided by the skeleton about an individual's sex and gender. Thus, **sexing a skeleton does not provide any information about the way in which an individual defined his or her own identity and therefore his or her gender**.

This difficulty can be illustrated by the case of a medieval Finnish burial (late 11th - early 12th century AD) containing fibulae, jewelry and weapons, discovered in 1968 at Suontaka Vesitorninmäki (Hattula, Finland). The deceased is identified as a woman due to the presence of fibulae and jewelry. According to archaeologists, the deceased may also have been a woman of power, or even a warrior, buried with at least one sword. But analysis of the ancient DNA (aDNA) from this skeleton suggests that the individual buried in this tomb had intersex characteristics in the form of aneuploid XXY chromosomes (Klinefelter's syndrome). The supernumerary X chromosome causes variable symptoms: while some individuals appear male, with no major physical differences from XY males, others develop symptoms ranging from infertility to hypospadias[415] and gynecomastia[416]. The variability of the effects is important, as a genotypic difference would not have been visible and therefore would not have had an impact on the life of this individual, whereas a phenotypic difference could have had significant consequences in everyday life. It is impossible to know whether the individual buried at Suontaka Vesitorninmäki had visible physical features of Klinefelter's syndrome, but the interpretation proposed by Finnish archaeologists for this individual buried with a sword, typical of male tombs, but with typically feminine clothing and ornaments, is as follows: the deceased would have been a respected person, since buried with precious material, of non-binary gender whose membership of a wealthy and/or influential family could have facilitated his/her integration into society[417]. It is therefore necessary, as Pamela Geller reminds us, for archaeologists not to consider sex in a strictly binary way, but as a continuum that can be just as fluid as gender, at the risk of obliterating individuals from the past who do not coincide with a binary vision of biological sex[418].

With this example, the question of gender quickly becomes intertwined with that of identifying the sex of the deceased. As we saw in the introduction, sex and gender are two distinct elements of the biological and social make-up of individuals. The question then arises as to what we can identify from a skeleton. Once sex has been established with varying degrees of certainty, what happens to gender? How can we establish with certainty the gender of a buried or cremated individual when the only data available to us is sex? Can we identify gender on the basis of funerary material alone? Archaeologists often tend to mix and match the two notions of sex and gender when faced with a funerary context[419]. As we have just seen (and will come back to in the next chapter), this poses problems when the grave contains objects whose 'gender' does not correspond to the biological sex of the deceased. What may be more important, however, is not so much our difficulty in reconciling the notions of sex and gender in these contexts, but to understand whether the distinction made sense to the communities who performed the funerals. Research into the Indigenous populations of North and Central America has contributed greatly to archaeologists' understanding of the sex/gender system. It has shown that the strict binarity of 'two sexes/two genders' did not exist in all societies[420]. One, two or three additional genders may exist in certain populations. Individuals may also transgress the norms we project onto the past and adopt the clothing and/or occupations of the other sex.

Furthermore, conceiving of sex as the primary way of dividing human societies sometimes obscures other divisions that make more sense for these societies[421]. Rosemary A. Joyce has demonstrated that, contrary to what had previously been written by other archaeologists, the most important social division in the tombs of the Tlatilco site south of Mexico City, which gave its name to the Tlatilco culture, was based on age rather than sex. The tombs at this site (*ca.* 1100–700 BC) were not located in a necropolis, but were for the most part integrated into the village, or even dug beneath the houses. Identical types of objects were found in both men's and women's graves. Two important elements were highlighted by Joyce. Firstly, the graves of young adults contained the most abundant and richest material, probably because potential social

412 Cohen C. 2016, 39–41.
413 Boucherie 2020, 42 ('Bien au-delà d'une simple binarité, les processus biologiques du sexe se caractérisent par une complexité inhérente qui n'interdit pas l'existence d'une intersexuation visible au niveau génétique, gonadique et/ou génital.'). See also Joyce 2008, 43–45. The morphological and skeletal implications of genetic and gonadal intersex variations have not been studied cf. Garofalo & Garvin 2020.
414 Sofaer 2006, 91. See also part 1.
415 A congenital condition in which the opening of the penis is positioned on its underside rather than at its tip.
416 Hypertrophy of the mammary glands in men.
417 Moilanen *et al.* 2022.
418 Geller 2008, 114. See also Geller 2005; 2008; 2017.
419 Geller 2017a, 81.
420 Geller 2005; Hollimon 1997; 2000; 2006; 2017.
421 Agarwal 2012, 324.

and economic alliances disappeared with them. Secondly, the graves of young adults were grouped together in the village or under houses, while the graves of older adults were isolated. In the funerary contexts of this society, the criterion of age was therefore of far greater importance than sex[422]. The gender roles that can be inferred from such a context are therefore particularly limited, and this should make us cautious[423]. As Joyce pointed out:

> 'We cannot begin our exploration of gender in archaeology by just looking for women and men, because that assumes that one kind of gender relations is universal, timeless, and more important than any other form of social distinction[424].'

In the case of children's burials, age may or may not be the primary social distinction. Using a new method of sex determination based on tooth enamel peptides, a team of archaeologists studied the burials of around 70 children under the age of 12 from one of the largest Early Bronze Age cemeteries in Europe, Franzhausen I (Austria, c. 2200–1600 BC). With the exception of one girl, the children were all buried in a flexed position, on their sides, with gender-specific differences in the orientation of the body (north-south for boys, south-north for girls), the side chosen (left for boys, right for girls) and the selection of funerary offerings. These tombs are an exact reflection of adult tombs and indicate an early consideration of the sex and gender roles of children[425]. In contrast, during certain periods of Greek Antiquity, age determined the type of funerary ritual, before any consideration of gender. Infants and immature youngsters were buried in large vases or other containers (*enchytrismos*), while adults were cremated[426]. At Çatalhöyük, on the other hand, a large Neolithic site in present-day Turkey, the study of bones showed no significant differences between men and women in terms of diet, physical trauma, infection or dental disease. Conversely, age seems to be the key variable at this site, since the oldest individuals were buried with objects, unlike the youngest, and show the most signs of individualisation in their choice of funerary offerings[427].

However, estimating biological sex is not the only information that can be obtained from an individual's skeleton: daily activities and diet leave traces on the body that shed light on other practices linked to gender, social class or age.

4.2. What marks bodies (I): differentiated activities and voluntary alterations

The skeleton has sometimes been seen as an element of material culture, to be studied in the same way as any other artefact[428]. Apart from biological sex, it can provide essential information, as many repeated behaviours and gestures leave marks on it. In some cases, these marks may be associated with differentiated socialisation and early learning of gender roles[429]. It is thus possible to study directly the way in which gender performance, or even class, leaves a mark on bodies: markers of musculoskeletal stress (size of muscle attachments, wear on joints), bone density, dental wear (linked to the use of teeth as tools), exostosis of the ear (associated with diving), etc. are all indications of particular bodily practices, which may mark a gendered division of tasks or its absence[430].

Repeated use of a muscle can exert a tensile force on the site of muscle insertion (enthesis) and repetitive work can damage joints. The study of these lesions enables anthropologists to propose interpretations of the amount and type of activity performed by an individual during his or her lifetime. For example, bone damage is particularly visible in the dominant arm bones of tennis players. The cortical bone in the humerus is 30% thicker on the dominant arm than on the other arm[431]. As Joanna Sofaer points out[432], studies of this type applied to ancient populations are now numerous and make it possible to identify or assume activities based on specific skeletal markers, such as archery, handling oars, grinding cereals or riding horses. Dental wear can also indicate specific activities requiring the use of the mouth and teeth[433]. In some cases, it is possible to identify a gender difference from the indicators left on the skeleton by repeated activities. This is the case, for example, in a study by Ted A. Rathbun, who found significant traces of degenerative disease in most of the skeletal joints of an enslaved population on a South Carolina plantation. The various elements indicated that the men carried heavy loads and that a sexual division of labour had been established: the joints most in demand in women were the knees and shoulders, while in men it was the elbow and hip[434].

This type of study can sometimes help to identify individuals belonging to a third gender in certain societies. Muscular or joint stress markers typically associated with female skeletons but appearing on male skeletons, or vice versa, as well as atypical markers on both male and female skeletons, may point to individuals belonging to a third gender, a fluid gender or a non-binary gender, as Sandra Hollimon points out in relation to the Indigenous populations of California[435]. In the Chumash necropolises studied by Hollimon, two burials contained the bones of two men whose skeletons showed marks typical of 'feminine' work. We will return to this case in the next chapter.

Episodes of violence can also leave marks on the skeleton[436]. In Giza, Egypt, during the Old Kingdom, the trauma

422 Joyce 2008, 46–51.
423 Moen 2019, 217.
424 Joyce 2008, 51.
425 Rebay-Salisbury *et al.* 2022.
426 Vlachou 2012, 382–384. See also Gilchrist 1999, 92.
427 Agarwal 2017.
428 Sofaer 2006; Hollimon 2006, 441.

429 For a good summary of the different types of analysis from a gendered perspective, see Hollimon 2011.
430 Brumfiel 2006, 37; Hollimon 2011, 153–156.
431 Sofaer 2006, 72.
432 Sofaer 2006, 72–73, 105–110.
433 Turner & Anderson 2003.
434 Rathbun 1987; for other examples, see Hollimon 2011, 153–156.
435 Hollimon 1997; 2000; 2017.
436 See for example Monge & Selinsky 2016.

observed on the deceased is an indicator of class and gender, since male and female workers suffered fractures more often than the elite, and men more than women[437]. However, interpretations of cases of violence often reinforce gender stereotypes[438]. Anthropologists tend to regard trauma and injuries to male skeletons as normal, and often approach female injuries not as evidence of their participation in violent episodes but as trauma resulting from domestic violence, especially when several factors known to be involved in cases of domestic violence overlap: fractures of the forearm (defensive injury), craniofacial fractures and age[439]. However, women's participation in warfare has been proven in certain regions and at certain times, particularly among the Scythians, where war wounds are frequently found on female skeletons. In one case, an arrowhead was found still embedded in the knee[440]. Similarly, there was a class of female warriors in Japan, the Onna-musha, who fought with the samurai. A study of the DNA of 105 skeletons unearthed at the site of the battle of Senbon Matsubaru (1580) revealed the presence of 35 women[441].

Alongside these alterations resulting from differentiated activities, the voluntary deformation of certain parts of the body can also constitute class and/or gender practices. For example, in imperial China, the fact that women with bandaged feet did not work was inscribed in their bodies and served to affirm the family's wealth. Indeed, footbinding was invented under the Northern Song dynasty, in power between the 10th and 12th centuries AD, and was practised by elite women before spreading more widely to the rest of society. The practice was finally banned by the government of the Republic of China in 1912, after several empresses and emperors had failed to do so. Footbinding involved strict control of women's bodies, subjecting them to a painful and even life-threatening procedure, and reducing their mobility[442]. However, recent work by Elizabeth Berger and her colleagues, based on a small sample of skeletons, shows that some elite women in Shaanxi did not bandage their feet at the end of the Ming dynasty, or did so in a much milder form. The study thus highlights the spread of gendered and specific bodily practices within Chinese society.

Other bodily practices are more difficult to interpret. Pamela Geller has studied dental modifications in individuals found in Mayan burials in Belize dating from 400 BC to 900 AD. These modifications involved, among other things, engraving the labial surface of the teeth, inlaying semi-precious stones such as haematite, jade or turquoise into the labial surface, or filing down the incisal edges of the teeth[443]. These alterations could have been carried out during rites of passage, signifying a change in status or identity for the individual – always an adult – who underwent the treatment. Both men and women had this type of dental alteration, with a slight prevalence of women in Geller's sample. However, certain patterns appear to be particularly associated with prominent members of society. The precise significance of these alterations, or lack of them, remains difficult to establish. The same is true of another type of bodily modification: the elongation of the skull in certain human groups by bandaging the head probably acts as a marker of identity, although its exact meaning is still debated: a mark of social class or ethnic affiliation[444]? Among the Mayans, where the practice is attested throughout their history, it should be noted that the modification of the cranium is not associated with rites of passage, like other types of body modification, because it takes place during childhood. Nevertheless, and precisely because it occurs at this time in life, this modification is a fundamental part of an individual's identity, though it is not gender-specific[445].

Another example of this type of body alteration is the use of the corset over a period spanning some four centuries between 1500 and 1900. The daily wearing of a corset deforms the ribcage and the spinous processes of the dorsal vertebrae. The ribcage changes from a bell shape to a cylindrical form, bringing the floating ribs towards the centre of the body. Similarly, the angle of the spinous processes of the dorsal vertebrae tends to become more acute. It should be noted, however, that the purpose of the corset was to support the torso and slim the waist, while marking the chest and hips, and that the deformation of the ribcage was not the primary aim but a consequence of the repeated wearing of this piece of clothing. The degree of violence between these different practices – cranial deformation, foot binding, corset, etc. – can vary widely. While the corset has often been decried as a patriarchal constraint imposed on women and possibly dangerous to their health, Rebecca Gibson's research has shown that the impact of ribcage deformations on the health of women wearing a corset was nil. What is more, wearing a corset is not an exclusively female practice, and some men, for example those with spina bifida or other conditions, did and still do wear them[446].

4.3. What marks bodies (II): differentiated diet

'It is around the production and control of food that all human groups, from hunter-gatherers to state-run societies, were originally organised[447]'. Food practices define a community and set it apart from others in a powerful way. Thus, for the ancient Greeks, the non-Greek, the barbarian, was, among other things, anyone who drank pure wine, whereas the 'civilised' practice was to mix it with water. Dietary practices define not only the contours of a given society but also its internal hierarchy, relying on dietetic reasoning to recommend diets suited to the elite, slaves,

437 Matić 2021, 35.
438 Hollimon 2011, 159.
439 Novak 2017.
440 Khudaverdyan *et al.* 2020.
441 Turnbull 2012, 6.
442 Berger *et al.* 2019; Lauwaert 2020. Darmangeat 2022, 267 notes in ethnography the example of certain Salish groups on the American north-west coast, where prepubescent girls from wealthy families were locked up for long periods in an uncomfortable room so that they would develop a deformity of the legs, which made them the most desirable parties.
443 Geller 2006.
444 Sofaer 2006, 73–74; Fox 2016, 655 reports the existence of this practice at the Neolithic site of Tharrounia in Evia (Greece).
445 Geller 2017b, 172–177.
446 Gibson 2020.
447 Quellier 2021, 7 ('C'est autour de la production et du contrôle de la nourriture que se sont originellement organisés tous les groupes humains, des chasseurs-cueilleurs aux sociétés étatisées.').

women, the elderly, children, etc. For example, in today's traditional societies in Côte d'Ivoire, men have priority over meat: 'In the case of the Seltaman, restrictions for women are placed on large game, and in the case of the Akyé, on small game, but in both cases, restrictions are placed on the meat most likely to be on the menu[448]'.

In Mesopotamia, large estates, palaces and temples employed large numbers of staff and paid them in the form of rations that depended on their sex, age, function and place in the hierarchy[449]. Similarly, in Egypt, 'the institutionalisation of hierarchies and social inequalities was achieved [...] through the official determination, by the authorities, of the dietary disparities between individuals of different social levels[450]'. Archaeology has highlighted this state of affairs, since at the site of Heit el-Gourob ('City of Workers' on the Giza plateau) the quality of meat and protein intake varied greatly according to the economic status of individuals: In the wealthy residential area, for example, the majority of meat consumed was that of cattle, gazelle, birds and Nile perch, whereas the inhabitants of the eastern part of the city, made up of a jumble of small houses, ate mainly mutton, goat, birds and pork[451].

It is estimated that a woman's daily caloric requirements are equivalent to two-thirds of a man's. Mesopotamian rations varied from region to region and from period to period, and are known to us from tablets listing the 'wages' in kind received by male and female workers. In the 3rd millennium, this portion was much lower for women, who received 1 liter of barley per day compared with 2 to 4 liters for men, even though the work they performed was just as physical and tiring as that of men (particularly the grinding of cereals). On the contrary, in the 14th century BC, in the Mesopotamian palace of Nuzi, the distribution appears to be more equitable and correspond to the caloric needs calculated according to sex[452].

In addition to caloric requirements, differential access to food resources and nutritional intake has repercussions on the body, leaving permanent traces known as stress indicators, particularly in the form of deficiencies visible on the skeleton. These bony stigmata include, for example, Harris lines, visible on long bones and which could indicate growth arrest, or the *cribra orbitalia*, marked by porosity of the orbit and probably indicating nutritional deficiencies[453]. Dental stigmata can be seen in the form of enamel hypoplasia, corresponding to a one-off deficiency during the formation of the dental crown and resulting in the presence of lines or grooves on the dental surface[454]. Conversely, the rich diet of the wealthier population is also visible on the bodies. In Egypt, excessively rich diet led to cardiovascular problems in high-ranking individuals, as revealed by analyses of their mummies[455]. On skeletons, an excessively rich diet can be revealed by hyperostosic disease, characterised 'by ossification of tendons, ligaments and joint capsules at their bony insertions, called entheses[456]'. This condition is associated, for example, with the high social status of the individuals buried in the cemetery of the Grey Nuns' Convent (*Couvent des Sœurs grises*) in Beauvais, in the Oise region, between the 15th and 18th centuries, and is more prevalent in males[457].

As Christine Delphy already noted in *L'ennemi principal*, an important sociological work on the question of women's unpaid productive and reproductive work in contemporary France, food consumption differs according to gender, age and the position of individuals within the family. She takes the example of rural families, which have low incomes and where we would expect to see the greatest degree of equity and equality in consumption. However, the quantity and quality of food varies greatly depending on the age and sex of the individual. In some cases, this differentiation in consumption means that access to certain types of food is restricted: sausages are kept in the parents' bedroom, sweets are kept high up, out of children's reach, etc. These restrictions are supported and justified by:

- a system of 'moral' beliefs: 'a drunk woman is ugly', 'men need more meat than women and children', etc,
- a presumed relationship between the size of individuals and their need for food (although even a puny man will always receive more food than a woman),
- the idea of differential energy expenditure: it is men who are in charge of 'heavy' jobs, which are more arduous than women's jobs, which are 'light'. However, this division between heavy and light work depends on the gender of the person doing it: a job is 'light' if it is done by a woman, and 'heavy' if it is done by a man. By definition, any work done by a woman will therefore be considered 'small'.

These normative beliefs and this hierarchy of family consumption do not disappear when we explore the more privileged social classes: rare and expensive foods are reserved for the father, while other family members eat less expensive foods. Using the example of family consumption of food, Delphy hypothesises that 'the rarest goods in each domain and the most prestigious areas of consumption are the object of privileged access[458]'. This theory is confirmed in the case of ancient Greece, where the diet of women and

448 Fournier *et al.* 2015 ('Dans le cas des Seltaman, les restrictions pour les femmes se font sur les gros gibiers, dans le cas des Akyé, sur les petits, mais, dans les deux cas, les restrictions se portent sur la viande susceptible d'être le plus fréquemment au menu.').
449 Michel 2012.
450 Mazé 2020, 66 ('l'institutionnalisation des hiérarchies et des inégalités sociales passe (…) par la fixation officielle, par le pouvoir, des disparités alimentaires entre individus de niveaux sociaux différents').
451 Mazé 2020, 64–65.
452 Lion 2021, 78.
453 It should be noted, however, that the aetiology of Harris lines is poorly known and little understood at present, and various factors could be the cause cf. Boucherie *et al.* 2017.
454 Bayard *et al.* 2019. Dental enamel hypoplasia has also been associated with other factors such as weaning, starvation, fever, low birth weight and congenital infections cf. Sofaer 2006, 74.
455 David 2010.
456 Kacki & Villotte 2006, 56.
457 Kacki & Villotte 2006. For another example, see Kacki *et al.* 2018.
458 Delphy 1998, 93 ('les biens le plus rares dans chaque domaine et les domaines de consommation les plus prestigieux font l'objet d'un accès privilégié').

slaves was different from that of men, and where the elite ate a more meaty and diversified diet[459]. A form of dietary hierarchy therefore emerged not only between the sexes, but also between classes (rich vs. poor), status (free vs. slave) and ethnic groups (Greek vs. non-Greek). Ancient authors, particularly those in the Hippocratic corpus, advocated reducing women's diets because they were considered less active than men. In addition to discrediting women's domestic work, this was above all about exercising power over women's bodies, as Jean-Manuel Roubineau explains:

> 'Medical treatises from the imperial period go so far as to see this reduced diet for young girls as an effective means of delaying the onset of puberty, and with it the desire to have sexual relations and bear children. In this way, the under-nutrition of young girls was part of a wider strategy of male control of the female body[460].'

It is therefore not uncommon to observe malnutrition problems on female skeletons, as well as a poorer physical condition than in men. Bones discovered in Egyptian necropolises from the Ptolemaic and Roman periods in the Kharga oasis in Egypt show that women died in excess between the ages of 12 and 40, and that their diet was much poorer than that of men. This excess mortality is probably the result of childbirth carried out in unhygienic conditions and without proper care. Harris lines, which may indicate arrested growth, are present on 42% of male skeletons compared with 68% of female skeletons[461].

In cases where there are no signs of dietary deficiencies or malnutrition, isotope analyses can be used to determine whether or not dietary practices were egalitarian between the sexes or social classes. For example, isotopic signatures show a higher consumption of animal protein among the elite, both men and women, in Bronze Age tombs at Pylos; in more modest tombs, the consumption of animal protein was higher among men than women[462]. Similarly, Christine D. White notes gender differences in diet among the Maya, and specifies that these were more pronounced among the elite, with elite men often consuming more animal protein than women. Elite men also consumed more foods that could be considered symbolically important, such as maize, maize-fed animals and marine resources, perhaps served as part of ritual meals in which women did not participate, or at least not to the same degree or with the same frequency. On the other hand, non-elite women appear to have consumed the same foods as their male counterparts. The elite men's preferential access to ritual foods ceased after the Spanish conquest, although their diet remained more meaty than that of the women[463].

Differentiated nutrition is one of the pillars of Priscille Touraille's theory on the dimorphism in stature between men and women in the modern era – a dimorphism that was not very marked in the *Homo* genus until the Neolithic period. While natural selection should, according to this researcher, favour tall women with a wide pelvis in order to facilitate childbirth, Touraille puts forward the hypothesis that two main factors have contributed, over the long course of human history, to making men tall and women short: on the one hand, a cultural preference on the part of men for women who are shorter than themselves and on the part of women for taller men, and on the other hand, a differentiated diet favouring men, in particular through a higher protein intake[464]. Pregnant and breast-feeding women have the highest animal protein requirements, not men, contrary to popular belief. Although Touraille's thesis has been widely controversial, it nevertheless has the advantage of deconstructing a phenomenon – differentiated diet – which is often perceived as a biological and immutable fact, by presenting it instead as a set of cultural norms[465].

While the body provides important information for archaeologists, funerary structures and assemblages – at least what remains of them in the form of non-perishable materials – provide significant additional information about the social structures of a given society[466]. For this reason, in the next chapter we will concentrate on the interpretation of objects found in tombs.

Where to start?

A. Boucherie, 'Approche archéo-anthropologique d'ensembles funéraires : question de sexe biologique ou de genre ?', *in* I. Algrain (ed.), *Archéologie du genre. Construction sociale des identités et culture matérielle*, Université des femmes, 2020, 41–59.

P.L. Geller, *The Bioarchaeology of Socio-Sexual Lives. Queering Common Sense About Sex, Gender, and Sexuality*, Springer, 2017.

S.E. Hollimon, 'Bioarchaeological Approaches to Nonbinary Genders. Case Studies from Native North America', *in* S.C. Agarwal & J.K. Wesp (ed.), *Exploring Sex and Gender in Bioarchaeology*, University of New Mexico Press, 2017, 51–69.

J. Sofaer, *The Body as Material Culture. A Theoretical Osteoarchaeology*, Cambridge University Press (coll. 'Topics in Contemporary Archaeology'), 2006.

459 Roubineau 2015, 155–172.
460 Roubineau 2015, 159 ('Les traités médicaux d'époque impériale vont jusqu'à voir dans cette alimentation réduite des jeunes filles un moyen efficace de retarder la venue de la puberté, et avec elle le désir d'entretenir des relations sexuelles et d'engendrer des enfants. En cela, la sous-alimentation des jeunes filles s'inscrit dans une stratégie plus large de contrôle du corps féminin par les hommes.').
461 Dunand 2004, 22.
462 Fox 2016, 652.
463 White 2005.
464 Touraille 2008.
465 Darmangeat 2022, 14–17.
466 Belard 2017, 69.

5

Funerary archaeology (II): 'female' vs. 'male' objects

Although funerary contexts provide valuable information about the beliefs and customs of ancient societies, they are not a mirror of the social organisation of the living. Funerary practices may vary within the same society, reflecting differences in social status, age or gender. They may also be influenced by cultural beliefs. Moreover, the burial provides a truncated image of the individual, anchored in the moment of death and probably not reflecting the different phases of his or her life. The objects associated with the deceased do not therefore constitute a complete biography of the various facets of their identity[467]. Nor do they provide information about an individual's gender identity, i.e. how they perceived themselves, but about their social identity, materialised by the living in attributes specific to their status, age or sex[468]. However, funerary assemblages are the best gateway for reconstructing social relations, particularly gender relations.

As we mentioned earlier, gender varies in time and space. Each society has its own complex sex/gender system. The material representation of this system, i.e. its embodiment in specific objects and material culture in the broadest sense, also varies over time and space. The study of gender through objects requires, on the one hand, a return to raw data, and on the other, a precise definition of the society under study and any regional and/or chronological variations. This object-based approach is essential for the archaeologist because 'much of the way we learn how to be men and women in any society comes, not through explicit discussion, but through the inexplicit experience of living in a world of things[469]'.

This return to raw data is made necessary by the fact that the first archaeological studies that looked at 'female' and 'male' objects did so by projecting the cultural norms of archaeologists onto the past. As a result, archaeologists frequently naturalised non-biological processes, giving the image of a past very similar to their own, with identical social relations between the sexes. On the one hand, this has reinforced contemporary social norms, which thus find legitimacy in an immutable and universal past, and on the other, it has masked the socio-cultural specificities of the past (see Figure 5.1)[470]. It should be pointed out, however, that while we are concentrating here on artefacts, any

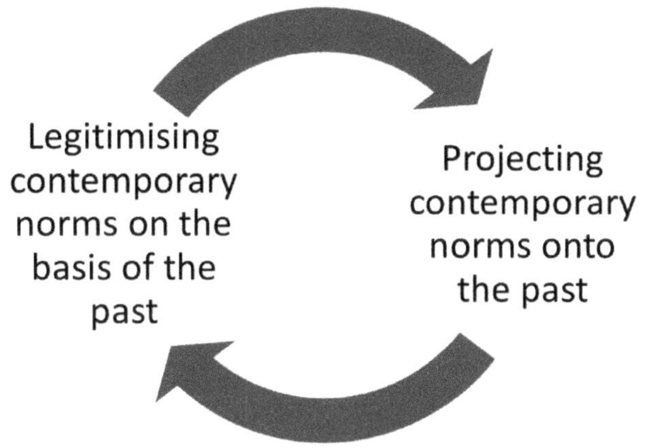

Figure 5.1. Self-reinforcing cycle between projecting present norms onto the past and legitimising those norms through historical narratives.

archaeological data relating to funerary contexts may be conditioned by gender (or other social factors): funerary arrangements or gestures – such as the architecture of the burial site, the funerary apparatus (structured architecture, coffin, shroud or pit in the ground), – the treatment of the body (cremation or burial), the orientation of the grave, the position of the body, and so on.

5.1. Gendered objects?

Objects do not determine gender, and even less so sex. Attempts to gender archaeological material are as old as the discipline itself. In caricature fashion, based on their own experience of the gender of objects, 19th-century archaeologists were quick to define objects that were typically masculine and feminine. 'These particular material things have acquired the status of metaphors par excellence of "malehood" and "womanhood" within archaeology[471]'. This bicategorisation of objects has sometimes been taken to ridiculous extremes. In a book published in 1898 by Frédéric Moreau, there is a depiction of an antique vase normally used to store food, but here depicted with a beautiful floral arrangement. The accompanying caption states that: 'You must not believe that these beautiful vases, with incised decoration, [...] were vases for storing food. They were ornamental vases for plants and flowers, and the Gallic woman was as

[467] Thomas 2022, 77.
[468] Belard 2017, 104–105; Augereau 2021, 36.
[469] Joyce 2008, 20.
[470] Walley 2020, 11.

[471] Hjørungdal 1994, 144, quoted by Sørensen 2000, 27.

curious and careful about them as a 19th-century French woman[472]'.

This division between 'feminine' and 'masculine' objects seemed perfectly natural in the 19th century, whereas in reality it stemmed from 'normative associations between sex and behaviour[473]'. The presence or absence of an object was enough to determine 'sex', in particular the presence of weapons to identify male graves and their absence to identify female graves. Since in our day and age, and in our Western societies, jewellery is associated with the feminine world and weapons are the preserve of men, it seemed logical to archaeologists that ancient societies should have made the same association. If we take the example of the Champagne region in the Iron Age (800–450 BC), the traditional approach was to make precisely this division: from the 19th century onwards, archaeologists distinguished between tombs with weapons, which were said to be 'masculine', and tombs with ornaments, which were said to be 'feminine'[474]. Yet these associations are sometimes far from obvious or universal. Natalia Berseneva notes that only 46% of the tombs of the Sargat, a nomadic population of the Eurasian steppes (6th c. BC - 3rd/4th c. AD), conform to gender stereotypes (weapons for men, jewellery for women) and that no object in these contexts is uniquely associated with either women or men (weapons are found in women's tombs and jewellery in men's tombs)[475].

It is true that 'analysing funerary objects by looking for preferential associations [seems to be a] logical approach [...]: in particular, it reflects the dichotomy of activities (sexual dichotomy in the world of the living, reflected in funerary objects but associated with other explanatory factors – age, status, etc.) and the possibility of exceptions to this rule (with contradictory situations between sex and gender or the possibility of multiple genders)[476]'. Indeed, the activities of men and women may differ as a result of the gendered division of labour (see introduction and chapter 7). For example, in Greek and Roman societies, weaving and preparing textiles were predominantly female activities, whereas defending the territory was a male activity. We might therefore expect to find in the burials a reflection of this division, with material preferentially associated with one of the two sexes. However, not all men's graves have weapons and not all women's graves have loom weights[477].

This apparent association of sex and material culture may appear to be a positive element that can facilitate the work of archaeologists. However, it can lead to a certain amount of confusion, since material culture does not reflect an individual's sex but his or her gender identity as experienced by that individual and as perceived by his or her community, since 'the dead do not bury themselves[478]'. The question of the 'gender' of objects is therefore one of the most important in the archaeology of gender, particularly in the study of funerary contexts. Yet, as Caroline Trémeaud points out, this method has a number of drawbacks, such as: 'confining our thinking to a binary system in which the masculine is opposed to the feminine; allowing only biological data (sex) to exist and ignoring the possibility of social data (gender); and, as a result, interpreting biologically data that is not biological, since it is obtained from artefacts[479]'.

Generally speaking, interpreting funerary material is not a problem as long as the biological sex coincides with the archaeological sex. However, archaeologists tend to insist on archaeological sex when an apparent contradiction between sex and material culture arises. For example, when a tomb with a female skeleton and extremely rich artefacts or weapons is discovered, a recurring pattern of problematic interpretation arises:

1. deny the evidence by saying that there has been a handling error, that the sample has been contaminated, that it does not in fact come from this context but has been mixed with other remains (see section 'Birka Bj 581: a simple burial with weapons or a female warrior's grave?');
2. propose an alternative solution by saying that, if a weapon is the mark of a warrior in a man's grave, its presence in a woman's grave in fact reflects the status of her husband or other male members of her family (see section 5.3, 'Transgression of norms (II): women and power');
3. turning to religion: rich women's tombs are those of priestesses because they cannot be the holders of any other type of power (see section 'The tomb of Vix');
4. falsely advocate open-mindedness by stating that this is an exceptional case of a third gender, of a 'transvestite', of a woman who lived under a male identity, which obviously undermines all the work carried out by archaeologists studying transidentity in ancient societies (see section 'The tomb of Vix').

472 Moreau 1898 quoted by Belard 2017, 36, fig. 3 ('il ne faut pas croire que ces beaux vases, à décors incisés, (...) étaient des vases à conserver des aliments. Ce sont des vases à ornements, pour recevoir plantes et fleurs, dont la Gauloise était aussi curieuse et soigneuse alors qu'une Française du XIXe siècle').
473 Sørensen 2000, 51.
474 Belard 2017, 8, 15–32.
475 Berseneva 2008, 142.
476 Trémeaud 2018, 19 ('effectuer l'analyse du mobilier funéraire en cherchant les associations préférentielles [semble être une approche] logique (...) : cela traduit notamment la dichotomie des activités (dichotomie sexuelle dans le monde des vivants, traduite dans le mobilier funéraire mais associée à d'autres facteurs explicatifs – âge, statut, etc.) et la possibilité d'exceptions à cette règle (avec des situations contradictoires entre sexe et genre ou la possibilité d'une multiplicité des genres)').
477 Belard 2017, 17.
478 Arnold 2012, 221 quoting Sørensen 2000, 52.
479 Trémeaud 2018, 2 ('enfermer la réflexion dans un système binaire, où le masculin s'oppose au féminin; ne permettre l'existence que de la donnée biologique (le sexe) et ne pas voir la possibilité d'une donnée sociale (le genre); par conséquent, interpréter biologiquement des données qui ne sont pas biologiques, puisque obtenues à partir du mobilier').

The tomb of Vix

The tomb of Vix, discovered in 1953, is an example widely used in archaeology to highlight the androcentric bias of research[480]. This chariot tomb found under a 38-meter-diameter tumulus in Burgundy is one of the richest of the period (late 6th century BC), and its position within the necropolis could attest to its importance in the 'aristocratic lineages[481]'. It contained, among other items, a monumental bronze crater from southern Italian workshops and material attesting to long-distance trade (coral, Baltic amber, Attic cup). The presence of rich ornaments and the absence of weapons clearly suggested a woman's tomb to archaeologists in the 1950s. She would become a 'queen', a 'princess' or even the 'Lady' of Vix, terms that reflect the difficulty of thinking about her status. Nevertheless, the gold torque found in the tomb, initially identified as a diadem, casted doubt on this identification, as it was then considered to be often associated with men. Other theories then appeared in the literature, attempting to deny the sex of the deceased: the Lady of Vix was a shaman-priest, a man who had no objection to wearing women's clothing, or a transvestite priest. To solve the problem, anthropologists analyzed the skeleton and confirmed the female sex of the deceased. Some analyses indicated physical defects that would explain her high social status and function as a priestess; other analyses finally indicated that the physical defects were not visible and did not affect the Lady of Vix's appearance. What seemed to archaeologists to be the problem with these numerous interpretative reversals was, in fact, the association of a female skeleton with particularly rich material, which went against their preconceptions of the role of women in Celtic societies. Even after the sex of the skeleton was confirmed, hypotheses continued to be put forward to explain the exceptional nature of the tomb (which would not have been the case had the skeleton been male). It was not until around 40 years later that the idea emerged that the Lady of Vix might have occupied a position of power. For Bettina Arnold, the gold torque is not a gender marker, but a marker of the deceased's important status. While this status remains difficult to pin down (especially in terms of the type of power held), it is in keeping with the phenomenon of rich female tombs studied by Caroline Trémeaud and is therefore in no way exceptional to this period.

[480] Arnold 1991 and 2012; Péré-Noguès 2011; Belard 2017, 39; Trémeaud 2018, 1–2.
[481] Milcent 2003, 324–325, quoted by Péré-Noguès 2011, note 9.

As we can see from these examples, it is essential to **go back to the raw data**. Moreover, if we want to highlight gender as a hierarchical system and the way in which it is expressed in material culture, it is also necessary to **analyse both women's and men's burials**. This approach sheds light on the construction of the masculine and feminine. Take, for example, Caroline Trémeaud's work on the North Alpine world (a region where the phenomenon of 'princely tombs' centred on the First Iron Age) from the Final Bronze Age to the middle of the Second Iron Age[482]. Using a corpus of more than 700 tombs, she first determined the different levels of wealth of the burials, potentially linked to the status of the individuals. She then defined which objects were associated with men, which with women and which were gender-neutral. She also analysed the assemblages within the burials, according to period. Finally, these data were compared with anthropological sex, where known, to see whether objects that were repeatedly found together were indeed associated with female or male skeletons. This method was also used to highlight transgressions, for example when 'feminine' objects were found in a man's grave and vice versa. We will come back to these transgressions later.

The results of this study, which combines the richness of burials with their archaeological gender, show that, depending on the period, the visibility of gender through funerary material can fluctuate. The female gender may be more perceptible in certain periods: 'the masculine is clearly dominant in the Final Bronze Age and Hallstatt C, but not in Hallstatt D and La Tène, where the proportions do not exceed 50%[483]'. However, the masculine is the most clearly defined: 'the masculine gender is always perceptible, while the feminine gender may fade away; there is at least a 20% proportion of neutral or mixed burials, so even in phases of strong gender distinction, a certain proportion of burials are deliberately non-gendered[484]'. The results also indicate that wealth is generally correlated with the feminine (Figure 5.2): in periods when the female gender is most visible in funerary material, this female gender also has access to the highest level of wealth[485].

The interpretation of these data and their significance for the social order are more complex. Firstly, the value of a gendered study based on the raw data from the rich burials is very clear. While the anthropological sex of the deceased can only be characterised for 4% of these burials, 96% of the burials could be characterised on the basis of gender. 22% of burials do not express gender, reflecting the fact that

[482] For the following paragraphs, see Trémeaud 2018 and 2019.
[483] Trémeaud 2018, 148 ('le masculin domine nettement au Bronze final et au Hallstatt C mais pas au Hallstatt D et au La Tène où les proportions ne dépassent pas les 50%').
[484] Trémeaud 2018, 148 ('le genre masculin est toujours perceptible alors que le féminin peut s'effacer; il y a a minima une proportion de 20% de sépultures neutres ou mixtes, donc même dans les phases de forte distinction du genre, une certaine proportion de sépultures est volontairement non genrée').
[485] Trémeaud 2018, 158–164.

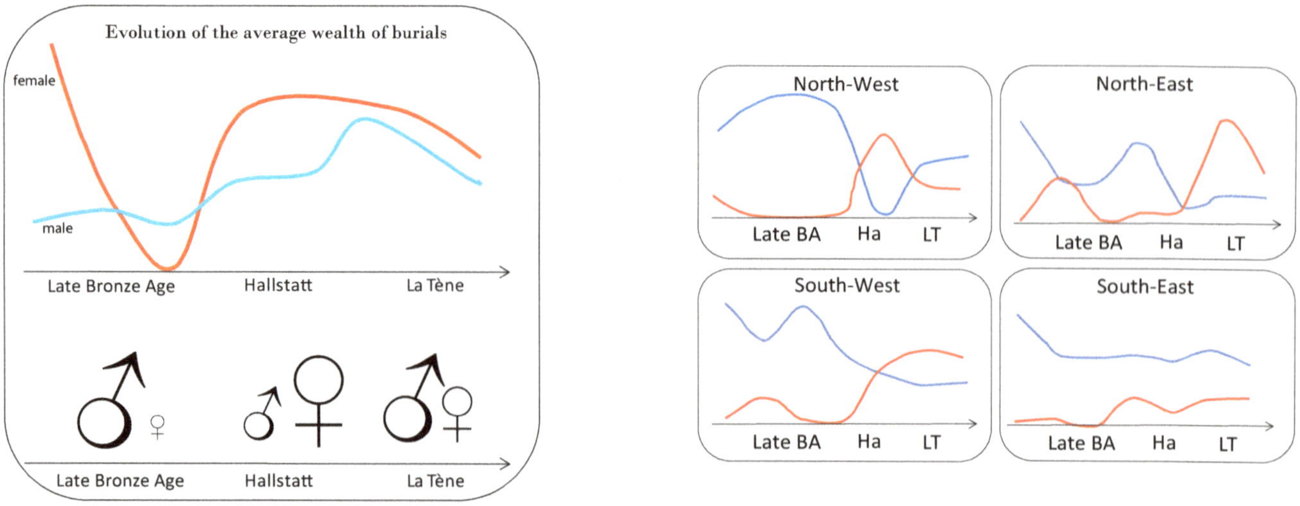

Figure 5.2. Changes in the average wealth of burials. After Trémeaud 2018, fig. 96.

this funerary elite can express gender in a more secondary manner, perhaps because in the case of these graves, status takes precedence over gender. The data also show that gender relations, and consequently the means of expressing gender through material culture, fluctuate from period to period.

These data also make it possible to re-examine previous research hypotheses in a new light. For example, the hypothesis of a male power vacuum that would have left the field open to women at certain periods is not sufficient to explain the extent of the phenomenon over such a vast region. The archaeological data do not allow us to establish to what type of status this wealth may be linked. We can, however, affirm that it is not solely an expression of the economic power of the family or the male entourage of the deceased (in particular, a symbol of the husband's power). If this were the case, we would see just as many rich male tombs. However, this is not the case, and the richest female graves, during periods of feminine ostentation, seem to function as a structuring element in necropolises.

The hypothesis put forward by Caroline Trémeaud is that these women probably took part in the process of the increasing complexity of societies, involving the expansion of territories and the appearance of urban complexes. These communities required a certain amount of logistics to ensure their survival, which enabled some women to gain access to positions of prestige and power similar to those of the male elites at the end of the Hallstatt period. Women successfully invested in the development of long-lasting exchange networks and thus gained easier access to power. The increased importance of contacts with the Mediterranean world may have played a role in the intensification of princely phenomena, particularly at the time of the creation of the Greek city-states. The existence of large-scale contacts and the influence of Mediterranean trade may have played a role in the emergence of the princely system. Thus, 'northern Alpine societies became more complex under the influence of Mediterranean contacts, but following a dynamic specific to the northern complex, gradually integrating women into positions of power similar to those open to men[486]'.

Other cases illustrate the variability in the expression of gender within tombs. Chloé Belard's re-evaluation of women's graves in Champagne during the Iron Age, particularly for the period from the last third of the 6th to the 3rd century BC, shows the presence of men's graves with weapons and women's graves with ornaments, but also the low representation of gender in other graves, since many of them contained neither weapons nor ornaments. These 'undetermined' graves often make up a higher proportion than the graves with weapons or ornaments, 'which clearly proves that this basis for classifying burial complexes is inappropriate[487]'. The study of funerary offerings also shows that only a minority of objects can be used to effectively classify burials: this is not the case for ceramics, food offerings or several types of metal objects. Some objects are preferentially associated with women, such as torques, but they are not present in all women's tombs, and there are a few instances of them in the funerary assemblages of men's tombs. The objects with the strongest connotations of male gender are razors, which also discriminate according to age since children's graves do not contain any, and weapons, which are present in only a quarter of the men's graves. In all, only 40% of the tombs studied by Chloé Belard contained objects indicative of gender; the others were devoid of such objects and contained objects independent of gender. The association of certain artefacts with each other, which is favoured in certain burials, seems to socially organise 2 or 3 groups of adults, depending on the period. This research

[486] Trémeaud 2018, 181 ('Les sociétés nord-alpines se sont complexifiées sous l'influence de contacts méditerranéens mais suivant une dynamique propre au complexe nord, en intégrant progressivement le féminin dans des situations de pouvoirs semblables à celles ouvertes au masculin.'). These contacts take place along two north-south axes (an eastern Adriatic-Baltic axis and a more western axis running along the Rhône and the Seine).

[487] Belard 2017, 24–25, 25 for the quote ('ce qui prouve bien que cette base de classification des ensembles sépulcraux n'est pas appropriée.').

highlights the multi-factorial nature of the choice of objects deposited in the grave: sex and gender are not the only categories that influence this choice; age and social status play an equally important role[488].

Finally, let's take the example of the Linear Pottery culture (LBK) of the Neolithic, which stretched from Central Europe to the Paris basin. Anne Augereau has recently published several works on the Western LBK (ca. 5500–4900 BC), approached from a gender perspective. Firstly, on a sample of 378 burials, she notes that more than 75% of men's tombs contained at least one object, whereas this is the case for less than 40% of women's tombs. The categories of artefacts are also more varied for men[489]. Around 25% of women's graves in the Paris Basin and Haute-Alsace contained items indicating that the deceased had been buried in full regalia, with more than three types of adornment (headdresses and necklaces made from rare and distant materials such as shells, breastplates, belts and garments embroidered with pearls, etc.). Some of these items also appear in male tombs, but in lesser numbers. The stone artefacts consisted mainly of punches, flint chips and grinding implements, all of which are gender-neutral[490]. The burial equipment associated with men's graves includes adzes, polished stone axes and maces, flint arrow frames, lighters and tools made from antlers, although not all the men were equipped with them[491]. In the LBK culture, male identities were clearly defined by specific items of equipment, associated with virility (hunting and warfare), while more generic items of equipment, not exclusive to women, accompanied the female deceased. The organisation of LBK culture necropolises is interesting in more ways than one. Generally speaking, there is a clear hierarchy in terms of wealth. The central grave is often that of a man carrying an adze, richly endowed with funerary equipment, who had lived locally since childhood – as indicated by the strontium isotope ratios of these individuals – and whose diet was richer in animal proteins than that of the other individuals in the necropolis, as indicated by the carbon and nitrogen isotope ratios. He was frequently accompanied by another richly endowed individual (male, female or immature). The other richly endowed tombs, those of men and then women, are organised around this remarkable tomb, while the tombs with no furnishings are located on the periphery[492]. In addition, analysis of strontium isotope ratios shows that women tended to be more mobile than men, who tended to remain anchored in their place of birth, suggesting a patrilocal matrimonial system[493].

5.2. Transgression of norms (I): atypical tombs

Queer theory's contribution to archaeology has made it possible to consider genders and identities situated on the margins of dominant and legitimate social norms. Queer theory seeks to challenge dominant categories and narratives that 'present restrictive social norms as natural[494]'. It emerged in the 1990s, notably following the publication of Judith Butler's work and in the wake of gay and lesbian studies. This research highlighted the constructed nature of both sex and gender, as well as the binarity of sex (male vs. female), gender (masculine vs. feminine) and sexuality (heterosexuality vs. homosexuality). By challenging norms, queer theory insists above all on the flexibility of identities and their culturally contingent nature[495]. Applied to archaeology, queer theory makes it possible to study practices that fall outside the dominant modern norms, but which can often be legitimate and within the norm according to the criteria of ancient societies. Sandra Hollimon defines queer archaeology as follows: 'As such, it is not a search for homosexuals in the archaeological record it is rather **a consideration of any persons or practices considered marginal in their own cultural contexts.**[496]'. Such approaches are all the more important when they concern societies that differ from the Western binary sex/gender system, and which possess more than two genders, for example. We will briefly discuss these cases before turning to binary societies (two sexes/two genders).

Since the late 1990s, Sandra Hollimon has been studying the California necropolises of the Chumash[497]. In keeping with the social structure of this society, she expected to find masculine and feminine marker objects in the graves, as well as clues to the identity of people belonging to a third gender. However, she noted that objects such as baskets, produced by women, were found in both men's and women's graves, with no apparent distinction, suggesting that gender is not a discriminating factor for the Chumash at burial. On the other hand, observation of the marks left on the bones by repetitive movements enabled her to identify markers typically found on female skeletons (osteoarthritis affecting the spine), caused by the repeated use of digging sticks, on two young male skeletons. Not only were these two young men buried with digging sticks – as is the case for other men – but they are the only men to also have baskets in their graves. Both types of objects are usually associated with gravediggers, an activity strongly associated with the third gender (*'aqi*) in Chumash society. Hollimon's research has shown that this third gender is not a fixed category. In fact, Chumash society is one in which part of the population expresses a certain gender fluidity: the third gender is not a fixed gender category or sexual identity, but a status acquired by certain people who can help the spirits of the dead make their journey to the afterlife. This spiritual status was linked to the reproductive capacity of individuals, implying that men whose primary partners were other men, celibates and women beyond menopause could belong to this *'aqi* group. Gender is therefore linked to sexuality in Chumash society, and can vary according to the period of an individual's life.

488 Belard 2017, 70–72, 89–108.
489 Augereau 2021, 111–112.
490 Augereau 2021, 123–128, 138.
491 Augereau 2021, 138–139.
492 Augereau 2021, 194–200.
493 Augereau 2021, 181–187.
494 Walley 2020, 37.
495 Walley 2020, 38.
496 Hollimon 2011, 161 (emphasis added).
497 Hollimon 1997; 2000; 2006; 2017.

Meghan Walley, a specialist in Inuit archaeology, notes that, while categorizations are useful for archaeologists to better apprehend and understand archaeological material, they also run the risk of limiting the conceptual framework, making it rigid and preventing us from going beyond the binarity of male/female or female/masculine[498]. Categories, if too rigid, can prevent us from seeing or considering intersex people in the study of biological sex, as well as a possible third gender or other types of transgression of our modern norms such as gender fluidity or non-binarity. For example, the gender fluidity present in Inuit societies is marked by very little gendered material in funerary assemblages but is clearly document by anthropologists[499]. For Meghan Walley:

> 'If we do not question the categories we apply to the past, then we bar ourselves from fresh perspectives ; we miss detail, and, worst of all, we risk naturalizing categories that are historically oppressive and perpetuate experiences of marginalization in the present[500].'

In binary societies (two sexes/two genders), after statistical studies of an entire necropolis, it is often possible to determine whether certain objects are preferentially associated with women or preferentially associated with men. There are also objects that are gender-neutral but which constitute typical funerary offerings or may be associated with individuals for other reasons (social class, age, etc.). In Classical Athens, for example, white-ground lekythoi were found in the tombs of men, women and children. These perfume vases were covered in a very fragile white slip that made them unsuitable for everyday use, and decorated with funerary themes (display of the body of the deceased, visits and rituals at the tomb, preparation of baskets of funerary offerings, scenes in the afterlife, etc.). White-ground lekythoi were produced specifically as funerary offerings. Alabastra, also perfume vases, have for a long time been associated exclusively with women in scientific publications, due to iconographic representations that show them mostly in the hands of women. However, in funerary contexts, they acquired the same use as lekythoi. The association of these two forms with the funerary world probably stems from the use of perfumed oils to prepare the body of the deceased, and not from the gendered use of these vessels and their contents[501].

The division of funerary material into 'masculine' and 'feminine' objects can pose methodological problems. It implies a de facto binarity of genders (masculine or feminine) which in some cases risks being reductive, as 'this method poses numerous problems (of objectivity and data reliability) and above all will erase particularly interesting situations of 'deviance'[502]'. These transgressions appear in two cases: when material that is both 'female' and 'male' is found in the tomb, and when the determination of sex seems to be contradicted by the 'archaeological sex'. We will take two examples to illustrate this point.

Laura Mary, for example, has challenged the binarity of sex identification of the deceased based on archaeological objects, taking as her starting point two burials from the Merovingian necropolis of Bossut-Gottechain (Belgium)[503]. This cemetery, which was in use from the last quarter of the 5th century to the third quarter of the 7th century AD, contained 437 tombs. Two of the tombs had atypical funerary furnishings. The other graves on the site generally contained either weapons (swords, shields, axes, scramasaxes, spearheads, arrowheads) and/or other everyday objects (chaplains, lighters, flints), or items of jewellery (fibulae, rings, pendants, pearl necklaces), fastenings (fibulae, shoe buckles) and/or items of transport (chatelaine, boxes, saddlebags). These two categories of furniture are traditionally used in Merovingian archaeology to define the sex of the deceased: 'male' for the former, 'female' for the latter. Tombs 137 and 260 contained both sets of material, along with several other non-gendered artefacts (ceramics, knives). Far from suggesting the existence of a third gender in Merovingian society, this configuration should encourage archaeologists to question the personal identity of these two deceased (did they transgress Merovingian social norms?), while also calling into question the 'gendered value' attributed to certain objects. For if objects thought to be 'feminine' or 'masculine' are found in the same burial site, are they really discriminatory? For Chloé Belard, 'graves with objects indicative of both genders are [...] not 'abnormal' or 'aberrant'; they highlight [the] social and emotional stakes by revealing the importance of funerary negotiation of the deceased's social identity. The deceased is not buried as a 'man' or a 'woman', but according to social needs and strategies[504]'. Transgression of norms or social negotiation? The question needs to be asked on a case-by-case basis, depending on the societies and regions studied.

As with the tombs mentioned above, the example of the tomb of Makareus can also be used to illustrate the presence of 'feminine' material in a man's tomb[505]. This 4th-century BC tomb, discovered in the Kerameikos necropolis in Athens, contained the skeleton of a young man accompanied by two ceramic pyxides and one marble pyxis, two lekanides, seven alabastra, a mirror and small animal figurines. The two Corinthian-style lekanides contained cerussite tablets and the pyxis contained pink powder, in other words, make-up products. The deceased was identified as Makareus, a young actor and poet whose

[498] Walley 2018 and 2020.
[499] Crass 2001, 111.
[500] Walley 2020, 1.
[501] Algrain 2014.
[502] Trémeaud 2018, 8 ('cette méthode pose de nombreux problèmes (d'objectivité et de fiabilité des données) et surtout va gommer les situations de "déviance" particulièrement intéressantes.').
[503] Mary 2021.
[504] Belard 2017, 106 ('les tombes présentant des objets indicatifs des deux genres ne sont [...] pas "anormales" ou "aberrantes"; elles mettent justement en évidence [l']enjeu social et émotionnel en révélant l'importance de la négociation funéraire de l'identité sociale du défunt. Celui-ci n'est pas inhumé en tant qu' "homme" ou "femme", mais en fonction des besoins et des stratégies sociales.').
[505] Algrain 2021b.

funerary monument, bearing his name and profession, was found nearby. Since the tragedian Thespis in the 6th century BC, it was customary for actors to paint their masks to enhance their facial features before performances. The presence of make-up and objects frequently associated with women, such as pyxides and mirrors, seem to indicate a difference between the biological sex and social sex (i.e. gender) of the deceased, at least as far as the funerary offerings deposited in the burial site are concerned. However, was it only because Makareus was an actor that make-up was found in his grave, or could it be that there is a certain gender fluidity[506] there that we do not recognise because it has not been studied? The question may be provocative, but it is necessary if we are to better understand the construction of gender identities in ancient societies.

The presence of 'atypical' graves in necropolises is far from an isolated phenomenon, and a number of studies have highlighted the need to re-evaluate funerary material through the prism of gender, while taking into account other factors whose importance may supersede gender, such as age or social class[507]. In the case of societies without writing, the interpretation of these tombs is obviously open to question. But since these tombs exist, and communities have seen fit to bury certain individuals in a position normally reserved for the other sex, or to offer them material usually associated with the other sex or with both sexes, it is not possible to be satisfied with an explanation such as 'this is a statistical error'. These examples show us that societies are capable of accepting and integrating these transgressions of norms, although they sometimes remain enigmatic for us and provide us with little information about how these individuals lived. In these cases, their social integration was sufficient for them to be buried in collective necropolises and to receive the appropriate funeral rites[508]. As Pamela Geller reminds us in her work, it is necessary to place socio-sexual identities and relationships within their specific cultural and historical frameworks, and to analyse the dynamics involved in their creation and transformationin order to give full scope to the gender variations that may have existed in the past societies we are studying[509]. These tombs should serve as a warning to us and encourage us to question the sex/gender systems of ancient societies[510]. It is also important to remember that, beyond the generalisations that can be made at the scale of a necropolis, it is above all individuals who bury and are buried.

The question of transgression of norms has two facets. On the one hand, there are transgressions of ancient social norms, acceptable or not, traceable or not in archaeological contexts, as the last two examples above have shown. On the other hand, what seems to us to be a transgression may sometimes reflect a social organization and sex/gender system different from our own. In this case, the transgression does not relate to the society studied, but to our modern Western standards[511]. Just think of the sex/gender systems of societies on the American continent, denigrated and erased by Europeans from the very start of the colonial period. In archaeology, populations with women warriors in their ranks are another good example.

5.3. Transgression of norms (II): women and power

Anthropologist and historian George W. Stocking writes that all those who research the past are 'undeniably conditioned in a thousand subtle ways by the present in which they write[512]'. It is not surprising, then, that archaeologists have long interpreted the rich tombs of women as simply reflecting the wealth of their husbands, or any other male relative, since women in modern times could not possess any wealth of their own. Conversely, precious objects, weapons and signs of power associated with men were seen as a sign of their own social and economic status, and marked a position of power in the community. Let's take the example of an interpretation of this type based on the study of rich graves from the Iron Age (La Tène) in the necropolis of Münsingen-Rain (Switzerland):

> '90.9% of the very rich graves are those with female burials [...] At first this seems to indicate that women have a higher status than men. At this point we have to abandon the assumption that wealth is also always equivalent to status [...] because the alternative is to postulate a matriarchal society –for which there is no ethnographical or historical parallel. An alternative interpretation of this phenomenon is that *the woman is being used to display her husband's wealth*; that she is a symbol of his status [...] that *a richly ornamented woman is a status symbol for a man*[513].'

However, this kind of explanation goes against everything we are taught in funerary archaeology, namely that funerary material is a reflection of the identity, social position and wealth of the deceased, staged by the living. Why should wealthy women be any different? Especially since, paradoxically, the argument is never used to explain the *poverty* of a woman's grave... In the case of the extract quoted above, several problems are worth noting: 1) The heteronormativity present in this extract is clearly visible: while we have no written source specifying the social organization, the author postulates that a woman

[506] On gender fluidity, this time in the Middle Ages, see the recent work by Maillet 2020.
[507] For example Díaz-Andreu & Tortosa 1998, 110; Bochnak 2010; Belard 2017, 211–216.
[508] Trémeaud 2018, 20.
[509] Geller 2017b & 2019.
[510] For this type of question about 'female' and 'male' material and atypical tombs, see in particular Weglian 2001.
[511] Lugones 2007.
[512] Stocking 1965, 216.
[513] Hinton 1986, 364–365 (emphasis added). This excerpt is far from isolated, and at best serves to exemplify a major research trend that was very much in evidence before the development of gender archaeology. Other researchers, working in a variety of regions and periods, have highlighted this phenomenon. See for example Gilchrist 1997, 46–47; Gräslund 2001, 91–95.

An original matriarchy?

The questioning of the place of women in past societies did not wait for the development of feminist studies and the concept of gender in the 1970s to emerge, even if it was rare before then. In 1860, J. J. Bachofen published a work entitled *Das Mutterrecht* in which he presented the theory of an original matriarchy whose origins could be 'clearly' read in ancient myths. He considered that all societies had their roots in a form of 'gynecocracy'[514]. This approach was also taken up by researchers such as James Mellaart and Marija Gimbutas, who postulated the existence of a form of matriarchy and worship of a 'Great Goddess' in Upper Palaeolithic and Neolithic societies[515]. However, archaeological evidence does not provide convincing evidence to support this hypothesis. Similarly, anthropology and ethnology have not been able to demonstrate the existence of any form of matriarchy in traditional societies. At best, some societies are organised not in a patrilineal fashion, like ours, but in a matrilineal fashion. In this case, it is not the women in the family who possess power, prestige and authority. These are indeed possessed by the men, but may, like property on certain occasions, be passed down through the maternal line. In this case, it is the men in the maternal line, the brother or uncle, who are the real holders of authority. It is therefore highly unlikely that prehistoric societies were based on a primitive matriarchy[516].

must necessarily be married to attain an important socio-economic position. He thus projects onto the past the modern belief in compulsory heterosexuality and the binarity of sexes and genders. 2) The author envisages a position of power for women only within the framework of a matriarchal society which, as he rightly points out, has no ethnographic equivalent. 3) If they symbolise the wealth of a husband or son, where are the graves of this husband or son at a time when rich female graves are most numerous?

Numerous examples in ancient and medieval texts alone show that women could occupy a position of power that varied according to place and time. As Anne Augereau has pointed out, there are different types of **power** (economic, social, political, coercive, religious, moral, etc.), which may or may not be exercised in combination: "power over', or the ability of an individual or social organisation to appropriate the actions of another; 'power to', which concerns the power of an individual or group to carry out, accomplish or conduct actions autonomously; and 'power with', which is exercised through interaction and exchanges of all kinds (cooperation, collaboration, discussion and dialogue, etc.)[517]'. Power and social status are closely linked, with individuals who hold power often occupying higher positions in social hierarchies. For Sherry Ortner, the three components of **status** are prestige, autonomy and control over others. For each individual, these three elements combine to varying degrees to give them a higher or lower social status[518]. Assigning power to women in ancient societies does not mean placing them in a position of absolute authority: it simply means recognising that it was possible for some women, depending on the region and the period, to exert a sometimes powerful influence in certain key areas of the social world.

The point of gender studies is to approach and apprehend archaeological material as neutrally as possible. Both andro-centric and gynocentric biases must be avoided. The re-evaluation of old material or the study of new material must be approached from the same angle, regardless of the sex of the deceased. As Caroline Trémeaud points out, 'the presence of female tombs as rich as the male tombs raises the question of the social position of these women, and above all their possible access to power. [...] However, while the relationship between wealth and the possession of power is commonly accepted for a male burial, it is not for a similar female burial. Yet, such a link must be considered for both, without presupposing a system of male domination[519].'

In her research, Vivi Saripanidi points out, for example, that burials of women with rich material and certain types of objects were regularly considered to be the tombs of priestesses in the necropolises of Temenid Macedonia between 570 and 490 BC[520]. What do the offerings tell us? Generally speaking, in the various necropolises we can observe a gendered approach to funerary arrangements, with burials oriented differently for men and women. Certain objects, such as offensive and defensive weapons, only appear in men's graves. When a miniature model of a bronze chariot is placed in the tomb, it is a 4-wheeled chariot for women and a 2-wheeled chariot for men. Rich women's tombs may include drinking vessels, vases usually associated with libation and religious practices in Greek cities such as Athens, metal miniatures of tables and chairs, andirons and spits. These items in particular have been used to justify the interpretation that the deceased were priestesses. However, the same objects appear in the

[514] Darmangeat 2022, 37–40.
[515] Darmangeat 2022, 46–49.
[516] Cohen C. 2016, 159–165, 174–176; Trémeaud 2018, 9; Darmangeat 2022, 86–88; Augereau & Darmangeat 2022, 9–17.

[517] Augereau 2021, 53–54 ('le "pouvoir sur" ou la capacité d'un individu ou d'une organisation sociale à s'approprier les actions d'un autre, le "pouvoir de" qui concerne le pouvoir d'un individu ou d'un groupe à réaliser, accomplir, conduire des actions de manière autonome, et le "pouvoir avec" qui s'exerce en interaction et au moyen d'échanges de tous ordres (coopération, collaboration, discussion et dialogue, etc.).').
[518] Ortner 1996, 139–172.
[519] Trémeaud 2018, 12 ('la présence de tombes féminines aussi riches que les tombes masculines pose la question de la place sociale de ces femmes, et surtout de leur éventuel accès au pouvoir. (…) néanmoins si la relation entre la richesse et la détention d'un pouvoir est couramment admise pour un défunt masculin, elle ne l'est pas pour une sépulture féminine semblable. Or, un tel lien doit être envisagé pour les deux, sans présupposer un système de domination masculine.').
[520] Saripanidi 2020.

tombs of men who are not considered to be priests. For Saripanidi, the funerary offerings mark the elevated status of part of the female population of the Temenid kingdom and their access to a form of economic and social power.

Another good example of research integrating both gender and social status is the study of the orientalising necropolises of Pontecagnano in Campania (8th-7th centuries BC). Mariassunta Cuozzo has studied them by cross-referencing the data provided by skeletal analyses with funerary arrangements, treatments and materials[521]. These various elements seem to reveal very clear gender and class relationships. Women's graves were located in the eastern necropolis, while men's graves were in the western necropolis. Funerary offerings of weapons were associated exclusively with men, while textile-making tools were deposited exclusively with women. In both necropolises, the highest hierarchical burial levels included objects denoting a high social status, identical for both men and women. The most interesting case is that of tomb 2465, a female chariot tomb containing a wealth of material including bronze tableware, iron objects, knives, tripods, spinning and weaving tools. Ornaments on the body include pendants, amber and precious metals. Mariassunta Cuozzo hypothesised that women in Etruscan society of this period had a particularly important status, as 'guarantors of continuity' of the family and the group, and proposed the existence of bilateral filiation, by mother and father, to explain this privileged situation.

5.4. Transgression of norms (III): women and weapons

While the rich graves of women may have posed a problem of interpretation, this problem is exacerbated in the case of women's graves containing weapons. One frequent interpretation is that the weapons symbolically refer to the husband or son of the deceased[522]. Kate Harrell notes the double standard of women buried with weapons in Greece[523]. While men's burials with weapons were considered to be warriors' tombs, this was not the case for women's burials. She takes the case of the woman buried with a dagger in the Lefkandi Toumba building, in a tomb dated to the Late Helladic IIIC (end of the 2nd millennium BC). The tomb also contained precious jewellery: a gold necklace and two bronze discs applied to the chest. In the same building was the tomb of a man whose ashes were placed in a bronze urn containing, among other things, a sword, a whetstone and a razor. A pit containing the bones of four horses was found close to the female tomb in the building. The woman herself was presented as a funerary offering, in the manner of the Indian *sati* rite: the crossed position of her limbs is said to be due to bonds, and the dagger is said to be the instrument of her death. Harrell points out the biases inherent in this type of interpretation. For example, the horses tend to be normally associated with the man, but could just as easily be associated with the woman, having perhaps been used to pull the funeral cart on which her coffin was placed. She also assumes that the two individuals, woman and man, must have played an important role in local power relations, since a necropolis is located directly in front of the building's entrance and is clearly organised around the presence of the building and the burials within it.

Moreover, there is now evidence of the presence of women warriors in certain ancient societies. For example, the identification of women warriors in the archaeological contexts of the ancient Eurasian steppe has been carried out on the basis of a wealth of tangible evidence. The social organisation of the Sauromates, Sarmates and, in Ukraine, the Scythians probably contributed to the birth of the Greek myth of the Amazons[524]. However, in most contemporary cultures, particularly around the Mediterranean basin, women were not generally involved in military activities. In order to identify the remains of women warriors, research must take into account a combination of factors, such as the marks or trauma present on the bodies of the deceased, the presence of weapons, horse equipment and other status symbols. Over the last decade, analyses of skeletons and funerary material have helped to answer some of the questions posed by researchers. Before 2010, the categories applied by archaeologists to the weapons found in women's graves ranged from 'weapons of war' to 'tools used for hunting or defence', in the case of arrowheads and knives. It should also be noted that – not surprisingly – the graves were sometimes sexed on the basis of the archaeological material and not on the study of the skeleton, as Bryan Hanks points out in relation to the Pokrovka tombs (southern Urals)[525].

Among the Sauromates (6th-4th centuries BC), between 20% and 29% of female burials contained weapons, mainly arrows. In the Early Sarmatian phase (4th-1st centuries BC), over 14% of female burials contained weapons. The proportions fall sharply after the beginning of our era[526]. The intersection of various factors, such as age and perhaps social class, with gender helps to refine our knowledge of the structure and hierarchisation of society in the Scythian populations. In 69% of the female burials with weapons, the deceased were aged between 16 and 30. It is also likely that they belonged not to the aristocracy but to the free 'middle' class, as weapons are much less common in aristocratic tombs[527]. In another case, around 20% of women's tombs in the Sargat kurgans (western Siberia) contained weapons, mainly arrowheads and, to a lesser extent, swords, daggers and spearheads, between the 2nd and 4th centuries AD[528].

Palaeopathological analysis of the skeleton of a woman in her twenties, buried on the Armenian high plateau between the 8th and 6th centuries BC, has revealed that the deceased was probably involved in combat. Her muscular

[521] Cuozzo 2008. Schmitt Pantel 2009, 105–107 for a summary of this research.
[522] Trémeaud 2018, 33–34.
[523] Harrell 2014.
[524] Jones-Bley 2008.
[525] Hanks 2008.
[526] Trémeaud 2018, 32.
[527] Trémeaud 2018, 34.
[528] Berseneva 2008.

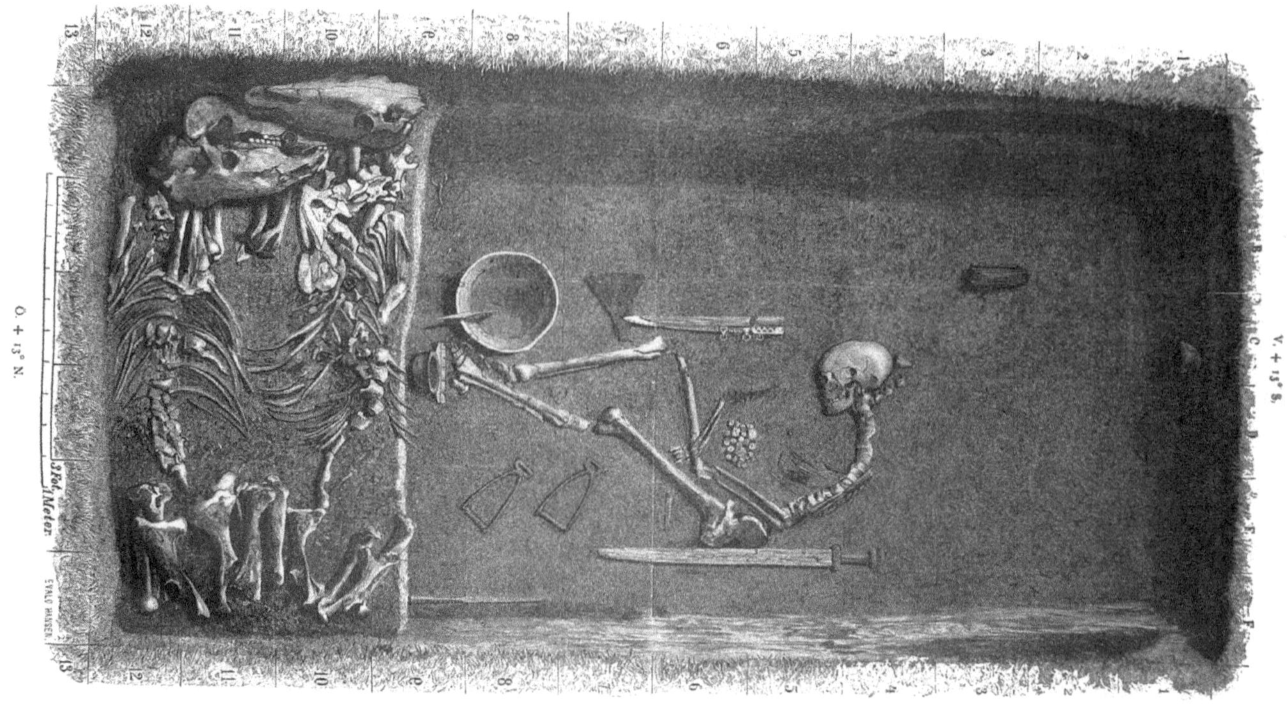

Figure 5.3. Engraving by Evald Hansen based on a plan drawn by archaeologist Hjalmar Stolpe, published in Stolpe 1889.

Birka Bj 581: a simple burial with weapons or a female warrior's grave?

An example of an armed woman's grave that has been in the news recently is grave Bj 581 in Birka, on Viking territory (Figure 5.3). Discovered in 1878 in Sweden, the 10th-century tomb contained a skeleton accompanied by a wealth of material: a sword, an axe, two spears, arrows, a combat knife, two shield parts, a pair of stirrups, a fibula, a horse's bit, two horses (a mare and a stallion) and a strategy game. During the excavation and until 2017, archaeologists had no doubt that this tomb belonged to a man, a warrior leader who had played a pre-eminent role at the time. But in 2017, a DNA analysis[529] carried out on the skeleton indicated that the warrior chief was in fact a woman... The team publishing this study concluded that the artifacts buried with the woman were proof that she was a high-ranking warrior. This conclusion was immediately challenged by some researchers, who argued that the artifacts were not evidence of this woman's participation in warfare in patriarchal Viking culture. Yet Hedenstierna-Jonson and her team reaffirmed their conclusions in a recent article[530]. Jóhanna Katrín Friðriksdóttir mentions, referring to Viking women, that: 'They were seen as future wives, mothers, housewives, and possibly future entrepreneurs, traders and craftswomen if their families practiced these trades, but probably not as warriors, poetesses, jurists, clan chiefs or independent rulers. That said, the fact that most girls were not trained for such roles does not mean that it was impossible for them to engage in some of these careers[531]'. However, she nuances the conclusions of Hedenstierna-Jonson and her team by questioning the gender of the deceased (was she a woman who had lived under a male identity?) and pointing out that children were also given weapons even though they had not been able to take part in any combat[532]. Furthermore, the number of women's graves is small in the Viking world, and these graves rarely contain a large number of weapons, as is the case with Bj 581, which reduces the possible number of "Viking women warriors"[533]. So, is Bj 581 a grave with weapons or a warrior woman's grave? In the absence of significant evidence (traces of battle-related trauma on the skeleton), it would be prudent to qualify this tomb as a "burial with weapons", rather than fall into the sensationalism of the "Viking warrior" media label. We must therefore avoid generalising the case of this tomb to the whole of Viking society, and distorting what we can learn from the archaeological material.

529 Hedenstierna-Jonson *et al.* 2017.

530 Price *et al.* 2019. *Contra* : Jesch 2017a; Jesch 2017b; Falk 2022, 87–99 lists the problems associated with this case study.

531 Friðriksdóttir 2020, 70.

532 Friðriksdóttir 2020, 111–118.

533 Falk 2022, 95.

attachments indicate that she was a frequent archer and horse rider. An arrowhead was embedded in her femur, but the wound had healed. She probably died in battle and three wounds caused by a hatchet and a sword are visible on her hip, thigh and left leg[534]. This tomb is far from being an isolated example, as numerous tombs of women warriors have also been unearthed or identified in recent years in these regions[535]. However, an understanding of gender dynamics in these steppe societies cannot be limited to the study of women warriors and, to provide a more nuanced vision that is faithful to reality, we must also consider the fate of women buried without weapons and who did not (or no longer) engage in combat-related activities.

While the presence of weapons in women's graves is far from limited to the tombs of the Eurasian steppes, we must be careful not to make these tombs into models to be applied to other ancient societies, as was the case with the much-publicised tomb of Birka: it is the combination of textual evidence (accounts by Greek authors), material evidence (weapons) and combat-related trauma on the skeletons that makes it possible to envisage the existence of 'women warriors'. The presence of weapons in societies where women do not traditionally take part in combat means that we need to be cautious when defining the activities of deceased women. The term 'graves with weapons[536]' is undoubtedly preferable and more neutral than 'warriors' graves'. Romilly-sur-Andelle, France, for example, weapons are found in the graves of women from the Merovingian period, perhaps indicating a specific social or economic position[537].

Where to start?

B. Arnold, 'The Vix Princess Redux: A Retrospective on European Iron Age Gender and Mortuary Studies', *in* L. Prados Torreira (ed.), *La Arqueología funeraria desde una perspectiva de género*, UA Ediciones, 2012, 215–232.

S.E. Hollimon, 'Sex and Gender in Bioarchaeological Research. Theory, Method, and Interpretation', *in* S. C. Agarwal, B. A. Glencross (eds.), *Social Bioarchaeology*, Wiley-Blackwell, 2011, 149–182.

R. A. Joyce, *Ancient Bodies, Ancient Lives. Sex, Gender, and Archaeology*, Thames & Hudson, 2008.

M.L.S. Sørensen, *Gender Archaeology*, Polity Press, 2000.

M. Walley, *Incorporating Nonbinary Gender into Inuit Archaeology. Oral Testimony and Material Inroads*, Routledge, 2020.

534 Khudaverdyan *et al.* 2020.

535 Guliaev 2003; Mayor, 2017; Guliaev *et al.* 2019. In North America, women's participation in warfare and hunting has also been studied, see for example Doucette 2001; Hollimon 2001.

536 Falk 2022, 92.

537 Colleter *et al.* 2014.

6

Performing gender

'The process of looking closely at another society which has very different patterns of behaviour from our own forces us to become aware of our own ethnocentric assumptions about social roles and behaviour[538].'

Judith Butler's theory of performativity posits that gender is not an inherent biological trait, but rather a social construct that is realised through repeated actions and behaviours. This theory maintains that gender is a repeated performance reinforced by social norms and expectations. The concept of performativity suggests that individuals are not simply born male or female, but that they learn and perform gender through a process of socialisation[539]. Gender socialisation refers to the process by which individuals learn and adopt the behaviours and attitudes that are considered appropriate for their gender in their culture. This process begins at a young age and continues throughout life, shaping the way in which individuals understand their own gender and the gender of others. It is a complex and ongoing process that is influenced by a variety of factors, including family, peers and education.

At the heart of gender socialisation is the development of gender identity, which refers to an individual's sense of self as male, female or other. This identity is shaped by a variety of factors, such as cultural norms and expectations as well as personal experiences. As individuals grow up and interact with the world around them, they internalise the messages they receive about what it means to be male or female and use these messages to adapt their own behaviours and attitudes. The impact of gender socialisation is significant and long-lasting. It shapes people's beliefs about their own capabilities and limitations, as well as their expectations of others. For example, gender socialisation can lead to the development of gender roles, which are sets of behaviours and expectations associated with being male or female. These roles can be restrictive, limiting people's choices and opportunities. However, they can also provide a sense of security and stability, helping individuals to navigate the complexities of gender and interpersonal relationships. Overall, gender socialisation plays a crucial role in how individuals understand themselves and the world around them[540].

In material culture, gender is expressed through the objects, clothing, spaces, symbols and activities that are associated with a particular gender. Social gender norms can influence the way objects are produced and consumed, as well as the way public and private spaces are designed and used. For example, certain toys may be considered to be for girls or boys, and certain colours may be associated with a particular gender. Together, these elements shape people's identities. In this chapter, we explore how gender is expressed in material culture and its impact on individuals throughout their lives. We will look at differentiated socialisation and the learning of uses specific to an individual's sex, the expression of gender identity through clothing, the use of spaces, archaeological traces linked to sexuality and masculinity, and finally the impact of disability.

6.1. Gender socialisation and learning

The length of childhood, the ages at which it begins and ends, and the rituals marking the transitions to the different age categories vary from time to time and from place to place. Sociologists make a distinction between chronological age (established by a form of calendar measurement), physiological age (a medical construct linked to the ageing of the body and physical damage) and social age (the age category to which an individual belongs and which requires compliance with social norms) [541]. Gender socialisation begins when a child is born and with the identification of its sex. 'It is not just a process of differentiation: it is also a matter of each gendered individual learning to situate himself and the objects and beings around him or her within a social and symbolic *hierarchy* between men and women, masculine and feminine[542]'. From then on, parents, family and community project onto the newborn the expectations and preconceptions specific to each sex. In our modern society, this process now takes place before birth, thanks to the identification of the foetus' sex by ultrasound. In ancient societies, the process of differentiated socialisation began at birth.

For a long time, in archaeological and historical research, children were not considered to be a subject worthy of interest, in particular because their participation in the economy and social fabric of ancient societies was largely underestimated. Indeed, 'being a child is to have a particular place in the social order[543]'. This place is

[538] Butler 2005 (1990).
[539] Nevett 1999, 12.
[540] Bereni *et al.* 2020, 89–154; Duru-Bellat 2017, 23–84.

[541] Gilchrist 1999, 89. For a summary of age-related issues in archaeology, see Lucy 2005.
[542] Bereni *et al.* 2020, 89 ('Il ne s'agit pas seulement d'un processus de différenciation : il s'agit aussi pour chaque individu sexué d'apprendre à se situer et à situer les objets et les êtres qui l'entourent eu sein d'une *hiérarchie* sociale et symbolique entre les hommes et les femmes, entre le masculin et le féminin.').
[543] Sofaer Derevenski 2000, 5.

subordinate to that of adults. It may, however, involve a material culture of its own or a participation, often invisible, in the material culture of adults. The participation of children and young people in the production of objects has been studied by archaeologists, particularly in the manufacture of lithic material[544]. Prehistorians have identified lithic remains on a number of sites that they attribute to a variety of profiles, ranging from beginners to the most experienced individuals: in-depth analyses of reconstructed assemblages within the framework of the *chaîne opératoire* identify differences in skill levels[545]. By reassembling the different flakes from the debitage on the nucleus, it is possible to reconstruct the different stages in the manufacture of a series of tools and to assess the degree of technical skill of the person who carried out the work. 'Novices have a limited grasp of basic techniques, produce few functional objects and have limited access to high-quality materials. They also tend to work in areas that are more peripheral to those used by adults[546]. It is obviously impossible to determine the age or gender of the novices. However, learning these techniques probably took place over long periods and must have begun when the novice was relatively young. The various tools discovered on the production sites could therefore attest to the existence of these sometimes lengthy learning phases, necessary for children to assimilate the most effective techniques and gestures. The learning of techniques from childhood has also been widely illustrated in ethnography[547].

What phenomena are visible at the intersection of age and gender? Depending on the society and the era, differentiation processes can take place with varying degrees of intensity, sometimes very early in a child's life. For example, Danièle Gourevitch looks at the difference in the way boys and girls were swaddled at Herculaneum[548]. She compared the skeleton of a 5–6 month old boy with that of a 2–3 month old girl. The osteological study revealed that the little boy had no traces of roughness on his femurs, which would tend to indicate that he had been swaddled loosely, or at any rate without force, whereas traces of roughness and erosion were present on the little girl's femurs, which could indicate tight swaddling. However, it is difficult to generalise from these two cases and to assert that there was a systematic difference in swaddling between boys and girls in Roman times.

As far as funerary archaeology is concerned, Joanna Sofaer Derevenski has generally observed two trends in the interpretation of children's graves and the material associated with them. On the one hand, children's graves with no material or containing specific material different from that of adults are interpreted as marking a clear difference in the construction of the different age groups. On the other hand, children's graves containing the same equipment as adult graves, in particular weapons, are interpreted as a sign of inheritance of the parents' status and wealth. The idea behind these interpretations is that children and adolescents cannot hold power or wealth in their own right, and this interpretation largely echoes the theories that women's tombs are a reflection of their husbands' wealth and power[549].

Careful interpretation of the funerary material in these tombs can, however, reveal important information. Sanne Houby-Nielsen has studied numerous ancient Athenian tombs of both adults and children, and their funerary material[550]. For children's tombs, she has compiled data from almost 2,000 Athenian tombs dated between the 12th and late 1st centuries BC. On the basis of the type of tomb and the nature of the funerary offerings, she was able to distinguish three age groups in the burials: babies (0–1 year), small children (1 to 3–4 years) and older children (3–4 to 8–10 years). This categorisation into 3 age groups peaks particularly between 720 and 400 BC. Adolescents, i.e. immature individuals over the age of 8–10, were not distinguished from adults in funeral rites. During the Protogeometric period (1050–900 BC), for example, there was a change in burial practices for adults. From then on, the majority of adults were cremated, a tradition that continued until the 6th century and was still present in the 5th and 4th centuries BC. However, children were not cremated and continued to be buried. It was during this period that babies and small children began to be buried in storage vases (*enchystrismos*). During the Protogeometric period, the division between adults and older children remained indistinct, but later became more pronounced. As far as funerary offerings are concerned, the older the children, the more frequently they are buried with objects that are gendered in the adult world. Generally speaking, babies are given vases for food, small children and older children are given toys, and older children are also accompanied by objects that can be related to the gender roles of adulthood (e.g. make-up, soap, instruments and objects related to textile work for girls; swords, arrowheads and strigils for boys).

6.2. Appearance, clothing and adornment

A significant proportion of our information on clothing, particularly accessories such as fibulae and belts, comes from funerary contexts. In very dry or very damp environments, these can sometimes be in an exceptional state of preservation. Iconography also has a role to play in defining the clothing attributes of different groups. This interest in clothing in relation to gender issues and an intersectional approach is far from anecdotal, as clothing and accessories play a part in the staging of social and cultural identity: depending on the region and the period, they can signal wealth, age, sex, change of social status or rites of passage (think of the wedding dress, for example), a particular function (for example, religious), ethnicity, maternity or the number of children, etc.[551]. As Marie

[544] Karlin & Pigeot 1989; Pigeot 1990; Grimm 2000.
[545] Grimm 2000, 54.
[546] Grimm 2000, 54.
[547] For example Greenfield 2000.
[548] Gourevitch 2011, 162–163.
[549] Sofaer Derevenski 2000, 6.
[550] Houby-Nielsen 2000.
[551] Belard 2017a, 176–177.

Louise Stig Sørensen points out, 'physical appearance is a powerful and meaningful mediation of social categories and identities. It is commonly used to signal how individuals are placed within society and to symbolise changes in their status[552]'. In this context, clothing and adornment, worn on the body, are very powerful signifying objects:

> 'Clothing has its place in the many procedures for shaping and controlling the body. It plays a very important role in the formation of identity and, in addition to its essential functions of protecting the body, preserving modesty and adornment, it acts as a sign, communicating the individual's identity, gender, condition and the particular circumstances in which they find themselves[553].'

The social function of clothing and adornment in Archaic and Classical Greece has been studied by Mireille M. Lee[554]. First of all, it should be noted that women were strongly associated with textiles, as the good wife is portrayed in texts as a producer of textiles for the household. In fact, women frequently made offerings of textiles in sanctuaries, for example offering belts to Artemis in the case of young girls of marriageable age. Various types of accessories were used to tie up and style the hair (pins, nets, hairnets, turbans, etc.), a compulsory practice since, by being associated with femininity, beauty and seduction, 'a woman's hair was ideologically associated with her sexuality[555]'.

In archaeological contexts, objects of adornment can refer to different elements of an individual's identity. For example, during the Iron Age in Champagne, earrings 'are involved in the representation of female identity[556] '. However, this was not their only significance, as they also marked social status. In fact, earrings were made exclusively of gold or bronze at La Tène A2 (430–390 BC) and are found in only 5% of tombs from this period, i.e. 'the highest levels of funerary hierarchy[557]'. Gold buckles only appear in the most prestigious tombs, the chariot tombs ('*tombes à char*'). Beyond this simple example, it should be noted that the type of objects used for adornment, their position on the body and the combinations of different adornments evolved over the course of the Iron Age. It was not until the 4th century BC that belts began to be differentiated according to gender, with ornamental belts for women and sword belts for men[558]. Some men and children also had pieces of jewellery and adornment. In the case of children, age has an impact on the type of jewellery (mainly bracelets, torques and pendants)[559].

6.3. Gendered space

The way in which gendered bodies inhabit, occupy, use and move around spaces, whether private or public, is significant[560]. On the one hand, private or domestic space refers to areas and environments designed to be used by isolated individuals or small groups, and are generally associated with the home and family life. These spaces are often seen as more personal, intimate and subject to less regulation and control from the public sphere. On the other hand, public space refers to areas and environments that are open and accessible to all. This includes spaces such as squares, public buildings and other similar areas. Public spaces are generally subject to more regulation and control as they are considered part of the common domain and are often used for collective activities such as socialising, leisure and socio-political events.

Private spaces can be gendered in different ways, with traditional gender roles and expectations often playing an important role. As early as the 1980s, feminist researcher Carole Pateman argued that the public/private dichotomy is not natural or inevitable, but is the product of historical and political processes that have constructed and maintained gendered power relations. According to Pateman, the public/private dichotomy creates a hierarchy in which the public sphere is associated with power, authority and masculinity, while the private sphere is associated with domesticity, emotionality and femininity. This division creates a system in which men are dominant in the public sphere and women are relegated to the private sphere[561].

While in modern Western societies the house is most often the dwelling place of the nuclear family, the situation is often more complex in ancient societies. Depending on the region and period under study, we therefore need to start by defining what we mean by family, house or household. As Julia A. Hendon points out, archaeologists began to study gender relations within the domestic space as early as the 1980s, while also paying attention to variations in these relations in different households as a function of class, social and/or economic status, and ethnicity[562]. The way in which social relations between family members are organised depends on various factors such as gender, age, seniority and place in domestic production. The domestic sphere also plays an important economic and social role, as it is both a place of production and reproduction of the social body.

> 'Standard social science definitions of the household emphasize cooperation, coresidence, and responsibility

[552] Sørensen 1997, 93.
[553] Beauvalet-Boutouyrie & Berthiaud 2015, 191 ('Le vêtement a sa place dans les multiples procédures de façonnage et de contrôle du corps. Il joue un rôle très important dans la constitution de l'identité et, au-delà des fonctions essentielles de protection du corps, de préservation de la pudeur et de parure, il assure une fonction de signe, servant à communiquer l'identité de l'individu, son sexe, son état et la circonstance particulière dans laquelle il se trouve.').
[554] Lee 2012.
[555] Lee 2012, 184.
[556] Belard 2017a, 178 ('sont impliquées dans la représentation de l'identité féminine').
[557] Belard 2017a, 179 ('les niveaux hiérarchiques funéraires les plus élevés').
[558] Belard 2012.
[559] Belard 2017a, 176–199. The ornaments in children's graves are often simple, unfinished objects that have been repaired and/or readjusted, unlike in adult graves.
[560] Alessandrin & Dagorn 2021.
[561] Pateman 1983.
[562] Hendon 2006.

for domestic tasks. Household members are economically interdependent through their participation in activities related to production and consumption[563].'

For example, in ancient Greece, the term *oikos* referred to both the house and all its inhabitants, including the family (possibly extended) and one or more slaves for families that could afford them. The term 'economy' is made up of two Greek words, *oikos* (house) and *nomos* (law) and refers to the management of the house. When Xenophon wrote his *Oeconomicus*, he was not referring to the proper management of the city, but giving advice on how best to ensure the proper management of the household – although the proper management of the household was a good starting point for the management of the city, according to the author[564].

In ancient Greece, the question of the organisation of domestic spaces is particularly relevant, since archaeologists have sometimes postulated the existence of a women's quarter (*gynaeceum* or *gynaeconitis*) or, at the very least, of highly gendered spaces. This hypothesis is based on a number of texts by ancient authors who, it should be remembered, depict power relations between men and women within the elite[565]. Respectable women were supposedly confined to their home, out of sight of men who did not belong to their family, or risked exposing themselves to scandal. However, Pauline Schmitt Pantel points out that 'the assertion of the seclusion of Greek women [was] forged in the 19th century on the model of the situation of women in the Ottoman Empire, and more particularly on the image of the harem[566]'. In fact, this situation probably only concerned a small number of women who belonged to the elite and did not need to work or perform certain tasks outside the home[567].

Lisa Nevett's research into domestic architecture has clearly shown that it is impossible to find any material trace of spaces reserved for women within the *oikos*[568]. On the contrary, the remains found in the houses of Olynth, destroyed in 348 BC by Philip II of Macedon, indicate that most of the rooms had no fixed function but were multi-functional. Different activities took place either simultaneously, or at different times of the day, or depending on the season[569]. The houses had a single entrance, which meant that visitors had direct access to the different areas of the house. The lack of separation between more private spaces and others open to visitors is all the more striking in that the banqueting hall, the *andron* – the dining room used by the men – is accessible via the inner courtyard of the house, and is therefore integrated into the other domestic spaces. It is therefore highly likely that women moved freely around the house, except perhaps during banquets, to which access was probably restricted, and then only on those occasions. At other times, the men and women of the house mingled without restriction in the various areas, including the *andron*, which was probably used for activities involving women and children. Generally speaking, regulating contact between the outside world and the inside of the house, as well as controlling the spaces that were open or visible to visitors, seem to have been the main concerns at the time of construction: this is reflected architecturally by an entrance that does not give direct visual access to the inner courtyard from the street and by means that allow the *andron* to be isolated (doors, antechamber with an off-centre entrance) [570]. Similarly, Julia Hendon's work on domestic spaces among the Maya of the classical period indicates that it is the public spaces controlled by power that are the most obviously gendered, and not domestic spaces[571].

Outside the domestic context, the study of architecture has also revealed attention to the issue of gender segregation in certain contexts. For example, in the Middle Ages, double monasteries developed an architecture that aimed to separate the male and female monastic communities as strictly as possible. At Fontevrault Abbey, for example, the nuns' cloisters were inside the walls, while the men's cloisters were outside. Inside the church, two choirs separated the two communities during services. Other convents also have traces of passageways reserved for women, to prevent them from coming into contact with men. The priest would enter the sacristy through a special passageway, again to avoid any contact with the nuns[572].

The question of a gendered spatial distribution on archaeological sites must, however, be approached with caution, particularly for societies where the sex/gender system is radically different from that of Western societies. For example, at most of the sites studied among the Inuit, there is no strict separation of spaces according to gender. The anthropological and ethnographic approach to these societies in the Far North also reveals a great deal of gender fluidity (see introduction) and an equally great deal of fluidity in the use of objects and the division of tasks. While a gendered division of tasks does exist in theory, it is not rigid and individual transgressions are possible and not stigmatised: a child can take on the gender roles of the opposite sex if he or she is born into a family with an unequal sex ratio[573].

563 Hendon 2006, 173.
564 Nevett 1999, 12–13.
565 Nevett 1999, 17–18.
566 Schmitt Pantel 2009, 107 ('l'affirmation de la réclusion des femmes grecques [s'est] forgée au XIXe siècle sur le modèle de la situation des femmes dans l'Empire ottoman et plus particulièrement sur l'image du harem').
567 Algrain 2014, 153–215; Nevett 1999, 16–17.
568 Nevett 1995; Nevett 1999, 71–72. The upper floors of the houses – for those that had them – have not been preserved.
569 Nevett 1999, 68–70.
570 Nevett 1999, 71–72; Hendon 2006.
571 Hendon 2006.
572 Gilchrist 2000, 94–96. Gilchrist 1994 explores in depth the archaeology of monastic spaces in the Middle Ages through the prism of gender, highlighting the differences between male and female monasteries, their position in the medieval environment and landscape, the organization of spaces and circulation in mixed spaces, etc.
573 Walley 2020, p. 21–34.

6.4. Archaeology of sexualities

Since the early 2000s, a series of publications has emerged on the archaeology of sexuality. According to Barbara L. Voss and Robert A. Schmidt, who draw on the work of Gayle Rubin (see introduction and chapter 1), the subject has taken a long time to develop, particularly in archaeological research, for a number of reasons: firstly, because of the belief that sexuality is a biological fact that is unaffected by culture and therefore has no historicity; a negative attitude towards sexuality and the researchers who study it; a hierarchy of sexualities whose apex is occupied by reproductive sex performed within a matrimonial framework; or conversely, a lascivious and hypersexualised treatment of images that are not, however, related to sexuality[574]. For a long time, these factors prevented any serious study of sexuality through the prism of archaeology, or any consideration of the variability of sexuality in ancient societies. Analyses published over the last twenty years or so have focused not only on marginal sexualities (homosexuality, prostitution, third and fourth genders, religious celibacy) – most of which were the subject of earlier studies – but also on heterosexuality, particularly in the context of marriage, which has been little studied because it is often essentialised and considered 'natural'[575]. These studies are important because they highlight the importance of the historical and geographical context for eminently social practices:

> 'Their essential point is that for as far back as one can gather historical evidence (from primitive artwork to the written word), humans have engaged in a variety of sexual practices, but that this sexual activity is bound to historical contexts. That is, sexual practices and societal understandings of them vary not only across cultures but over time as well[576].'

These recent analyses have also made it possible to overcome certain prejudices expressed by researchers in the 19th century, particularly with regard to the sexuality of prehistoric societies. At the time, prehistoric sexuality was seen as primitive, based on the stereotype of the caveman and on ethnological comparisons with traditional hunter-gatherer societies. The way of life of these communities – often misunderstood and poorly described in literature – was seen as a reflection of the living conditions of prehistoric men and women[577]. Stereotypes abounded, constructing prehistoric mores in opposition to Judeo-Christian values: primitive promiscuity in which there were no taboos on incest, homosexuality, and adultery; a high birth rate leading to infanticide; sexual bestiality; abduction of women; ignorance of the reproductive function of sexuality, etc. These constructions of sexuality in bygone eras also highlighted the eugenic considerations of the 19th century, since this 'history' of sexuality presented the strongest and most beautiful males as the only ones capable of reproducing with the most beautiful (and least hairy) women, while the weakest and/or oldest males were killed off and left to be scavenged.

In concrete terms, how can archaeology contribute to the study of sexuality when these practices leave no material traces? Barbara L. Voss gives an example in her article on the structuring of colonial spaces by Spanish missions in California in the late 18th and early 19th centuries[578]. Until the beginning of Spanish colonisation in 1769, archaeology tells us that the Native villages of California were organised into scattered dwellings along a creek or the coast. Collective activities (men's sweat lodge, women's menstrual lodge, dance area, etc.) and production (food preparation, basketry, leatherworking, etc.) took place on the outskirts of the villages. As a result of the repeated sexual assaults and rapes suffered by Native women at the hands of Spanish soldiers, a new organisation was gradually put in place over the following decades. Dwellings were grouped together and production activities took place in spaces within dense groups of houses. Here, the social factor of sexual violence has a direct influence on domestic and urban architecture.

Violence was also endemic within the Christian missions against converted and baptised Native women. Colonial architecture gradually established a separation between the soldiers' quarters, initially integrated into the mission, and the homes of the Indigenous families, probably at the instigation of the priests and missionaries. This architecture, designed to control the sexuality of Native women, culminated in the *monjerío*, the women's barracks, found in every mission. Young girls and unmarried women were confined to this building located in the immediate vicinity of the mission, with its high, barred windows and a single entrance that was locked from the outside. Women only left the building to go to church. This isolation disrupted traditional social organisation, as it 'disrupted indigenous adolescent initiation rites, interrupted transmission of cultural lore and technologies, and altered traditional courtship rituals and marriage arrangements[579]'. It was an attempt – sometimes unsuccessful – to regulate the sexuality of Indigenous women who were otherwise living 'in sin' by having sex outside the bonds of Christian marriage.

6.5. Gender and ethnicity

The concept of ethnicity is still often debated by archaeologists but there is no clear definition of what 'ethnicity' means. The history of research into ethnicity calls for great caution. For example, as far as Egyptology is concerned, the concept and definition of ethnicity have hardly been called into question. Ethnicity has often simply been used to replace the problematic notion

574 Voss & Schmidt 2000, 3–5.
575 Voss & Schmidt 2000, 18–19.
576 Fausto-Sterling 2000, 12.
577 Manias 2015.

578 Voss 2000b.
579 Voss 2000b, 43. Poor hygiene and the spread of disease within the buildings led to their closure in 1834.

of 'race' and, in fact, covers the same ideas[580]. Indeed, 19th-century archaeologists, including the Egyptologist William Flinders Petrie, frequently used racial theories to study ancient Egypt and sometimes to justify the inferior status and conditions in which non-European populations were held (see chapter 2). In archaeological research, this initially took the form of a biased association: 'culture = people', i.e. it was considered – and is still sometimes considered – that the archaeological material of a given culture reflected the presence of people belonging to that culture, including – and especially – outside its cultural area[581]. But as Reine-Marie Bérard points out:

> 'From an archaeological point of view [...], while it is indeed possible to attribute the production of an artefact to a particular people, this in no way predicts the ethnic origin of the person using it. The archaeological study of elements of material culture may make it possible to determine the ethnicity of the producer, but not the ethnicity of the user[582].'

An almost caricatural example is the presence of Nubian kitchen ware in an Egyptian fort at Askut, in Nubia[583]. This kitchen ware would indicate not only the adoption by Egyptian soldiers of Nubian culinary practices, but also the presence of Nubian women who would have been in charge of food preparation in the fort and may have become the wives of Egyptian soldiers. Obviously, the presence of Nubian pottery does not necessarily indicate the presence of Nubians in the fort, and even less a form of Egyptian-Nubian ethnic hybridisation. This very generalist shortcut is rooted in the stereotype of the woman as cook and provider of food, whereas military organisation within a fort probably implies an organisation very different from that found in a domestic context. The colonial model also has an impact on this type of interpretation by reproducing the stereotype of the settler, warrior or soldier, who marries an Indigenous woman.

Uroš Matić notes that, in sometimes very recent publications, Egypt, Greece, Rome and the United Kingdom are placed in the same sequence of great imperial powers[584]. Egypt is thus placed on a pedestal and presented as a predecessor of the great Western powers. As a result of this bias, Egyptologists sometimes tend to play down the importance of productions that they do not feel measure up to this ideal. For example, dry stone constructions are considered cruder and attributed to foreigners, and not to Egyptians[585]. Interpretations of this kind also tend to overlook the fact that communities did not live in isolation, but that there were contacts and exchanges between different populations.

Rebecca Futo Kennedy, for her part, has studied metics, i.e. the non-citizens living in Athens in the 5th and 4th centuries BC, with a particular focus on women[586]. Citizenship in Athens was rooted in the myth of autochthony, according to which its first inhabitants were born of the land: it separated citizens from non-citizens extremely sharply, as the latter could not own land[587]. As the author reminds us, research has often presented Athenian women in two blocs: respectable citizens and all the others, most often assimilated to prostitutes and studied from the point of view of 'gender and sexuality instead of ethnicity and legal status[588]'. However, a careful study of the sources reveals a much more nuanced picture of these women, free but non-citizens, who were foreigners, freedwomen or even daughters of citizen fathers but non-citizen mothers (sometimes considered non-citizens depending on the period). For example, the iconography of the funerary stelae of these women in the 5th and 4th centuries BC shows how well integrated they were into the social fabric. Like citizens, they are depicted in their roles as wives and mothers, and also as workers, including midwives, doctors, seamstresses and tavern keepers[589].

6.6. Gender and disability

Living with a disability can have different repercussions for women and men, depending on the social class to which they belong[590]. At present, while research into disability in ancient societies is flourishing, there are few archaeological studies that specifically examine the intersection of gender and disability. Nevertheless, a few interesting avenues can be explored. In her study of disability in ancient Rome, Caroline Husquin uses the term 'physical impairment', as there is no equivalent term in Latin for 'disability'. It is important to understand that, in ancient societies, 'physical impairment was not at all considered in the same way as it is today. What we call disability had no real equivalent among the Romans, who made no distinction between the disabled and the able-bodied; in Rome, people with physical impairments did not constitute a separate social category, a distinct group that could be clearly identified. Moreover, the Ancients did not perceive physical impairment in terms

[580] Matić 2020.
[581] Matić 2020, 24–34.
[582] Bérard 2014, 155–156 ('Du point de vue archéologique (…), s'il est effectivement possible d'attribuer la production d'un artefact à un peuple particulier, cela ne présage en rien de l'origine ethnique de celui qui l'utilise. L'étude archéologique des éléments de culture matérielle peut éventuellement permettre d'atteindre l'ethnicité du producteur, pas celle de l'utilisateur'). In this article, the author summarises the debate surrounding the fibulae discovered in the Pithekoussai necropolis (mostly 8th century BC tombs), often considered to be evidence of 'mixed marriages' between colonists and Native women.
[583] Matić 2020, 42.
[584] Matić 2020, 23. This attitude is not unique to Egyptology. Ancient Greek scholars have also described the regions colonised by the Greeks as being populated by culturally 'inferior' individuals. See Bérard 2014, 146–147.
[585] Matić 2020, 32.
[586] Kennedy 2014.
[587] According to Nicole Loraux, the myth of autochthony enables the construction of a 'civic imaginary' and the exclusion of women from citizenship. Women transmit citizenship, but are not citizen themselves in the same way as men. See Loraux 1981.
[588] Kennedy 2014, 59, note 1.
[589] Kennedy 2014, 56, 107.
[590] In the Roman world, for example, speech-impaired or mute citizens belonging to the elite had enormous difficulty integrating into society, as oratory was so much a part of the definition of a citizen. See Husquin 2020, 242–250.

of a medical problem, as is the case in our societies[591]'. Disability and its perception are therefore conditioned by the social and aesthetic norms in force in a given society, and are as variable, chronologically and geographically, as the concept of gender[592].

The intersection of disability with other discriminatory categories such as social class provides data on the inclusion or exclusion of people with physical impairments in society[593]. Caroline Husquin reports the case of an elderly woman from Herculaneum who died during the eruption of Mount Vesuvius in 79 AD, suffering from bilateral dislocation of the hip. However, analyses carried out on her remains indicate a marked use of the upper limbs, especially the right arm. Furthermore, her body was found on the beach, a good distance from the centre of the city, which would suggest that those around her had taken care to help her move around in search of shelter[594]. This is not an isolated case, and people with disabilities were employed to the best of their ability. The fact that they were buried in necropolises tends to show that they were not excluded from society, either in life or in death, at least for most of them[595].

For more recent periods, at the Jacobins convent in Rennes for example, analysis of the bone remains of individuals buried between the 13th and 18th centuries shows that:

> '(...) the deceased buried at the Jacobins Convent do not seem to have been equal in the face of disability. They are slightly more numerous in certain burial spaces, some conditions affect one sex more often than the other and adults are more affected. Although the statistical links are not always clearly established for most conditions, it seems that women, particularly those buried in privileged areas, died at an older age than men. It is perhaps this later age at death that explains why they are more affected by severe degenerative pathologies and are significantly more toothless. With advancing age, the most privileged subjects [...] were more exposed to the risk of disability, particularly in terms of mobility[596].'

Debby Sneed's research has also provided some interesting leads[597]. She has revisited the issue of infanticide in ancient Greece, with particular reference to children with physical disabilities. She points out that numerous publications indicate that the practice of infanticide or exposure of newborn babies with disabilities, particularly girls, was common in ancient Greece[598]. By re-examining the texts that mention this phenomenon, compiling data from bioarchaeology and cross-referencing it with archaeological material, Sneed demonstrates that child infanticide was far from the norm. Adults with disabilities have been found in necropolises, testifying to the care they received as children and their ability to adapt and integrate into the economic and social life. As far as archaeological material is concerned, ceramic feeding bottles, often found in children's tombs, could have helped children with cleft lips and/or palates to eat.

Where to start?

C. Belard, 'Les ceintures de l'âge du fer en Champagne : genre et archéologie', *in Clio. Histoire, femmes et société* 36, 2012, 183–190.

U. Matić, *Ethnic Identities in the Land of the Pharaohs. Past and Present Approaches in Egyptology*, Cambridge University Press, 2020.

L.C. Nevett, *House and Society in the Ancient Greek World*, Cambridge University Press, 1999.

R.A. Schmidt et B.L. Voss (ed.), *Archaeologies of Sexuality*, Routledge, 2000.

M.L.S. Sørensen, 'Reading Dress: The Construction of Social Categories and Identities in Bronze Age Europe', *in Journal of European Archaeology* 5/1, 1997, 93–114

591 Husquin 2020, 13 ('L'atteinte physique n'est absolument pas envisagée comme aujourd'hui. Ce que nous qualifions de handicap n'a pas d'équivalent réel chez les Romains qui ne distinguent pas handicapés et valides; les personnes atteintes de déficiences physiques ne constituent pas, à Rome, une catégorie sociale à part, un groupe distinct clairement identifiable. En outre, les Anciens ne percevaient pas l'atteinte corporelle en termes de problème médical, comme c'est le cas dans nos sociétés.').

592 Covey 1998; Husquin 2020, 13–14.

593 Delattre 2018.

594 Husquin 2020, 97–98, 134–135.

595 Husquin 2020, 101–106.

596 Colleter 2021 ('les défunts inhumés au couvent des Jacobins ne semblent pas avoir été égaux face aux handicaps. Ils sont un peu plus nombreux dans certains espaces funéraires, quelques affections touchent plus souvent un sexe que l'autre et les adultes sont davantage impactés. Bien que les liens statistiques ne soient pas toujours clairement établis pour la plupart des affections, il semble que les femmes, notamment celles inhumées dans des zones privilégiées, mouraient plus âgées que les hommes. C'est peut-être cet âge au décès plus tardif qui explique qu'elles soient plus touchées par des pathologies dégénératives sévères et significativement plus édentées. En avançant en âge, les sujets les plus favorisés (…) ont davantage été exposés au risque de handicap, notamment en termes de mobilité.').

597 Sneed 2021.

598 Exposure is not necessarily synonymous with infanticide, as the newborn is probably abandoned in a place where it can be adopted. See Sneed 2021.

7

Gender and division of labour

'Whatever the origin of the gender division of labour, it is a prerequisite for the social inferiority of women[599].'

The origins of the gendered division of labour have been widely debated, but no evidence can be considered as clear proof of its appearance at a given date – assuming that it appeared and was not always there – and no hypothesis has been verified[600]. 18th- and 19th-century scholars believed that the origin of the gendered division of labour could be traced back to pre-agricultural societies, where tasks were divided according to the physical abilities of men and women. In these societies, men would generally have been hunters and protectors, while women would have been gatherers and would have provided care work[601]. According to this scenario, with the advent of agriculture and the development of sedentary communities, the gendered division of labour became more complex. The development of different trades and techniques would have led to the specialisation of work, which would have reinforced the gendered division of labour, based on cultural beliefs and norms associating certain tasks with one sex or the other.

In reality, it is impossible to date the emergence of the gendered division of labour. We can, however, measure its effects in our contemporary societies. We can still see the effects of a gendered division of labour that has been institutionalised and reinforced by laws, policies and economic systems that restrict women's access to education, training and certain types of employment. As a result, gender inequality persists in the workplace, with women often paid less, working in lower-level jobs and facing barriers to promotion[602].

Care

In feminist studies, the concept of 'care' refers to the domestic and emotional work involved in maintaining relationships and meeting the needs of others. Care is often gendered, with women expected to perform the majority of care tasks both inside and outside the home. Feminist academics have argued that this gendered division of labour reinforces gender inequality and perpetuates systems of oppression, and have called for a re-evaluation and redistribution of care work.

[599] Kirsch 1977, 37 ('Quelle que soit l'origine de la division sexuelle du travail, elle est un prérequis à l'infériorité sociale des femmes.').
[600] Darmangeat 2022.
[601] Dahlberg 1983b, 13 points out that the start of the gendered division of labour is also debated, since it is sometimes located at the beginning of hominid evolution and sometimes at more recent periods.
[602] Bereni *et al.* 2020, 223–267.

Just as it is probably illusory to date the 'appearance' of the gendered division of labour, the date of appearance of male domination is also indeterminable. Even if male domination is present in varying degrees, ranging from relative equality to strong domination, the following fact can be observed in all traditional societies[603]: the material foundations of gender relations are manifested in this gendered division of tasks, which is one of the four invariants observed by structuralist anthropologists (see introduction). Françoise Héritier points out that:

> 'At the same time as the symbolic apparatus of language was taking shape, human groups developed solutions that were structurally similar because they obeyed the laws of limited possibilities: regulation of sexual relations, recognition of a principle of filiation classifying individuals in the group into those who could be married and those who could not, development of principles of alliance based on the prohibition of incest, and finally, to stabilise relations between individuals, *the gendered division of tasks intervened to make them dependent on each other within the couple because of their respective incapacities artificially established*[604].'

Whatever the society studied, including the most egalitarian traditional societies, and for all the ancient societies where written documents enable us to reconstruct the division of labour, we can see that this division exists and separates the activities of women and men[605]. This division of tasks is not rooted in biology for physical reasons, but for symbolic reasons linked to the differential value of the sexes and justified a posteriori by biology. It implies a symbolic hierarchy between masculine and feminine, between men's and women's tasks. The division of labour is therefore usually accompanied by a devaluation of women's tasks. Proof of this hierarchical structure can be seen in the research carried out by French sociologist

[603] Darmangeat 2022, 190.
[604] Héritier 1991, 275 (emphasis added) ('En même temps que l'appareil symbolique du langage prenait forme, en leurs différents points d'émergence et soumis aux mêmes nécessités, les groupes humains ont élaboré des solutions structurellement ressemblantes parce qu'elles obéissaient aux lois de possibilités limitées : une réglementation des rapports sexuels, la reconnaissance d'un principe de filiation classant les individus du groupe en épousables et non-épousables, la mise au point de principes d'alliance fondé sur la prohibition de l'inceste, enfin pour stabiliser les rapports entre les individus, la division sexuelle des tâches intervient pour les rendre dépendants l'un de l'autre au sein du couple en raison de leurs incapacités respectives artificiellement établies.'). See also Bourdieu 1998, 53.
[605] Augereau & Darmangeat 2022, 22.

Christine Delphy on domestic work on French farms, where there is a hierarchical, gendered classification of tasks into 'heavy work' and 'light work'.

> 'Yet this classification is not based on the energy expenditure required by the activity in question, but on the nature of the activities. However, the technical operation itself is not the real criterion for classification: carrying water is considered 'light work', carrying manure 'heavy work'; nor is the arduousness of the task: harvesting with a scythe is 'heavy work', bundling and tying are considered 'light work'. Throughout France, carrying water and bundling are or were exclusively women's work, while other carrying and harvesting are men's work. The criterion for classifying work as 'big' or 'small' was in fact the status [male or female] of those who usually carried it out. *Some work, reserved for men and therefore considered 'heavy' in certain regions, is reserved for women in others and loses its qualification*[606].'

In traditional societies, 'a great many activities may be performed by women (preferably or exclusively), or by men. This is the case, for example, with weaving, pottery, much agricultural work and tending domestic animals. As for the constants, certain activities are universally, or almost universally, reserved for one sex only[607]. The tasks most commonly carried out exclusively by women or men include caring for and bringing up young children in the case of the former, and hunting big game, warfare and metalworking in the case of the latter[608]. When it comes to ancient societies and what archaeology can tell us about the division of labour, it is important to confine ourselves to the clues provided by the material and remains, avoiding hasty generalisations or hype. It has been said often enough that gender varies in time and space, and it is likely that there are major variations between 'feminine' and 'masculine' tasks, depending on whether you are in the Dordogne during the Upper Palaeolithic, among the Scythians in the 6th century BC or in Pompeii shortly before the eruption of Mount Vesuvius.

7.1. A prehistoric division of labour?

In archaeology, the emblematic example of this division of labour is the split between the male hunter and the female gatherer in prehistoric societies. Pamela Geller traces the beginnings of this theory to the Age of Enlightenment[609]. At that time, medical science redefined the sexes and their differences, and was used to support a vision of women as physically and intellectually inferior, like children and other 'races'. For most 18th- and 19th-century scientists, starting with Darwin, women's reproductive, child-rearing and caring tasks were the result of their love and feminine qualities[610]. In evolutionary terms, this meant that women's contribution was non-existent, as they simply bore the children of male hunters.

From the 1950s onwards, American anthropologists developed various scenarios to explain prehistoric societies and human evolution, in particular the 'man the hunter' scenario[611]. The development of humankind and its social organisation would be linked to hunting, in particular to the need to develop new technologies, through tools and weapons, as well as social practices that enabled hunting to be carried out collectively[612]. This social organisation would be based on an exchange in which men bring women the fruits of their hunt in exchange for sexual favours. However, when we look for empirical evidence of a division of labour in prehistoric times, we find that there really was none. These hypotheses are based on the prejudices of scholars who, from the Enlightenment to the 20th century, believed that a division of labour between the sexes was a 'natural' and immutable fact. To justify the existence of this division in ancient societies, research has often resorted to anthropological comparisons with contemporary populations[613].

The same assertions are often made, namely that men's greater physical capacity would have made them better suited to carrying out tasks away from the domestic sphere, while motherhood, childcare or the care of other members of the group would have tended to tie women to the domestic sphere, implying that their tasks were necessarily carried out close to the base. But this hypothetical division of labour is just one 'example of the naturalisation of culture[614]'. This scenario, which completely ignores women and their contribution to human evolution, was called into question as early as the 1960s, notably by Lewis Binford, who emphasised the importance of carrion gathering for the earliest periods, an activity that does not require any particular skill and can be practised by an entire human group[615].

Moreover, over the last forty years, feminist anthropologists have demonstrated the biases of the studies that preceded

606 Delphy 1998, 82–83 (emphasis added) ('Or, cette classification n'est pas établie d'après la dépense d'énergie requise par l'activité considérée, mais par la nature des activités. Cependant, l'opération technique elle-même n'est pas le critère réel de la classification : le portage d'eau est considéré comme un "petit travail", le portage de fumier un "gros travail"; la pénibilité de la tâche non plus : le moissonnage à la faux est "un gros travail", le bottelage et le liage sont regardés comme un "petit travail". Partout en France, portage d'eau et bottelage sont ou étaient exclusivement des travaux de femmes, les autres portages et le moissonnage des travaux d'hommes. Le critère de classification des travaux en "gros" et "petits", réside en fait dans le statut [homme ou femme] de ceux qui les effectuent ordinairement. Certains travaux, réservés aux hommes et donc réputés "gros" dans certaines régions, sont réservés aux femmes dans d'autres et y perdent leur qualification.').

607 Augereau & Darmangeat 2022, 23 ('de très nombreuses activités peuvent être ici féminines (préférentiellement ou exclusivement), là masculines. C'est par exemple le cas du tissage, de la poterie, d'une bonne partie des travaux agricoles ou de l'entretien des animaux domestiques. Du côté des constantes, certaines activités sont universellement, ou quasi universellement, réservées à un seul sexe.').

608 Darmangeat 2022, 187–189; Augereau & Darmangeat 2022, 23.

609 Geller 2017b, 132.

610 Zihlman 1983, 76–78; Schiebinger 1986; Geller 2017b, 134–135.

611 Zihlman 2013, 26–27; Cohen C. 2016, 122–124.

612 Zihlman 1983.

613 Geller 2017b, 137.

614 Geller 2017b, 132.

615 Binford 1981.

them, in particular the fact that male ethnographers tended to focus more on men's activities and to underestimate the importance of gender relations[616]. They also showed that the contribution of hunters to the subsistence of the group is disproportionately emphasised to the detriment of the tasks of female gatherers. For example, among the !Kung San of South Africa, a group of hunter-gatherers, big game hunting accounts for only a third of food intake[617]. Among the Hidatsa of the North American plains in the 19th century, women procured and processed all the food, with the exception of one task, the slaughter of animals[618]. Similarly, activities related to hunting but carried out by women – flushing out game, transporting it, eviscerating it, cleaning it, preparing it, packing it – have often not been classified by anthropologists as hunting activities, which tends to naturalise the division of labour.

The causes of the gendered division of labour have been extensively researched, particularly in relation to hunting. In many cases, women in traditional societies come up against prohibitions: they are forbidden to kill prey when hunting big game, and they are forbidden to handle the most lethal weapons, or even to touch them. 'In the vast majority of cases, [the peoples concerned] invoke a set of extremely strong magico-religious beliefs, all of which revolve around the danger of women's blood (particularly their menstrual blood) coming into contact with the blood of game[619]'. For anthropologist Christophe Darmangeat, this a posteriori justification legitimises a mode of operation which, while it ultimately devalued women's work, enabled greater profitability through the specialisation of tasks[620].

Androcentric biases can also be observed in bioarchaeological analyses. Pamela Geller gives the example of research into musculoskeletal stress markers on the forearms of the skeletons of 37 individuals, 21 men and 16 women, dating from the Upper Palaeolithic and Mesolithic periods, covering a period of 12,000 years[621]. On 4 male skeletons, the researchers interpreted the markers as evidence of javelin throwing. From these 4 individuals, they deduced a gendered division of hunting tasks that extended to all Palaeolithic individuals. However, some of the female skeletons show exactly the same marker, without the authors providing any explanation.

Finally, it is worth noting an important exception to the gendered division of labour, highlighted by ethnographic evidence, particularly among the Iroquois and on the North West coast of North America: slavery. In this case, individuals may be required to perform tasks that would not normally be done by people of their own sex, because they are 'in a way deprived of their human person, [...] of their sexual identity[622]'. Here, social status disrupts gender roles.

7.2. Revaluing women's work

The aim of gender archaeology is neither to refute the antiquity of the gendered division of labour nor to present the situation of women in ancient societies as idyllic. On the contrary, its aim is to highlight the crucial roles that women, just like men, played in the past. When we talk about revaluing women's work, we are obviously talking about revaluing this work in current research. There can be no question of revaluing work which, in a given society, was devalued, minimised or made invisible because it was carried out by women. The important point of this approach is to show that the devaluation of these tasks is a social construct of the society studied, and even of contemporary thought, and that this work done by women did in fact have a social and economic value.

For a long time, researchers considered that women's work in prehistoric times was unimportant, if not impossible to study from archaeological contexts: on the one hand, 'male' production left clearly visible traces, since men would have worked hard materials (flint knapping, wood and animal bone carving), while 'female' tasks left no traces in the archaeological material (basketry, leatherwork, plant collection)[623]. Worse still, before the second feminist wave, many texts associated the notion of activity with men and passivity with women. This is all the more paradoxical given that the same texts described women's activities: bogged down by pregnancy and breastfeeding, they would have been busy picking fruit, nuts and berries and gathering roots and tubers[624]. We can appreciate the genius of making these different activities seem passive. In the early 1990s, a number of articles shook up these certainties. Alice Kehoe showed that, in the literature, traces of activities such as trap-making had been ignored in favour of stone tool-making[625]. Joan Gero challenged the generally accepted idea that only men were involved in making stone tools, and put forward the hypothesis that women could make the tools they used on a daily basis themselves, as attested by ethnography[626].

In this latest study, Joan Gero also deconstructed each of the reasons that might have prevented women from taking part in stone tool-making (lack of strength and/or skill, incompatibility of the task with pregnancy, reduced

[616] Geller 2017b, 138. See also Tabet 1979; Spector 1983; Zihlman 2013, 29–30.
[617] Cohen C. 2016, 127.
[618] Spector 1983.
[619] Darmangeat 2022, 205 ('Dans l'immense majorité des cas, [les peuples concernés] invoquent un ensemble de croyances magico-religieuses extrêmement fortes, qui tournent toutes autour du danger que représenterait le rapprochement entre le sang des femmes (en particulier leur sang menstruel) et le sang du gibier'). This theory was first proposed by Testart 1986.
[620] Darmangeat 2022, 205.
[621] Geller 2017b, 140–141, quoting the research of Villotte *et al.* 2010.
[622] Darmangeat 2022, 194 ('en quelque sorte privés de leur personne humaine, (...) de leur identité sexuelle').
[623] Gilchrist 1999, 36–45.
[624] Watson & Kennedy 1991.
[625] Kehoe 1990.
[626] Gero 1991. This is also attested by ethnography in Australia and New Guinea, cf. Bird 1993. Gero's theory is followed in particular by Sassaman 1992. See also Finlay 2013.

mobility) and criticised the over-representation of men in experimental studies aimed at reproducing prehistoric techniques, which would in fact introduce an androcentric bias into the research. Her case study was the Huaricoto site in Peru, where she put forward three hypotheses as to the involvement of women in the production of stone tools. 1) It was likely that women's stone-cutting activities took place in or near domestic contexts. 2) Even if it is traditionally assumed that men obtained rare and/or distant stones themselves because of their greater mobility, nothing prevented women from obtaining stones close to their homes. 3) The notion of 'tool' is also called into question. According to Gero, research to date had focused on modified or reworked tools, to the detriment of simpler but equally useful tools. Can these hypotheses be proven? Given our current state of knowledge, it is impossible to determine who made and who used Palaeolithic tools and other objects. Gero's hypotheses have also been criticised on the grounds that they tend to reinforce gender stereotypes (low mobility of women, attribution of less sophisticated tools to women)[627]. Even though ethnography probably cannot account for all the diversity in terms of the division of tasks that existed during prehistory, ethnographic studies show that, depending on the hunter-gatherer society, women sometimes followed this pattern and, in other cases, took part in the distant collection of raw materials or made axes[628].

In the case of the Neolithic populations of the north-east of the Iberian Peninsula, between the middle of the 5th and the middle of the 4th millennium BC, the use-wear analysis of funerary material seems to support the hypothesis of a division of tasks. Aside from projectiles probably used for hunting or even warfare, the tools associated with men were used for butchery and woodworking, while those associated with women were smaller and used to process hides. Other tools, such as scrapers and bone punches, used in the manufacture of leather and pottery and for processing certain types of plant, are significantly associated with women. In addition, men are buried with a greater number of tools, and these are more often made from exogenous materials[629]. Although these results cannot be generalised to the Neolithic as a whole, nor can they be considered an exact reflection of the situation in the Palaeolithic, they do tend to confirm in part the hypotheses proposed by Joan Gero in 1991. These results are also a reminder that great caution is called for in gender studies. Claims for fairness and equality are eminently modern and it would be damaging, both for research and for current claims, to try at all costs to bring to light an equality of prehistoric women and men that probably never existed.

While the lithic production is recurrently associated with men, the manufacture of ceramics in prehistoric times, on the other hand, is associated with women in many publications, on the basis of ethnographic studies showing that this task was mostly – but not exclusively – carried out by women[630]. This idea of women making pottery was quickly adopted by prehistorians, as this activity 'is relatively monotonous and does not require great concentration, can be carried out in spite of interruptions and can be easily resumed[631]'. The situation changes when societies become more complex and pottery-making becomes a commercial activity, or when a technological innovation, such as the wheel, is introduced. It is then the men who take charge of the production, with an opposition between female domestic production and male specialised production[632]. Once again, the wide variations in traditional societies make it possible to find examples that confirm and refute this hypothesis, which goes to show that using examples taken from ethnography must be done with the utmost caution. In archaeology, Saro Wallace has for example highlighted the increased standardisation – seen as a sign of specialisation – of Cypriot vases at the end of the Chalcolithic period, a time when vases were made without a potter's wheel and produced on a domestic scale, which runs counter to commonly accepted theories[633]. In the Harappean civilisation (Indus Valley, Bronze Age), large-scale production took place in a domestic context[634].

According to Rita P. Wright, the dichotomous vision of male-potter vs. female-potter does not hold up because it does not take into account the '*chaîne opératoire*'[635]. In the case of pottery production, a strong division of tasks is necessary to arrive at the finished product. Just because a vase is made by a man or a woman does not mean that all aspects of the '*chaîne opératoire*' are handled by either men or women. For example, the harvesting and preparation of raw materials, the decoration and even the management of the firing can be carried out by people of different sexes[636]. Wright argues instead for the existence of a **collaborative model**, as opposed to the model of the isolated craftsman, highlighting the participation of a group of individuals. This group can be made up of people of different sexes and different ages, because the learning period is an important factor to take into account.

For other ancient societies, such as those of Greco-Roman antiquity and the Middle East, written and iconographic sources provide a slightly clearer picture of the gendered division of labour, particularly as regards the production of pottery. In the 6th and 5th centuries BC, the production of vases – in particular in Athens – was a major commercial enterprise, involving large-scale trade throughout the Mediterranean basin and beyond. The representations of pottery workshops, the signatures of painters and potters, the marks of the intermediaries responsible for exporting the vases clearly show that it was men who controlled this

[627] Finlay 2013, 147.
[628] Finlay 2013, 153.
[629] Masclans *et al.* 2019.

[630] Bolger 2013, 161–162.
[631] Arnold 1985, 101.
[632] Wright 1991, 195; Bolger 2013.
[633] Wallace 1995, quoted by Bolger 2013.
[634] Wright 1991, 209–213.
[635] Wright 1991.
[636] Hendon 2006, 182 explains that certain members of the household are perceived as 'potters' in Southeast Asia, but that women and children regularly take part in the manufacturing process.

Figure 7.1. A group of women at work grinding grain during the Copper Age. Source: Proyecto Pastwomen. Historia material de las mujeres. Illustration by Andrés Marín.

activity. The collaborative model proposed for prehistoric pottery is well illustrated in this production, with vases sometimes signed with the names of two craftsmen, one a painter and the other a potter[637]. This model invites us to rethink our ideas of the ancient craftsman as an artist, a kind of solitary creative genius in the manner of 19th and 20th century artists, and to think in terms of collaboration rather than individuality[638].

Conversely, the preparation of food was often the responsibility of women and slave labour, and formed a significant part of the domestic work carried out by these two groups. In Upper Mesopotamia, Queen Uqnitum of Urkeš had a female cook called Tuli, whose cylinder seal shows food production activities (butchery, churning milk) [639]. The grinding of cereals using a standing millstone and a hand millstone is attested in archaeological contexts. The importance of this activity in the tasks carried out by women can be seen in texts, particularly in Mesopotamia. They mention millstones, cauldrons and jars in the dowries of young girls. For example, in the 39th year of Hammurabi's reign (1753 BC), the dowry of a consecrated woman named Dulluqtum, from the elite of the city of Sippar, included several millstones[640]. In the city of Umma, at the time of Ur III, a tablet dated to the 4th year of the reign of Shu-Shîn (2034 BC) mentions a group of 37 state-owned female millers, whose work was subject to production quotas[641]. If we go back to the neolithic Linear Pottery culture (LBK), the grinding of cereals and plants using a hand millstone may have left traces on the bones of women (Figure 7.1). In fact, their muscular attachments indicate great robustness, comparable to that of modern rowing champions, and could be the result of this activity[642].

Finally, textile production was also an activity carried out mainly by women[643]. Cathy Lynn Costin points out that this essential activity has long been neglected by archaeologists, mainly because it left few traces[644]. Another factor contributing to this neglect is the underestimation of

[637] Boardman 2001, 139–146.
[638] Wright 1991, 199; Bolger 2013, 172.
[639] Otto 2016, 132.

[640] Cousin 2015.
[641] Lafont 1994.
[642] Macinthosh *et al.* 2017.
[643] Esposito & Pollini 2021; Gilchrist 1999, 51 notes a change from the 11th century onwards in northern Europe. The technical development of the loom gradually turned it into a tool requiring greater specialization. It gradually moved out of domestic contexts and became the prerogative of professionals – men – organised into guilds. Women's share of textile work was reduced to meticulous finishing and embroidery, or to elite women who produced textiles for the Church or tapestries.
[644] Costin 2013.

the time needed to produce the various types of textile: the manufacture of one square metre of fabric on a loom requires 200 to 300 hours of work if we count spinning but exclude the harvesting of the fibre (plant or animal), carding, dyeing, and so on. These various points have contributed to under-valuing, and even devaluing, women's work, especially as the work carried out by women in a domestic context was free work in the sense understood by materialist feminists, and therefore invisible[645]. Moreover, as with pottery, textile work was not the work of a single person, but a collaborative activity. Men and women may have taken on different tasks in the fabric manufacturing chain, and a considerable workforce may have been mobilised for this purpose. For example, in the palatial or religious productions in and around the city of Ur at the end of the 3rd millennium BC, there were 13,000 workers responsible for spinning textile fibres, engaged in this activity because of their status as refugees, slaves (because of debts) or prisoners of war[646].

The degree of technicality, dexterity, skill and strength required is also often underestimated[647]. Emily Wilson, the first woman to translate the *Odyssey* into English in 2017, noted that the male translators before her had often chosen to translate certain terms ambiguously, or even incorrectly. For example, the *Odyssey* refers to Penelope's hands, who is known to spend a lot of time weaving, as 'thick' (*pachus*). However, the male translators chose either not to translate the adjective or to translate it as 'stable', as the idea of a thick female hand does not fit in with the modern vision of women, who should have fine and delicate hands[648]. Wilson, on the other hand, chose to translate the adjective as 'muscular', because intensive weaving develops the muscles of the hands. Generally speaking, the study of textiles in ancient Greece bears witness to the central role played by women in the economy of cities, whether in domestic production or public production for sanctuaries and divinities[649].

7.3. Conventional and unconventional work

Beyond the recurrent association of women with domestic tasks, the presence of women in employment, sometimes in professions considered masculine, is far from anecdotal in ancient sources. Literary texts, epigraphy and iconography provide clues as to the occupations held by women. For example, the archives of the Persepolis fortifications, a collection of tens of thousands of tablets produced by the Persian administration around 500 BC, provide a wealth of information on the activities carried out by women and men, as well as the food rations they were given. The women of the royal family-owned lands and estates throughout the territory dominated by Persia. They employed their own labour, were supported by administrative officials and approved rations with their seal. This was the case of Irdabama, a woman at the court of Darius I, who had a workforce of around 480 workers[650]. Outside the royal family, some women, like the men, performed supervisory tasks. The tablets mention the names Sadukka and Matmaba, for example, each in charge of supervising a group of women and children[651]. The tasks carried out by these groups are not always known or clear, as the translation of the tablets is complicated. There does, however, seem to have been a division of labour between male professions (scribe) and female professions (preparation of food and rations), even though certain tasks, particularly service tasks, were performed by both men and women[652]. The importance of women's work outside domestic context is also attested in earlier periods, notably by the Code of Hammurabi. This code mentions the existence of female tavern-keepers – always written in the feminine form. They ran social venues and could grant beer loans, repayable in barley at the next harvest[653].

In Greco-Roman antiquity, numerous examples of women exercising a profession or being involved in an economic activity appear in the sources. In Athens, during the Classical period, the household, the *oikos*, was a centre of production, trade and economic activity, which led Christiane Sourvinou-Inwood to say that it was 'the basic economic unit of the city[654]'. Women's involvement and role in the economy was therefore far from negligible. Elite women, particularly widows, were able to exercise considerable control over the management of the family fortune. Other women were involved in financial transactions (loans, for example), practised as doctors or midwives, and were very active in the sale of sesame, honey, incense, salt, bread, figs, herbs, clothes, crowns, ribbons and perfumes, among other things[655].

Current research is also reassessing the place of women in ancient artistic and craft productions. For a long time, it was generally accepted that men's work was art, while women's work was craft[656]. Recent research has focused on women's participation in what we call 'art'. For example, in the collective unconscious, rock art was long considered to be an exclusively male endeavour. It was hard to imagine that women could have ventured into the darkness of caves to paint or engrave the well-known Upper Palaeolithic bestiary associated with the great hunts, and therefore with a 'masculine' world. The association of cave art with men has been all the stronger since, among the well-known representations of animals on the walls, we find vulvas, female silhouettes and other feminine symbols: these have been interpreted as the erotic, even pornographic, creations of adolescents hunting in groups[657]. However, a number of

645 Delphy 1998.
646 Costin 2013, 188–190, 194.
647 Costin 2013, 181–182.
648 Wilson 2017, 89–90; Pottier 2018.
649 Vlachou 2020.
650 Brosius 1996, 135–144.
651 Brosius 1996, 149, 155.
652 Brosius 1996, 151.
653 Lion 2021, 80–81.
654 Sourvinou-Inwood 1995, 113 ('l'unité économique de base de la cité').
655 Cohen E.E. 2016, 716–717. For evidence of working women in texts, see Kennedy 2014, 123–161; in iconography, see Lewis 2002, 91–129.
656 Díaz-Andreu 2005, 32.
657 Cohen 2016, 142–144.

prehistoric specialists have recently analysed the 'negative hands' frequently found in caves, and their findings suggest that women were involved in artistic activities. These prints, most often of left hands, were made by blowing or dabbing pigments onto the hand with the fingers spread out on the wall. In most of the caves studied by Dean Snow, the archaeologist suggested, by means of statistical computer processing of the data, that in a large number of cases these were women's hands, as at Pech Merle, for example[658]. The presence of both men and women has also been assumed following the study of negative hands in Palaeolithic caves in Borneo[659]. This research was based on the Manning index, which measures the proportion between the index and ring fingers, but serious objections have been raised against it[660]. For the time being, it remains impossible to determine whether it was men or women who painted and/or engraved the prehistoric fauna and other motifs in all these caves. But the merit of these studies is that they invite us to seriously reconsider the question of women 'artists' in prehistory, and to think beyond the norm.

Another study, this time on ancient Greece, looked at the involvement of women in ceramic production between 1200 and 650 BC[661]. According to the authors, women probably played an important role in the stylistic developments of ceramics at the beginning of the Protogeometric period (1200–900 BC), since the scale of production was essentially domestic during this period, at least for the vast majority of it. In the ethnographic examples, it is the women who manage production on this scale. Furthermore, the motifs used are more in keeping with women's experience than men's, since they may bear a strong resemblance to textile and basketry designs. In this way, they attempt to highlight the important role that women may have played in the production of material culture in Iron Age Attica, and challenge traditional notions of craft production as a male-dominated sphere. This is all the more true given that, in later periods, production was clearly dominated by men, as we have seen above, which seems to have obscured the question of the identity of craftsmen in the Protogeometric period. This re-examination of the place of women in craft and artistic production is all the more necessary if we are to better understand the social and economic history of ancient societies.

Where to start?

A. Augereau, 'Change and Continuity: Gender and Flint Knapping Activities During the Neolithic in the Paris Basin', *in* J. K. Koch & W. Kirleis, *Gender Transformations in Prehistoric and Archaic Societies*, Sidestone Press, 2019, 435–458.

C.L. Costin, 'Gender and Textile Production in Prehistory', *in* D. L. Bolger (ed.), *A Companion to Gender Prehistory*, Wiley-Blackwell, 2013, 180–202.

Ch. Darmangeat, *Le communisme primitif n'est plus ce qu'il était. Aux origines de l'oppression des femmes*, Smolny, 2022, troisième édition.

J. Gero, 'Genderlithics: Women's Role in Stone Tool Production', *in* J. Gero & M. Conkey (ed.), *Engendering Archaeology: Women and Prehistory*, Basil Blackwell, 1991, 163–193.

---

658 Snow 2013.
659 Cohen 2016, 145–146.
660 Brůžek *et al.* 2012.
661 Murray *et al.* 2020.

8

Iconography

Gendered representations in art have been a topic of discussion for decades. The focus is on how gender is represented and on challenging traditional representations. Before the 20th century, the representation of the human body was widely discussed in terms of artistic styles, forms and techniques. However, it was only in the 20th century, with the rise of feminist criticism, that the discussion of gender representation in art became more specific. Feminist art historians, such as Linda Nochlin, wrote extensively both about the under-representation of women artists and about the way in which women were represented in art[662]. Critics such as Griselda Pollock have explored the ways in which gender is constructed and how this construction reflects and reinforces patriarchal values[663].

Art has often reinforced gender stereotypes by representing men and women in a way that conforms to societal norms and expectations. These stereotypical representations of gender can have a powerful impact on how individuals understand and experience their own gender as well as how they perceive others[664]. For example, when women are systematically portrayed as passive and submissive, this reinforces the idea that women are inferior to men and reinforces patriarchal power structures. Similarly, when men are portrayed as powerful and active, it reinforces the idea that men are better suited to positions of power and women are better suited to subordinate roles.

In the case of ancient societies that have left a large number of monuments and figurative objects, the study of figurative art can reveal gender role expectations and stereotypes through the representation of gendered activities, clothing and attributes. For example, representations of women engaged in domestic tasks, wearing distinctive clothing and depicted with specific attributes can provide an insight into expected behaviour and social norms for women. The same applies to iconography of activities related to the masculine gender roles expected of men. In this way, figurative art can be a valuable resource for understanding gender roles in ancient societies. However, it is important to bear in mind that artistic representations are not a carbon copy of reality, but are more often than not idealised, and therefore tend to reinforce stereotypes[665]. Variations in the way gender is represented in different artistic media within the same society are also important: these variations are to be expected rather than uniform conventions, especially as different activities are represented depending on the medium used[666]. Just think, for example, of the differences between art commissioned by the state or the elite in ancient Greece (for example, the Parthenon and the Panathenaeum frieze) and terracotta figurines depicting domestic activities. The audience is different, the message is different, and the means of reaching both are different. Elizabeth M. Brumfiel points out that:

> 'the public nature of representational art makes it a useful tool in enforcing gender norms. Thus, when representational art depicts women and men and other genders engaged in different activities, these depictions may constitute ideological statements about gender roles rather than direct reflections of reality[667]'.

Images are therefore not there to help us understand directly how ancient societies were structured, but rather to show us how artists and craftsmen transcribed the elements that seemed relevant to them in the construction of masculinity, femininity and the social relationships of their contemporaries. In this chapter, we will look at a few examples of studies of representations from a gendered perspective.

8.1. Iconography of violence

Egyptologist Uroš Matić has studied the representations of violence in both texts and iconography and its consequences for different social categories according to gender, age and ethnicity[668]. In the Theban tomb of Intef (11th Dynasty), there is a battle scene depicting the capture of a Syro-Palestinian town by Egyptian soldiers. One of the registers shows that the Egyptians have taken three enemy soldiers prisoner. The soldiers are naked and the one furthest to the left is shown with a flaccid penis. This last point is important because it contrasts with Egyptian representations of masculinity, where men and deities are systematically depicted – when their genitals are visible – with an erect penis. Two registers down, the Egyptian soldiers have gathered captives, this time women and children. The actions of the Egyptian soldiers are violent: the captives are tied with ropes or pulled by the hair. In particular, the motif of the soldier holding a foreign woman by the hair is reminiscent of the scenes in which the king strikes a single enemy or a group of enemies whom he holds by the hair using a weapon that he raises above the head (mace, javelin, sword, etc.). This motif indicates domination over the enemy and has existed from the beginning of Egyptian history right through to the

[662] Nochlin 2021 (1971).
[663] Pollock 1988 et 1999.
[664] Levin 2020.
[665] Brumfiel 2006, 40–41.
[666] Brumfiel 2006, 33.
[667] Brumfiel 2006, 40–41.
[668] The following paragraphs are based on Matić 2021, 91–98.

Roman period. Given the symbolic importance of hair in the construction of female identity in ancient Egypt, the motif of the enemy held by the hair has implications in terms of gender. The male enemy held by the hair is thus equated with a woman, and therefore with the notion of passivity. The feminisation of enemies, whether in texts or iconography, is a frequent motif, not only in Egypt but also in other ancient societies in the Mediterranean basin[669]. In Egyptian bas-reliefs from the New Kingdom, this feminisation culminates in the depiction of the counting of slain enemies: hands and penises are cut off and presented in a heap before the pharaoh, while scribes proceed with the counting[670].

From the New Kingdom onwards, war scenes were no longer found in private tombs. Instead, they were engraved on official monuments, particularly temples. In these bas-reliefs, violence against women and children is not depicted, even though it is mentioned in the texts. In the context of the private tombs of nobles, scenes of violence include the presentation to the pharaoh of tribute, taxes or spoils of war. Foreign women and children feature prominently among these spoils. These women and children were then distributed to the temple workshops to carry out various tasks, such as weaving, processing cereals or meat. The representations also show a certain categorisation by age and gender, with women of childbearing age accompanied by children shown first, before nubile girls and little girls. Referring to the work of Maria Lugones on the coloniality of gender[671], Matić also considers that this categorisation by gender and age is imposed by Egypt's colonial sex/gender system on these foreign captives who may have had a different social organisation in their country of origin. More generally, gender coloniality – the way in which colonialism, as a system of power and domination, shaped gender roles, identities and relations in colonised societies by imposing the norms and values of the colonising country – also implies that foreign captive women have an inferior status in Egyptian society.

The motif of the king striking down enemies was also used by Hatshepsut in her iconography as pharaoh[672]. In some scenes, Hatshepsut is represented not as a queen but as a king, notably in her funerary temple at Deir el-Bahari, where she appears as a male sphinx trampling on enemies who, in this case, are men. For other New Kingdom queens, such as Tiye and Nefertiti, the iconography is different: the queens never hit or trample on male enemies, but only women, most often personifying Egypt's enemy countries[673]. Unlike researchers who have previously focused on the identity of queens by emphasising their power, Matić notes that 'rather than mark Nefertiti's and Tiye's unprecedented high status, these representations indicate their subordination in visual and gender hierarchy since they do not trample or smite male enemies. Such enemies are only associated with kings. When Hatshepsut is depicted trampling male enemies, she is a female depicted as a king[674]'.

8.2. Respectable women or prostitutes?

Athenian black-figure vases, then red-figure vases, were produced during the Archaic and Classical periods and decorated with scenes from mythology, everyday life or funerary scenes. Among these scenes, images of women at a fountain constitute an important series of representations on Athenian vases from the late Archaic period, between ca. 530 and 470 BC[675]. Although they appear on other shapes, they are usually painted on hydria, the same vessels used in the images to draw water. The scenes of women drawing water from the fountain follow a pattern that varies little (Figure 8.1). The fountain is depicted as a building with a roof, housing one or more lion's head mouths from which water pours into a basin. In these images, the women carry the hydria on their heads, either standing or lying down when empty. Their hand gestures indicate that they are conversing, which seems to make the fountain a place of female sociability. These images sometimes contain meaningless inscriptions and women's names (which are often names of flowers such as Rhodon, Anthylle, etc.).

Identifying these scenes is more complex than it might at first appear, not because of problems with the subject matter depicted, which is relatively explicit, but because the social and economic status of the women depicted has been much debated (Figure 8.2). Far from being limited to fountain scenes, this debate is part of a general problem concerning all iconography relating to women in the context of everyday life in both the Archaic and Classical periods. With the exception of clearly identified scenes, such as wedding rituals or visits to the tomb by family members, in which the status of the women (wives or daughters of citizens) is not in doubt, the research navigates between two extremes: the virtuous wife and the prostitute. Sian Lewis has noted that, in contemporary publications, women 'who converse with men, women who receive gifts of any kind, women who dance, play music, or drink, and even those who engage in tasks such as spinning or textile work[676]' are regularly identified with *hetairai* or prostitutes (). 'In its most extreme form, this theory can label a woman who stands fully-clothed making a cushion, or who is alone in a room holding a mirror as a prostitute[677].'

[669] On the feminisation of enemies in Athenian iconography in the 5th century BC, see for example Cartledge 1998; Algrain 2022; it also appears in Hittite and Assyrian texts, etc. See Matić 2021, 113–114.
[670] Matić 2021, 123–131.
[671] Lugones 2007.
[672] Matić 2021, 98–105.
[673] Matić 2017.
[674] Matić 2021, 104.
[675] Hannestad 1984, 252.
[676] Lewis 2006, 33.
[677] *Ibid.*

Figure 8.1. Hydria attributed to the Class of Hamburg 1917.477. The Metropolitan Museum of Art, New York, inv. 06.1021.77. Rogers Fund, 1906. *Ca.* 510–500 BC (www.metmuseum.org).

Figure 8.2. Fragmentary kylix attributed to the Kiss Painter. The Metropolitan Museum of Art, New York, inv. 07.286.50. Rogers Fund, 1907. *Ca.* 510–500 BC (www.metmuseum.org).

When art historians interpret fountain representations as religious scenes, the women are seen as members of aristocratic Athenian families, who frequently played important roles in the city's cults and festivals[678]. On the other hand, when these scenes are interpreted as scenes of everyday life, the women are often identified as *hetairai* (courtesans), prostitutes or slaves. Alan Shapiro relies mainly on the names of the women depicted and the *kale* cheers to identify them as *hetairai*. However, recent onomastic studies show that the names of the women painted on the Attic vases could be the names of 'citizen' women or foreigners[679]. This identification is also made because of the occasional presence of men in the image, but also because the task, described in some texts as difficult and performed by slaves, does not fit well with the 'modern' vision that some researchers have of Athenian women, who are supposed to be recluse in the *gynaeceum*, away from any contact with members of the opposite sex[680].

In the scenes at the fountain, for example, there is no evidence to support the hypothesis that the women were *hetairai*[681]. The names sometimes attached to these women are not specific to a group and do not allow us to state that they belonged to the groups of slaves, foreigners or courtesans. Although it is likely that women from the wealthier classes sent servants or slaves to the fountain, less fortunate women probably had to carry out this task themselves.

Against the previous theories, Victoria Sabetai proposes that, in most cases, the drawing scenes should be read more specifically as images of *parthenoi*, young girls between childhood and adulthood, about to be married. In at least two cases, the inscriptions painted on the hydriae name the fountain as Kallirhoe, i.e. the spring from which the water for the nuptial bath was drawn during the rituals leading up to the wedding. There are several additional arguments in favour of identifying these women as *parthenoi*[682]. For example, in several of these scenes, the women hold a flower in their hands and inhale its fragrance. In various ancient poetic texts, we repeatedly find excerpts that compare young girls with flowers, deer or other young animals. The women's names are also linked to flowers, such as Rhodon, Elanthis, Rodopis or Anthyllè. The flower thus becomes a symbol which, in certain contexts, enables *parthenoi* to be identified[683]. As for the identification of young girls with wild animals, a hydria preserved in London features a scene in which women holding flowers go to draw water from a fountain in the company of deer,

[678] Manakidou 1992–1993. The status of women is sometimes considered irrelevant, since the festival promotes class mixing.
[679] Shapiro 2003, 96–98. Contra Lewis 2002, 107–110 for the onomastic study of women's names in Attic ceramics.
[680] For example Williams 1993, 92–106.
[681] Hannestad 1984, 254–255 for the refutation of slave status.
[682] Sabetai 2009, 103–114.
[683] It can also be a symbol of the girl's fragrance. In the case of married women, this symbol seems to have been replaced by a controlled, tamed and no longer wild version of the flower's perfume in the form of perfumed oil contained in an alabastron. See Algrain 2015.

while in the Homeric Hymn to Demeter, young girls are compared to deer and heifers[684].

Representations of women on other types of scene, especially if accompanied by men, are also regularly interpreted as images of *hetairai*. However, if we measure them against their male counterparts, images of women can be understood as a feminine equivalent of representations of the male elite. The images thus offer us a glimpse of the expected social roles and activities of the wives and daughters of citizens. It is no longer a question of images of seclusion within the *gynaeceum*, but of a gilded life where the women, surrounded by their families and household staff, organise the activities of the *oikos*[685]. Not having to work or do hard labour is a symbol of the privileged social status of the wives of wealthy citizens[686]. Rebecca Futo Kennedy comes to the same conclusion and recommends the utmost caution when using terms that refer, in the imagination of modern researchers, to different forms of prostitution. At the time these images were produced, literary references to the term '*hetaira*' (often translated as 'courtesan') did not refer to prostitution but to a form of non-contractual union between a citizen and women excluded from marriage (for example, women from citizen families without a dowry or metic women)[687].

8.3. Iconography of masculinities

According to sociologist Raewyn Connell, there are several types of masculinity. Among these, hegemonic masculinity corresponds to men in a position of domination and holding a form of political hegemony. It refers to an ideal that is often unattainable and is constructed in opposition to femininity and other types of masculinity, which are non-hegemonic[688]. Just as gender and femininity evolve over time, hegemonic masculinity is not static and evolves according to historical, cultural and social contexts.

Ilan Peled's study of cult servants, known in Mesopotamian texts as *gala* (Sumerian) / *kalû* (Akkadian) and attested from the middle of the 3rd millennium to the end of the 1st millennium BC, is a good example of an approach focusing on the variability of masculinity[689]. Their primary activity was to perform certain funeral rituals. In particular, they were professional mourners, a task previously reserved for women. Their functions gradually took on greater importance at the end of the 3rd millennium, and they were integrated into the cult of Inanna/Ištar, a gender-ambivalent divinity linked to eroticism, sexuality and war. The *gala* / *kalû* utter laments in a dialect called *emesal*, which is used exclusively by them and the female divinities. In the texts, they are mocked for their supposed sexual passivity.

In order to define the specific features of *gala* / *kalû* masculinity and its deviations from norms, Peled begins by recalling what hegemonic masculinity meant in ancient Mesopotamia:

> 'Mesopotamian men of hegemonic masculinity possessed the following characteristics: they operated in a patriarchal system and had superiority over women and non-hegemonic men; demonstrated physical strength and, occasionally, military prowess; exhibited penetrative sexuality, avoided receptive sexuality, and were expected to produce offspring; were involved with the public arena and not with the domestic one; and had expertise and exclusive proficiency in skilled crafts[690].'

However, the various sources clearly indicate that the *gala* / *kalû* deviates from this form of masculinity. Firstly, the fact that they took on an activity that had previously been carried out exclusively by women (the lamentations) already points to a deviation from gender roles. The same applies to the dialect spoken by these servants of the cult. The way in which they pronounced these laments is interesting, as they did so in a high-pitched voice considered inappropriate for men. The iconography also shows how the masculinity of these cult servants stood in stark contrast to hegemonic masculinity and its visual construction. In Mesopotamia during this period, men were generally depicted with a full beard, one of the signs of virility. The *gala* / *kalû*, on the other hand, are shown beardless. It is possible that they shaved their beards to give themselves an effeminate, youthful appearance that matched their high-pitched voice and marked their membership in a non-hegemonic form of masculinity.

Masculinities vs. masculinism

Masculinity refers to the traits, behaviours and characteristics associated with men and with being a man. The characteristics generally promoted or used to define masculinity are physical strength, independence, competitiveness, rationality and aggressiveness. However, research in the social sciences (notably that of Raewyn Connell, see chapter 3) has highlighted the existence of different forms of masculinity, varying according to social status, age, sexual orientation, race, etc. Masculinism, on the other hand, is a social and political movement that focuses on defending and promoting men's rights and interests. Masculinists seek to challenge the idea that gender inequalities exist, often in response to feminist movements and social changes that have challenged traditional gender roles, and adopt misogynist and anti-feminist attitudes and behaviour[691].

684 Manfrini-Aragno 1992, 127–148; Hymne à Déméter, 172–178.
685 See Xenophon, Oeconomicus, 7, 35–36: The wife's role was to supervise the work of the slaves and servants in the household, who were involved in making textiles and bread, as well as ensuring the proper management of the *oikos'* food resources.
686 Algrain 2014, 213–214.
687 Kennedy 2014, 112–117.
688 Connell 2014 (1995).
689 Peled 2016.
690 Peled 2016, 162.
691 Dupuis-Déri 2018; Bard *et al.* 2019; Algrain & Lootvoet 2019.

Another example of this type of research is Hans van Wees' study of the expression of feelings in the context of Greece from the 8th to the 6th centuries BC. Starting from the premise that the expression of emotions is a cultural fact, the researcher looked at the gendered expression of grief and mourning in texts and iconography[692]. He noted a gradual change in the ideology associated with the expression of emotions, particularly those linked to grief, for women and men during this period. Van Wees began by analysing the Iliad and the Odyssey, which show men openly expressing their emotions, particularly sadness and grief. Generally speaking, he found no significant difference between the emotions expressed by men and women in these texts, apart from at funerals, where men are expected to behave calmly while women display their grief intensely. In contrast, during the classical period, there was a clear emphasis on self-control on the part of men. Plato even goes so far as to say that passages in Homer's works where the heroes are crying and expressing their emotions should be deleted. He also adds that self-control and emotional control distinguish men from women[693], a distinction that Homer did not make. The first evidence of the association between the expression of emotions and feminine nature appeared in the 7th century. It was at this time, therefore, that we saw a change in the construction of masculinity.

How was this development reflected in iconography? A study of funeral scenes, particularly those depicting the display of the body of the deceased (*prothesis*) on ceramic vases, showed a gradual differentiation in the roles assigned to men and women. In the 8th century, mourners raised one or both hands to their heads in a gesture typical of expressions of grief. Initially, the difference in gender roles with regard to the expression of emotions intensified between the end of the 8th and the middle of the 7th century. By the end of the Geometric period (late 8th century), gestures of lamentation were clearly gendered: women raised both arms above their heads in mourning and grief, while men raised only one (Figure 8.3). The women who are closest to the body on display, and who presumably belong to the immediate family, are sometimes seated, but gradually these female figures are no longer seated but kneel (in Homer, sitting on the floor is a sign of intense pain). From the mid-7th century onwards, the gestures were even more dramatic. On vases and terracottas alike, women lacerated their cheeks with their fingernails, leaving bloody trails. Self-mutilation was seen as a profound mark of respect. Women's weeping and wounding thus contributed to male power dynamics. For a family burying its dead, a *prothesis* and public funeral with crowds of mourning, self-lacerating women became a potent display of assertion against rival families[694]. After 580 BC, this motif disappeared and mourning was once again expressed by raising the hands to the head. For Van Wees, there is a clear link with a Solonian law of 594 BC, which forbids self-mutilation at funerals.

Figure 8.3. Krater attributed to the workshop of the Hirschfeld Painter. The Metropolitan Museum of Art, New York, inv. 14.130.14. Rogers Fund, 1914. *Ca.* 750–735 BC (www.metmuseum.org).

The segregation of the sexes also increased over time in funeral scenes. Between the late 8th and early 6th centuries, men and women gradually occupied clearly demarcated areas on the vases and practised different activities (lamentations for the women, processions and dances for the men). By the end of this period, and until around 580 BC, all images depicted were of women. This segregation of images also seems to reflect the consequences of the Solonian laws of 594 BC, which reinforced the differentiation of roles between men and women at funerals. The law of 594 forbade women who were not close relatives from taking part in the funeral and required them to walk behind the men in the funeral procession. This legislation made the display of the body of a deceased a private, domestic and therefore female affair, rather than a public one, while the funeral procession, which was eminently public, was dominated by men.

8.4. Gender and skin

On Attic black-figure pottery from the Archaic period (6th century BC), women's skin was mostly highlighted in white, contrasting with that of men, which was left in black. The rare examples of Archaic wall paintings or polychrome sculptures also confirmed this practice of painting male

692 Van Wees 1998.
693 Platon, *République*, 605 D 7-E 1.
694 Van Wees 1998, 42.

Figure 8.4. Amphora attributed to Exekias. The Metropolitan Museum of Art, New York, inv. 17.230.14a. Rogers Fund, 1917. *Ca.* 540 BC (www.metmuseum.org).

flesh in darker tones (Figure 8.4). The explanation most often put forward to justify this difference is that women were confined to the home and kept their skin pale, while men carried out various activities outdoors and therefore had tanned skin. White was used not only to distinguish women from men, but also to highlight the feminine nature of monstrous creatures such as the Gorgon[695]. Skin colour was also invoked in texts to mark the difference between Greeks and non-Greeks, particularly Persians. The former had tanned skin because they exercised naked in the palestra; the latter were portrayed by ancient authors as white-skinned slobs who did not engage in any kind of physical activity. The description of their skin colour feminised them and served as a mechanism for making them seem inferior. In iconography, this difference was illustrated by Greek hoplites in heroic nudity pitted against Oriental warriors covered from head to toe in clothing[696].

For Mireille M. Lee, physical exercise, bathing and body care performed in a public (palestra) and homosocial setting, under the gaze of other citizens, characterised the bodies of male citizens. They involved a form of controlled bodily modification that contrasted with women's body care (bathing, perfume and cosmetics, hair removal, hair care, etc.) performed in a private domestic setting and intended solely for the gaze of the woman who performed them[697]. These 'performances', as Judith Butler understands them, had to be repeated daily for both men and women. They allowed not only the staging of gender, but also of class and ethnicity. They showed the opposition between women and men, between aristocratic elites and the rest of the population who did not have the time (for the poorest) or were forbidden (for slaves) to practice at the palestra, between Greeks and Barbarians. In the latter case, the opposition was all the more marked as the Barbarians were the bearers of *permanent* body modifications (circumcision or tattoos), whereas the modifications proposed by the Greeks were not. Yet, no 'Greek' body modification allowed Barbarians to free themselves from their ethnicity.

Where to start?

I. Algrain, 'Gender, Perfume and Society in Ancient Athens', *in* U. Matić (ed.), *Beautiful Bodies. Gender and Corporeal Aesthetics in the Past*, Oxbow Books, 2022, 153–175.

B. Jensen & U. Matić, *Archaeologies of Gender and Violence*, Oxbow Books, 2017.

S. Lewis, *The Athenian Woman: an Iconographic Handbook*, Routledge, 2002.

U. Matić, *Violence and Gender in Ancient Egypt*, Routledge, 2021.

695 Eaverly 2013.

696 Algrain 2022.

697 Lee 2009.

9

Disseminating and popularising research

Researchers in the field of gender archaeology carry out a wide range of studies on how museums popularise archaeological discoveries for the general public. Their work focuses not only on permanent and temporary exhibitions, but also on the way in which stereotypes present in archaeological research are disseminated to the general public through the media, films and series, and video games. For example, at the time of the discovery of the Vix tomb in 1953, the media, and in particular Paris Match magazine, broadcasted artist's views of the 'Lady' of Vix, presented as a young, pretty blonde woman. This representation corresponded in fact to the Western feminine ideal of the 1950s embodied by Brigitte Bardot, but went against the facial reconstruction of the Lady of Vix and did not correspond to her age, estimated at between 30 and 55[698]. School textbooks can also convey stereotypes about the role of women. In the first half of the 20th century, in these books, Celt and Gallic women were confined to domestic activities such as cooking and textile work, which were always carried out close to home. Men, on the other hand, carried out outdoor activities such as hunting and fishing. This tended to naturalise and essentialise the roles of men and women, presenting them as immutable and universal. In fact, the authors of these books applied to the Celts and Gauls the model of the 'good wife' as it existed in society in the first half of the 20th century[699].

In this chapter, we will be looking in particular at how archaeological museums present the roles of women and men in ancient societies, the research carried out on this theme and the solutions proposed to remedy the spread of stereotypes in these institutions. The presentation of stereotyped behaviour in exhibition halls is an integral part of the history of museums. We know the role of museum institutions in the construction of a '*roman national*' for nation-states during the 19th century. Following the work of Michel Foucault, in particular *Surveiller et punir. Naissance de la prison*, published in 1975, research into gender and the inclusion of minorities in museums has highlighted the disciplinary nature of institutions such as museums[700]. 'The museum takes its place as part of a cultural apparatus aimed at keeping the working class and other "troublesome" persons (such as females and homosexuals) in line by offering them instruction in approved culture and behaviors[701]'.

Gender stereotyping is far from confined to archaeological museums. An interesting example is provided by Donna Haraway, who in 1984 examined the way in which animals were displayed in natural history museums, pointing out that this mode of display reflects and reinforces patriarchal norms[702]. In this way, museums naturalise power structures that are in fact human, by setting up specific images, particularly in dioramas. In the case of animals living in large groups, museums display just a few animals – a large, vigilant male, one or two females, a baby – recreating a nuclear family structured by a supposedly 'natural' division of male and female roles. It is therefore, unconsciously, a way of spreading a message about social dynamics, human behaviour and gender roles, and of reiterating these values in a public space, namely the museum.

The research carried out on the specific subject of stereotypes in archaeological museums, mainly in the English-speaking world, Spain and Germany, has focused on the stereotypes and biases that permeate both permanent and temporary exhibitions, whether or not they deal specifically with the role of women in ancient societies. They have also proposed original solutions to compensate for this lack of visibility of women and to offer a more nuanced view of social relations in ancient societies. These studies and proposals form part of the wider framework of research into gender in museology[703]. They also respond to the concerns of ICOM, which in 2013, among other things, adopted a resolution on 'Museums, Gender Mainstreaming, and Inclusion'. It recommends that museums 'analyse the narratives being told from a gender perspective', 'work with audience, staff and programmes from a gender perspective and at the same time with the embodiment of ideas' and use an intersectional perspective 'to realise the idea of inclusiveness in museums'[704].

9.1. Paradox: the presence and absence of women in museums[705]

A great deal of research into museology and the history of archaeology points to a paradox. On the one hand, women and minorities are largely absent or under-represented in museum collections and, on the other, since the emergence of public archaeological museums in the 19th century, they have made up a greater or lesser proportion of the contractual and/or voluntary staff of these museums, sometimes with great variations depending on the period and the region.

698 Belard 2017, 44–45; Trémeaud 2018, 1.
699 Belard 2017, 44–48.
700 Nixon Chen 2013; Tyburczy 2016, 1.
701 Levin 2010b, 5. See also Nixon Chen 2013, 407.
702 Haraway 1984.
703 For example Levin 2010; Adair & Levin 2020.
704 ICOM 2013; see also Sanz 2017.
705 This section is largely based on a presentation already published on this theme by one of the authors. See Algrain 2023.

The choice of objects on display in museums is a key factor in building a narrative about the past. Certain activities traditionally associated with women have left little archaeological trace and are therefore often not presented in showcases, such as basketry, textile work or other subsistence activities. It is also often because objects associated with daily life and women's activities are less prestigious and/or made from less precious materials that they are not displayed. Objects traditionally associated with the masculine world, such as metal weapons and polished axes, are more likely to be found in display cases than kitchen ware. It is therefore essential to allow objects in museum collections to reveal stories about traditionally marginalised groups, such as women, the elderly and children[706]. By showing little of the diversity of ancient societies and projecting the present – and its stereotypes – onto the past, we make women and other minority groups invisible; we also tend to attribute little value to the activities associated with them.

Objects in collections that are supposedly made by men are often exhibited repeatedly, without there being the slightest questioning of the fact that they were indeed produced by men. The example of lithic material from prehistoric times is interesting in this respect, as there is no scientific evidence to identify the sex of the people who made it. Since the 19th century, it has been 'traditionally' accepted – and this tradition has produced androcentric stereotypes – that these tools were made by men, whereas it is probable that each individual had to produce his own tools, as ethnographic examples show[707]. Other recurring stereotypes concern, for example, the exclusion of women from exhibition themes such as hunting in prehistoric times, even though we know that cooperation was essential for the survival of the group, which involved working together to butcher animals[708].

Moreover, the spaces devoted to women in archaeological museums are often limited. Their presence is mentioned through objects in domestic spaces and their tasks related to care and subsistence for the group. These care and subsistence activities, which include caring for children and the elderly, educating children, making textiles and basketry, processing and preparing food, etc., although essential, are not considered to be of real importance, or at least of equal importance to male activities[709]. The insistence on the model of the 'housewife', confined to the domestic space where she takes care of her family, is the result of a phenomenon of 'iconisation' and stereotyping[710]: in this way, the museum reinforces the stereotype, created by archaeologists as early as the 19th century, that women's place has always been in the home and that they did not participate with men in outside activities.

The presence of women among museum staff has also been well studied (see Part Three). Kate Hill, for example, has devoted a book to the presence of women in English museums between 1850 and 1914. She points out that a large number of women worked in or around museums. When archaeology began to be professionalised at the end of the 19th century, it was still difficult for women to gain access to archaeological sites, or they were confined to menial roles. Museums offered them the opportunity to work on objects, if they could not take part in excavations. They constituted a workforce that was considered to be under-qualified and unprofessional and, as a result, very cheap. Their history is difficult to trace, however, because the roles they play in museums tend not to be considered important enough for their contributions to be recorded and archived. The first reason for this was that the majority of curatorial jobs – the most prestigious in museums – were held by men, as the management of collections was considered to be an intellectual undertaking suitable for a gentleman, as was the management of curiosity cabinets in the past. Women often found themselves confined to roles deemed appropriate to their feminine status, such as educational services dedicated in particular to popularising science and supporting the general public and children, but in which they would bring added value that would benefit the institution as a whole. Only one woman in Kate Hill's entire study period was a curator; the other women involved in English museums at the time were curatorial assistants (usually on temporary contracts), caretakers, cleaners, secretaries, printers, lecturers, donors or volunteers (especially in the case of married women)[711].

In the first decade of the 21st century, the number of women in museums is high. In the United States, for example, 63% of museum staff are women[712]. In 2014, UNESCO published an analysis of gender in the cultural sector, with a particular focus on museums. The results show that the majority of staff in these institutions are women and that there is a division of labour. As in the past, male employees tend to have higher qualifications, work in research and are often responsible for fieldwork, photo shoots and physical tasks. Women, on the other hand, are more likely to be working as tourist guides, educators and restorers[713]. In France, there is strong vertical segregation in cultural institutions: while in 2012, 80% of students in the Ministry of Culture's 'heritage' courses (École du

706 Wood & Cotton 1999, 33; Prados Torreira 2016, 22. In modern art museums, we have also noted the over-representation of male artists and the large number of representations of female nudes, making the modern art museum a masculine space *par excellence*. See Duncan 1995, 111–132.

707 Prados Torreira 2017, 32.

708 Prados Torreira 2016, 18; Maceira-Ochoa 2017, 78. The stereotype of the prehistoric male hunt has its origins in Charles Darwin's book, *The Descent of Man, and Selection in Relation to Sex*, published in 1871. In it, the author asserts as an irrefutable scientific truth a difference in the intellectual faculties of the two sexes, obviously to the advantage of men. Hunting, an exclusively male activity according to Darwin, was a key factor in the hominisation process and contributed to the evolution of brain size. See Querol 2017, 57.

709 Prados Torreira 2016, 18.

710 Maceira-Ochoa 2017, 83.

711 Hill 2016, 17–40, 163–169.

712 Schwarzer 2010, 17. Museum staff in Spain are also heavily feminised cf. Baquedano *et al.* 2017.

713 UNESCO, *Égalité des genres : patrimoine et créativité*, Paris, 2014, [Accessed 3 February 2023, https://unesdoc.unesco.org/ark:/48223/pf0000230304].

Louvre and INP) were women, only 25% of women held management positions[714].

While the majority of museum staff are women, the extensive research carried out into the representation of women and men in exhibitions shows that the men of the past are most often the 'bearers' of the narrative. They are the main actors and subjects of the story, while women often play an ornamental role. They are not essential to understanding the subject[715]. This is not the only paradox of museum institutions which, despite a strong presence of women among their staff, have difficulty changing their discourse on women and minorities.

9.2. 'What the museum does not tell becomes marginal[716]'

Nick Merriman points out that the 'analysis of museum cultures tends to show that museums have historically produced authoritative versions of the past that have – intentionally or not– served to educate the public in the ways of the dominant culture[717]'. Within a museum, the archaeological collection is used to tell a story. It may seem radical to assert that this story is fabricated by research and museums, but it is necessary to remember that the objects themselves are devoid of meaning and that this meaning is given to them by the researchers and curators[718]. The choice of exhibiting certain objects rather than others and the way they are presented reflect the social norms of the dominant culture and the curators' interest in certain themes[719]. The curators give meaning to the objects and can therefore either confirm the stereotypes held by the public or, on the contrary, encourage the public to question them. 'We believe that visitors interpret museum exhibitions using their existing mental framework, which is shaped by socialisation and learning. Most museums reinforce this framework, helping to perpetuate the gender stereotypes and prejudices that visitors already had before seeing the exhibitions. [...] The language used in exhibitions has the power to validate current stereotypes and prejudices against women[720]'.

Not surprisingly, national policies and attitudes towards gender, sex and sexuality permeate some museums and can contribute to the discrimination or invisibilisation of women and minority groups, including those from the LGBTQIA+ community[721]. Following the discovery of numerous objects linked to sexuality in the ruins of Pompeii in the 18th century, 'secret museums' sprang up in major museums, with an audience made up of elite men. The images, deemed pornographic and obscene, were considered inappropriate for women, children and the working classes – 'vulnerable' sections of the population[722]. Presenting this type of object to the public still seems problematic. The Museum of Fine Arts in Boston, for example, has the largest collection of Greek vases decorated with erotic scenes, assembled by Edward Perry Warren (1860–1928), a wealthy patron of the arts who was openly homosexual and donated them to the museum during his lifetime. These vases were exhibited from 1964 onwards without any public outcry, and it was at this time that the overpainting hiding the erect genitals of the figures was removed[723]. In the new museography presented to the public in December 2021, only one of these numerous vases, decorated with a heterosexual erotic scene, is still on display to the public. The other vases, and in particular those depicting homosexual scenes, have been placed in storage[724]. We might well wonder whether a certain puritanism, or even a form of censorship, was behind the rearrangement of the rooms. Jonathan Katz refers to a form of 'covert censorship' when it comes to not exhibiting certain objects or works of art, or adding a statement to the label of certain pieces to the effect that they are 'offensive' because they simply do not correspond to the dominant heteronormative culture[725].

The way in which objects are described in labels, in exhibition halls or in museums' online catalogues can also help to highlight or erase LGBTQIA+ experiences. Åsa Johannsesson and Clair Le Couteur note that on the label describing the frieze from the temple of Bassae from the late 5th century BC, now in the British Museum, Kaineus' gender transformation is mentioned. In mythology, Kainea, born a woman, is raped by Poseidon, then transformed into a young man by the god because she no longer wishes to be penetrated. When the strongest of the centaurs, Latreus, realised that Kainea had been born a woman, he mocked him and challenged him to a fight. Outraged by Kaineus' victory, the centaurs bury him under stones. The frieze illustrates this moment. While the label does mention this gender transformation, the online catalogue does not. Furthermore, neither the label nor the catalogue mentions the rape of Kainea by Poseidon, and so ignores the issue of violence against women[726].

---

714 Dufrêne 2014.

715 Prados Torreira 2016, 18–19; Sánchez Romero 2016, 28–29; Sørensen 2000.

716 Izquierdo Peraile 2016, 19 ('aquello que el museo no cuenta se convierte en marginal').

717 Merriman 1999, 4.

718 Wood & Cotton 1999, 28–29 refer to 'representation', 'sampling', 'interpretation' and 'creation' in the case of permanent exhibitions.

719 Izquierdo Peraile 2014, 18; Dionísio Rechena 2016, 56.

720 Dionísio Rechena 2016, 56–57 ('Assim, consideramos que os/as visitantes interpretam uma exposição museológica com o quadro mental de referência que possuem, quadro esse formado no processo de socialização e de aprendizagem. A maioria dos museus confirma esse quadro mental de referência, contribuindo para homologar estereótipos e preconceitos de género que os/as visitantes já possuem antes de contactar com as exposições. [...] a linguagem utilizada nas exposições tem poder para validar os estereótipos e preconceitos atuais relativos às mulheres').

721 Levin 2020.

722 Tyburczy 2016, 25–29. For example, the Raccolta Pornografica at Museo Archeologico Nazionale di Napoli and the Secretum at the British Museum.

723 Vermeule 1969.

724 Thompson 2022.

725 Katz 2018; Tyburczy 2016, xiii-xviii.

726 Johannsesson & Le Couteur 2020. In museums of modern and/or contemporary art, this concealed censorship can take the form of minimising or invisibilising LGBTQIA+ relationships. For example, exhibition catalogs devoted to Gertrude Stein either do not mention or refer to her homosexual relationship with Alice Toklas as a 'friendship'. See Hunt 2020.

The presentation of LGBTQIA+ sexualities or sexualities that do not have procreative aims as 'alternative' sexualities is also problematic, since they are only 'alternative' in relation to modern Judeo-Christian sexuality and not necessarily in relation to ancient norms[727].

The binary presentation of female versus male objects can also be questioned, particularly in societies with more than two genders. This is the case, for example, for certain populations in North America, which also included two-spirit individuals, or in imperial China and during the Byzantine period, where eunuchs constituted a third gender[728]. Luz Maceira-Ochoa points out, for example, that the Museo Nacional de Antropología in Mexico City, in the rooms devoted to the cultures of Oaxaca, makes no mention of the existence of a third gender, which was present even before colonisation and is still represented by the *muxe* among the Zapotecs[729]. This type of presentation erases from history sex/gender systems or sexualities that differ from the Western model. Researchers such as Maria Lugones have analysed the social mechanisms that, during colonisation, led to other gender systems being supplanted or even erased by the colonisers[730]. For example, the free sexuality of Inuit women and expressions of female desire were repressed and shamed by the colonisers because they did not conform to the Judeo-Christian ideology of purity and chastity[731]. The diversity of gender systems and sexualities needs to be recognised by museums, because education for equality requires, among other things, recognition of the contingent nature of gender and the possibility for Indigenous populations to have a space in which to tell their own stories.

9.3. Sexist stereotypes in archaeology museums: words

The presence of gender stereotypes in archaeological museums has long been highlighted by researchers. The objects on display, the texts, images and other dioramas tend to present the public with a very dichotomous view of gender roles and, even in museums where the presentation is intended to be as gender-neutral as possible, making the texts and visuals inclusive is not always an easy task, as Kirsten Eppler has shown for the Landesmuseum Württemberg in Stuttgart (Germany)[732]. In the case of dioramas, Stephanie Moser notes that prehistoric women are often depicted either at the entrance to a cave, with a child on their hip, or processing skins. Women are often not represented in activities other than those related to care and 'domestic' tasks. Conversely, men are depicted as hunters. In this way, the diorama seems familiar to the public, showing them the supposed antiquity of the social institutions of our Western societies, primarily heteronormative structures and the nuclear family, while sidestepping other possible types of social organisation[733].

Designing a coherent and inclusive message, both in the text and in the illustrations, is nonetheless essential for issues of equality education. The Museum of Natural Sciences in Brussels (Belgium) is not an archaeology museum, but part of its collections dedicated to human evolution bears similarities to the displays frequently found in museums or galleries dedicated to prehistory, and includes originals and reproductions of skeletons from different human and prehuman species, as well as a few artefacts. Visitors enter the 'Galerie de l'Homme', inaugurated in 2015, through a corridor decorated with a poster featuring seven figures from different human groups, including four women. The name of the gallery is displayed next to the figures in four languages: it is translated into Dutch as 'De Galerij van de mens', into German as 'Die Galerie des Menschen' and into English as 'The Gallery of Humankind'. With the exception of French, all the languages used refer to the notion of humanity, which is much more neutral than the term 'Man'. Names such as 'prehistoric man', 'Cro-Magnon man', 'the gallery of man', etc. used on panels and labels are commonplace in museums. But the universal use of the masculine gender to designate both sexes is far from neutral. On the contrary, these formulations tend to erase women from the narrative because, for the reader, the subject of the action is male[734]. This mechanism is important because it can contribute to reinforcing gender stereotypes: 'when History is written in the masculine, the women of the past become non-existent and the classic and harmful opposition between the visible and active masculine and the invisible and passive feminine is reinforced[735]'. The use of inclusive language is easy to implement, however, and other formulas exist to designate 'the evolution of humanity', 'prehistoric populations', 'humans', etc. Languages such as French or Spanish make this exercise a little more complicated than English, for example, because their grammar includes the masculine and feminine genders.

In the 75 museum texts (labels, explanatory texts) displayed alongside the display cases in the Brussels Museum of Natural Sciences, the number of occurrences of the generic terms used to describe human and prehuman beings is neutral in over 54% of cases, but refers to the masculine gender in over 42% of cases (Table 4). Specific mention of the feminine is limited to 3%. This phenomenon is common and has been noted in other museums, such as the Archaeological Museum of Barcelona, where the word 'man' is used as a 'neutral' term in museum texts[736].

In Brussels, most of the texts are written in the third person singular and in the masculine, and women or

---

[727] Challis 2015.
[728] Algrain 2021a.
[729] Maceira-Ochoa 2017, 75–76.
[730] Lugones 2007.
[731] Georgeson-Usher 2020.
[732] Eppler 2017.
[733] Moser 1999, 105; Dowson 2006, 95–96. Rovira Hortalà 2017, 191 also notes the androcentrism of a diorama, showing a man painting in a cave, and the accompanying text at Barcelona's Archaeological Museum.
[734] Argelès, Piqué & Vila 1991; Prados Torreira 2016, 24–25; Prados Torreira 2017, 33–34; Maceira-Ochoa 2017, 78–80.
[735] Querol 2017, 53–54 ('cuando se hace Historia utilizando un lenguaje en masculino, las mujeres del pasado se convierten en inexistentes y además se afianza la clásica y dañina oposición entre lo masculino visible y activo y lo femenino invisible y pasivo').
[736] Rovira Hortalà 2017 A great deal of archaeological and linguistic research has been carried out on this subject, including Fernández 1999; Querol 2005; Fernández Poncela 2012; Viennot 2014.

Table 4. Occurrences of different terms in the labels at the Museum of Natural Sciences in Brussels (after Algrain 2023).

Homme (Man)	28	Reference to masculine: 42,55%
homme (man)	8	
mâle (male)	4	
femme (woman)	0	Reference to feminine: 3,19%
femelle (female)	3	
humain (human - noun)	20	Neutral: 54,26%
humain (human - adjective)	20	
préhumain (prehuman - noun)	11	

mentions of the feminine are almost absent. The result is not neutral, since the terms used to describe prehumans and humans refer to qualities traditionally associated with the masculine. While a male and a female of the species *Paranthropus boisei* are presented in the form of sculptures, the title of one of the panels explaining the differences in stature between the sexes is entitled 'Strong males'. *Homo erectus* is an 'explorer' ('*explorateur*', masculine form), *Homo heidelbergensis* is a 'big strapping fellow' ('*grand gaillard costaud*', there is no indication whether the female of this species is also a big strapping fellow or a puny little creature) and *Homo sapiens* is a 'conqueror' ('*conquérant*'). About *Australopithecus garhi*, the label asks: 'could he have used rudimentary tools?' ('*aurait-il pu utiliser des outils rudimentaires ?* ') an is *Homo habilis* 'the first craftsman' ('*le premier artisan ?*'). Paradoxically, while the touch screens for finding out more about each species show an individual corresponding to the skeleton on display on the home screen, the text remains in the 'neutral' masculine, even when the skeletons are female. The screen devoted to *Homo floresiensis* illustrates a woman, next to a sculpture of a woman, but is entitled 'The smallest man' ('*Le plus petit homme*').

9.4. Sexist stereotypes in archaeology museums: images

The evocation of different human groups over several million years alongside the artefacts associated with them is the norm in museums devoted to prehistory. The Altamira Museum in Spain adopted a progressive policy towards gender issues when it renovated the institution in the early 2000s. The museum team deliberately chose to use a man and a woman in each of its life-size illustrations of four human representatives (*Homo habilis*, *Homo heidelbergensis*, *Homo neanderthalensis* and *Homo sapiens*). Despite this, there are still more representations of men than women in the exhibition rooms at the Altamira Museum[737]. Similarly, at the Muséum des Sciences naturelles in Brussels, the illustration next to the entrance of the '*Galerie de l'Homme*' shows male and female specimens from several hominid groups. To explain the poster illustration, the museum's website states that it wanted to 'break the clichés' associated with human evolution: 'And while we were at it, we chose to break one last cliché by also using women to illustrate the evolution of Man (sic) [738]!' The iconographic effort is commendable, but the persistent use of the word 'Man', both in the title and in the explanation, to refer to the whole of humanity makes it somewhat shaky.

This situation is far from unusual. Maria Ángeles Querol Fernández studied the illustrations used in six Spanish museums refurbished or created after 2000, specifically the scenes in which at least two characters interact (whether in drawings, videos, educational comics or other media). The highest percentage of female representations is 33% for the Museum of Almeria. However, although many women are represented, only 50% are standing and 28% are kneeling to carry out various tasks in what Querol Fernández describes as 'a position of total humiliation stemming from artistic ideology', while only 10% of the men are represented in this position. The tasks carried out by the women in these images are not very varied, and are related to cooking and care, but paradoxically not to crafts (only 15%)[739]. Another problem encountered in the illustrations may be the sexualisation of the female characters[740].

What is known as 'overspecificity' is a sexist mechanism in the construction of knowledge that consists of presenting attitudes or tasks that could be both masculine and feminine as specific to a single sex[741]. For example, the participation of women in the production of Palaeolithic cave paintings was not considered for a very long time because of a tendency to consider that most material culture – and art in particular – had been produced by men[742]. But in the case of Palaeolithic paintings, this division between male/art and female/crafts associations has been frequently called into question since the early 2010s. The poster for the exhibition *Arte sin artistas. Una mirada al Paleolítico* (18 December 2012 – 7 April 2013), at the Museo Arqueológico Regional in Madrid, caused a stir in the scientific sphere because it showed a Palaeolithic woman with two young children painting the ceiling of the Altamira cave (see chapter 7, section 7.3 'Conventional and unconventional work')[743].

9.5. Integrating the gender dimension into exhibition rooms

Whether in the context of temporary exhibitions or in the exhibition rooms of archaeological museums, since the early 2000s the teams of many Spanish museums have begun to

737 Fatás Monforte & Martínez Llano 2016.

738 [Accessed 09 July 2022, https://web.archive.org/web/20220705132446/naturalsciences.be/fr/museum/exhibitions-view/771/2762/697] ('Et tant que nous y étions, nous avons choisi de casser un dernier cliché en utilisant aussi des femmes pour illustrer l'évolution de l'Homme (sic) !').

739 Querol Fernández 2016, 48 ('la postura de humillación total del ideario artístico').

740 Prados Torreira 2017, 35–36.

741 Maceira-Ochoa 2017, 80–81.

742 Prados Torreira 2016, 18.

743 Escobar García & Baquedano Pérez 2016,136–137.

reflect on the integration of gender issues, with the idea that 'archaeological museums can and must transmit an inclusive history that helps to make traditionally marginalised groups in society visible, in order to contribute to education for equality[744]'. This reflection is far from systematic and does not always concern all the departments within a single institution, but the efforts made, the teaching methods implemented and presented in the publications show the dynamism of this research theme in the Iberian Peninsula. In order to integrate the gender dimension into the exhibition rooms and to ensure an inclusive and non-discriminatory perspective, this notion must be present at the very conception of the exhibition, must participate in the selection of the objects, in the elaboration of the accompanying texts and in the production of the visual material[745].

For example, during the renovation of the Ancient Greece exhibition rooms at the National Archaeological Museum in Madrid, it was decided to completely overhaul the presentation of the collection of Greek vases[746]. Rather than presenting these objects in their typo-chronological development, the museum team has chosen to highlight themes that will enable visitors to understand the social, political and economic aspects of everyday life in ancient Greece. The exhibition is based around the words of Thales of Miletus, 'I thank the gods that I am a man and not an animal, that I am a man and not a woman, that I am a Greek and not a barbarian[747]', and therefore around the identity of man. The aim is to explain the exclusion of the other, the different, by contrasting the Greek man, the citizen, with the otherness of women, foreigners and elements linked to nature. Two parallel themes illustrate the separation of the domestic sphere associated with women, 'Oikos. The home', and the public sphere associated with men, 'Polis. The city'. 'The aim is to show everyday Greek life and to highlight, from a gender perspective, the construction of a social and political system that establishes and sanctions inequality and exclusion[748]'. In analysing social organisation and the manufacture of inequalities in Greek society, the museum team avoids the pitfalls of naturalisation and dehistoricisation, since 'there is often no systematic effort to show social organisation, relations and practices as the product of each society and each period [...], but as if they had always had the same character, the same meaning, the same organisation, etc., essentialising them and immobilising the social world[749]'. Similarly, the team at the Museo Arqueológico Regional de la Comunidad de Madrid (MAR), which opened its permanent exhibition in 2003, has given considerable thought to the subject. Particular attention was paid to the images, which depict both men and women, all in active attitudes, as well as children and the elderly. The museum's aim was to show visitors that the tools displayed in the showcases could have been used by any individual from ancient human groups[750].

The actions undertaken by the Spanish researchers are not limited to the study of museography and the reorganisation of exhibition rooms. Based on the observation that the iconographic material used for educational purposes (school textbooks, academic publications and publications for the general public, websites, etc.) is particularly limited when it comes to representing the role and activities of women in prehistoric and ancient societies, in 2007 they developed the *PastWomen - història material de las mujeres* project (https://www.pastwomen.net). The project presents an inclusive version of history and aims, among other things, to offer a repertoire of inclusive images that can be used in any type of dissemination of historical and archaeological research (Figure 9.1). The images, texts and objects analysed on the site cover five main themes: caring for community members, providing food, building a community, living spaces and everyday technologies[751]. In 2022, to celebrate the 15th anniversary of the project, a virtual exhibition, *Otras miradas al pasado* (https://otrasmiradas.pastwomen.net), set out to show the contribution of feminist and gender archaeology and to reaffirm the central role of women and minorities, who are often invisible, in the community life of prehistoric and ancient societies.

In France, the Musé·e·s association was founded in 2021 by a collective of eight young professionals working in museum institutions and the cultural world. They define themselves as a group of women 'committed to inclusive, feminist and intersectional museums'. The association's website offers resources for tackling issues of gender and intersectionality in museums and the cultural sector[752]. The association has also published a book in French in 2021 entitled *Guide pour un musée féministe*[753].

The impact of these and other initiatives around the world, whether in archaeological museums or other types of museum institutions, is real. An analysis of their approaches shows that integrating a gender perspective contributes 'to the empowerment and social participation of women, to raising social awareness of certain issues of concern to women, to promoting gender equality and to changing social patterns[754]'. Minorities also benefit from an approach centred on gender and the deconstruction of stereotypes[755].

744 Prados Torreira & López Ruiz 2017, 11 ('los museos arqueológicos pueden y deben transmitir una Historia inclusiva que ayude a visibilizar a los grupos tradicionalmente marginados de la sociedad, con el fin de contribuir a una educación en igualdad.').
745 Prados Torreira 2017.
746 Cabrera Bonet 2016.
747 Diogenes Laertius 1, 34.
748 Cabrera Bonet 2016, 105 ('El objetivo es mostrar la vida cotidiana griega y subrayar, desde una perspectiva de género, la construcción de un sistema social y político que establece y sanciona la desigualdad y la exclusión.').
749 Maceira-Ochoa 2017, 86 ('no hay una labor sistemática para mostrar los arreglos, relaciones y prácticas sociales como producto de cada sociedad y momento, más bien "se colocan en el pasado pero como si hubieran tenido desde entonces el mismo carácter, sentido, organización, etc., eternizándolas, inmovilizando el mundo social".').
750 Baquedano *et al.* 2017.
751 Sánchez Romero 2016, 32–35.
752 [Accessed 15 May 2023, https://associationmusees.wordpress.com/].
753 Association Musé·e·s 2022.
754 Maceira-Ochoa 2017, 89 ('al empoderamiento y la participación social de las mujeres, a la sensibilización social respecto a ciertos temas de interés para las mujeres, y a la promoción de la equidad de género y el cambio de modelos sociales').
755 Clayton & Hoskin 2020.

Figure 9.1. Example of an inclusive image available on the Pastwomen project website: flint and bone work in the Upper Palaeolithic. Source: Proyecto Pastwomen. Historia material de las mujeres. Illustration by Andrés Marín.

Where to start?

I. Algrain, 'Exposer l'humanité. Les musées d'archéologie face à la problématique du genre, entre surexposition des hommes et sous-exposition des femmes. Réflexions à partir de l'Espagne et de la Belgique', *in Les Cahiers de Muséologie* 3, 2023 [online: https://popups.uliege.be/2406–7202/index.php?id=1387].

L. Maceira-Ochoa, '¿Vestigios para un futuro igualitario? Pensar la educación en los museos arqueológicos desde una perspectiva feminista', *in* L. Prados Torreira & C. López Ruiz (eds.), *Museos arqueológicos y género. Educando en igualdad*, UAM Ediciones, 2017, 69–103.

L. Prados Torreira, 'Why Is It Necessary to Include the Gender Perspective in Archaeological Museums? Some Examples from Spanish Museums', *in Museum Worlds: Advances in Research* 4, 18–32.

L. Prados Torreira, '¿Abogan los museos arqueológicos del siglo XXI por una educación en igualdad?', *in* Prados Torreira Lourdes & López Ruiz Clara (eds.), *Museos arqueológicos y género. Educando en igualdad*, Madrid, UAM Ediciones, 2017, 23–49.

Part Three

The place of women and minorities in the profession

10

Sexism

10.1. Joan Gero and 'the woman-at-home ideology'

In 1985, the American archaeologist Joan Gero published 'Socio-Politics and the Woman-at-Home Ideology'. In the introduction to this article, she stated:

> 'In this case study, we look not only at how unexamined assumptions about gender structure our interpretations of the past, but also at how these assumptions underwrite the gender relations among archaeologists today to produce in our research conclusions and in our professional lives, the same society, past and present[756].'

She added that archaeology is a conservative field dominated by White middle-class men where the image of a certain masculinity prevails. For this reason, archaeologists – whom she calls 'the cowboys of science' in her introduction – have been slow to adopt a feminist approach in their analyses. She then drew a parallel between the stereotypical image of the Palaeolithic hunter (active, robust, exploratory) portrayed in archaeological studies and the model of masculinity (dominant, destructive, conquering) promoted on excavation sites. Finally, she looked at women, who until then had been either absent from the studies or relegated to a passive role in the home. She noted that, like these women of the past, women archaeologists tend to be relegated to the laboratory, the museum or the dig house, where they carry out tasks that receive little or no recognition, such as receiving, cleaning, sorting and cataloguing archaeological material – what she calls 'archaeological housework'.

To support this reflection and examine the way in which the gendered division of labour manifests itself in archaeology, she used a series of data: 1) current fieldwork in Central America reported in the journal *American Antiquity*; 2) doctoral theses listed in *Dissertation Abstracts International*; 3) and the distribution of funding from the National Sciences Foundation. She noted that the majority of archaeologists carrying out archaeological research in Central America were men. They were also more likely to complete a thesis involving fieldwork and received more funding to carry out their research, both outside and in the field. Women were more likely to obtain funding from the National Sciences Foundation if their project did not involve fieldwork.

By providing the first quantitative data on the subject, Joan Gero has paved the way for future publications on the place of women and minorities within the profession.

To date, work on sexism in archaeology has gone through two main phases. From 1985 to 2000, studies focused more on female archaeologists and their research within the history of the discipline, how they were made invisible in this history, the gendered division of labour, pay inequalities, differences in promotion, in obtaining a degree or a scholarship, and disparities in publications. From the 2000s onwards, attention has been focusing on new themes such as menstruation, pregnancy and maternity, sexist and sexual violence and masculinities.

10.2. Invisible women in archaeology: the Matilda effect

Theorised in 1993 by science historian Margaret W. Rossiter, the 'Matilda effect' refers to the systematic denial or minimisation of women's contributions to science. It complements the 'Mathieu effect' described in 1968 by the American sociologist Robert K. Merton as 'a kind of 'halo effect' experienced by well-known scientists who find work attributed to themselves which they did not do (or did not do totally alone)[757]'. In her article translated into French in 2003 by Irène Jami, Rossiter develops:

> 'Although Dean Keith Simonton has recently stated that scientific reputations once made persist for generations, this is often not the case for women in science. Not only have those unrecognized in their own time generally remained so, but others that were well-known in their day have since been obliterated from history, either by laziness or inertia, or by historians with definite axes to grind[758].'

Women scientists tend to disappear from history (Figure 10.1). Their contributions to research are forgotten, invisible, or relegated to acknowledgements and footnotes. Their work is attributed to or monopolised by their male colleagues, their spouses/collaborators or their research supervisors. In archaeology, a relatively famous case is that of Mary Ross Ellingson (1906–1993). Mary Ross was an archaeologist who worked on the site of Olynthus in Greece during the 1930s. She was responsible for supervising the workers and for photography. She was also involved in the study of terracotta figurines, the subject of her master's thesis, which she later developed in her doctoral dissertation. After completing her thesis, she married Rudolph Conrad Ellingson and left the academic world. She returned to teaching in the 1960s. Officially,

[756] Gero 1985, 343.

[757] Rossiter 2003 ('l'espèce d' 'effet de halo' qui fait attribuer à des scientifiques célèbres des travaux qu'ils n'ont pas (ou pas entièrement eux-mêmes) réalisés.').

[758] Rossiter 2003.

Figure 10.1. An unknown woman working on an archaeological excavation with the Swedish Expedition in Cyprus, 1927–1931. Excavation, documentation, archaeologist, Swedish Cyprus Expedition. Photograph by Lindros, John - The Museum of Mediterranean and Near Eastern Antiquities, Sweden – CC0.

Mary Ross's work has never been published. Her supervisor, David Moore Robinson, plagiarised her work and published it under his own name. Ross's dissertation forms volume VII of Robinson's *Excavations at Olynthus* series, her thesis the opening chapters of volume XIV. She is mentioned briefly in the introductions to both volumes. In the acknowledgements to volume XIV, Robinson writes:

> 'I thank especially my former students and members of my staff, Mary Ross (now Mrs. R. C. Ellingson of Evansville, Ind.), Eleanor Lay (now Mrs. Arthur Ross of Syracuse, New-York), and I owe much to my deceased daughter (Mrs. Wilson)[759].'

This plagiarism was highlighted in 2014 by Alan Kaiser, who also indicated that Robinson had not only stolen Ellingson's work but also, to a lesser extent, that of three other students: George Hanfmann, Eleonore Ross and Meredith Vestling[760].

[759] Kaiser 2014, 145.
[760] Kaiser 2014, 174–180.

In archaeology, marriage could be synonymous with disappearance from the academic world and/or the field, as in the case of Mary Ross Ellingson, or with the invisibility of the work carried out. This was particularly true in the 19th and early 20th centuries, when there were few women in archaeology[761]. Opting for celibacy so as not to hinder their professional careers was the solution adopted by archaeologists such as the Frenchwomen Madeleine Colani (1866–1943), who excavated over 130 sites in East Asia[762], and Suzanne Cassou de Saint-Marthurin (1900–1975), who studied the Palaeolithic art of Angles-sur-l'Anglin with the British archaeologist Dorothy Garrod[763]. However, overcoming social pressure and remaining single did not always save women from invisibility. British Egyptologist Margaret Murray (1863–1963) is a case in point. She was one of the first women archaeologists to work at University College London, led a series of excavations and published numerous works on Egyptology, but she was still overshadowed by her colleague William Flinders Petrie[764].

Women married to archaeologists are not unusual either, even if their influence and investment in their husbands' careers are presented as anecdotal or simply go unrecognised. This is particularly true of Hilda Petrie (1871–1956), the wife of William Flinders Petrie[765]. She took part in his excavations in Egypt, produced his drawings and edited his texts, but most of her work went unrecognised and her husband rarely mentioned her name in his publications. Similarly, Tessa Wheeler (1893–1936), Mortimer Wheeler's wife, co-directed a number of excavations with her husband[766]. She was responsible for the organisation, finances and cataloguing of the material, and was even considered by some to be a better researcher than her husband. Yet her work received little recognition. Despite her pioneering work in palaeopalynology, Arlette Leroi-Gourhan (1913–2005) also remained in the shadow of her husband, André Leroi-Gourhan[767]. She worked as director of the pollen analysis laboratory at the Musée de l'Homme in Paris, which she set up and developed, but had no official post or funding. Her husband, who was in charge of prehistory at the CNRS at the time, asked her not to apply to the same institution so as not to be accused of nepotism. They only co-authored one article together.

10.3. Rehabilitating and promoting: biographies of women archaeologists

Archaeology is an androcentric discipline, both in terms of interpreting the material remains of the past and in reconstructing its own history. The major syntheses, the most popular historiographies in archaeology and the

[761] Algrain 2022b; Algrain & Mary 2023.
[762] Coudart 1998, 68–69.
[763] Coudart 1998, 71.
[764] Champion 1998, 191; Whitehouse 2013, 120–127. See also Sheppard 2013.
[765] Champion 1998, 178.
[766] Champion 1998, 178.
[767] Coudart 1998, 73.

biographical collections are mostly written by men and focus on research carried out by men[768]. In these books, women seem at best to have played only a minor role, at worst to be absent from the texts. In order to combat this marginalisation and invisibilisation of women's contributions, a whole process of rehabilitation was needed. From the 1990s onwards, researchers began to write biographies of women who had contributed to archaeology both before and after its recognition as a scientific discipline. Marie Louise Stig Sørensen has shown that women have played a part in the history of archaeology from its very beginnings. She put forward a series of arguments demonstrating the need to highlight women and their work: to identify role models for future generations of archaeologists, to gather information on the distribution of gendered roles within the profession at any given time, and to show how sexism affects the production of knowledge[769].

According to Elisabeth Arwill-Nordbladh, a biography 'can enlighten the process of how science is fabricated, how scientific knowledge is established, and the character of that knowledge[770]'. At the same time, it provides an opportunity to pay tribute to a leading scientist and his or her achievements. In archaeology, these biographies take the form of collective works[771] or articles[772] on different personalities; monographs or articles focusing on a single archaeologist[773]; summary biographies[774] or online videos[775]. These publications are written and produced by archaeology professionals and non-professionals alike, but all have the same aim: to raise the profile of little-known or invisible figures in archaeology. Research into the role of women in the history of archaeology clearly shows that women pioneers in archaeology, some of whom have been working on excavation sites since the 18th century[776], have had to contend with forms of sexism that are still prevalent today. Obstacles prevented them from taking an active part in archaeological digs from the end of the 19th century, when archaeology became more professional. The archaeological site was seen as a male domain, and the tasks that women were given were relegated to the menial roles of housekeeping, looking after the workers, cataloguing and drawing artefacts, revising manuscripts and so on.

As a result, women were often relegated to the dig houses to carry out the delicate and meticulous work of cataloguing archaeological material while the men developed their brute strength to dig on site (or rather supervised workers who digged on site) (Figure 10.2). They were confined to studying so-called feminine material (jewellery, textiles, terracotta, etc.), while the men wrote general summaries or concentrated on architecture, sculpture and so-called masculine objects such as weapons. Women published little, or mainly in local and national journals, whereas men published internationally. They were often employed in museums, while men held the majority of academic positions. They were torn between their role as mothers and their role as researchers and fieldworkers[777].

Figure 10.2. Archaeological excavations southeast of Borg Church at the ruins of Borgholm Castle. Three medieval settlement levels were identified, dating from the 12th century to the end of the 14th century, 1961. Source: Excavated memories From Skedemosse to Sandby Borg. Editors Kjell-Håkan Arnell & Ludvig Papmehl-Dufay, text by Stibéus. Bernving, Allan – Kalmar County Museum, Sweden – Public Domain.

More recently, the desire to highlight the work of women in archaeology has moved into the virtual world. The *Trowel Blazers* project was originally a Tumblr created in 2013 by four researchers: Brenna R. Hassett, Suzanne Pilaar Birch, Rebecca Wragg Sykes and Victoria Herridge. It later took the form of a participatory digital platform aimed at increasing the visibility of women in the fields of archaeology, geology and palaeontology by writing and sharing biographies on social networks (Twitter, Facebook)[778]. The profiles put forward by the project are varied and no longer limited to the United States and Europe[779]. In 2020, the *Pacific Matildas: Finding the*

768 Diaz-Andreu & Sørensen 1998, 1.
769 Sørensen 1998, 31–56.
770 Arwill-Nordbladh 2008, 139.
771 See Reyman 1992; Claassen 1994; Diaz-Andreu & Sørensen 1997; Koch & Mertens 2002; Cohen & Joukowsky 2004; Fries & Gutsmiedl-Schümann 2013.
772 Among others, Bender 1991; Claassen 1993; Nelson 1991; Chilton 1994; Weedman 2001.
773 For example, Gran-Aymerich & Gran-Aymerich 1991; Smith 2000; Howell 2010; Pope & Davies 2023; Pope & Davies 2025.
774 For example, TrowelBlazers [Accessed 23 August 2021, https://trowelblazers.com/]; Breaking Ground: Women in Old World Archaeology website [Accessed 23 August 2021, https://www.brown.edu/Research/Breaking_Ground/].
775 For example, on YouTube: La Prof 'Gertrude Bell - Gentes Dames Badass #6' [Accessed 23 August 2021, https://youtu.be/Gv6etRwpWMs].
776 Hill 2016, 159.
777 Hill 2016, 163–166.
778 TrowelBlazers Tumblr [Accessed 27 August 2021, http://trowelblazers.tumblr.com/]; TrowelBlazers website [Accessed 27 August 2021, https://trowelblazers.com/].
779 See the 'Women of African Archaeology' series, referencing the lives and works of Intisar Soghayroun el-Zein, Nthabiseng Mokoena and Sada Mire.

women in the history of Pacific archaeology project aimed to document the lives and research of the first women to carry out archaeological work in Oceania from the end of the 19th to the middle of the 20th century[780].

It should be noted that all the works cited in this section focus almost exclusively on White women from the middle and upper classes. However, Black women were not absent from excavation sites in the early 20th century (see section 10.5.2, 'Irene Mound (Georgia, USA): at the intersection of sexism, racism and classism').

10.4. A glass ceiling stronger than steel

The glass ceiling represents 'the set of visible and invisible obstacles that separate women from the top of professional and organizational hierarchies[781]'. A series of studies have shown that women are increasingly rare as one moves up the hierarchy (the so-called 'leaky pipeline' phenomenon). They also show that women are still in the minority in management positions to which stereotypically masculine qualities are attached (authority, composure, charisma)[782]. Archaeology has not been spared this phenomenon. Researchers based in the United States, Australia and Norway were the first to investigate the place of women in archaeology[783].

These publications include the collective work *Equity Issues for Women in Archaeology* edited by Margaret C. Nelson, Sarah M. Nelson and Alison Wylie. Published in 1994, it grew out of a round-table discussion on women in archaeology organised by Alison Wylie and Diane Gifford-Gonzalez in 1991 and two sessions at the annual meeting of the Association of American Archaeologists in 1992[784]. The aim of this book is to document inequalities and gender bias within the profession. The topics covered range from differences in salary, specialisation, obtaining a position, a promotion or a fellowship, to difficulties encountered in different working environments and disparities in publication. The thirty or so articles cover the United States, Australia, South America, including Argentina, and a number of European countries, including Spain and Norway. In the preface, however, the editors of the book stress its lack of diversity:

> 'The demographic of contributors to this volume, and of the subjects they describe, reflects the discipline as a whole: white, middle class, heterosexual, First World, and ablebodied[785].'

It is, however, the first book to list the various ways in which gender inequalities manifest themselves in archaeological practice.

10.4.1. In the United States

Since the 1970s, a great deal of research has been carried out in the United States on the issue of gender inequality within the profession[786]. In particular, publications focusing on the impact of the glass ceiling on women's careers have provided an overview of the situation.

Between 1976 and 1986, a majority of women took archaeology courses, and they generally obtained better marks. They also graduated in greater numbers than men. The trend is reversed thereafter: only 36% of women obtain their doctorate in archaeology[787] with less funding than their male colleagues[788]. They are even less likely to obtain a post-doctoral contract and an academic position[789], which is often part-time and in less prestigious universities, where they are also paid less than men for an equivalent job[790]. Finally, a minority of women are appointed as professors, while the majority opt for a non-academic career[791]. Outside academia, women are in the majority but are still fewer in managerial and supervisory positions[792]. Between 1979 and 1980, of the 117 excavation projects in Central America listed by *American Antiquity*, 91 were directed by men and 26 by women, 9 of whom co-directed with a man (who was often their husband)[793]. This general trend continued into the 2000s. At university, women are paid on average 5.5% less than men for the same work; in the public and private sectors, they are still paid between 11.2 and 13.7% less than their male colleagues for the same job[794]. Men predominate in management positions, and women are more likely to hold temporary positions[795].

10.4.2. In Australia

The first study to examine the place of women in Australian archaeology dates from the late 1980s[796]. The first collective work to examine the issue in part was published in 1993. Edited by Hilary du Cros and Laurajane Smith, *Women in Archaeology: A Feminist Critique* was drawn from the first colloquium on women in archaeology held at Charles Sturt University in 1991. In addition to occasional articles, two general surveys of the profession were also conducted in 2005 and 2010[797].

---

780 Dotte-Sarout 2021.
781 Laufer 2004, 118.
782 Bereni *et al.* 2020, 259.
783 In the United States: Stewart 1977; McLemore & Reynolds 1979; Wildesen 1980; Gero 1983; Gero 1985; Kramer & Stark 1988; Stark 1991; Ford 1992; Nelson *et al.* 1994; Claassen 1994. In Australia: Beck & Head 1989; du Cros & Smith 1993; Balme et Beck 1994; Beck 1994. In Norway: Holm-Olsen & Mandt 1974; Mandt & Naess 1986; Lillehammer 1988; Dommasnes 1992.
784 Sessions *Equity Issues for Women in Archaeology* et *Women Archaeologists' Equity*.
785 Nelson *et al.* 1994, xi.
786 Mary 2020.
787 Kramer & Stark 1994, 19.
788 Kramer & Stark 1994, 17–18; Nelson 1994, 199; Wildesen 1980, 5; Yellen 1991.
789 Kramer & Stark 1994, 18–20.
790 Stark 1991, 188.
791 Kramer & Stark 1994, 18.
792 Nelson & Nelson 1994, 231; Zeder 1997, 189.
793 Gero 1994, 40.
794 Association Research Inc. 2005, appendice C.
795 Neal 2008, 32–34.
796 Beck & Head 1989.
797 Beck 1994; Smith & du Cros 1994; Smith & Burke 2006; Ulm *et al.* 2013.

During the 1990s, women made up over 50% of archaeology students and 40% of doctoral students, but they held only 22% of academic posts. These positions are generally at the lower end of the academic hierarchy, which means that salaries are low[798]. In 2005, more women were working in archaeology in the academic world. They held 61% of research posts, but only 31% were appointed as lecturers[799]. Seven women (compared with 21 men) hold the positions of associate professor and professor. The Australian National University, for example, has no female professors. Six of the country's 13 universities have only one woman professor[800]. In 2010, the trend is continuing: younger women are more numerous within the discipline, while older men are more numerous in stable positions of responsibility. Most of the figures relate to universities, but it should be noted that although women are in the majority in the private sector, they do not occupy more senior positions[801].

10.4.3. In Norway

In Norway, the first article on the subject dates back to 1974[802]. However, it was not until the 1980s that Norwegian archaeologists really got to grips with the issue, as evidenced by the creation of the organisation Kvinner i arkeologi i Norge (Women in Archaeology in Norway) in 1985 by archaeologists Jenny-Rita Naess and Gro Mandt[803], and the proliferation of articles on the subject, first in Norwegian[804] and then in English[805] in order to reach the international community.

Between the 1950s and 1970s, Norwegian women already outnumbered their male counterparts at university. They obtained excellent marks and sometimes pursued other studies at the same time in order to secure their professional future as best they could. Once they graduated, they managed to get jobs in museums or in the field. A few even managed to become honorary professors. According to Dommasnes and her colleagues, the fact that the emergence and professionalisation of archaeology in Norway are strongly linked to museums may to some extent explain why many women were able to enter the discipline very early on[806]. Work in museum institutions was less well paid and less prestigious than that of a university professor, and was therefore considered acceptable for women. However, the situation was far from ideal. By 1970, women graduates had all found jobs in archaeology, but these were generally temporary and/or menial positions. They were also absent from management positions in the museum and university sectors[807]. At the beginning of the 1990s, the situation changed: of the 11 professorships in archaeology, 5 were held by women; 2 of the 5 positions as archaeological museum directors were held by women[808]. Despite this, women still found it more difficult than their male colleagues to climb the hierarchical ladder. Most of them worked part-time and on fixed-term contracts[809].

Today, women are still in the majority in Norwegian archaeology. A recent study showed that, in 2010, 75% of archaeology graduates were women[810]. They also held 63% of jobs in archaeology. Despite a favourable political environment for women, pay differentials persisted. Women aged 41 and over earned only 89.1% of what their male colleagues earn for the same work. Disparities also persisted at the level of the hierarchy: men, despite being in the minority within the profession, occupied 75% of management positions in the private sector.

10.4.4. Across the globe

From the 1990s onwards, other countries also began to address this issue, including Canada, Denmark, Germany, Greece, Poland, Spain and the United Kingdom[811]. Generally speaking, the conclusions of the studies carried out there are the same as those shared by Sarah M. Nelson and Margareth C. Nelson[812]. More women than men graduate in archaeology and generally do better, but fewer obtain a PhD and go on to full-time employment. Even when they are in the majority in the profession, they are in the minority in positions of responsibility, both in academia and in the public and private sectors. They progress much more slowly in the profession than their male colleagues. They also receive less funding to carry out their research and are paid less for equal work.

In 2014, the *Discovering the Archaeologists of Europe* survey took stock of the situation in archaeology in 21 countries and provided a series of data on the number of archaeologists, their age, gender and whether they are disabled. It also provided information on the types of contract and average salaries. Unfortunately, the age/gender/disability parameters were not systematically cross-referenced with the data on contract types and salaries. On average, there were slightly more women (50.7%) than men in European archaeology in 2014[813]. In some countries, they even represented a large majority. Greece, for example, is the European country with the highest proportion of women (76.1%). There, women

798 Beck 1994, 101.
799 Smith & Burke 2006, 15.
800 Smith & Burke 2006, 15: these are the universities of Adelaide, James Cook, Macquarie, New England, Queensland and Wollongong.
801 Ulm *et al.* 2013, 35–37.
802 Holm-Olsen et Mandt, 1974.
803 Dommasnes 1992, 7; Dommasnes & Montón-Subías 2012, 371.
804 Kleppe 1985; Mandt & Naess 1986; Lillehammer 1988.
805 Dommasnes & Kleppe 1988; Dommasnes 1992; Engelstad *et al.* 1994; Dommasnes *et al.* 1998.
806 Dommasnes *et al.* 1998, 109.
807 Dommasnes 1992, 2–3; Dommasnes *et al.* 1998, 115, 117; Kleppe 1985, 63.
808 Dommasnes *et al.* 1998, 105.
809 Dommasnes 1992, 8.
810 Lazar *et al.* 2014.
811 Germany: Kästner *et al.* 1998. Canada: Kelley & Hill 1994. Denmark: Fonnesbeck-Sandberg *et al.* 1972; Jogersen 1998. Spain: Diaz-Andreu 1998; Diaz-Andreu & Gallego 1994; session on women in archaeology *Reunión de Arqueología Teórica* in 1992. Greece: Kokkinidou & Nikolaidou 1998. Poland: Bialecka & Bochenek 1981; Janik & Zawadzka 1998. United Kingdom: Hamilton 2014; Morris 1992.
812 Nelson & Nelson 1994, 229–235.
813 Aitchison *et al.* 2014, 27.

headed 84% of archaeological services. In universities, there were 38 women professors and associate professors (compared with 34 men)[814]. Conversely, in countries such as Poland, men were still in the majority (61.5%). Women were under-represented in academia and the private sector, but they were more numerous in public institutions such as museums and foundations[815]. In academia, only 35% of women completed their doctoral thesis (compared to 55% of men), and 14 women (compared to 59 men) were professors of archaeology[816].

France and the French-speaking community of Belgium (Wallonia and the Brussels-Capital region; Flanders did submit its figures) are the two major absentees from this report. An overview of the situation is provided in 2020[817]. No specific study has been carried out, but some information can be gleaned from an article and more general reports on gender equality in the field of culture in France. In 2018–2019, women are in the majority among doctoral students (107 out of 185) and lecturers (11 out of 17), but are in the minority among professors (3 out of 13) in the archaeology doctoral school at the University of Paris 1[818]. At the Institut national de la recherche archéologique préventive (Inrap), the majority of management positions are held by men. Between 2015 and 2017, 72% of the heads of territorial commercial archaeology departments were men[819]. In 2018, 36% of operation managers were women. There are also pay inequalities, with women being paid an average of 3% less than their male colleagues as operation managers and an average of 4% less as operation technicians[820].

10.5. Glass walls and gendered division of labour

Complementary to the glass ceiling described above, the **glass walls** phenomenon is defined as the mechanism 'favouring exclusion and the differentiation of opportunities, which varies according to the economic sector[821]'. To take an example formulated by Paola Cappellin, 'when women manage to reach a high level on the hierarchical ladder, they in fact find themselves in sectors or departments considered to be of less central importance, with a less strategic role in the organisation of the company (human resources or administration)[822]'. In archaeology, this horizontal segregation can be seen both in the **distribution of work** and the **subjects studied**.

10.5.1. The prestige of the dig

Joan Gero returns to the subject of the professional and social prestige associated with fieldwork, which is all the more important when it comes to managing an excavation site[823] :

> '[...] archeology is excavation or it is nothing. Status in archeology still accrues primarily from running field excavations ("big digs") rather than from the analysis of archeological materials, and even the great theorists or grand synthesizers must serve at least an apprenticeship as a field archeologist in order to earn their bona fides. [...] archeological research that does not include the collection of primary data is subtly evaluated as less compelling, less original work, and the non-digging archeologist is considered a less important contributor or even (ironically!) a lesser scholar[824].'

In the United States, she notes that between 1967 and 1979, almost 75% of the funding allocated by the National Science Foundation went to field projects. The prestige of the field goes hand in hand with sexism:

> 'Not only is the "real" archeologist an excavating archeologist but he is also a MALE. Fieldwork, in fact, embodies the central cultural ideals of male roles in our society: active, aggressive, exploratory, out-of-doors, dominant, managerial, risk-taking, and bringing-home-the-goodies[825].'

Of the 74.9% of funding distributed by the National Science Foundation to field-related projects, Gero also points out that 93% went to men.

10.5.2. Gendered division of labour

The stereotype of 'hard-drinking cowboys[826]' or 'men in pith helmets[827]' is a hard one. Men and women do not generally occupy the same positions, and do not get involved in archaeology in the same way[828].

These disparities were present from the very beginning of the institutionalisation of the discipline. For a long time, women were excluded from fieldwork, whether implicitly or not. Many site managers felt that women were a distraction to the other male members of the team and did not belong on site[829]. The most explicit example is the case of the archaeologist Harriet Boyd Hawkes (1871–1945), who was repeatedly forbidden by the director of the American School of Athens to undertake excavations on mainland Greece because she was a woman[830]. One

814 Initiative for Heritage Conservancy 2014, 13–15.
815 Liibert *et al.* 2014, 39.
816 Liibert *et al.* 2014, 40.
817 Mary 2020.
818 Procopiou 2019.
819 Ministère de la Culture 2021, 38, table 28.
820 *Ibid.*, 61, table 84.
821 Cappellin 2010, 36 ('favorisant l'exclusion et la différenciation des chances, variable selon le secteur économique').
822 Cappellin 2010, 36 ('lorsque les femmes arrivent à atteindre un haut niveau sur l'échelle hiérarchique, elles se retrouvent en fait dans des secteurs ou des services considérés comme ayant une importance moins centrale, un rôle moins stratégique dans l'organisation de l'entreprise (ressources humaines ou administration).').

823 For this part, see Gero 1994, 38–40.
824 Gero 1994, 38.
825 Gero 1994, 40.
826 Gero 1985.
827 Beck 1994, 99.
828 Among others Gero 1994; Hays-Gilpin 2000; Kramer & Stark 1988; Moser 1996; Mary *et al.* 2019; Wylie 1994.
829 Wylie 1994, 67; Hays-Gilpin 2000, 91.
830 Dìaz-Andreu & Sørensen 1998, 8; Picazo 1998, 202; Sørensen 2000, 30.

of the first women to carry out archaeological research, Hanna Rydh, was an exception, as she was asked to direct excavations in her native Sweden as early as 1916[831], one of the countries where the situation for female archaeologists was the least unfavourable (Figure 10.3). Some of the forerunners of European archaeology, such as Gertrude Bell (1868–1926), opted for a career abroad in order to get round the (in)formal ban[832]. Yet, a few male archaeologists encouraged women to work in the field. As early as the late 1920s, Alfred V. Kidder allowed women onto his excavation sites and trained them in fieldwork alongside other male students. In 1929, he also appointed women (Isabel Kelly, Frances Watkins and Eva Homer) as directors of excavations at the Tecolote site[833].

Irene Mound (Georgia, USA): at the intersection of sexism, racism and classism

The prehistoric site of Irene Mound was excavated between 1937 and 1940. Although the project was led by four men, the work was actually carried out by women: 32 White women and 87 Black women. This is one of the first examples of a site in the United States where Afro-descendant women took part in archaeological excavations[834]. The names of all the White women involved in the project are known. They were responsible for analysing and interpreting the material remains, making drawings and writing excavation reports. Catherine McCann, one of the few women to have actually studied archaeology at university, also co-wrote the final report[835]. White women were not allowed to work in the field, unlike Black women, who at the time were not recognised as women but rather as cheap labour[836]. Almost all their names are unknown to us. One of these workers is called Gussie White[837]. Her name and her story have come down to us thanks to the testimony of her son, John White, in an audio recording made by Gail Whalen[838]. In the field, these women carried out a variety of tasks[839]: cutting down trees, digging trenches, clearing the land, excavating graves, collecting material remains, and so on. This work received little or no recognition. For equivalent work, they were paid less than their male Black colleagues working on other sites, who were themselves paid less than their White colleagues[840].

Figure 10.3. Ulf Erik Hagberg and possibly Margareta Beskow are conducting archaeological surveys in Bredsättra parish, 1970. Bernving, Allan - Kalmar County Museum, Sweden - Public Domain.

In addition to the field, women were generally not welcome within archaeological societies and universities. For example, it was not until 1939 that Dorothy Garrod (1892–1968) became the first woman to hold a professorship at Cambridge University[841]. On the other hand, it was easier for women to gain access to museums, which were perceived as less prestigious and requiring feminine qualities. In Spain, for example, it was very difficult for women to enter the academic world and receive a salary between 1939 and 1960, but it was easier for them to enter museums, where the pay was lower[842].

This situation continues to this day (see section 10.4, 'A glass ceiling stronger than steel'). In Australia, women tend to be invited to speak at conferences and symposia less often than men[843]. In France, the report by the Observatoire de l'égalité entre femmes et hommes dans la culture et la communication (Observatory for equality between women and men in culture and communication) tells us that fieldwork is still predominantly a male domain: 60% of operations technicians and 64% of operations managers are men[844]. Women are more likely to be found in the laboratory: 63% of specialists are women[845].

This division of labour is accompanied by a hierarchical structure. The tasks performed by women are generally devalued and therefore rarely paid. This low level of recognition is linked to the fact that these tasks are not considered to be the result of an apprenticeship, but

[831] Arwill-Nordbladh 1998, 157.
[832] Dìaz-Andreu & Sørensen 1998, 14.
[833] Hays-Gilpin 2000, 92.
[834] Battle-Baptiste 2016, 68.
[835] Claassen 1993, 92, 96–98.
[836] Claassen 1993, 96, 103.
[837] Claassen 1993, 107.
[838] The recording can be listened to on this site: [Accessed 24 March 2021, http://www.siarmstrong.edu/Irene/oral.html].
[839] Claassen 1993, 98.
[840] Rashid & Grieve s.d.

[841] Dìaz-Andreu & Sørensen 1998, 16.
[842] Dìaz Andreu & Sanz Gallego 1994, 122.
[843] Smith & Burke 2006, 20.
[844] Ministère de la Culture et de la Communication 2019, 56, table 67.
[845] Mary 2020.

rather are linked to the supposedly 'natural' qualities of women, such as patience, attention to detail, tidiness and care. Women are expected to do more interior work, because it is sedentary, 'passive' and carried out in a safe environment[846]. Some researchers, such as Liv Helga Dommasnes and Joan Gero, link these tasks to domestic work[847]. These essential but invisible activities include cleaning, encoding, descriptions, drawings, excavation site accounting, administrative management, organising collections, preparing lessons and correcting copies.

When they have the opportunity to participate fully in excavation sites, women are sometimes listed as 'assistants' but not as 'researchers' or 'archaeologists'[848]. They are not involved in the thinking and decision-making processes[849]. A gendered division of labour within excavation sites is also highlighted by the sharing of English- and French-language accounts produced by three projects: Every Dig Sexism (created in 2015 by Hanna Cobb and Catherine Poucher), Paye ta Truelle (created in 2017 by Laura Mary) and the Archéo-Sexisme exhibition (opening in 2019 and organised by Laura Mary, Béline Pasquini and Ségolène Vandevelde). This unequal distribution of tasks is evident from the very first contact archaeology students have with the field during the 'field schools': the male students do the heavy work with pickaxe and American shovel; the female students carry and empty the buckets and wheelbarrows, clean up the area before photography, sieve and manage the dig house (cooking, tidying up). This discrimination 'results in partial training for male and female students, which helps to reproduce (and not to call into question) the gendered division of tasks currently observed in archaeology, whether in the commercial sector, at university or on other work sites[850]'.

10.5.3. Disparities in research topics

> 'Former UNM student Florence Lister recalls two pieces of advice from Florence Hawley, her mentor, in the early 1940s: to break into the discipline, a woman must "find some aspect of the work that the men did not enjoy and then to become a specialist in it", and "Your best bet is to marry an archaeologist". Lister became a pottery specialist and married a National Park Service archaeologist she met at the Chaco Canyon field school[851].'

The question of whether archaeologists take up certain types of subject because of their gender or gender expectations is a complex one. The exclusion of women from the field and from academia seems in any case to have played a role in the way women became involved in archaeology. From the very beginning of the discipline, women carried out research on subjects traditionally rejected by men because they were considered feminine (and therefore less prestigious), such as textiles, jewellery, ceramics and artistic representations[852]. There are also more women working on periods neglected by their male colleagues. In Norway, for example, women were quick to take up research themes associated with the Iron Age and the Middle Ages[853]. In Australia, the regional survey method was developed by women, while major stratigraphic excavations were mainly carried out by men[854]. In the United States, according to publications in the journal *Historical Archaeology* between 1967 and 1990, women were more involved in ceramic studies and the analysis of beads and faunal remains than in general on-site studies and theoretical subjects[855]. Generally speaking, women were more likely to receive funding if their research topics corresponded to what was expected of them within the patriarchy, i.e. working indoors and on a very specific type of material[856].

However, despite the work carried out by Joan Gero as early as 1985, there has been very little research into this issue. It was not until 2019 that researcher Laura Heath-Stout took up the subject again. In the conclusion to her doctoral thesis, she notes that for the United States:

> 'Straight white cisgender men conduct a plurality or majority of archaeological research across almost every subfield, region, method, and topic[857].'

The only two exceptions are iconographic analyses and subjects related to gender archaeology and feminist archaeology[858].

10.6. Publications and gender inequality

Another way in which researchers try to measure gender inequalities within the profession is through publications. The majority of these studies originate in the United States and therefore focus mainly on American articles, but some occasional information can also be found in Australian, British, Spanish, Polish and Norwegian publications[859]. In 1994, the main archaeological journal in Australia (*Archaeology in Oceania*) had only 35% female authors[860]. Before 1980, few women published articles in two of Spain's leading journals (*Zephyrus* and *Congresos Nacionales de Arqueología*)[861]. A more global study shows that between 1970 and 2020 only 30% of women published articles in Spanish scientific archaeological journals, with a slight increase in their number over time[862]. Between 1945 and 1997, the vast majority of authors in the four main African

846 Gero 1994, 41.
847 Dommasnes *et al.* 1998; Gero 1985.
848 Arwill-Nordbladh 1998, vi.
849 Wylie 1994, 67.
850 Mary *et al.* 2019, 216 ('a pour conséquence une formation partielle des étudiants et des étudiantes, laquelle participe à reproduire (et à ne pas remettre en question) la répartition genrée des tâches actuellement observée en archéologie, que ce soit dans le secteur préventif, à l'université ou sur des chantiers associatifs.').
851 Hays-Gilpin 2000, 91.

852 Diàz-Andreu & Sørensen 1998, 9–10.
853 Sørensen 2000, 30; Sørensen 2013, 397.
854 Moser 1995.
855 Victor & Beaudry 1992; Beaudry 1994.
856 Gero 1985.
857 Heath-Stout 2019, 204.
858 Heath-Stout 2019, 204.
859 Australia: Beck 1994; Spain: Diàz-Andreu & Sanz Gallego 1994; Díaz-Andreu 1998, 139; Pastor Quiles & Mateo Corredor 2022. Poland: Janik & Zawadzka 1998. Norway: Dommasnes *et al.* 1998, 118–119; United Kingdom: Hanscam & witcher 2022.
860 Beck 1994, 100.
861 Diàz-Andreu & Sanz Gallego 1994, 124–125.
862 Pastor Quiles & Mateo Corredor 2022.

archaeological journals were men: 84.5% for the *South African Archaeological Bulletin*, 84% for *Azania*, 95.7% for the *West African Journal of Archaeology* and 72.4% for the *African Archaeological Review*[863]. In Poland between 1957 and 1994, only a quarter of the articles in the periodical *Archeologia Polski* were written by women[864]. Emily Hanscam and Robert Witcher analysed the publications of Antiquity for the United Kingdom. They noted that, in '1990, 24.1% of all listed authors and 23.2% of first-named authors were female. By 2020, 33.2% of all listed authors were female, and 38.8% of first-named authors were female[865]'.

American studies are far more numerous. They focus either on a single journal, such as *American Antiquity*[866], *Journal of Field Archaeology*[867] and *Historical Archaeology*[868], or on several journals[869]. All of them focus solely on the gender of the authors. Heath-Stout is the only one to take account of race, sexual orientation and gender identity (cisgender/transgender) in her parameters. Her results will be developed in the following chapters[870].

The first finding of these studies is that, on average, **women are published less than men**. Of the 974 articles published between 1967 and 1990 in the journal *American Antiquity*, 23% were written or co-authored by women[871]. A similar percentage was calculated for *Historical Archaeology*[872]. Between 1967 and 1990, 17% of the journal's articles were written by women, with a clear increase from 0 articles in 1967 to 48% of articles by women in 1990. More recently, a similar observation was made for the *Journal of Field Archaeology*[873]. Between 2014 and 2018, a minority (27%) of its articles were published by women. Researcher Laura Heath-Stout also conducted a survey of articles published between 1999 and 2017 in 21 archaeology journals. On average, between 50% and 70% of the authors were male. Three of the most prestigious journals (*Annual Review of Anthropology*, *Current Anthropology*, *American Antiquity*) have more than 70% male authors[874]. Between 2000 and 2013, the majority of publications in archaeology in the south-western United States remained the work of men (74%)[875].

In terms of **citations**, the results are more mixed. In *American Antiquity* and *Historical Archaeology*, women were cited less than men on average between 1967 and 1990[876]. Between 1990 and 2000, there was no significant difference in citations in the journals *American Antiquity*, *Journal of Field Archaeology* and *Ancient Mesoamerica*, but in *Southeastern Archaeology*, researchers cited their female colleagues less often. Hutson also notes that in the journals *American Antiquity* and *Ancient Mesoamerica*, the number of works by women cited for a given research subject is significantly lower than the actual number of works written by women on this subject. A difference is in fact detected among male and female researchers working on theoretical subjects: men are less likely than women to cite the work of women[877]. Heath-Stout also notes that women cite more sources in their articles than men. She hypothesises that women feel a greater need to prove their knowledge through longer bibliographies[878]. Or that they are simply more rigorous and intellectually honest.

In relation to the previous two points, studies have shown that **women submit fewer articles than men**. Between 2009 and 2010, men submitted more articles than women to the journal *American Antiquity*. Even though men are in the majority among the journal's reviewers (64%), the acceptance rate for an article is the same regardless of the gender of the author[879]. However, women are less likely to resubmit their articles after peer review[880]. In 1994, researcher Mary Beaudry investigated the reasons why women submit fewer articles and encouraged them to be more self-confident[881]. In 2014, Dana Bardolph took this analysis a step further. She argues that women certainly lack self-confidence because of the gendered upbringing they have received, but that above all they have less time to devote to research than men. They spend more time on administrative, teaching, domestic and parental tasks than their male colleagues. They have fewer opportunities to receive feedback and advice from their colleagues and research supervisors. They are also less likely to fragment their research into several small articles[882].

A few studies have examined the **link between the prestige of a journal and the gender of the people who publish in it**. Dana Bardolph, for example, compared the publications of five major journals (including *American Antiquity*) and five smaller archaeological journals between 1990 and 2013[883]. She found no difference: men remain in the majority and make up 71% of first authors, regardless of the journal. However, Tushingham and her colleagues noted that more women publish in the non-refereed journal *The Society for California Archaeology's Proceedings*, while men dominate publications in the three prestigious journals *California Archaeology*, *Journal of California* and *Great Basin Anthropology*[884]. They called this phenomenon the '**peer review gap**' and showed that men have a monopoly on certain prestigious sub-fields of the discipline, while the research carried out by women is often little recognised and undervalued. A veritable vicious circle can thus be revealed: more men than women submit articles to a prestigious journal, so more of them are published, the journal is cited

863 Weedman 2001, 3.
864 Janik & Zawadzka 1998, 98–101.
865 Hanscam & witcher 2022, 88.
866 Beaudry & Victor 1992; Gero 1985; Rantman 2012.
867 Heath-Stout 2020b.
868 Beaudry 1994; Beaudry & White 1994.
869 Bardolph 2014; Bardolph & Vanderwarker 2016; Hutson 2002; Heath-Stout 2019; Tushingham *et al.* 2017.
870 Heath-Stout 2019.
871 Beaudry & Victor 1992, 14.
872 Beaudry & White 1994, 153.
873 Heath-Stout 2020b, 138.
874 Heath-Stout 2019, 96.
875 Bardolph & Vanderwarker 2016, 14.
876 Beaudry & Victor 1992, 16; Beaudry & White 1994, 155.
877 Hutson 2002, 340.
878 Heath-Stout 2019, 155–156.
879 Rautman 2012, 25–26.
880 Bardolph & Vanderwarker 2016, 15.
881 Beaudry 1994, 227.
882 Bardolph 2014, 534–535.
883 Bardolph 2014.
884 Tushingham *et al.* 2017.

more often as a result, so it is perceived as even more prestigious and its metric index rises, encouraging more men than women to submit an article, etc. In short,

> 'Despite increasing numbers of women engaged in the field of archaeology, women publish less often than men do, and their work is cited less often. Women are more represented in the less-prestigious, unrefereed publications like conference proceedings and edited volumes, while refereed journals remain maledominated. Labor in archaeology is thus divided into more prestigious work done by men and the housework that is important but undervalued and is conducted by women[885].'

Finally, in connection with inequalities in publications, a number of studies have looked at the place occupied by women in conferences. Hilary Du Cros and Laurajane Smith looked at the annual conferences organised by the Australian Archaeological Association in 1988, 1989 and 1990. They found that 66% of post-conference questions and comments were formulated by men, even though they made up only 40% of the audience, and that their speaking time was 50% longer than that of women[886]. Despite an increase in the number of women on organising committees in the United States during the 1990s, men are still more often invited to conferences[887]. This observation also applies to the years 2000 to 2013[888].

10.7. Sexist and sexual violence

10.7.1. Sexist comments and behaviour

Paternalism, sexist 'jokes', systematic reference to physical appearance, questioning of professional skills, 'manterrupting', 'mansplaining', etc. Sexist comments and behaviour are not uncommon in archaeology. They sometimes take the form of benevolent sexism, sometimes hostile sexism. Benevolent sexism is defined by Peter Glick and Susan T. Fiske as 'a subjectively positive attitude that describes women as pure creatures, to be protected and adored by men'. Benevolent sexism refers to implicit behaviours that seem to 'even differentiate favourably between women [...]. Nevertheless, by suggesting that women are fragile and need men's protection, benevolent sexism also suggests that they are inferior and less capable than men[889]'. Taking a pickaxe out of women's hands on an excavation site on the pretext that the tool is heavy and that it is not a job for them, or relegating them to the laboratory because laboratory work is perceived as less arduous, are examples of this.

> **Definitions**
>
> Manterrupting: behaviour in which men cut women off during discussions[890].
>
> Mansplaining: behaviour in which men explain to a woman something she already knows – or is a recognised expert on – in a potentially paternalistic or condescending tone[891].

Hostile sexism is 'an explicitly negative attitude towards women, who are seen as manipulative, feminist and aggressive, using their seduction to better control men[892]'. Sexist jokes, comments and insults, sexual harassment and sexual assault are all expressions of this. In archaeology, hostile sexism takes the form, for example, of remarks associating women with the traditional role of 'housewife' when they are cleaning an area prior to photography, systematic references to their physical appearance when they are wearing shorts or a tank top, or the appropriation of their ideas in work meetings (for other examples, see also section 10.7.2, 'Sexual harassment, assault, and rape').

Both benevolent and hostile sexism contribute to maintaining social inequalities between women and men. This is sometimes compounded by internalised sexism, which is both perpetuated and suffered by women in relation to themselves and their peers. In archaeology, these insidious and difficult-to-quantify manifestations are little studied[893]. In 1994, Alison Wylie deplored the fact that:

> 'There is virtually nothing in print, and little included here, that deals with the linkages between forms of inequity, harassment, and discrimination that run along gender lines[894].'

Yet women have faced discrimination from the very beginnings of the discipline. In 1930, the archaeology student Clara Lee Tanner complained in her excavation notebook that her site manager, Dean Byron Cummings, occasionally sent female site students to the dig house to look after the children of VIPs invited to visit the site[895]. Edward Burgess also used to ask his female students on site to look after his children and bring him food during breaks[896]. Other American archaeologists such as Alfred Kroeber, Fay-Cooper Cole and Alfred Tozzer also made it their mission to discourage female students from

885 Heath-Stout 2019, 51–52.
886 du Cros & Smith 1993, xviii.
887 Claassen *et al.* 1999, 95.
888 Bardolph & VanDerwarker 2016.
889 Glick & Fiske 1996; Sarlet & Dardenne 2012, 438. ('une attitude subjectivement positive, qui décrit les femmes comme des créatures pures, qui doivent être protégées et adorées par les hommes [...] qui a une apparence anodine et qui semble même différencier favorablement les femmes en les décrivant comme chaleureuses et sociables. Néanmoins, en suggérant l'idée que les femmes sont fragiles et qu'elles ont besoin de la protection des hommes, le sexisme bienveillant suggère également qu'elles sont inférieures et moins capables qu'eux.')
890 Bennet 2015.
891 Solnit 2012.
892 Glick & Fiske 1996; Sarlet & Dardenne 2012, 438. ('attitude explicitement négative envers les femmes qui sont considérées comme des manipulatrices aux idées féministes et agressives, usant de leur séduction pour mieux contrôler les hommes.')
893 Mary *et al.* 2019, 215–216; Tavera Medine 2019, 239–260.
894 Nelson *et al.* 1994, 3.
895 Hays-Gilpin 2000, 92.
896 Browman 2013, 116.

continuing their studies[897]. On 9 April 1931, Mary Ross Ellingson, then a doctoral student in archaeology, wrote in a letter to her mother:

> 'The other night, I asked him [Robinson] where the men were going to be paid, & he said "would you like to pay them? You're the prettiest girl here, you can be Miss Olynthus, & pay the men." And the other day when my hand was swollen from a flea bite, he said, "You have a pretty neck, I hope it doesn't swell up"[898].'

In 2000, anthropology professor Kelley Hays-Gilpin suggested, not without sarcasm, that:

> 'Many male field directors felt that women distracted male crew members and got in the way of highly valued masculine activities such as cursing and working without a shirt[899].'

In 2005, Jane Eva Baxter highlighted in her survey of members of the Society of American Archaeology that men perceived sexist violence to be rare or very rare within the profession, while the majority of women said that it was commonplace[900]. Historically, the publicising of individual accounts of sexual harassment in the workplace led to the emergence of a legislative framework from the 1980s onwards in the United States, notably on the basis of the work of Catharine MacKinnon, who 'demonstrated that sexual relations between two people of different professional status were necessarily coercive[901]'.

In 2015, word also spread on the Internet[902]. The impetus came from social networks such as Tumblr, Twitter, Facebook and Instagram. As a space for autonomous content creation and a place for political expression and education, the Internet was rapidly taken over by women and minorities in the 1990s[903]. From the 2010s onwards, archaeologists began to reappropriate the tools of online struggle, in particular by posting testimonies online. Inspired by the Every Day Sexism project, the English-language Every Dig Sexism project was created in 2015 by Hanna Cobb and Catherine Poucher to compile accounts of sexism in archaeology and other heritage professions. Very active between 2015 and 2017, the project took the form of an online platform and a Twitter account responsible for sharing the accounts received via the hashtags #everydigsexism (#sexismesurtousleschantiers) and #archswan (in reference to the British Athena Swan Scheme, which promotes equality in science).

Every Dig Sexism's French-language counterpart, the Paye ta Truelle collective, was founded in 2017 by Belgian archaeologist and feminist activist Laura Mary. It follows in the footsteps of other 'Paye ton/ta' projects that emerged in the wake of Paye ta Shnek, an initiative founded in 2012 by Anaïs Bourdet to combat sexist harassment in the public space. Paye ta Truelle began as a Tumblr to collect and share stories of sexism in archaeology via social networks. It now includes other forms of discrimination (racist, LGBTQIAphobic, validist, classist) and has expanded into the offline sphere by organising conferences, seminars, training courses and one-day conferences. In partnership with the Archéo-Éthique association, Paye ta Truelle is also trying to shake up archaeology with a travelling exhibition of illustrated testimonials, 'Archéo-Sexisme' (Figure 10.4). It was inaugurated at the Maison des Sciences de l'Homme Mondes in Nanterre on 8 March 2019, International Women's Rights Day. It has since been circulating in Belgium, France, England, the United States, Greece, Switzerland and Quebec, with the aim of raising awareness of discrimination among archaeology students and professionals.

10.7.2. Sexual harassment, sexual assault and rape

In addition to sexist jokes, remarks and insults, hostile sexism takes the form of sexual harassment, sexual assault and rape. These forms of discrimination are almost invisible, or even difficult to recognise, even for the victims.

American researcher Rita P. Wright was one of the first people to take an interest in the issue[904]. In an article published in 2008, she states that she first raised the issue in 1996 when she was a member of the Committee on the Status of Women in Archaeology (COSWA). Between 1996 and 2002, she also tried to change the situation within the Society of American Archaeology (SAA), in particular by insisting on the introduction of working regulations that included a section on sexual harassment and assault. In 2008, she deplored the fact that 'at this date, no specific action on this issue has been taken by the SAA[905]'. In 2015, the SAA finally introduced a procedure and a guide to combat all forms of harassment and assault within the institution.

In the mid-2010s, archaeology really got to grips with the issue. Sexist and sexual violence was the subject of several sessions at the annual meetings and colloquia of the Society of American Archaeology, the Society of Historical Archaeology, the American Antropological Association, the European Archaeological Association, the Theoretical Archaeology Group at University College London and Stanford University. A one-day colloquium on 'Féminismes et archéologie. Égalité, diversité et

[897] Meyers *et al.* 2018, 2.
[898] Kaiser 2014, 28.
[899] Hays-Gilpin 2000, 91.
[900] Baxter 2005, 8.
[901] Froidevaux-Metterie 2021, 221, n. 3 for the quote ('a démontré que des relations sexuelles entre deux personnes n'ayant pas le même statut professionnel étaient nécessairement coercitives.'); MacKinnon 1979.
[902] These issues were already being documented and discussed in the United Kingdom in the 1990s. See Pope & Teather 2025.
[903] Jouët, Niemeyer & Pavard 2017.

[904] Wright 2000, 2002 et 2008.
[905] Wright 2008, 27.

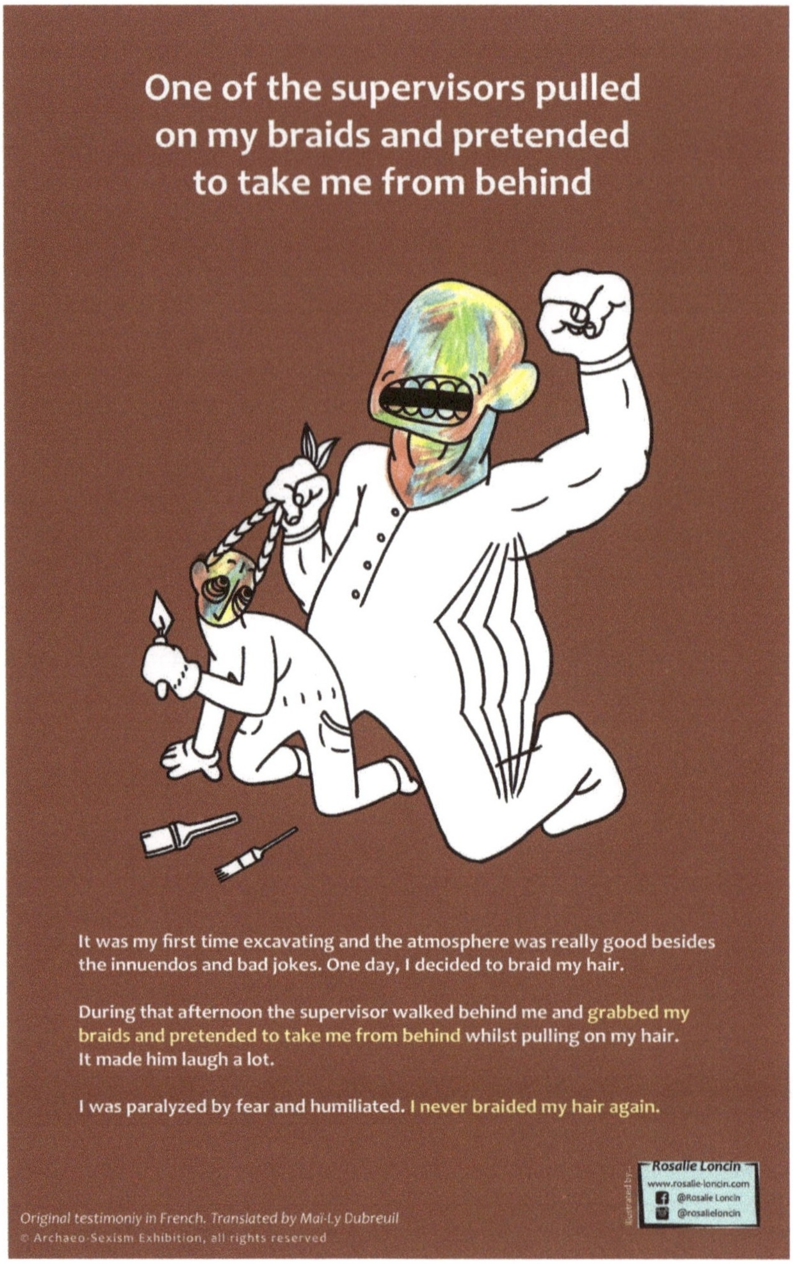

Figure 10.4. Example of a panel from the Archéo-Sexisme exhibition, illustrated by Rosalie Loncin.

convergence des luttes : pour une archéologie de la subversion' was also organised in Brussels in 2020.

Gender-based and sexual violence are omnipresent in archaeology. Two types of source make it possible to document their presence, quantify their frequency and measure their impact: eyewitness accounts and surveys. In English-, Spanish- and French-speaking circles, the Every Dig Sexism, MeTooArquelogía and Paye ta Truelle projects and the Archéo-Sexisme exhibition are the main initiatives relaying accounts of sexual violence in archaeology on social networks and offline. Other projects, such as the Australian collective MeTooAntropo, which fights against sexual harassment and assault in anthropology and archaeology, and the US initiative The Fieldwork Initiative, also occasionally relay these anonymous accounts online. Some archaeologists, such as Sasja van der Vaart-Verschoof, also choose to speak out on their blogs or personal websites[906].

Surveys, on the other hand, are rare. They focus almost exclusively on the gender parameter and concentrate above all on the United States (see Table 5)[907]. Although rapes do occur on archaeological sites[908], none of the studies listed below mention them. They follow on from an initial study carried out by Kathryn Clancy and her colleagues in 2014. SAFE (Survey of Academic Field Experiences, online) does not focus exclusively on archaeology, but on all professions requiring fieldwork. It recorded the responses of 666 people, a quarter of whom were archaeologists.

[906] van der Vaart-Verschoof 2019.

[907] Meyers *et al.* 2015 et 2018; Radde 2018; VanDerwarker *et al.* 2018. See also Voss 2021b.

[908] Boutboul & Bredoux 2019.

Table 5. Results of surveys on sexual harassment and assault in archaeology.

Surveys	Percentage of respondents who have experienced sexual harassment	Percentage of respondents who have experienced at least one sexual assault
Clancy *et al.* 2014	70% women and 40% men	26% women and 6% men
Meyers *et al.* 2015	7% women and 27% men	77% women and 19% men
Rade 2018	45% women and 20% men	20% women and 5% men
Coto-Sarmiento *et al.* 2019	51% women and 15% men	No information
Hodgetts *et al.* 2020	21,7% women and 4,1% men	6,3% women and 2,7% men
Coltofean-Arizancu *et al.* 2023	45% women and 8% men	10% women and 2% men

64% of these people (70% of women and 40% of men) said they had already been sexually harassed on site and 20% (26% of women and 6% of men) said they had been sexually assaulted. The majority of victims were female students and post-doctoral researchers, while the majority of harassers and assailants were male.

Published in 2015, the preliminary results of the survey carried out by Maureen Meyers and her colleagues focus on archaeologists working in the south-eastern region of the United States (Florida, Texas and Louisiana)[909]. This is the first survey to focus specifically on archaeology. There were 382 responses. The survey revealed that 71% of the women questioned had been sexually harassed on excavation sites (compared with 27% of the men) and that 77% of the women had been sexually assaulted (compared with 19% of the men). The majority of victims are students. Just over a quarter of the respondents to the survey said that sexual harassment had had a negative impact on their career: some had left archaeology, others had changed their place of work or voluntarily put their career on hold for a while.

Hugh Radde's 2018 survey focuses on California and makes similar findings. The majority of victims of sexual harassment are women (45% compared with 20% for men). More women than men are sexually assaulted (20% compared with 5%). Harassers and aggressors are most often heterosexual men[910]. Similar results were reported in another study, also conducted in California[911].

Outside the United States, Beth Alper Nakhai distributed questionnaires in 2014, 2015 and 2019 on the safety and well-being of women archaeologists working in the field in the Mediterranean Basin, the Middle East and North Africa. The results of the *Surveys on Field Safety: Middle East, North Africa, and Mediterranean Basin* are only partly published online[912] but have been presented on several occasions at the annual meeting of the American Schools of Oriental Research[913]. Sexual violence was reported on 20% of the worksites listed.

In 2019, archaeologist Maria Coto-Sarmiento and her colleagues published the first survey of sexual violence in archaeology to be conducted in Spain[914]. There were 358 participants. 51% of the women surveyed (compared with 15% of the men) said that they had already been sexually harassed at work, and some of them (19%) had left archaeology as a result. In 89% of cases, the harassment had no consequences. The vast majority of harassers (89.86%) were men in higher hierarchical positions than the victims.

In 2020, the survey conducted by the Canadian Archaeological Association's Equity and Diversity working group received 564 responses[915]. The pattern already identified in the other studies was repeated. Generally speaking, more women than men are verbally abused (66.5% compared with 49.7%), sexually harassed (21.7% compared with 4.1%) and sexually assaulted (6.3% compared with 2.7%). The majority of perpetrators of verbal and sexual violence are male superiors.

Is archaeology a particularly favourable environment for the development of sexist and sexual violence? Alongside these investigations and testimonies, archaeologists are looking into systemic violence. In 2018, the National Academies of Sciences, Engineering, and Medicine (NASEM) published a report on sexual harassment of women in science, engineering, and medicine. In it, NASEM lists five factors that tend to create environments where harassment and assault are more likely to occur: 1) a general tolerance for inappropriate sexual behaviour; 2) a professional environment dominated by men and where positions of responsibility are predominantly held by men; 3) an organisational structure of hierarchical power, with a strong dependence from lower levels of the hierarchy to higher levels; 4) an emphasis on individual responsibility, not structural responsibility; and 5) an authority that does not intentionally prioritise or focus on measures to reduce and eliminate inappropriate sexual behaviour[916]. Transposing these factors to archaeology, Carol E. Colaninno and her colleagues conclude that:

909 Meyers *et al.* 2015, 20. See also Meyers *et al.* 2018.
910 Radde 2018, 240–241.
911 VanDerwarker *et al.* 2018.
912 Nakhai 2017.
913 Nakhai 2018.
914 Coto-Sarmiento *et al.* 2019, 21.
915 Hodgetts *et al.* 2020, 32–35.
916 NASEM 2018, 3–4; Voss 2021a.

> 'Given the hierarchical nature and structure of field schools, enrolled students are particularly susceptible to harassment and assault [917].'

Other archaeologists, such as Stephanie Moser and Robert Muckle, speak of the 'culture of fieldwork', referring to the special atmosphere and mentality of archaeological excavations ('what happens in the field, stays in the field')[918].

> 'Fieldwork is a highly social experience in which people have to live together and co-operate as part of a group, therefore those who work well in a team and who "fit in" socially are seen to have the necessary skills to pursue a career in the subject. [...] It is in the field that unspoken rules and ideas about the nature of archaeology are learnt; being good in the field is not just about troweling techniques, it is also about coping with working outdoors in conditions that are often tough, enduring the ordeals and hardships associated with living in remote regions, and participating in the spirit of the whole enterprise that is fieldwork[919].'

In an attempt to define this 'spirit', the archaeologist Mary Leighton has developed the concept of 'performative informality'. When a profession such as archaeology is presented as 'fun', 'open', 'friendly' and 'meritocratic', individuals wishing to pursue a career in the profession are encouraged to take part in a series of events in addition to their work (which can take place both on and off site) and to 'perform informality' in the 'right way' (drinking, laughing and using sexist humour, for example) in order to project a 'good image' to people who can then potentially support their applications for funding or jobs[920]. During these events, the consumption of alcohol and/or drugs is strongly encouraged, blurring the boundaries between the professional and the private, as well as hierarchical relationships. This makes it all the more difficult to put words and limits to inappropriate behaviour. In the survey conducted by Beth Alper Nakhai in 2017, 58% of respondents said that drug and/or alcohol abuse was a major problem in the 'fieldwork culture' and had an impact on their well-being at work[921].

To combat this anxiety-provoking 'fieldwork culture', archaeologists from academia and the public and private sectors in various countries are calling for the creation of charters and protocols to make everyone aware of the ethics and rules of good conduct to be adopted in archaeology. They encourage these documents to be widely distributed to managers, employees, students and volunteers, and recommend that training courses be set up for everyone. Some also advocate the introduction of 'dry field programmes', archaeological excavations where the consumption of alcohol is prohibited[922]. In 2012, for example, the Australian Archaeological Association developed and disseminated a code of ethics within its institution, which must be scrupulously respected both outside and in the field. The same applies to the Canadian Archaeological Association, the Association des Archéologues du Québec, the Archaeological Institute of America, the Institute of Archaeologists of Ireland and the World Archaeological Congress. More recently, the British Archaeological Jobs Resource published an online guide to combating harassment in archaeology in the UK[923].

In the French-speaking world, the Paye ta Truelle collective and the Archéo-Éthique association developed a 'Chantier-Éthique' charter and an anti-discrimination vademecum in 2019, which are freely available on their respective websites, with the support of the French Ministry of Culture. In the United States, the National Science Foundation financed a project against sexual harassment in science in the same year, in which archaeologists from the Arkansas Archaeological Survey and Mississippi State University took part. The aim of the research team was to develop protocols that school site directors can implement to prevent sexual harassment and make fieldwork safer and more inclusive for undergraduate students who aspire to become archaeologists. In 2021, the Archaeology of Gender in Europe group and the Paye ta Truelle collective set up a survey to determine the extent of various forms of harassment and aggression in the various European archaeological communities. 82% of respondents said they had experienced at least one form of harassment in the course of their studies or work. Given the scale of the phenomenon, the researchers behind the initiative called for more charters, training and real enforcement of work regulations in the event of a problem, regardless of the hierarchical level of the alleged perpetrator[924].

10.8. Menstruation hygiene on excavation sites

Archaeologists have been slow to take up the issue of menstruation and menstrual hygiene on excavation sites. The British initiative Seeing Red and the French collective Paye ta Truelle have shared numerous testimonies on this subject on social networks in 2019 and 2020. They detail the difficulties encountered in the field by menstruating people: lack of toilets or a place where they can change in peace and quiet, lack of toilet paper, a water tank and soap to wash their hands or rinse their menstrual cup, lack of a rubbish bin to dispose of their used tampons and pads, toilets that do not comply with hygiene standards or that are not adapted (for small people or people with disabilities, for example), etc. These problems are more common in the case of excavations organised by university academics or researchers, but they are no less common in the case of commercial archaeology.

917 Colaninno *et al.* 2020, 113.
918 Moser 2007; Muckle 2014, 32.
919 Moser 2007, 246–247.
920 Leighton 2020, 444–458.
921 Meyers *et al.* 2018, 10; Nakhai 2017.
922 Colaninno *et al.* 2020, 118; Meyers *et al.* 2018, 10.
923 *RESPECT - Acting against Harassment in Archaeology*, [Accessed 29 March 2021, http://www.bajr.org/BAJRGuides/44.%20Harrasment/Sexual-Harassment-in-Archaeology.pdf].
924 Coltofean-Arizancu *et al.* 2023.

On-site sanitary facilities are generally designed by and for cisgender men. Deemed "unnecessary", they can be subtracted from the excavation budget to save money. When they are present, they tend not to comply with basic hygiene standards.

The issue of menstruation remains invisible in archaeology. It has been observed that, in the absence of any interest in the issue and any concern for it on the part of those in charge, menstruating workers sometimes opt for solutions that are dangerous to their health, such as keeping a tampon in for longer than the recommended four hours, thereby exposing themselves to toxic shock syndrome. Some people even confide in their testimonies that the fact that menstruation is not dealt with on site is one of the reasons why they left archaeology[925]. This taboo has an even more negative impact on people suffering from miscarriage or endometriosis. The risks of vaginal mycosis, cystitis and other urinary tract infections are also rarely taken into account.

To combat the invisibility of menstruation in archaeology, the British group Mentoring Womxn in Archaeology & Heritage is developing the Seeing Red in 2020 initiative. Spearheaded by archaeologist Amy Talbot, the project consists of a free downloadable guide to menstrual hygiene[926] and a free on-demand menstruation pack including sanitary towels in different sizes, several types of tampon, soap, hydro-alcoholic gel, towels, tissues and a bin bag. To promote the initiative, Amy Talbot regularly speaks at training courses, seminars and online and offline conferences. The project is well received in the UK and is supported by organisations such as the British Archaeological Jobs Resource (BAJR) and the Federation of Archaeological Managers and Employers (FAME). The menstruation pack has been adopted by a number of organisations, including the York Archaeological Trust, Headland Archaeology and Wessex Archaeology. In December 2020, FAME announced that from 2021 it would be making sanitary protection bins and dispensers available free of charge on all its sites. In France, a menstruation kit was introduced in 2020 by the social and economic committee of the commercial archaeology operator Archeodunum following awareness-raising by the Mentoring Womxn in Archaeology & Heritage group and the Paye ta Truelle collective. It consists of six sanitary towels of three different types, packed in an airtight bag, and a reminder of the hygiene measures recommended by occupational medicine. In 2022, the Paye ta Truelle collective and the Archéo-Éthique association also produced a short guide to menstruation on excavation sites, as well as a video aimed at making life easier for menstruating people on sites by sharing practical advice that respects both the bodies of the people concerned and the environment[927].

[925] For examples of testimonies on this issue, see Paye Ta Truelle Tumblr [Accessed 29 June 2023, https://www.tumblr.com/payetatruelle/].

[926] [Accessed 30 May 2021, https://mentorwomxn.org/2020/06/05/seeing-red/].

[927] [Accessed 30 May 30 2021, https://payetatruelle.wixsite.com/projet/menstruations-chantier-fouilles].

10.9. Pregnancy, maternity and parenthood

> 'We're not supposed to have kids anyway. Actually, we're not supposed to get married. Archaeology is not a career path that is conducive to children and things are particulary bad if you're a field archeo[928].'

As with the issue of menstruation on the field, the subject of pregnancy, motherhood and parenthood is not widely discussed in archaeology. No statistics have been published, but occasional accounts suggest that it is a subject of great concern to women archaeologists, mainly in heterosexual couples[929]. Since the 1980s, information has been disseminated in a number of articles. Leslie Wildesen points out that fieldwork can conflict with traditional female roles of motherhood and childcare[930]. Archaeologist Wendy Beck also noted in 1994 that the working conditions of Australian women archaeologists in the academic world were better than in other countries because they are entitled to maternity leave (12 weeks paid). She added that there were also government-subsidised childcare facilities on most campuses[931]. However, the subject was not officially addressed until the *Motherhood, Institutional Change, and the Future of Women in Archaeology* forum organised during the 73rd annual meeting of the Society for American Archaeology. The speakers, all mothers and archaeologists, addressed issues such as the challenges and choices imposed by motherhood on their careers, the personal strategies developed to cope with them, and the solutions that institutions need to put in place to support archaeologists in their desire to have and raise children. In her article published in 2008, archaeologist Maxine Oland reports on some of these discussions:

> 'Women reported being forced out of CRM firms for getting pregnant or not hired because they had children, and being denied maternity leave and other support in both businesses and universities. Women in many situations felt they had to hide pregnancies, and to seek the support of unions before telling their superiors. [...] Some women feel in a double bind—when parental leave time is offered, they feel pressured not to accept it for fear that it will reflect poorly on their scholarly commitment[932].'

Other more subtle constraints can also be mentioned, such as a lack of facilities for breastfeeding or breast pumping in offices, conference centres or dig houses, the absence of any possibility of adapting fieldwork during pregnancy, compulsory activities taking place outside day-care hours, or the absence of day-care facilities in or near workplaces[933]. Following this forum and Oland's article, the Society for American Archaeology committee nevertheless agreed to

[928] [Accessed 30 May 30 2021, http://www.succinctresearch.com/archaeologists-arent-allowed-to-have-kids-anyway/].

[929] Oland 2008, 22.

[930] Wildesen 1980, 6.

[931] Beck 1994, 101.

[932] Oland 2008, 23.

[933] Oland 2008, 23.

set up a childcare system for their next annual meetings and encouraged parents to bring their children[934].

More recently, testimonies shared on social networks or blogs continue to demonstrate just how complicated it remains for women to be both pregnant and/or a mother in archaeology. On her blog, archaeologist Siân Halcrow shares in an article dated 21 February 2017:

> 'As I am a (bio)archaeologist, having children poses some real difficulties for the logistics of my work, [...]. I missed a major fellowship deadline when my baby was a newborn, which could have been a career changer for me. Although I was working long hours and being successful and productive there was a 'dip' in my research[935].'

She also mentions some positive changes. Some universities in England such as Durham recognise, she says, the need for parental leave and additional support for young parents when they return to work, given the impact it has on their research. Archaeologist Becky Wraggs Sykes also blogs on 11 July 2014 about the relief of being able to take paid maternity leave when her first child was born.

> 'I was extremely fortunate to be on a good contract that guaranteed me the same rights to maternity leave as a French employee (thanks to it being a Marie Curie Fellowship). Coming from the UK, the 16 weeks I was entitled to felt quite short [...] but as I work for the Universite Bordeaux, a public sector entity, I would receive full salary for the period of leave. I'm well aware that compared to US archaeological colleagues, I was very lucky indeed- they often only get paid 2 weeks, if any[936]!'

Added to this is the testimony of archaeologist Bill White. On his website, he confides in 2014:

> 'It's hard to be a husband, dad and field archaeologist. [...] How can you raise a kid if you don't make much money, have to work out of the town all the time, and don't know if you'll have a job next year. As a man, [...] I don't have first-hand experience of the plight of a working mom but [...] I see what happens to my female archaeologists colleagues with regard to how parenthood effects their career[937].'

Today, women still do the majority of domestic and parental work in heterosexual couples[938]. This is due less to an alleged 'maternal instinct' than to an unequal division of labour based on gender. In recent years, there has been a shift in the role of fathers in certain circles: from a fatherhood based on status, which consists of providing his children with a comfortable material environment by working outside the home, to a fatherhood based on intention, where certain investments that were previously considered 'maternal' (such as changing nappies) are valued. However, their involvement generally remains lower than that of mothers and the professional consequences are more limited. Since it is a personal choice rather than a social injunction, choosing to become involved in fatherhood is less costly for men, both financially and socially[939]. In France in 2010, 'women were responsible for 64% of domestic work excluding parental work (compared with 69% in 1985)[940]'. Since 1986, the time spent by men on domestic tasks has increased by just 17 minutes a day.

In 2017, the archaeologist Suzanne Pilaar Birch, who was pregnant at the time, asked women archaeologists on Twitter to share their experiences of pregnancy in the field[941]. The hashtag #pregnantinthefield was filled with photographs and anecdotes from women archaeologists, but not only! Volcanologists, palaeontologists and geologists all joined in, demonstrating that being pregnant does not prevent you from taking part in fieldwork, albeit with a few adaptations. Following this hashtag, biologist Emily Sohn published a guide in *Nature* in 2018 on the risks and recommendations for pregnant people working in the field. However, the emphasis is more on individual rather than institutional responsibilities. Recognition of pregnancy, motherhood and parenthood would nevertheless be an important step towards equity within the profession. On 15 February 2022, Katharina Rebay-Salisbury organised an online round table entitled 'Motherhood in archaeology and matricentric feminism'. Some of the topics discussed related to this issue.

10.10. The issue of masculinities

Until the 1980s, masculinity was traditionally seen as a fixed block: all men, at all times and in all places, expressed themselves and behaved in the same way. This was taken to mean that they exercise 'domination over women in the same way, with the same privileges, costs and benefits[942]'. To go beyond this essentialist definition, Australian sociologist Raewynn Connell has proposed a new model: *masculinities*, which she sees as processes and power relationships that vary according to context and are open to challenge and renegotiation[943]. The interest of this model is twofold: it makes it possible to analyse the processes by which a certain category of men (hegemonic masculinity) imposes its domination both on women and on other categories of men[944] (see chapter 3).

---

934 Rizvi 2008, 6.

935 [Accessed July 3, 2021, https://childhoodbioarchaeology.org/2017/02/21/having-babies-as-an-academic-archaeologist/].

936 [Accessed April 12, 2021, https://www.dayofarchaeology.com/maternity-leave-archaeological-style-blogging-and-breastfeeding/].

937 [Accessed April 12, 2021, http://www.succinctresearch.com/archaeologists-arent-allowed-to-have-kids-anyway/].

938 Bereni *et al.* 2020, 108–112.

939 *Ibid.*

940 Bereni *et al.* 2020, 227 ('Les femmes assurent 64% du temps de travail domestique hors travail parental (contre 69% en 1985).'); INSEE, surveys 1986 and 2009–2010.

941 Carter 2017.

942 Tuaillon 2019, 53–54 ('une domination sur le groupe des femmes, avec les mêmes privilèges, les mêmes coûts et les mêmes bénéfices').

943 Connell 2014 (1995).

944 Alberti 2006, 413; Connell 2014 (1995), 72–80; Tuaillon 2020, 54–55.

A few studies have looked at men and masculinities in archaeological practice[945]. All have taken the field as their starting point, because 'the mythology of fieldwork and excavation remains at the core of our disciplinary identity[946]'. In archaeology, the excavation site is the preferred place for future professionals to learn what it means to be an archaeologist. It is also the place where gendered identities and behaviours are constructed and maintained. Commenting on her ethnographic research on the Arroyo Seco site in Argentina, Joan Gero notes:

> 'Fieldwork is the common denominator of all archaeological research, the baseline of production that unifies archaeologists of historic and prehistoric, classical and anthropological, New World and Old World, hunter– gatherer and complex society persuasions[947].'

She also demonstrates how fieldwork conforms to a 'masculinist style of research', which emphasises and privileges men[948].

> '[The archaeological practice is] coded with values and messages about gender and power, where the most successful styles of practice are undertaken by males, but even more critically, where the practices most venerated as "scientific" are symbolically and rhetorically charged as "male" [949].'

This is also the observation made by Stephanie Moser in her research on Australian archaeology[950]. In this article, she identifies the field as the area where the gendered regimes of archaeological practice are established. Historically, fieldwork has been linked to a series of so-called masculine values. These values are constructed and maintained by popular culture (films, series, comic strips, video games), the media and by archaeologists themselves.

> 'My thesis is that, through fieldwork, the disciplinary culture of archaeology expresses a gender regime that valorizes everything connected with the active (and actively) heterosexual male, or perhaps more specifically, everything connected with a certain type of masculinity[951].'

For Moser, this masculinity is intrinsically linked to the romantic image inherited from the 19th century of the enthusiastic and free explorer or adventurer who braves all dangers to set out and discover new sites and territories to conquer[952]. This first image is reinforced by that of the 19th century settler who sets out to conquer the world dressed in a khaki safari suit and wearing a salacot, and who must be courageous, robust and physically capable of surviving in the face of the Native people and wild beasts[954]. She points out that this military connotation also persists today in the vocabulary used ('campaign', 'trench', 'zone') and the discipline established on the sites (hierarchical structure, waking up before dawn, strict timetable, regulation and compulsory equipment for everyone)[955].

Whiteness

Whiteness is a concept coined by researcher Judith Ezekiel that 'designates the white social, cultural and political hegemony faced by ethnoracial minorities, as well as a mode of problematizing social relations of race[953].'

Taking up the concept developed by Connell[956], Moser argues that hegemonic masculinity in archaeology is above all based on values and behaviours such as action, a taste for exploration and destruction, outdoor work, strength, physical prowess and the consumption of large quantities of alcohol. A similar description is offered by Geller in 2016[957]. The term 'cowboy' is used by Gero as well as by Woodall and Perricone to describe this stereotypical but valued representation of the archaeologist in the United States who likes to live rough, drink heavily and take risks, in isolated, sometimes hostile terrain, in mountains, deserts or caves[958].

Moser also points out that fieldwork is not only masculine, but also fiercely and fundamentally heterosexual. To illustrate this point, she uses the definitions proposed by archaeologist Michael Shanks in *Experiencing the Past: On the Character of Archaeology*:

> 'Michael Shanks [...] characterizes fieldwork as an erotic enterprise: excavation is described in terms of the metaphor of "striptease", layers, like clothes, are "peeled off slowly, tantalizing us with glimpses of something we hope to see completely exposed"[959].'

The many recent surveys, testimonies and studies on sexist and sexual violence support these statements. The survey carried out by the Canadian Archaeological Association's Equity and Diversity working group, for example, showed that moral harassment, sexual harassment, sexual assault and physical violence in archaeology mostly take place on excavation sites, and that men are mostly responsible[960].

945 Geller 2016; Gero 1983, 1985, 1994 et 1996.; Hart 2020.; Moser 2007.; Woodall & Perricone 1981.
946 Moser 2007, 243.
947 Gero 1996, 225.
948 Gero 1996, 252.; Moser 2007, 248.
949 Gero 1996, 274.
950 Moser 2007.
951 Moser 2007, 259.
952 Moser 2007, 249–250.
953 Ezekiel 2002, quoted by Cervulle 2012, 39.
954 Moser 2007, 250–251.
955 Moser 2007, 254.
956 Connell 1995.
957 Geller 2016.
958 Woodall & Perricone 1981; Gero 1983 et 1985.
959 Shanks 1992, 192–193 quoted by Moser 2007, 253.
960 Hodgetts *et al.* 2020, 36–39.

> 'There is a pervasive "old boys" culture in archaeology that requires women to take abuse from male subordinates and colleagues or risk being seen as "difficult" or "unable to take a joke" [961].'

This hegemonic masculinity not only imposes a hierarchy between men and women, but also a hierarchy between men themselves. In 2018, Hugh Radde points out in the results of his study of Californian archaeology that 'students who identified as women or as a member of a marginalized group, such as people of colour and LGBTQ+ archaeologists, experience remarkably more verbal and physical harassment than do men[962]'. He also notes that 'students who do not identify as heteronormative are also significantly targeted for physical harassment[963]' from their colleagues and superiors[964]. Drawing on the work of Gero, Moser and Connell, researcher Siobhan Hart sets out to demonstrate how whiteness reinforces the hierarchies established on excavation sites and how fieldwork is designed by and for able-bodied heterosexual White men[965].

Moser and Geller note that virility is not only perpetuated by men, but that women may also seek to embrace this identity or be encouraged to do so in order to gain acceptance within the group ('to become [...] one of the blokes')[966].

Where to start?

M. Díaz-Andreu & M. L. S. Sørensen (eds.), *Excavating Women. An History of Women in European Archaeology*, Routledge, 1998.

J. M. Gero, 'Excavation Bias and the Woman at Home Ideology', *in Archeological Papers of the American Anthropological Association* 5/1, 1994, 37–42.

S. Moser, 'On Disciplinary Culture: Archaeology as Fieldwork and its Gendered Associations', *in Journal of Archaeological Method and Theory* 14, 2007, 235–263.

M. Nelson, S. M. Nelson & A. Wylie (eds.), *Equity Issues for Women in Archaeology*, American Anthropological Association, 1994.

A. Wylie, 'Workplace Issues for Women in Archaeology: The Chilly Climate', *in* H. du Cros et L. Smith (eds.), *Women in Archaeology: A Feminist Critique*, Department of Prehistory, Research School of Pacific Studies, Australian National University, 1993, 245–258.

[961] Hodgetts *et al.* 2020, 39.
[962] Radde 2018, 235.
[963] Radde 2018, 236.
[964] Radde 2018, 239.
[965] Hart 2020, 55–58.
[966] Moser 2007, 259; Geller 2016.

11

Racism

11.1. Minorities in the profession

There are few studies and surveys on the discrimination faced by racialised people in the profession. Deeply marked by racism (see chapter 2), the archaeological community is predominantly made up of White people, the only exception being excavation site workers[967]. Since the late 1990s, researchers based in South Africa, Kenya, the United States, the United Kingdom and Australia have published some data on the place of minorities in the discipline and the discrimination to which they are subjected.

11.1.1. In South Africa

Generally speaking, Scott MacEachern notes that Black researchers are in constant danger of becoming second-class citizens in their own discipline, as they do not have access to the same financial resources as foreign archaeologists and find it difficult to make their research known outside the African continent[968]. William Carruthers also mentions the fact that 'most of the archaeological work carried out in Kenya and published in Euro-American journals during the twentieth century, that lens was overwhelmingly white and male[969]'. He goes on to say:

> 'My grandfather Karisa Ndurya died when I was very young, and I have no recollection of him. I managed to gather some information on his archaeological work via family accounts and books written by his boss, a British archaeologist called James Kirkman. They worked together during and after the period of British colonialism in Kenya, exploring and excavating sites all over East Africa, including Gede Ruins and Fort Jesus, from the 1940s to the 1970s. At that time, James Kirkman was Warden of the Coastal Historical Sites of Kenya, and grandad was the Foreman. During my visit to Fort Jesus in Mombasa, my uncle recounted a memory of his dad and Kirkman discovering the ancient Portuguese art that hangs in the Fort. Yet when I walked around the site, there was only one name inscribed in historical descriptions of the archaeological work. It was Kirkman's[970].'

Only three studies deal with the place of minorities and women in the field of African archaeology, and all of them focus on South Africa[971]. In this country, race played a more important role than gender in the training and recruitment of archaeologists following the policies of apartheid. However, Diane Lyons points out that 'it is certain that there are far fewer indigenous women archaeologists than men in most African countries[972]', especially South Africa.

Wadley's survey of four South African universities highlights the fact that the majority of archaeology students are White South Africans[973]. Only one Black woman and a handful of Black men were employed in archaeology in 1997. The situation remains unchanged in 2019. Ndukuyakhe Ndlovu states that 'South African archaeology remains dominantly White[974]' and mentions that 'little transformation has taken place within the discipline since the fall of the apartheid regime[975]'. Of the 53 archaeologists accredited by the Association of Southern African Professional Archaeologists, two are Black and neither is from South Africa. Yet Ndlovu argues that Black people have always played a leading role in archaeology, but that their work is rarely recognised. He also highlights the lack of support and opportunities for Black students to participate in archaeological research, as well as the absence of Black researchers on the editorial boards of various African scientific journals[976].

> 'Rather than only having African labourers within archaeology, we need to encourage the training of professional African archaeologists who can take their place within our ranks[977].'

11.1.2. In the United States

In 1997, Maria Franklin, a Black American archaeologist, asked the question: 'Why are there so few black archaeologists in the United States?' She noted that 'nearly every American archaeologist is white[978]' and wondered 'why, in a discipline with a 100-year history in the US, there is a relative absence of blacks from the archaeological scene[979]'. The latest survey on the state of the profession in the United States, carried out in 1994 by the Society of American Archaeology, the country's largest organisation of professional archaeologists, shows that 98% of the 1502 respondents are 'European American', in other words, White[980]. Two identified themselves as African-American, 4 as Asian, 15 as Hispanic and 10 as Native

967 Fryer & Raczek 2020, 15.
968 MacEachern 1996.
969 Carruthers *et al.* 2021, 3.
970 Carruthers *et al.* 2021, 3–4.
971 Lyons 2006, 596.
972 Lyons 2006, 598–599.
973 Wadley 1997, quoted by Lyons 2006.
974 Ndlovu 2009, 91.
975 Ndlovu 2009, 91.
976 Ndlovu 2009, 91–92.
977 Ndlovu 2019, 91.
978 Franklin 1997b, 799.
979 Franklin 1997b, 799.
980 Zeder 1997, quoted by Carruthers *et al.* 2021, 2.

American[981]. Franklin also mentions that in 1997, only four African-Americans obtained a doctorate. The first Black woman, Theresa Singleton, was awarded a doctorate in archaeology in 1980[982], while Helen Magill became the first White woman to receive the title in... 1877[983]. There are also very few Black people working in public services, national parks, museums and historic sites as professional archaeologists with a Master's degree[984]. This observation is shared by Sonya Atalay for the Indigenous people[985]. The first Native American to become an archaeologist was Arthur C. Parker. He began his career at the beginning of the 20th century, but was not to be emulated[986]. Atalay also gives the example of the Michigan Archaeological Society: 'although the MAS, as a whole, is extremely interested in Native Americans and the Indigenous cultures of early Michigan, it is doubtful that a Native American has ever been a member of the MAS[987]'.

For many archaeologists, the low percentage of racialised people in archaeology can be attributed to the 'barriers instituted and perpetuated by racism[988]'. Franklin also points out that the majority of Black Americans who have been able to access higher education have chosen fields such as medicine or law because of the higher salary prospects and to meet the immediate needs of Black communities[989]. Those who opted for archaeology or anthropology, however, focused on the study of the African diaspora. Similar patterns can be found among people from Indigenous populations[990]. Some of these people nevertheless manage to become archaeologists and reach important positions within organisations made up almost exclusively of White people[991]. For example, the president of the Society for American Archaeology (SAA) from 2019 to 2021, Joe Watkins, was a member of the Choctaw tribe[992].

In 2020, Franklin and her colleagues argue that the increase in the number of Black archaeologists is partly linked to the Black Lives Matter movement and the development of anti-racist organisations, in particular the Society of Black Archaeologists[993]. They also link this phenomenon to the growth in research on people of African descent[994], but for Anna Agbe-Davies as well as Ayana Omilade Flewellen and her colleagues the development of archaeological studies on the African diaspora is not enough to attract and retain Black archaeologists in the profession[995]. The exact number of Black people employed as archaeologists remains unknown. Data collected by the SAA in 2003, 2010 and 2015 indicate that 'the percentage of people who identify as African American has remained at less than 1 percent of the total number of American archaeologists, growing at the slow pace of 0.1 percent roughly every five years[996]'. However, there was an improvement in the total number of non-White SAA members between 2003 (9.9%) and 2015 (22.3%)[997]. In 2021, Ayana Omilade Flewellen and her colleagues conclude that overall, 'our numbers remain low, [...] and disciplinary practices and the professional environment continue to privilege whiteness[998]'.

Flewellen and his colleagues also note that 'Black archaeologists continue to experience implicit and overt forms of antiblack racism in our field[999]'. Minorities have reported feeling discouraged and ostracised by the professors responsible for mentoring them during their studies[1000]. In 2018, a survey on mentoring was conducted among members of the Society for California Archaeology[1001]. Of the 407 respondents, 83.8% identified themselves as White. The majority reported that their relationship with their mentor was encouraging and caring. The trend is reversed for racialised people. They report, for example, that their mentors included them less often in research projects (16% less). On average, fewer of them were able to get regular meetings and they also received less support in writing their publications. 'We (the PhD experts as Blacks) had no credibility[1002]'. Michael Blakey talks about the difficulties encountered by African-American archaeologists in carrying out their research: 'We were surrounded by White archaeologists and city and national preservation bureaucracies that sought to contain us at every turn[1003]'. Their voices are delegitimised, if not simply silenced, particularly in the sector devoted to the study of Indigenous sites or the African diaspora, where the researchers are almost exclusively White but very few of them have followed a course in African-American or Indigenous studies at university[1004]. In terms of publications, the editors of the Society for American Archaeology's journals admit that at present, none of them are Black or Indigenous, and there are only a few racialised people on their editorial teams[1005]. There are also a few occasional testimonials online. William White recounts:

> 'I (William) know many white archaeologists who have fundamental misunderstandings about Black people. In addition to the crew member not offering me sunscreen because he didn't think I could get a sunburn, I've had archaeologists tell me I have a natural resistance to chigger bites and say I will be better suited for

981 White & Draycott 2020.
982 Flewellen *et al.* 2021, 225.
983 Spongberg *et al.* 2005, 12.
984 Franklin 1997b, 779–780.
985 Atalay 2006, 290.
986 Colwell-Chanthaphonh *et al.* 2010, 234.
987 Atalay 2006, 282.
988 Lee & Scott 2019, 85. See also Atalay 2006; Blakey 2020; Brown 2018; Flewellen *et al.* 2021; Franklin 1997a and b; Franklin *et al.* 2020; Fryer & Raczek 2020; Lee & Scott 2019; Odewale *et al.*. 2018; White & Draycott 2020.
989 Franklin 1997b, 780.
990 Atalay 2006, 290.
991 Bruchac 2014, 2070.
992 White & Draycott 2020.
993 Franklin *et al.* 2020, 756.
994 Franklin *et al.* 2020, 755.
995 Agbe-Davis 2002, 27; Flewellen *et al.* 2021, 227.
996 Odewale *et al.* 2018.
997 Brown 2018, 201.
998 Flewellen *et al.* 2021, 227.
999 Flewellen *et al.* 2021, 227.
1000 Brown 2018, 202.
1001 Brown 2018, 200.
1002 Blakey 2020, 189.
1003 Blakey 2020, 188.
1004 Blakey 2020, 184.
1005 Gamble *et al.* 2020, vi.

a job because I have a natural resistance to heat and humidity. This is all based on pseudoscientific 19th-century anthropology continuing into the 21st century. I have also seen white archaeologists "correct" Native American and African American narratives, sometimes speaking over the voices of community elders[1006].'

In *Black Feminist Theory in Prehistory*, Kathleen Sterling also shares:

> 'As a prehistorian working in Western Europe, I have also had my interest in my research area questioned, since it was assumed that as a Black woman (of mixed ancestry) I would want to study "my own people". I have also been treated as a potential informant about Black or Caribbean cultures, depending on how much the person knew about my ancestry[1007].'

Quantitative data on harassment and assault is patchy. The first survey within the profession does not provide any information about the violence faced by racialised people[1008]. Clancy and his team indicate that racialised people are under-represented in the discipline, and by extension in their data. Hugh Radde's 2018 survey of members of the Society for California Archaeology provides a little more information. The majority of respondents to the survey identified themselves as White (82.3%). The remaining percentage included Native Americans, Asians, Black people and Hispanics. Among the results obtained, the majority of racialised people, particularly women, indicated that they had been the target of physical harassment[1009].

11.1.3. Across the world

For the rest of the world, information is much rarer. In the United Kingdom, the *Profiling the Profession* survey published in 2013 reported that 99.2% of archaeological professionals and 97% of archaeological volunteers identified themselves as White[1010]. Only one person in the professional group identified as Black. In Australia, Indigenous people are still under-represented in the discipline. According to the latest survey of the profession by the Australian Archaeological Association in 2010, 'there were under ten members of AAA who identified as Indigenous' and 'three people who identifies as Indigenous archaeologists[1011]'. In 2019, only three students from Aboriginal communities completed their doctoral thesis in archaeology. No Aboriginal person was a professor. The authors of the article 'Pursuing Social Justice Through Collaborative Archaeologies in Aboriginal Australia' hope that it will not be 'another 20 years before the first Aboriginal professor is hired [at an Australian university] [1012]'.

11.1.4. Working with and for archaeologists

While Black and Indigenous people are in the minority among archaeologists, they are much more numerous among excavation workers (see section 10.5.2, 'Irene Mound (Georgia, USA): at the intersection of sexism, racism and classism'). In the Middle East and Africa, the majority of these workers were men. From the earliest days of the discipline, they were involved in the excavation of major sites such as Great Zimbabwe and Mapungubwe[1013]. These men 'dug, sieved, sorted, located sites and "finds", fetched and carried, pitched camp, cooked and served food, negotiated with local chiefs and suppliers, and assisted in the interpretation of artefacts and events[1014]'. Although they feature prominently in the films and photographs taken during the excavations, they remain little-known and are 'forgotten' in reports, articles and historiographical works[1015]. For example, Robinson noted in his report on the Great Zimbabwe excavations that he was assisted by 'six Africans', whom he did not name, and that 'the most intelligent came from the Rozwi group[1016]'. These people were not regarded as unofficial archaeologists or producers of knowledge, but at best as assistants, at worst as 'little hands' or 'boys'[1017]. Nick Shepherd conducted an investigation to try and identify these people in the photographic archives of archaeologist John Goodwin (1900–1959) for his sites in South Africa and Nigeria[1018]. This is also the work undertaken by Allison Mickel for the Petra and Çatalhöyük sites[1019].

11.2. Solutions to fight discrimination

> 'The future of archaeology is antiracist or it is nothing[1020].'

'The diversification of archaeology will take time[1021]'. In 1997, Maria Franklin, then one of only a handful of African-American archaeologists, suggested that one way of bridging the gap between White and Black archaeologists would be simply to hire more Black people. For her, it is the responsibility of archaeologists to create links with the Black community and invite these people 'to participate in the construction of their histories[1022]'. Franklin also suggests the need to create a broad network of Black researchers, not only in archaeology but also in history, social anthropology, literature and so on.

At the end of the 1990s, the Society for American Archaeology, the World Archaeological Congress and the America Anthropological Association included a section on responsibility, public education and awareness, and mentoring

1006 White & Draycott 2020.
1007 Sterling 2015, 103.
1008 Clancy *et al.* 2014.
1009 Radde 2018, 240.
1010 Aitchison & Rocks-Macqueen 2013, quoted by White & Draycott 2020 and Carruthers *et al.* 2021.
1011 Wilson 2014, 3791.
1012 Smith *et al.* 2019, 545.

1013 Chirikure 2014, 3834.
1014 Sheperd 2003, 335.
1015 Chirikure 2014; Mickel 2021; Sheperd 2003.
1016 Chirikure 2014, 3834.
1017 Chirikure 2014, 3834; Sheperd 2003, 335.
1018 Sheperd 2003.
1019 Mickel 2021.
1020 Flewellen *et al.* 2021, 238, quoting a tweet from W. Battle-Baptiste.
1021 Franklin 1997a, 45.
1022 Franklin 1997a, 47.

in their codes of ethics[1023]. Since 2011, the Society of Black Archaeologists has been fighting for the integration of Black people into archaeology and the development of studies on the archaeology of the African diaspora. Its European counterparts, The European Society of Black & Allied Archaeologists, and its Brazilian counterpart, Rede de Arqueologia Negra, pursue the same objectives. The Indigenous Archaeology collective is setting up similar initiatives for Indigenous people across the globe.

For Kaitlin Brown, Peggy Brunache and her colleagues, as well as Ndukuyakhe Ndlovu, mentoring is one of the ways of effectively combating racism and the under-representation of minorities within the profession[1024]. It plays a crucial role in students' decisions as to whether or not to pursue a career in archaeology. Supportive and encouraging mentoring can also help to establish professional networks and facilitate career opportunities. Franklin and his colleagues add that 'those of us who are in the position to recruit BIPOC students should actively work to do so[1025]'.

Ayana Omilade Flewellen and her colleagues also stress the importance of representativeness and encourage the hiring of more racialised people in universities. It is imperative that students recognise themselves in their professors, their field supervisors, their peers and in the studies they are expected to undertake[1026]. They add that the procedures for obtaining a grant, evaluation and tenure need to be more transparent, that teachers and academic staff need to be trained in the issues and treatment of discrimination, and that study programmes and course outlines need to be revised to incorporate a greater diversity of perspectives[1027]. On the latter subject, Maxine Oland recently published a guide[1028]. Kylie Quave and her colleagues also suggest that course books should include chapters on the colonial origins of archaeology, feminist archaeology, anarchist archaeology, nationalist recuperations of archaeology, etc.[1029].

11.2.1. 'An antiracist archaeology is about rebuilding internally as well as externally[1030]'

A number of archaeologists stress the need for collaboration with Indigenous communities, anti-racist associations and all those working in small associations to preserve local heritage, at every stage of archaeological and museum work[1031]. 'Archaeology cannot be just for archaeologists[1032]'.

Flewellen and her colleagues write that:

> 'It is our collective responsibility to reconcile with the violence this field has done to Black, Latina/o, Asian, Arab, and Indigenous, and other historically marginalized communities in both the past and present and to take an active role in creating an antiracist place of belonging for all[1033].'

André Cicalo shows how archaeologists working on structures linked to the history of slavery in the port region of Rio de Janeiro (Valongo Wharf) have collaborated with activists from the Brazilian anti-racist movement[1034]. Tânia Lima, the archaeologist in charge of the Valongo site, involved the activists in the process of interpreting the material remains unearthed. Their association has also led to the establishment of a charter ('carta do Valongo') for the preservation and enhancement of the remains, and the creation of a memorial circuit within the city, one of the milestones of which is the port site. In the United States, Alicia Odewale is researching the human bones unearthed in the Greenwood district of Tulsa, in conjunction with members of the city's Black community[1035].

Nicholas C. Laluk's research on, with and for the Ndee (Apache) is another example. Laluk encourages 'more "Ndee-controlled" processes to guide anthropological research and helps Ndee communities to better preserve and protect their culture, heritage, and identity in Ndee terms[1036]'. The Kashaya Pomo Interpretive Trail project set up by UC Berkeley, the California Department of Parks and the Kashaya Pomo tribe[1037], the Clanwilliam Living Landscape project in South Africa[1038] and the excavations at the Ganeshwar-Jodhpura complex in India[1039] are three other examples of fruitful collaborative projects between archaeologists and the local community.

The Tulsa Massacre (Oklahoma, United States)

The Tulsa massacre (30 May-1 June 1921) was one of the worst outbursts of murderous violence perpetrated by the White population against the African-American community. In the space of one day, this racist riot claimed the lives of more than 100 African-Americans and caused the destruction of an entire neighbourhood, leaving more than 8,000 people homeless[1040].

1023 Franklin 1997, 47.
1024 Brunache *et al.* 2021, 294–298; Brown 2018, 188; Ndlovu 2009, 91–92
1025 Franklin *et al.* 2020, 761–762.
1026 Flewellen *et al.* 2021, 232.
1027 Flewellen *et al.* 2021, 232–237.
1028 Oland 2020.
1029 Quave *et al.* 2021.
1030 Flewellen *et al.* 2021, 231.
1031 Entre autres Cicalo 2015; Curtoni & Politis 2006; Flewellen *et al.* 2021; Franklin *et al.* 2020; Kelvin & Hodgetts, 2020.
1032 Schumann 2019, 2.
1033 Flewellen *et al.* 2021, 231.
1034 Cicalo 2015.
1035 Franklin *et al.* 2020, 758.
1036 Laluk 2021, 54.
1037 Gonzalez 2016.
1038 Chirikure 2014.
1039 Rizvi 2019.
1040 Odewale & Slocum 2020.

11.2.2. The role of allies

> 'For those who refuse to remain silent there are multiple ways to get involved[1041].'

Many anti-racist archaeologists insist that this fight is everyone's business. In this sense, listening to the criticisms levelled at us, understanding them and modifying our behaviour as a result is essential. Self-education is also crucial, because we should not expect the victims of racist discrimination to take responsibility for our own education. 'We must educate ourselves and our peers, and hold each other accountable[1042]'and 'BIPOC archaeologists alone cannot do the work that is needed to radically change archaeology[1043]'. The foundations of an anti-racist archaeology must be built alongside allies, who can 'use their privilege to bring about change through action[1044]' through concrete action at universities, in the field and in the various archaeological associations.

Since 2009, the Transformation Task team within the Association of Southern African Professional Archaeologists has been working to attract more Black students to archaeology. Following the Black Lives Matter protests in the summer of 2020, the main archaeological associations in the United States (the Archaeological Institute of America, the Society for American Archaeology, the Society for Historical Archaeology and the World Archaeological Congress) issued statements in support of the anti-racist struggle[1045]. The editors of SAA journals have also stated their willingness to change the under-representation of racialised researchers on their editorial boards and peer review systems, to include more articles dealing with colonialism in their publications, to encourage more racialised people to publish in their journals and to combat inequalities within the profession more widely[1046]. Since 2020, the anarchist collective The Black Trowel has also been supporting racialised students through micro-bursaries.

Where to start?

S. Atalay, 'Indigenous Archaeology as Decolonizing Practice', *in American Indian Quarterly* 30, n°3/4, 2006, 280–310.

W. Carruthers, J. C. Niala, S. Davis, B. Challis, P. A. Schiappacasse, S. Dixon, M. Milosavljevic, L. Moore, R. Nevell, A. Fitzpatrick, H. Abd el Gawad & A. Stevenson, 'Special Issue: Inequality and Race in the Histories of Archaeology', *in Bulletin of the History of Archaeology*, 2021.

A. O. Flewellen, J. P. Dunnavant, A. Odewale, A. Jones, T. Wolde-Michael, Z. Crossland & M. Franklin, 'The Future of Archaeology is Antiracist: Archaeology in the Time of Black Lives Matter', *in American Antiquity* 86/2, 2021, 224–243.

M. Franklin, '"Power to the People": Sociopolitics and the Archaeology of Black Americans', *in Historical Archaeology* 31/3, 1997, 36–50.

N. Lee & J. N. Scott, 'Introduction: New Directions in Africa Diaspora Archaeology', *in Transforming Anthropology* 27/2, 2019, 85–90.

[1041] Franklin *et al.* 2020, 762.
[1042] Kelvin & Hodgetts 2020, 11.
[1043] Franklin *et al.* 2020, 762.
[1044] Flewellen *et al.* 2021, 234.
[1045] Franklin *et al.* 2020, 757.
[1046] Gamble *et al.* 2020.

12

Classism

12.1. Classes, capitalism and archaeology

Our society is structured into several differentiated and hierarchical social classes, with the higher classes dominating the lower classes and benefiting from this domination. An individual's social class is determined in particular by the function he or she occupies in economic production: for example, blue-collar workers are traditionally attached to the working class, schoolteachers belong to the middle classes and managers to the upper classes. In France, the nomenclature of professions and socio-professional categories is drawn up by INSEE (Institut national de la statistique et des études économiques). In addition to occupation, other criteria are used to determine who belongs to a particular social category, such as employment status (permanent/contractual, public/private sector), cultural capital (level of diploma or language, for example), economic capital (salary, family wealth), social capital (network, relationships), etc. Classism refers to the discrimination suffered by a person or group of people at the hands of an individual or group of individuals belonging to a more privileged social class. These discriminations range from ordinary class contempt to the impossibility of access to certain spaces, via the normalisation of free labour and precariousness.

> 'Archaeologists do not, however, just confront class, it also confronts us. Class and class relations permeate all aspects of capitalist society and as a part of that society archaeology embodies these relations[1047].'

In archaeology, the question of classism is rarely addressed. In the introduction to their article 'Class Confrontations in Archaeology', Randall McGuire and Mark Walker note that the subject remains largely a non-issue within our discipline, even though many archaeologists have pointed out that archaeology, whether in terms of its history, its practitioners or its public, is 'a middle-class product and that it tends to express the ideology of that class[1048]'. Bruce Trigger, for example, links the emergence of archaeology to the rise of the bourgeoisie in Europe and argues that the discipline was used as a tool to legitimise its privileges[1049]. In other words, the knowledge produced by archaeologists is part of the symbolic capital that a well-educated person must possess[1050]. The majority of archaeologists therefore come from this class. For McGuire and Walker, it is because archaeology serves the interests of the bourgeoisie that it tends to attract individuals from this class and to repel people from the working classes, who may perceive archaeology as elitist[1051]. McGuire and Reckner add that 'the problem with archaeology is that too often we [archaeologists] are speaking only to ourselves or to a small audience of aficionados who share our sometimes-arcane interests[1052]'. In order to create 'an archaeology of the American working class that speaks to a working-class audience', the Colorado Coal Field War project brought together students and archaeologists from the universities of Denver and Binghamton, descendants of the Ludlow massacre and unionised workers from southern Colorado[1053].

> **Ludlow Massacre**
>
> The Ludlow Massacre was one of the most violent events of the Colorado coal strike (1913–1914). On 20 April 1914, the Colorado National Guard attacked the strikers and their families in Ludlow with machine guns and then set fire to their camp. Twenty people were killed that day, including two women and twelve children.

Classism in archaeology takes many forms: the discipline is unattractive to the working classes, access to material remains is restricted, volunteer work is valued and standardised, students are exploited in excavations organised by university academics or researchers and professionals in commercial archaeology, manual work is devalued, etc. Although feminist archaeologists agree that class discrimination is present in archaeology, their reflections are more in the form of occasional comments than quantitative and qualitative studies[1054]. The work of Laura Heath-Stout and Elizabeth Hannigan on the lack of accessibility of excavation sites for students and that of Heath-Stout on the recruitment of future archaeologists in the United States are exceptions[1055]. The few publications dealing with this issue are written by archaeologists who may or may not identify themselves as Marxists or anarchists[1056]. *Archaeology and Capitalism: From Ethics to Politics*, edited by

[1047] McGuire & Walker 1999, 159.
[1048] McGuire & Walker 1999, 160.
[1049] Trigger 1989, 14, quoted by McGuire & Walker 1999, 162.
[1050] McGuire & Walker 1999, 160.
[1051] McGuire & Walker 1999, 160–163, 165.
[1052] McGuire & Reckner 2003, 83.
[1053] McGuire & Reckner 2003.
[1054] Heath-Stout & Hannigan 2020, 2.
[1055] Heath-Stout & Hannigan 2020.; Heath-Stout 2021.
[1056] Berggren & Hodder 2003; Everill 2007; Kolhatkar *et al.* 2020; McGuire & Reckner 2003; McGuire & Walker 1999; Minkoff & Morris 2016; The Black Trowel Collective; Zorzin 2015a and b.

Yannis Hamilakis and Philip Duke, includes a section devoted to an anti-capitalist approach to the profession and looks at the situation in Brazil, the United States, the Middle East, the United Kingdom and Peru[1057]. The cases of Canada, Quebec and Japan are developed by Nicolas Zorzin[1058]. Anti-classist reflections also appear in the studies carried out by anti-racist archaeologists (see chapter 2). Finally, scattered accounts can be found on the various social networks.

> 'By denying or overlooking its existence we ignore an important factor that affects the histories that we write and that structures the audiences for which we write. Finally, by denying class we conceal the class inequities that exist within our own discipline[1059].'

12.2. The opposition between intellectual and manual labour

> 'The old theoretical debate about the separation between data and interpretation in archaeology partly has a social basis. It is not an abstract philosophical discussion. It is about who is empowered to interpret. And on the whole the answer has been "not the excavator".[1060]'

Asa Berggren and Ian Hodder suggest that the 'development of excavation field methods in archaeology is closely tied to the social position of fieldworkers[1061]'. They go on to point out that some of the problems encountered today in European and American archaeology stem directly from the fact that manual work on site was discredited at the start of the professionalisation of the discipline because it was carried out by prisoners, the unemployed, volunteers and low-paid workers[1062]. A strict separation of manual and intellectual work is the norm in archaeological excavations, particularly those carried out in a colonial context, but not exclusively. On Mortimer Wheeler's digs in India, for example, Wheeler and a few British assistants were in charge of recording and interpretation, while dozens and dozens of local workers dug and removed the sediment. These men were considered to have no practical or theoretical knowledge, even though some had been employed on the site for several years, others came from families that had worked in archaeology for several generations, and still others sometimes worked without supervision. Their work was also ignored in publications. For Berggren and Hodder, this division of labour has continued to the present day. While the extraction of the raw materials needed for archaeological research is at the heart of the construction of archaeologists' professional identity, and fieldwork acts as a marker of membership of the professional community, 'the more archaeological knowledge one had, the further away from the actual excavation one was placed in the hierarchy[1063]'. On the sites, the archaeologists do the intellectual work that is valued and paid for, while the technicians, amateur archaeologists, volunteers and students are the voiceless, invisible and low-cost workforce. To remedy this problem, some sites such as Heathrow Terminal 5 in England or Catalhöyük give excavators the opportunity to interpret the structures they are working on. This process is documented and incorporated into the teams' publications[1064].

For McGuire and Walker, this disregard for manual work is also reflected to some extent in the relationship between archaeologists and looters or detectorists, who often come from the working classes[1065]. They point out that 'clearly those people who loot archaeological sites and advocate cult archaeologies have a different concept as to the value of the past than we do as archaeologists[1066]'. According to McGuire and Walker, it is therefore up to archaeologists to understand why these individuals engage in such activities in order 'to change both their and our behavior[1067]'.

Detectorism

In the United Kingdom, this activity is permitted and regulated by law for the protection of heritage. For example, detectorists cannot detect on Scheduled Monuments or in Areas of Archaeological Importance (AAIs). Organisations such as the National Council for Metal Detecting (NCMD) provide resources to help detectorists document their finds. In France, the looting of archaeological sites by prospecting with metal detectors is prohibited by the law of 18 December 1989. Finding an object without documenting its context is of no archaeological interest, and the practice actually destroys our heritage. The French Heritage Code also states that 'no-one may use equipment to detect metal objects for the purpose of researching monuments and objects that may be of interest to prehistory, history, art or archaeology, without first obtaining an administrative authorisation issued on the basis of the applicant's qualifications and the nature and methods of the research[1068]'.

[1057] HAMILAKIS & DUKE 2007.
[1058] ZORZIN 2015b.
[1059] MCGUIRE & WALKER 1999, 159.
[1060] BERGGREN & HODDER 2003, 425.
[1061] BERGGREN & HODDER 2003, 421.
[1062] BERGGREN & HODDER 2003, 421.
[1063] BERGGREN & HODDER 2003, 424.
[1064] BERGGREN & HODDER 2003, 427–428.
[1065] MCGUIRE & WALKER 1999, 165. See also HODDER 1984, POTTER 1994.
[1066] McGuire & Walker 1999, 165.
[1067] McGuire & Walker 1999, 165.
[1068] Art. L. 542–1 ('Nul ne peut utiliser du matériel permettant la détection d'objets métalliques, à l'effet de recherches de monuments et d'objets pouvant intéresser la préhistoire, l'histoire, l'art ou l'archéologie, sans avoir, au préalable, obtenu une autorisation administrative délivrée en fonction de la qualification du demandeur ainsi que de la nature et des modalités de la recherche.')

12.3. The 'archaeological proletariat'

In a paper presented at the annual meeting of the Society for American Archaeology in 2021, Laura Heath-Stout discusses the discrimination experienced by students from working-class backgrounds and highlights the crucial role played by mentors in recruiting and supporting these students[1069]. Based on around a hundred interviews with archaeologists, she reports:

> 'We've all heard stories like my own, of the child who discovers archaeology through a book, movie, museum visit, educational vacation, or all of the above. Those who did tell childhood stories were disproportionately White and from middle- or upper-class backgrounds. Their privilege facilitated early access to knowledge of archaeology, whether through expensive travel, parents with weekends off from work to take children to museums, or school curricula that incorporate topics that are rarely covered on standardized tests. My less privileged interviewees were [...] less likely to have come across archaeology as children, or if they had, it had not occurred to them as a viable career path. But once they got to college, they would find themselves in an anthropology or archaeology classroom due to general education requirements, friends' recommendations, or even administrative mix-ups, and they would catch the bug.'

She also looks at the cost of the field schools. The tuition, admission and travel fees, as well as the incompressible daily expenses, prevent a whole category of people from pursuing a course in archaeology. The fact that the majority of these field schools take place during the summer, a period when precarious students can earn money through seasonal employment, further reinforces these inequalities[1070]. Study and research grants are available, but there are very few of them and they never cover all the expenses. In the United States, the average cost of a training site is 4065 dollars. Grants provide an average of $2268.33 to cover costs[1071]. The authors note that 'the cost of participating in these work-schools primarily affects students from marginalized communities, helping to maintain archaeology as a discipline of privileged, predominantly White, upper-middle-class researchers[1072]'. For Heath-Stout and Hannigan, these scholarships are not the solution: work camps should be freely accessible to all students[1073]. Heath-Stout goes one step further in his 2021 paper, recommending that students be paid for their work on these sites[1074]. In 2022, Stanford University is the only institution to cover the full cost of participation. Some universities, such as Harvard and Brown, also have workcamps on or near their campuses, which are accessible to students during the academic year, and for which the cost of entry is included in the tuition fees. But these fees are already a barrier in themselves for people from lower socio-economic backgrounds. Some of them end up entering archaeology through paid employment in museums.

On the French-speaking side, the literature is almost non-existent, but there are a few more occasional comments and online testimonials. Anne Lehoërff wrote in her article 'L'enseignement de l'archéologie en licence dans les universités françaises' published in 2009 that 'the economic difficulties encountered by some students in expensive cities are detrimental to certain establishments, particularly in Paris, where the figures show a greater stagnation [in student numbers] than in some regional universities[1075]'. In 2022, a footnote in the article 'Enquête au pays des démagogues' published by the participatory magazine *Notre Condition* explicitly denounced the free work done by archaeology students:

> 'Students, whose experience is generally limited to excavations organised by university academics or researchers are obviously not prepared for what is known as commercial archaeology. Worse still, under the pretext of offering an opportunity to put one's passion for the discipline into practice, they are accustomed to not being paid for their scientific output. In other words, this normalisation of unpaid work instils in the minds of young archaeologists a form of servility that they accept when they are confronted with working conditions that really need to be improved. This situation masks the transition from one precarious situation to another[1076].'

In their press release of 22 February 2022, also published in *Notre Condition*, the members of the Groupes Archéo en Lutte focused on the lack of funding for excavations organised by university academics or researchers and voluntary work, showing how this exacerbates the economic insecurity of students[1077]. On Twitter, students, doctoral candidates, young researchers and precarious workers are also sharing the difficulties they face in archaeology. The issue of free work comes up frequently. Between volunteer excavation placements, unpaid lectures and articles, reports written outside working hours, unpaid transport and accommodation costs, underpaid and sometimes unpaid salaries for part-time lecturers,

[1069] Heath-Stout 2021.
[1070] Heath-Stout 2021; Heath-Stout & Hannigan 2020, 124–125.
[1071] Heath-Stout & Hannigan 2020, 127.
[1072] Heath-Stout & Hannigan 2020, 127.
[1073] This view is also shared by Minkoff & Morris 2016.
[1074] Heath-Stout & Hannigan 2020, 129.

[1075] Lehoërff 2009, 11 ('les difficultés économiques que rencontrent certains étudiants dans des villes onéreuses nuisent à certains établissements, en particulier parisiens, où les chiffres révèlent une stagnation [du nombre d'étudiant·e·s] plus forte que dans certaines universités régionales.').
[1076] GAEL 2022a ('Les étudiant.e.s, dont l'expérience se borne généralement aux fouilles programmées ne préparant évidemment pas à ce que l'on appelle le préventif. Pire, qui sous prétexte d'offrir une possibilité de mettre en pratique sa passion pour la discipline, habitue à une non rémunération de la production scientifique. Autant dire que cette normalisation du travail gratuit ancre dans les consciences des jeunes archéologues une forme de servilité consentie lorsqu'ils/elles seront confronté.e.s à des conditions de travail nécessitant en réalité de nettes améliorations. Cette situation masque le passage d'une précarité à une autre.').
[1077] GAEL 2022b.

and the scarcity of doctoral contracts, not everyone can study archaeology and then pursue a successful career in the field. In a series of tweets posted on 17 January 2022, Audrey Vincent-Pennec returns to the case of programmed archaeology, which relies for the most part on the free work of students[1078]:

> 'All programmed excavations, whether on a field schools or not, emphasize training as a means of recruitment. [...] Just like any free internship in a company, we need manpower, and we sell you training and experience so we can exploit you for free. And in archaeology, as elsewhere, it works because you need it afterwards to build up your CV in an extremely competitive field where there are so few jobs. You can imagine the inequalities in training that this entails, and the rather drastic consequences it can have for precarious students, who simply do not have the means to spend the summer digging, and who can't put this experience to good use on their CV.'

Vincent-Pennec then extends the discussion, arguing that this free work has consequences not only for students in precarious employment, but also for the profession as a whole, which it helps to make more precarious:

> 'Now that you've got used to working for free every summer, and have [maybe even] struggled [for] 4 years with an unfunded thesis, [when] you're offered a fixed-term contract paying minimum wage after a Master or a PhD, what do you think? JACKPOT![1079]'

Berggren and Hodder share this observation for the United States, where the work of field technicians in particular is very poorly paid. According to a national survey carried out by The United Archaeological Field Technicians in the early 2000s, 70% of them are homeless and 90% have no health insurance or retirement savings[1080]. McGuire and Walker add that archaeology 'has followed a trajectory typical of most capitalist industries[1081]', and that it cannot therefore escape the problems of labour exploitation and precariousness, both in academia and in commercial archaeology. They compare the large number of precarious technicians in the commercial sector to an inexhaustible supply of exploitable workers, 'the new archaeological proletariat'[1082]. This expression and that of 'invisible diggers' are also used by Paul Everill in his article on archaeology in the United Kingdom and Nicolas Zorzin in his research on Quebec archaeology to refer to this mass of interchangeable, undervalued and underpaid individuals[1083]. In France, precariousness in archaeology has also been the subject of a number of recent articles[1084]. The preliminary results of the survey carried out by the Groupe Archéo en lutte in 2020 highlight the working conditions of archaeologists: an increase in the number of short, fragmented contracts, a rise in the number of 'CDIs' (open-ended contracts) for worksites/missions, a median salary after a Master's degree of 1,380 euros, an average of one to two months' free work per year to write reports and articles and take part in conferences, and so on[1085].

> 'The guild model of apprenticeship justifies the exploitation of graduate students/adjuncts and field technicians by portraying these statuses as temporary rites of passage that must be endured to achieve mastery. In reality these positions have become permanent career tracks that most individuals can only escape by leaving the discipline[1086].'

12.4. Solutions to fight discrimination

> 'This "proletarianisation" has contributed to the instillation in every digger and archaeologist of the sense that he or she is dispensable, that his or her right to work is a privilege and a fragile and permanently threatened one to say the least[1087].'

In its response to the cut in budgets for programmed excavations, Archéo en Lutte lists a series of measures that would effectively combat precariousness within our discipline. These include: 'hiring in line with needs and under the conditions of an open-ended contract; aligning the salary progression conditions of fixed-term contracts with those of open-ended contracts; rejecting seasonal contracts and project contracts; abandoning the 'site-independent contract', the corollary of the University's 'project-independent contract'; involvement of "technicians" in the organization of field and post-excavation phases; respect for a proportion of time spent in the field and time spent post-excavation (75% field, 25% post-excavation), taking into account the arduous nature of the job for all[1088]'.

[1078] @EnskaWho. Shared with her permission, thanks to her. ('Toutes les fouilles programmées, chantier-école ou pas, mettent en avant la formation pour recruter. [...] Comme n'importe quel stage gratos en entreprise, on a besoin de main d'œuvre, et on vous vend la formation et l'acquisition de l'expérience pour pouvoir vous exploiter gratuitement. Et en archéo, comme ailleurs, ça marche parce qu'on en a besoin ensuite pour faire valoir son cv dans un milieu extrêmement concurrentiel du fait du peu de postes. Vous vous doutez des inégalités de formation que cela entraîne, et des conséquences assez drastiques que ça peut avoir pour les étudiant·e·s précaires, qui n'ont tout simplement pas les moyens de fouiller l'été, et qui ne peuvent pas faire valoir cette expérience sur leur cv.').

[1079] ('Maintenant qu'on vous a habitué·e·s à travailler gratos tous les étés, que vous avez en [en plus peut-être] galéré [pendant] 4 ans en thèse non financée, [quand] on vous propose un contrat en CDD payé le smic bac+5 ou 8/9, vous vous dites quoi ? TROP BIEN !')

[1080] Berggren & Hodder 2003, 423.

[1081] McGuire & Walker 1999, 171.

[1082] McGuire & Walker 1999, 172 and 177 for the quote.

[1083] Everill 2007; Zorzin 2015a.

[1084] Goutas *et al.* 2020; Procopiou 2019; Trémeaud 2020.

[1085] Goutas *et al.* 2020; Trémeaud 2020.

[1086] McGuire & Walker 1999, 177.

[1087] Zorzin 2015a, 123.

[1088] GAEL (Groupe Archéo en Lutte), online. ('embauche à hauteur des besoins et dans les conditions d'un CDI; alignement des conditions d'évolution des salaires des CDD sur celles des CDI; refus des Contrats saisonniers et des Contrats de Projets; abandon du "CDI-chantier", corollaire du "CDI-projet" de l'Université; association des "techniciens" à l'organisation des phases de terrain et de post-fouille; respect d'une proportion de temps passé sur le terrain et de temps passé en post-fouille (75 % terrain, 25% post-fouille), prise en compte de la pénibilité du métier pour toutes et tous').

To combat these inequalities, the international anarchist collective The Black Trowel awards micro-scholarships in the English-speaking world ranging from 5 to 300 dollars/pounds/euros to archaeology students and doctoral candidates. The collective takes its inspiration from the Sportula initiative[1089], which helps students studying classics. The Black Trowel also helps people in need to obtain funding for larger sums. On their website, they state:

> 'We recognize that academia in its current form is ethnicity, class, ability, and gender-biased and discourages or even effectively forbids minorities and people from working classes from attending programs by enforcing prohibitively high tuition fees, expensive mandatory field schools and ignoring the often harsh reality of these students' lives outside of the academic bubble. All too often, we and our students have to work double shifts to get the extra money needed to buy a book, attend an excavation project, pay rent or internet bills to have access to online university materials from home, or even just buy a proper meal so that they do not have to attend the next class on an empty stomach! It is our goal to erode these barriers to make them more permeable for the next generation of archaeologists[1090].'

In 2022, there are no other similar initiatives. McGuire and Walker conclude that 'it is naive to believe that the archaeological proletariat will receive respect, living wages, benefits, and decent working conditions simply because it is humane. [...] Those of us who have stable employment need to assist temporary and part-time workers to organize and fight for respect, fair treatment, and security[1091]'.

Where to start?

A. Berggren & I. Hodder, 'Social Practice, Method, and Some Problems of Field Archaeology', *in American Antiquity* 68/3, 2003, 421–434.

L. Heath-Stout & E. M. Hannigan, 'Affording Archaeology: How Field School Costs Promote Exclusivity', *in Advances in Archaeological Practice* 8/2, 2020, 123–133.

R. McGuire & M. Walker, 'Class Confrontations in Archaeology', *in Historical Archaeology* 33/1, 1999, 159–183.

[1089] Sportula website [Accessed 23 April 2021, https://thesportula.wordpress.com/].

[1090] The Black Trowel website [Accessed 23 April 2021, https://blacktrowelcollective.wordpress.com/].

[1091] McGuire & Walker 1999, 178–179.

13

LGBTphobias

13.1. Queer archaeology and the critique of the heteropatriarchal system

The term 'heteropatriarchy' refers to a socio-political system based on the interweaving of patriarchy and heterosexuality. In this system, people who do not respect certain norms (masculine, cisgender, heterosexual) are discriminated against as being 'abnormal', 'deviant', 'perverse' or 'dangerous'. This is the case for homosexuals and transgender people, for example.

This discrimination is reinforced if these individuals also belong to other marginalised groups (women, racialised people or people with disabilities). Conversely, being a heterosexual cisgender man (whose gender identity corresponds to the gender assigned to him at birth) in this same system has a series of advantages, such as[1092]:

- not having to hide their sexual orientation or gender identity at work;
- not having to worry that their potential discovery will have negative economic, emotional or physical consequences;
- being able to express affection for their partner in public places without fear of judgement, discrimination or violence;
- having role models to identify with all around them (in the media, in films, at work, etc.);
- not having to defend their sexual orientation or gender identity, and even having the luxury of forgetting about them.

Archaeology is no exception to this system.

> 'Traditionally, archaeology is not a queer-friendly space. Fueled by machismo, it has created a hostile environment for those who do not fit the historic straight-white-male mold[1093].'

Homosexuality and the WHO

The World Health Organization removed homosexuality from the list of mental illnesses on May 17, 1990. Transidentity, on the other hand, was not removed until May 27, 2019.

[1092] DYLLA *et al.* 2016, 31.
[1093] DYLLA *et al.* 2016, 31.

Prior to the 2000s, research focused primarily on the discrimination faced by heterosexual cisgender women in the profession. Nevertheless, a few comments in certain publications indicate that archaeologists of the time were aware that the profession lacked diversity. For example, Alison Wylie noted in the introduction to *Equity Issues for Women in Archaeology* that the profile of the contributors to the book, as well as the subjects covered, were a reflection of the discipline as a whole: White, middle-class, heterosexual, Western and able-bodied. At the same time, she encouraged her colleagues to tackle the issue[1094]. Mobilising the tools developed by queer theory has a dual impact:

> 'Queering archaeology is relevant to our entire discipline, from the diversity of its members to the interpretation of the past itself[1095].'

However, the first writings claiming to be queer archaeology, i.e. concerned with all sexual and gender minorities, and by queer archaeologists, did not appear until the year 2000.

13.2. The 2000s: emergence with Claassen and Dowson

In 2000, the American archaeologist Cheryl Claassen showed how homophobia excluded women from archaeology in the United States from the very beginning of the institutionalisation of the discipline and continues to have a negative impact on the careers of women archaeologists today[1096]. She focuses on the period between 1880 and 1950. At that time, lesbianism was viewed in the United States solely from a psychiatric and medical perspective: homosexuality was considered an illness, a deviance. A woman who desires or has relations with another woman disrupts the established order, i.e. the understanding of what it means to 'be a man' or 'be a woman'. Claassen draws a parallel between this pathologisation of homosexuality and the exclusion of women from excavation sites. For her, this exclusion must be seen in terms of both sexism and homophobia. Women wishing to work in archaeology, and more specifically in the field, a masculine environment par excellence, cannot be real women because they aspire to fulfil themselves in a sector that is not intended for them. They are therefore classed as suspicious and abnormal, and seen as a threat to the social balance.

[1094] NELSON *et al.* 1994, xi.
[1095] DYLLA *et al.* 2016, 31.
[1096] CLAASSEN 2000.

Sexism and homophobia can also be combined with racism. Claassen points out that this denial of femininity is total when it comes to Black women. It is not acceptable to use 'masculine' White women or 'women turned into men' (lesbians), but there are no restrictions when it comes to Black women. From the earliest excavation sites, archaeologists have not hesitated to exploit Black women, because they are seen first and foremost as cheap labour before they are seen as women.

> 'This was one of the supreme ironies of slavery: in order to approach its strategic goal – to extract the greatest possible surplus from the labor of the slaves – the black women had to be annulled as woman, that is, as woman in her historical stance of wardship under the male hierarchy[1097].'

Cheryl Claassen concludes by saying that today, homophobia has not disappeared. Homosexual students are still forced to keep their sexual orientation secret. Homophobic insults, sexual harassment and aggression towards members of the academic community who are recognised as lesbians or who may be lesbians are still very much present. She points out that this discrimination also affects gay men[1098].

In the introduction to his article 'Why Queer Archaeology? An Introduction', the American archaeologist Thomas Dowson says:

> 'For some time after "coming out" I strongly believed my sexuality had nothing to do with me being an archaeologist[1099].'

At the time, he did not want to talk about it in his professional environment and thought that this choice of silence was a personal decision. He is now revising his opinion:

> 'It derives from an unspoken social rule whereby academic homosexual men and women are forced to maintain an authority to act by denying or downplaying their sexuality[1100].'

For Dowson, homosexual people have to constantly negotiate how they can acquire and maintain the right to speak, to be heard and to be taken seriously without denying or hiding their sexual orientation. It is not just a question of being able to be publicly homosexual, but of being able to preserve a de-demonised link between their homosexuality and their scientific credibility. This is not an easy task:

> 'It should come as no surprise then that many archaeologists with a homosexual identity, or even those who are assumed to be homosexual, have been or are excluded from various aspects of archaeology at one time or another[1101].'

He points out that rejection used to be more frontal and that exclusion has now become more pernicious and harder to prove.

> 'I heard of a young male student who was reluctant to take my undergraduate courses because he feared his peers would discover he was gay. That fear of being thought of as un-manly also affects heterosexual men who suffer the pressures of having to live up to certain expectations of what a man should be[1102].'

In addition to exclusion, homophobia is used to explicitly or implicitly discredit certain research projects. For Dowson, heterosexual male archaeologists have an epistemological privilege over homosexual archaeologists. This privilege also legitimises a certain vision of the past[1103].

13.3. From the 2000s to 2020

> 'We need both qualitative and quantitative narratives about queer experience in archaeology[1104].'

Twenty years have passed since the seminal articles by Claassen and Dowson, and there is still relatively little data in archaeology. For example, there are no specific surveys on the place of LGBTQIA+ people in archaeology, as there are for cisgender women. In 2020, the English-language LGBTQ+ Field Network published a questionnaire entitled 'Being Out in the Field' on the place of queer people in the field. The results have not yet been published. However, data can be obtained from a number of general studies conducted from an intersectional perspective[1105]. For example, Laura Heath-Stout concludes in her thesis defended in 2019:

> 'Straight white cisgender men conduct a plurality or majority of archaeological research across almost every subfield, region, method, and topic[1106].'

It also shows that the majority of publications in archaeology in the United States are written by White cisgender heterosexual men[1107]. Gender archaeology and feminist archaeology are the fields with the most diverse researcher profiles: 23% of them do not identify themselves as heterosexual. In the other fields, between 92% and 95% of researchers are heterosexual[1108].

There are also few testimonies, and few concrete measures and solutions put in place to combat such discrimination. The majority of works come from the United States, Canada

[1097] Claassen 2000, 177, quoting Davis 1971, 7.
[1098] Claassen 2000, 178.
[1099] Dowson 2000, 161.
[1100] Dowson 2000, 161.
[1101] Dowson 2000, 162.
[1102] Dowson 2000, 162.
[1103] Dowson 2000, 162.
[1104] Danis 2016, 38.
[1105] Cook 2019; Fryer & Raczek 2020; Heath-Stout 2019.
[1106] Heath-Stout 2019, 204.
[1107] Heath-Stout 2019, 111–113.
[1108] Heath-Stout 2019, 184.

and the United Kingdom[1109]. These issues have also recently spread to Peru[1110] and the French-speaking world[1111]. The *Queer forum: Queer Scholarship and Queer Experience* round table, held at the Society of Historical Archaeology's annual meeting in 2014 in Quebec City (Canada), was the first event in archaeology to address this issue[1112]. The Society for American Archaeology was the first in the United States to organise a one-day conference focused on this theme, in San Francisco in 2015. The session *Queering the Field: Archaeologies of Sexuality, Gender, and Beyond* had several aims, including defining what queer is and how it can be applied to archaeology. Five of the six lectures focused on academia and the use of queer theory in the interpretation of material remains. Casey Campetti's *Out in the Field? Queer Archaeologists, Queer Archaeology, and CRM* [Cultural Resource Management], looked more specifically at the case of archaeologists working in the public sector. The archaeologist noted that, even with the arrival of queer issues in archaeology, the situation of cultural resource managers had not really changed and they remained relatively invisible compared to LGBTQIA+ archaeologists in academia.

> 'In addition to very real issues in seeking employment and receiving fair promotions, the work environments (particularly the field) for CRM archaeologists can be wilfully ignorant of LGBTQ issues or outwardly hostile[1113].'

Volume 16 of the *SAA Archaeological Record, Toward an Inclusive Queer Archaeology*, comes to the same conclusion by exploring what it means to be a queer archaeologist today, how heteronormativity affects the exclusion of queer people within archaeology, and the possibilities for building more inclusive and safe spaces for study and work[1114].

> 'Archaeologists have increasingly recognized the need to diversify our discipline, yet there is still little discussion of the heteronormative assumptions that linger in research, fieldwork, and classrooms— assumptions that affect both archaeological perspectives and the composition of its practitioners[1115].'

This point of view was also shared in February 2022 by Gabriela Oré Menéndez in her lecture *Redefining (My) Archaeological Practice Through Queer Lens* at Cambridge University.

13.4. Discrimination

Our experience of archaeology is shaped as much by our sexual orientation as by our gender identity. Queer archaeologists learn very early on which spaces they are welcome in and which are closed to them. We know about the discrimination experienced by these archaeologists from a few articles and testimonials posted on the web.

Definition

Transphobia: rejection, contempt and hatred of transgender people.

Chelsea Blackmore and her colleagues describe the dangers and problems faced by LGBTQIA+ archaeologists in the field. In their view, the field is the place where most of the tensions are crystallised, with the valorisation of a certain type of masculinity, heterosexuality as the norm and the sharing of living and working spaces[1116]. To support their arguments, they draw on a series of testimonials from academia and the public sector. Similar experiences are posted online on the *Queer Archaeology* platform. In the French-speaking world, a number of accounts of homophobia and transphobia with similar content are also being shared via the Paye ta Truelle collective and the Archéo-Sexisme exhibition.

Among the problems listed, the most recurrent is the fact of **forcing LGBTQIA+ archaeologists to remain invisible** coupled with **ostracism**, leading to a feeling of shame and illegitimacy. Some queer archaeologists are out in the workplace and are relatively comfortable with this, but this comfort depends above all on a series of variables such as social position and gender identity.

> 'Among my peers (i.e., other archaeologists in senior positions or other consultants), many seemed to avoid me at meetings and conferences. occasionally sensed discomfort by some (always men), it never became a point of contention. Part of this too, I think, was that people were never confronted by the reality of my sexual identity. I was a "safe" queer, if you will— I didn't have boyfriends/partners/husbands to go to meetings or social events with me[1117].'

Carla Hernándès, a bisexual archaeologist married to a woman, reports in an article on the website *Queer Archaeology*:

> 'So, long story short: I am bisexual, and married to a wonderfully smart and beautiful woman who is in the same field as me, and who more than once has joined me on fieldwork projects. [...] When I started in archaeology, I didn't know this would be an issue. I didn't know that there would be always this wall between me and the people I work with[1118].'

Because of this, many researchers are reluctant to talk openly about their sexual orientation because they fear the consequences for their careers. In 2019, Katherine Cook reminded us that queer academics are more likely

[1109] Springate 2020.
[1110] Tavera Medine 2019.
[1111] Mary, Pasquini & Vandevelde 2019; Mary 2020.
[1112] Springate 2014.
[1113] Campetti 2015.
[1114] Rutecki & Blackmore 2016.
[1115] Rutecki & Blackmore 2016, 9.
[1116] Blackmore *et al.* 2016, 18–19.
[1117] Blackmore *et al.* 2016, 19–20.
[1118] [Accessed 30 April 2021, https://queerarchaeology.com/2018/02/21/queer-in-the-field/].

to be excluded from conventional funding opportunities, publication structures and career models[1119].

> 'Until recently [I] never met an out gay man on a field crew. I think this is due in large part to archaeology, especially CRM, still being permeated with a cowboy mentality, which encourages a pronounced machismo[1120].'

These insidious forms of discrimination are compounded by **homophobic and transphobic insults, moral and sexual harassment, and physical and sexual assaults**. Hugh Radde's survey of Californian archaeology shows that the majority of people who are the targets of harassment and physical assault are LGBTQIA+ people[1121]. Men are generally physically attacked because of their real or assumed sexual orientation. The majority of perpetrators are their male colleagues or superiors.

> 'As an archaeologist, I've been let down by peers, colleagues, and friends who claim to be liberal allies. I've seen men assume an effeminate gait for a few laughs. I once heard a colleague question the "manliness" of trans men[1122].'

An anonymous lesbian archaeologist testifies:

> 'Working in CRM, and particularly on site with construction or related crews, verbal harassment is frequent. In a limited number of such instances I have felt unsafe, particularly as a gay woman[1123].'

Similar situations are reported by another queer archaeologist in Laura Heath-Stout's 2019 thesis. She recounts how difficult it is to be a woman in archaeology, but even more so to be a queer woman. Through homophobic insults and constant questioning of her skills, her male colleagues make her feel that she is not welcome in the field, that it is not her place[1124].

Micro-aggressions are also common. Several archaeologists point out that the field is a particularly hostile place for transgender people and denounce the general climate of misogyny and transphobia in archaeology[1125]. For transgender people, these micro-aggressions can be found in the rooming arrangements in the excavation houses, the absence of non-gender-segregated toilets at conferences or the absence of rubbish bins in all the toilets and bathrooms, for example[1126].

> 'Having your gender identity invalidated every time you need to wee seems an unnecessary attack, and one that can be easily avoided. Especially during field work, having appropriate facilities is essential[1127].'

For transgender people, this is compounded by the denial of their identity through the use of a 'deadname' (birth name, different from the new name chosen by the person) or misgendering (use of a gender in which the person does not recognise him or herself). The effect of this discrimination is to create a hostile environment, with consequences for both the mental and physical well-being of queer people.

13.5. Solutions to fight discrimination

For the last twenty years or so, a minority of archaeologists have been fighting against this discrimination within the discipline. For Chelsea Blackmore, awareness-raising, education and the creation of exchange and working networks are essential. In 2015, she created the Queer Archaeology initiative, which took the form of a website, a Twitter account and a Facebook group designed to relay testimonies from queer people as well as providing information and resources for queer and allied people.

In concluding his investigation, Hugh Radde stresses the importance of recognising one's privileges and questioning oneself[1128]. He calls for the introduction and dissemination of procedures that are easy to understand and follow in the event of an incident. Finally, he stresses the urgent need for training for operations managers, excavation site managers and teachers. These conclusions are shared by Cobb and Croucher[1129], as well as by Rutecki and Blackmore, who point out that by 'undervaluing the importance of heteronormative critiques and maintaining the status quo, we fail as social scientists[1130]'.

In the UK, the Equality and Diversity Group was set up in 2016 with the support of the Chartered Institute for Archaeologists, the Federation of Archaeological Managers and Employers and Prospect Archaeology to challenge the lack of equality and diversity within the profession. As part of their actions, a code of conduct and ethics has been drawn up and distributed to a number of sites. It aims to combat inequalities based on gender, race, sexual orientation and disability, and to improve working environments for archaeologists. In the French-speaking world, the Chantier-Éthique charter and vade-mecum created by the Archéo-Éthique association and the Paye ta Truelle collective pursue the same objectives. The conferences, round tables and study days organised by these three organisations also aim to raise awareness and train students and professionals in these issues.

1119 Cook 2019, 400.
1120 Blackmore *et al.* 2016, 20.
1121 Radde 2018, 235–243.
1122 Dylla *et al.* 2016, 33.
1123 Radde 2018, 243.
1124 Heath-Stout 2019, 271.
1125 Dylla *et al.* 2016, 20; Jorgensen-Rideout 2017, 23; Radde 2018; VanDerwarker *et al.* 2018.
1126 Dylla *et al.* 2016, 33; Jorgensen-Rideout 2017, 23.
1127 Jorgensen-Rideout 2017, 23.
1128 Radde 2018.
1129 Cobb & Croucher 2016.
1130 Rutecki & Blackmore 2016, 10.

American researchers Emily Dylla, Sheena A. Ketchum and Carol McDavid list a series of recommendations for being a good ally in archaeology[1131]. These include:

- Make it clear that harassment based on sexual orientation and gender identity is not tolerated;
- Teach ourselves LGBTQIA+ history, concepts and terminology, because the LGBTQIA+ community is not responsible for our education;
- Learn to listen to criticism, apologise and change our behaviour, rather than instinctively reacting with anger or rejection;
- Take concrete action at individual and collective level, such as providing financial support to organisations fighting for the rights of LGBTQIA+ people.

Some advice focuses more specifically on microaggressions and on the behaviours and infrastructures to be built. In 2011, for example, the Fort Davis archaeological project led by Laurie Wilkie and Katrina Eichner set up a form where archaeology students and archaeologists could indicate their preferred pronouns and room arrangements before the start of the excavations. In 2014, the Queer Archaeology Interest Group was created within the Society of American Archaeology with the aim of recognising, raising the profile of and supporting lesbian, gay, bisexual, transgender, queer and intersex students and archaeologists. At the group's request in 2016, gender-neutral toilets were installed in all areas hosting conferences and symposia organised by the SAA[1132]. Since 2019, the Seeing Red project has also been campaigning in the UK to ensure that the problems associated with menstruation on excavation sites are recognised for cisgender women, transgender men and non-binary people alike.

Where to start?

Ch. Blackmore, L. Drane, R. Baldwin & D. Ellis, 'Queering Fieldwork. Difference and Identity in Archaeological Practice', *in The SAA Archaeological Record* 16/1, 2016, 18–23.

Ch. Claassen, 'Homophobia and Women Archaeologists', *in World Archaeology* 32/2, 2000, 173–179.

T.A. Dowson, 'Why Queer Archaeology? An Introduction', *in* P.L. Geller & M.K. Stockett (ed.), *Feminist Anthropology. Past, Present, and Future*, University of Pennsylvania Press, 2006, 89–102.

E. Dylla, S. A. Ketchum & C. McDavid, 'Listening More and Talking Less. Being a Good Ally', *in The SAA Archaeological Record* 16/1, 2016, 31–35.

D. M. Rutecki & C. Blackmore, 'Towards an Inclusive Queer Archaeology. An Overview and an Introduction', *in Special issue of The SAA Archaeological Record* 16/1, 2016, 9–11.

[1131] Dylla *et al.* 2016, 34–35.
[1132] Danis 2016, 37.

14

Ableism

14.1. Disabilities, ableism and archaeology

According to the World Health Organization (WHO), 'a disabled person is one whose physical or mental integrity is temporarily or permanently impaired, either congenitally or as a result of age or accident, so that his or her independence, ability to attend school or hold a job are compromised'. Sociologist Erving Goffman defines 'stigma' as the gap between others' stereotypical expectations of our identity and our actual identity[1133]. At the same time, he distinguishes between 'visible' and 'invisible' stigmas. 'Visible disability' commonly refers to any motor handicap (paraplegia, tetraplegia, malformation, etc.). The 'invisible handicap' covers both mental disorders (autism, dyslexia, depression, etc.) and physical disorders (deafness, visual impairment, heart problems, endometriosis, arthritis, etc.). Both are subject to discrimination.

The term **'disablism'** was coined around thirty years ago in the United States as part of the field of disability studies[1134]. These studies focus on the perception of disability as a social construct. People with disabilities are not excluded from society because of their 'shortcomings', but because of the physical, social and economic barriers created by society itself[1135]. Paul Miller, Sophia Parker and Sarah Gillinson define 'disablism' as 'discriminatory, oppressive or abusive behaviour, rooted in the belief that people with disabilities are inferior to others[1136]'. In 2019, French anthropologist Clara Lecadet proposed a relatively similar definition, saying that it refers to 'the system of norms and values that organises life in society around the figure of the able-bodied person[1137]'. In this system of power, people with disabilities are made inferior, relegated to the margins of the public arena and perceived as mistakes and failures because they are 'abnormal', outside the norm.

The discrimination faced by people with disabilities in our society is numerous: less access to employment, housing, education and public spaces; insults; and physical and sexual aggression. Once again, archaeology is not spared by this system. Tim Phillips and Roberta Gilchrist note that:

> 'Archaeology, especially fieldwork, has long been seen as the preserve of young, fit, and healthy people. Indeed, fieldwork can be both physically and mentally demanding, and perhaps appears to be an environment that is neither suitable nor welcoming to people with disabilities[1138].'

Not only does this image of the profession discourage students with disabilities from enrolling in archaeology courses, but a person with a disability wishing to pursue a career in the discipline may also be perceived as lacking professional credibility. For archaeologist Doug Rock-Macqueen, this is why many people with a disability in archaeology hide it from their employer: the fear of being sacked or not finding a job afterwards is real in a system that operates largely on small, fixed-term contracts, word of mouth and nepotism[1139].

There are few studies on the subject in archaeology. A few researchers based in England and the United States timidly took up the issue at the end of the 1990s. Their studies are largely based on the work undertaken by feminist archaeologists in the 1980s and 1990s. The first conference on the subject dates from 1995. Presented by Nyree Finlay as part of the Theorical Achaeology Group (TAG) organised at the University of Reading in England, it gave rise in 1999 to a special issue in the journal *Archaeological Review from Cambridge* on the issue of disability in archaeology. Entitled *Disability and Archaeology*, the issue in fact focused mainly on the place of disability within past societies, but the articles by Nyree Finlay ('Disabling Archaeology: an Introduction') and Tom Shakespeare ('Commentary – Observations on Disability and Archaeology') laid the foundations for further reflection.

Inclusive, Accessible, Archaeology was created a few years later in England. Led by Roberta Gilchrist, it is a collaborative project founded by the Department of Archaeology at the University of Reading, the School of Conservation Sciences at Bournemouth University and the Inclusive Environments research group at the University of Reading. The aim of the project is to raise awareness of disability issues in archaeology and to improve the integration of people with disabilities in the field. To this end, it works in collaboration with both the academic world and public services such as the Council for British Archaeology, the Institute of Field Archaeologists, and English Heritage and Oxford Archaeology. It was as part of this project that the first survey on the issue of disability in archaeology was carried out in 2005. *Disability and Archaeological Fieldwork* takes stock of the situation in the United Kingdom[1140]. The results show that disability affects between 2% and 10% of archaeologists and 14% of archaeology students[1141]. Most of the disabilities identified are invisible to both professionals and students: dyslexia, autism, deafness, arthritis, asthma,

1133 Goffman 1975.
1134 Albrecht *et al.* 2011, 47.
1135 Phillips & Gilchrist 2012, 3–4.
1136 Miller *et al.* 2004, 9.
1137 Lecadet 2019, 47 ('du système de normes et de valeurs qui organisent la vie en société autour de la figure de la personne valide.').
1138 Phillips & Gilchrist 2012, 2.
1139 Rocks-Macqueen 2014.
1140 Phillips & Gilchrist 2005.
1141 Phillips & Gilchrist 2012, 7.

epilepsy, heart problems, depression, etc. Motor disabilities affect 8.5% of those surveyed.

In addition to this survey, four conferences on the same theme were presented at the TAG in Exeter in 2006. In the United States, a doctoral thesis was completed in 2006 by researcher Meredith Fraser, who looks in particular at how to make archaeology truly accessible to all. Laura Heath-Stout also looks at the discrimination faced by people with disabilities in archaeology[1142]. On 27 January 2022, a webinar entitled *Accessing Archaeology: A Conversation on Equity and Ethics* was organised by six speakers, archaeologists with disabilities, and supported by the Smithsonian[1143]. A number of experiences are also being shared by archaeologists directly concerned online, via the Inclusive, Accessible, Archaeology project website, personal blogs[1144] and social networks.

Information can also be gleaned from surveys of the profession in general. For example, the survey carried out in England in 2013 indicated that 1.8% of archaeologists have one or more forms of disability[1145]. The study *Discovering the Archaeologists of Europe 2012–14: Transnational Report* published in 2014 reports that there are 1.1% of archaeologists with disabilities across Europe. Germany is the country with the highest number of disabled people working in archaeology (5%). Countries such as Denmark, Greece and Slovenia, on the other hand, have none. The survey concludes that 'disabled people may be excluded from working in the archaeological sector in many countries[1146]'.

One of the most active figures in the field between 2014 and 2019 was British archaeologist Theresa O'Mahony, who passed away on September 22 2019, a specialist in disability in archaeology and herself suffering from a motor disability. Her master's thesis, *Archaeology for All? An Examination of Attitudes Towards Disability Within Archaeology* led to a series of conferences in the United Kingdom, the publication of an article[1147], the creation of an *Enabled Archaeology* guide, available in open access on the British Archaeological Jobs Resource website[1148], and the formation of the Enabled Archaeology Foundation collective.

14.2. Discrimination

In 2005, one of the respondents to the *Archaeology and Disability* survey confided:

> 'The concept of anyone who is physically or mentally impaired being involved with field archaeology, particularly excavation, is absurd[1149].'

[1142] Heath-Stout 2022.
[1143] On Youtube: [Accessed May 2, 2021, https://youtu.be/G2B--jL7KtY].
[1144] For example Rathbone 2013; Rock-MacQueen 2014.
[1145] Aitchison & Rocks Macqueen 2013; Cobb & Croucher 2016.
[1146] Aitchison *et al.* 2014, 31–32.
[1147] O'Mahony 2016.
[1148] O'Mahony 2015.
[1149] Phillips & Gilchrist 2005.

However, archaeology is an ageing discipline, and many of the health problems and disabilities listed may arise as a result of the repetitive nature of the work, insecure pay and status, and poor general working conditions (climate, pollution, lack of suitable equipment, inadequate protective measures), such as back or knee problems, osteoarthritis or depression[1150]. For example, in an article posted on his personal website, the American archaeologist Stuart Rathbone recounts the following:

> 'There are some interesting connections that can be made between the lifestyle of contract archaeologists, the occurrence of mental illness, and the levels of alcohol and drug misuse. The development of mental illness and drink and drug problems are believed to be influenced by a complex combination of factors relating to the genetic makeup of a person and the nature of their environment. The important part for the archaeological profession is that whatever the biological and sociological background of our compatriots may be, there are other factors that have a substantial impact on wellbeing. It is within our collective power to make alterations to these factors if we can identify avoidable problems and find appropriate ways of negating them[1151].'

At the same time, a study carried out in 2010 identified the difficulties encountered by disabled people in archaeology[1152]:

- **A general lack of knowledge about disabilities**

Of the twenty-two files shared by people with disabilities on the *Inclusive, Accessible, Archaeology* website, Paul, who is partially deaf, testifies:

> 'There have been very few problems with fieldwork. [...] At odd times the supervisors on site were a bit quiet, I sometimes turned up the volume, but at no time did I have to ask them to speak louder. I tried to opt for normality and cope by using the technology. [...] I did not have any real problems working as part of a team, as we worked in loose groups. If I had wanted 100% communication, I would have had to tell the whole group about the condition and tell them to look at me when speaking. I often said: "Sorry, say that again"[1153].'

- **Lack of knowledge about disability legislation and the support available to employers.**

Sarah, an archaeologist who has had a motor disability and a coordination problem (dysprasia) since the age of 9, shares:

[1150] Goutas *et al.* 2020; Phillips & Gilchrist 2012; Trémeaud 2020; Tufféry 2019.
[1151] [Accessed April 29, 2023, http://rmchapple.blogspot.com/2013/09/the-four-and-half-inch-pointing-trowel.html].
[1152] Phillips & Creighton 2010.
[1153] Inclusive Accessible Archaeology [Accessed 29 April 2023, https://doi.org/10.5284/1000211], Downloads, Case Studies, 02 Paul.

'On my training dig ten years later, it became apparent fieldwork was not for me. [....] What made it worse was the Site Director did not believe anything was wrong with me. [...] I am now working as a computer archaeologist, desk-based and office work and quite happy doing it. Websites are my major hobby and getting paid for doing it is a bonus. I do miss the fieldwork a bit[1154].'

- **A reluctance to declare a disability or ask for an adaptation of working conditions for fear of being refused or losing a job.**

Theresa O'Mahony recounts her difficulties in gaining acceptance into archaeology after declaring her disability:

'I had volunteered at digs before I started university. In all I applied to 38 different training schools, museums and archives but I kept being rejected, in total 36 times. [...] On one occasion I was called a "freak on three legs" (I walk with a cane), "a witch" and "evil". I also experienced people as a group (around 30 people), turn their backs on me as I walked into a room[1155].'

- **A lack of adapted facilities** (e.g. access to infrastructures and excavation sites, adjusted office equipment, modified working hours, toilets up to standard, etc.).

- **A focus on output and production that fails to take into account the fact that not everyone is capable of doing everything at the same speed and with the same level of skill.**

Simon, who suffers from dyslexia, arthritis and is unable to fully control his upper limbs following a motorbike accident, tells:

'When I started [archaeology], I just wanted to dig. With my physical limitations two weeks of digging was as much as I could cope with. Even with the flotation sieving there are times when I have to take a break. [...] My supervisor had not been made aware of my condition. I had to sit down with him and explain my problems. It would have been nice if there had been a little more interaction in the first place where they could have known what to expect. [...] There was a bit of disagreement about the value of what I was doing with the site boss and I felt very under pressure, unnecessary pressure[1156].'

Those who receive the best support from their institution are those who already have a permanent contract and undergraduate and masters students[1157]. In the study by Phillips and Creighton, the university appears to be the place where disability issues are best dealt with, but there are very few arrangements in place from doctoral level onwards[1158]. Furthermore, very little work is done in the field schools, despite the fact that the field is seen as essential and instructive from the very first years of university. As a result, many students with disabilities find themselves forced to change direction mid-course or are driven to depression, and even suicide in the most serious cases[1159].

'One of my dissertation research participants, a man on the autistic spectrum, committed suicide and I believe the very negative experiences of his fieldwork training were a contributory factor in his death. During my interview with him, he kept saying "I'm invisible, just empty space"[1160].'

14.3. Solutions to fight discrimination

'Whether in the field or in the laboratory, professional archaeologists are often exposed to organizations and working conditions that do not always take into account the fragility of the individuals themselves. Paradoxically, the attitude of prevention and care towards heritage seems to be greater than that towards the individuals in charge of it[1161].'

Nowadays, almost all codes of ethics in archaeology include a reference to people with disabilities. Legal obligations exist in most countries. However, concrete action remains rather rare and is driven more by the individuals directly concerned than by the institutions[1162]. In England, public bodies have each developed their own internal policy, under the banner of the Heritage for All project, 'all' including people with disabilities. Since then, a number of projects have been set up to encourage people with disabilities to take part in excavations and surveys. The Newcastle Society for the Blind (NSPB), for example, organises visits to rock art sites in Northumbria and study days to interpret the representations recorded[1163]. Despite all these regulations, there is no qualitative data on the actual experience of the disabled public.

Generally speaking, the solutions put forward by the various players fighting for the recognition of people with disabilities in archaeology are the same:

- Procedures to be put in place at school excavation sites to ensure that students with disabilities have access to all services;

[1154] Inclusive Accessible Archaeology [Accessed 29 April 2023, https://doi.org/10.5284/1000211], Downloads, Case Studies, 08 Sarah.
[1155] O'Mahony 2018, 216.
[1156] Inclusive Accessible Archaeology [Accessed 29 April 2023, https://doi.org/10.5284/1000211], Downloads, Case Studies, 03 Simon.
[1157] Phillips & Gilchrist 2012, 8.

[1158] Phillips & Creighton 2010, quoted by Phillips & Gilchrist 2012, 11 et 14.
[1159] Phillips & Gilchrist 2012, 14.
[1160] O'Mahony 2018, 216.
[1161] Tufféry 2019, 130. ('Sur le terrain ou en laboratoire, les archéologues professionnels sont souvent exposés à des organisations et des conditions de travail qui ne prennent pas toujours en compte des fragilités des individus eux-mêmes. Paradoxalement, l'attitude de prévention et de soin apporté au patrimoine semble plus grande que celle apportée aux individus qui en ont la charge.')
[1162] Tufféry 2019, 135.
[1163] Phillips & Gilchrist 2012, 5.

- Possibility of work adjustments, which must be agreed and discussed with the students and professionals concerned;
- Training for supervisors, with advice and examples of good practice;
- Improved physical access to sites, buildings, premises and toilets;
- Improved access to written and oral documents.

Very active on Twitter, Instagram and TikTok, deaf American archaeologist Amelia S. Dall has been offering archaeologists her sign language translation services for courses, seminars and conferences since 2020[1164]. She also produces a variety of content on social networks to raise awareness of deafness among the general public, whether or not they come directly from the heritage field.

The Inclusive, Accessible, Archaeology project has also created a guide entitled *Including Disabled Students and Self-Evaluation in Archaeological Fieldwork Training*, which includes recommendations for making field schools and university outings more inclusive, as well as excavation sites more accessible to the general public[1165]. It also aims to raise awareness in the fields of archaeology and heritage by collecting and disseminating widely online and offline experiences of people with disabilities. Finally, a toolkit for students has been developed. It takes the form of a questionnaire that enables individuals to identify their ability to carry out the various tasks required on site by answering a series of questions about everyday activities that are similar to archaeological activities. Depending on the results, any necessary adjustments can be identified and requested, and even modified after an initial field experience. The Archaeology and Heritage: Mental Health and Wellbeing working group at the University of Winchester has also produced a guide to raising awareness of the issue of mental health and well-being in archaeology[1166].

Via the All Inclusive Archaeology group on Facebook, Theresa O'Mahony also opts to raise awareness among archaeology students and professionals to combat 'the fear, ignorance and suspicion encountered by people with disabilities within archaeology and society in a broader sense'. In 2018, she created the Enabled Archaeology Foundation to continue the work. The aims of this collective are twofold: to empower, equip and enable all people with disabilities to work in archaeology, and to combat validism within archaeology.

> 'My name is Theresa a mature disabled (some mobility probs) archaeology post-graduate student at University in London. Time and again, I found myself hitting attitude barriers, disabled, being thought of as physically incapable of doing any archaeology. [...] This is why I am raising awareness, then soon I will go out into the world and tell anyone who will listen, if attitudes are changed then we could have equality in and outside of archaeology. By setting up the Enabled Archaeology Foundation for both able-bodied and disabled/enabled to be equipped to know that we can all participate in archaeology, and smash the attitudinal barriers of fear, suspicion and at times outright prejudice to disabled/enabled involvement in archaeology today. Us disabled folk just need one chance[1167].'

The actions undertaken take place both online (website, Twitter, Facebook, podcast) and offline (training courses, lectures, one-day conferences), such as the first global one-day conference on disabilities in archaeology organised in 2018. The movement launched by the late Theresa O'Mahony continues. The Enabled Archaeology Foundation is now reaching out to the Australian archaeological community[1168]. With its list of practical tips (trenches adapted for wheelchair users, trowels with straps, documents in Braille, etc.), the *Enabled Archaeology* guide is now used as a reference in the United Kingdom[1169].

Where to start?

L. Heath-Stout, 'The Invisibly Disabled Archaeologist', *in International Journal of Historical Archaeology*, 2022, [online: https://doi.org/10.1007/s10761–022–00653–8].

T. O'Mahony, *Enabled Archaeology Guide 41*, 2015, [online: http://www.bajr.org/BAJRGuides/41_Enabled_Archaeology/41EnabledArchaeology.pdf].

T. O'Mahony, 'Archaeology from a Disabled Enabled Perspective', *in London Archaeologist* 14/10, 2016, 265–269.

T. Phillips & J. Creighton, *Employing People with Disabilities: Good Practice Guidelines for Archaeologists*, Institute for Archaeologists (Institute for Archaeologists Professional Paper 9), 2010, [online: https://www.archaeologists.net/sites/default/files/Disabilitypaper.pdf].

Website *Inclusive, Accessible, Archaeology*: https://doi.org/10.5284/1000211

1164 @ameliathearchaeologist.
1165 [Accessed April 20, 2021, https://www.advance-he.ac.uk/knowledge-hub/number-5-guide-teaching-and-learning-archaeology].
1166 [Accessed April 12, 2021, https://www.solent.ac.uk/research-innovation-enterprise/research-at-solent/projects-and-awards/documents/march-plus-guidelines-summary.pdf].
1167 On Facebook [Accessed April 12, 2021, https://www.facebook.com/allinclusivearchaeology].
1168 O'Mahony 2018, 217.
1169 [Accessed April 12, 2021, http://www.bajr.org/bajrguides/41_enabled_archaeology/41enabledarchaeology.pdf].

Conclusion

Archaeology is not – and has never been – apolitical. As archaeologists, we cannot operate outside of society because we are deeply embedded within it. Our work, institutions and interpretations are all shaped by the social, cultural and political contexts in which we live. This means that we are both agents and, at times, victims of the patriarchal structures that govern our world. The sexism, racism, ableism, classism and homophobia we encounter in archaeology are not unique to the discipline; they reflect broader societal systems of inequality. Claiming that archaeology can remain neutral or objective in the face of these realities is not only naive, it is also complicit. In a world where academic freedom is under increasing threat and words such as 'gender', 'race', 'trans', 'bias', and 'LGBT' are censored or politically targeted, we must acknowledge the inherently political nature of our discipline.

It is precisely within this context that gender archaeology emerges as both a scholarly approach and a political stance, one that challenges dominant narratives and seeks to expose the power dynamics at work in both past societies and contemporary research practices. Throughout this book, we have explored how gender archaeology, rather than offering a fixed methodology, invites a critical rethinking of how we interpret the past, and how we conduct archaeology itself. Beginning with a reflection on the definitions of sex and gender, we highlighted the dynamic, socially constructed, and intersectional nature of identity. In tracing the history of gender archaeology, we examined the influence of feminist thought, the challenges it posed to androcentric narratives, and the ways it intersected with decolonial, queer, and Indigenous approaches.

The second part of the book is a series of case studies demonstrating the various ways in which gender can be interpreted – and misinterpreted – in the archaeological record. We showed how material culture both reflects and constructs gendered identities, examining topics ranging from funerary contexts and labour divisions to iconography and museum practices. We also emphasised the importance of critically questioning our own assumptions, as well as the contemporary ideologies that shape interpretation.

Finally, we turned the lens inward and interrogated the structures of our own profession. We examined the persistent inequalities within archaeology itself: who has a voice, who is silenced, who is represented and who remains invisible? Adopting the premise that 'a patriarchal discipline can only produce a patriarchal past[1170]', we advocated for a more inclusive, critical and socially engaged archaeology.

Ultimately, gender archaeology is about more than just uncovering the lives of women and marginalised individuals in the past. It is also about transforming the frameworks through which we conduct archaeological research, the narratives we create and the values we uphold as a scholarly community. It acknowledges that archaeology is inherently political and that, as scholars, we have a responsibility towards the past, present and future of our discipline.

However, this book is not just a review of past and present debates in gender archaeology. It is also a call to action. As well as documenting the evolution of the field and offering critical insights, we hope that this volume will serve as a practical and transformative tool to support current and future archaeologists in making the discipline more inclusive, reflexive and socially responsible. Yet, our aim is not merely to highlight the challenges and inequalities faced by the discipline, but also to propose concrete solutions to improve the situation and foster meaningful change.

As this book has demonstrated, the current situation remains far from ideal. Education is an important first step, but structural change is also required. Specifically, this includes:

Improving education and awareness:

- Mandatory courses and training in gender archaeology should be integrated into the curriculum to teach students and professionals how to incorporate gender perspectives into their research. This should include the analysis of archaeological material, site interpretation and theoretical frameworks. This approach fosters a critical understanding of how gender intersects with other social categories to shape past societies and archaeological practice.
- Incorporate queer, feminist, postcolonial, decolonial and intersectional perspectives into archaeological curricula and research agendas to broaden analytical frameworks and challenge dominant paradigms.

Enhancing access and representation:

- Facilitate equitable access to the discipline by offering scholarships and financial support for fieldwork participation, as well as mentorship programmes dedicated to supporting women and minorities.
- Increase the visibility and inclusion of women and marginalised groups in university programmes and academic positions. Recognise their contributions as essential to the development of archaeology.
- Work with concerned communities must become systematic. Local and Indigenous voices must be integrated into the scientific process.

[1170] Pope 2021.

Ensuring safe and inclusive working environments:

- Establish and enforce zero-tolerance policies against harassment, assault and discrimination in universities and on excavation sites.
- Develop clear procedures with trained, dedicated advisors to support victims and handle complaints effectively.
- Redesign fieldwork sites and training programmes to accommodate the specific needs of all participants and ensure they are safe, respectful and inclusive spaces.

Based on these recommendations, we wrote this book to serve as the handbook we wished we had had as students and early-career researchers starting out in the field. We hope that it will become a valuable resource for students, non-specialists, professors and experts alike, facilitating the wider dissemination and deeper integration of gender-based archaeological research.

Our aim is for this volume to support archaeologists at all levels in approaching archaeological contexts and material culture with a more nuanced, less biased and more intersectional perspective. Furthermore, we hope that it will serve as a catalyst for change, encouraging the recognition of the importance of gender not only within academic curricula, but also across the profession and in fieldwork environments.

By fostering greater awareness and understanding, we believe this book can contribute to the development of a more inclusive and socially conscious archaeology that honours the diversity of human experience, both past and present.

Bibliography

Abrunhosa & Valdez-Tullet 2021: A. Abrunhosa & J. Valdez-Tullet, 'The Role (or Lack of) Gender Theory in Portuguese Archaeology', poster, *1st Virtual Conference for Women Archaeologists and Paleontologists*, 7–8 mars 2021, Toulouse.

Adair & Levin 2020: J.G. Adair & A.K. Levin (eds.), *Museums, Sexuality, and Gender Activism*, Routledge, 2020.

Agarwal 2012: S. C. Agarwal, 'The Past of Sex, Gender, and Health: Bioarchaeology of the Aging Skeleton', *in American Anthropologist* vol. 114/2, 2012, 322–335.

Agarwal 2017: S. C. Agarwal, 'Understanding Sex- and Gender-Related Patterns of Bone Loss and Health in the Past. A Case Study from the Neolithic Community of Çatalhöyük', *in* S. C. Agarwal, J. K. Wesp (eds.), *Exploring Sex and Gender in Bioarchaeology*, University of New Mexico Press, 2017, 165–188.

Agbe-Davies 2002: A. Agbe-Davies, 'Black Scholars, Black Pasts', *in The SAA Archaeological Record* 2/4, 2002, 24–28.

Agbe-Davies 2010: A. Agbe-Davies, 'Concepts of Community in the Pursuit of an Inclusive Archaeology', *in International Journal of Heritage Studies* 16/6, 2010, 373–389.

Aimers & Rutecki 2016: J. Aimers & D. M. Rutecki, 'Brave New World: Interpreting Sex, Gender, and Sexuality in the Past', *in The SAA Archaeological Record* 16/1, 2016, 12–17.

Aitchison & Edwards 2008: K. Aitchison & R. Edwards, *Archaeology Labour Market Intelligence: Profiling the Profession 2007/08*, Institute for Archaeologists, 2008.

Aitchison & Rocks-Macqueen 2013: K. Aitchison & D. Rocks-Macqueen, *Archaeology Labour Market Intelligence: Profiling the Profession 2011–2012*, Landward Archaeology, 2013.

Aitchison *et al.* 2014: K. Aitchison *et al.*, *Discovering the Archaeologists of Europe 2012–14: Transnational Report*, York Archaeological Trust, 2014.

Alberti 1997: B. Alberti, *Archaeology and Masculinity in Bronze Age Knossos*, thèse de doctorat, Université de Southampton, 1997.

Alberti 2001: B. Alberti, 'Faience Goddesses and Ivory Bull-leapers: the Aesthetics of Sexual Difference at Late Bronze Age Knossos', *in World Archaeologies* 33, 2001, 189–205.

Alberti 2006: B. Alberti, 'Archaeology, Men, and Masculinities', *in* S. M. Nelson (ed.), *Handbook of Gender in Archaeology*, AltamiraPress, 2006, 401–434.

Alberti & Danielsson 2018: B. Alberti & I.-M. Danielsson, 'Gender, Feminist, and Queer Archaeologies: USA Perspective', *in* C. Smith, *Encyclopedia of Global Archaeology*, Springer, 2018, 2988–2997.

Albrecht *et al.* 2011: G. L. Albrecht, J.-F. Ravaud & H.-J. Stiker, 'L'émergence des disability studies: état des lieux et perspectives', *in Sciences Sociales et Santé* 19/4, 2011, 43–73.

Alessandrin & Dagorn 2021: A. Alessandrin & J. Dagorn, 'Femmes et déplacements: différents contextes, différentes expériences ?', *in Dynamiques régionales* 12/3, 2021, 63–82.

Algrain 2014: I. Algrain, *L'alabastre attique. Origine, formes et usages*, CReA-Patrimoine – Université libre de Bruxelles, 2014.

Algrain 2015: I. Algrain, '"À l'ombre des jeunes filles en fleur". Women and Flowers on Attic Pottery', *in* E. Trinkl & C. Lang-Auinger (eds.), *ΦΥΤΑ ΚΑΙ ΖΩΙΑ. Pflanzen und Tiere auf griechischen Vasen. Internationales Symposion, 26.–28. September 2013*, Verlag der österreichischen Akademie der Wissenschaften, 2015, 47–54.

Algrain 2020a: I. Algrain (ed.), *Archéologie du genre. Construction sociale des identités et culture matérielle*, Université des femmes, 2020.

Algrain 2020b: I. Algrain, 'Introduction. Pourquoi une archéologie du genre ?', *in* I. Algrain (ed.), *Archéologie du genre. Construction sociale des identités et culture matérielle*, Université des femmes, 2020, 7–20.

Algrain 2021a: I. Algrain, 'Genre et diversité dans les contextes archéologiques', *in Revista de Arqueologia Pública* 16/1, 2021, 95–110 [online: https://periodicos.sbu.unicamp.br/ojs/index.php/rap/issue/view/1843].

Algrain 2021b: I. Algrain, 'Un exemple de genre fluide dans la nécropole du Céramique ?', *Frontière·s, Revue d'archéologie, histoire & histoire de l'art* 5/1, 27–36, [online: https://publications-prairial.fr/frontiere-s/index.php?id=849].

Algrain 2022a: I. Algrain, 'Gender, Perfume and Society in Ancient Athens', *in* U. Matić (ed.), *Beautiful Bodies. Gender and Corporeal Aesthetics in the Past*, Oxbow Books, 2022, 153–175.

Algrain 2022b: I. Algrain, 'Les pionnières de l'archéologie. De Lady Stanhope à Gertrude Caton-Thompson', *in* L. Cattelain, M. Gillard & A. Smolderen (eds.), *Archéologues Malgré-Tout. Apporter sa pierre pour y voir clair. Mélanges offerts à Claire Bellier et Pierre Cattelain*, Éditions du Cedarc / Musée du Malgré-Tout, 2022, 321–328.

Algrain 2023: I. Algrain, 'Exposer l'humanité. Les musées d'archéologie face à la problématique du genre, entre surexposition des hommes et sous-exposition des femmes. Réflexions à partir de l'Espagne et de la Belgique', *in Les Cahiers de Muséologie* 3, 2023 [online: https://popups.uliege.be/2406–7202/index.php?id=1387].

Algrain & Lootvoet 2019: I. Algrain & V. Lootvoet (coord.), *Les dominations masculines: des origines aux antiféminismes*, Université des Femmes, 2019.

Algrain & Mary 2023: I. Algrain & L. Mary, 'Gertrude Bell (1868–1926): une vie impropre au mariage', *in* J. Eyméoud & C.-L. Gaillard (eds.), *Une histoire des célibats. Naissance d'un statut social (XVe-XXe siècles)*, Presses Universitaires de France, 2023, 119–133.

Anderson 2017: C. Anderson, 'A Female Viking Warrior? A Tomb Yields Clues', *in The New York Times*, 14 septembre 2017, [https://web.archive.org/web/20170921034740/https://www.nytimes.com/2017/09/14/world/europe/sweden-viking-women-warriors-dna.html?emc=eta1].

Angelbeck & Grier 2012: B. Angelbeck & C. Grier, 'Anarchism and the Archaeology of Anarchic Societies', *in Current Anthropology* 53/5, 2012, 547–587.

Angelbeck *et al.* 2018: B. Angelbeck, L. Borck & M. Sanger, 'Anarchist Theory and Archaeology', *in* C. Smith (ed.), *Encyclopedia of Global Archaeology*, Springer, 2018, 1–8, [https://doi.org/10.1007/978-3-319-51726-1_2627-1].

Angelbeck & Jones 2018: B. Angelbeck & J. Jones, 'Direct Actions and Archaeology: The Lil'wat Peoples Movement to Protect Archaeological Sites', *in Journal of Contemporary Archaeology* 5/2, 2018, 219–229.

Argelès *et al.* 1991: T. Argelès, R. Piqué & A. Vila, 'La importancia de llamarse hombre en prehistoria', *in Revista de Arqueología*, n° 121, 6–9.

Arnold 1985: D. Arnold, *Ceramic Theory and Cultural Process*, Cambridge University Press, 1985.

Arnold 1990: B. Arnold, 'The Past as Propaganda: Totalitarian archaeology in Nazi Germany', *in Antiquity* 64 (244), 1990, 464–478.

Arnold 2005: B. Arnold, '"Arierdämmerung": Race and Archaeology in Nazi Germany', *in World Archaeology* 38/1, Race, Racism and Archaeology, 2005, 8–31.

Arnold 2012: B. Arnold, 'The Vix Princess Redux: A Retrospective on European Iron Age Gender and Mortuary Studies', *in* L. Prados Torreira (ed.), *La Arqueología funeraria desde una perspectiva de género*, UA Ediciones, 2012, 215–232.

Arnold *et al.* 1988: K. Arnold, R. Gilchrist, P. Graves & S. Taylor, 'Women and Archaeology', *in Archaeological Review from Cambridge* 7, 1988, 2–9.

Arwill-Nordbladh 1998: E. Arwill-Nordbladh, 'Archaeology, Gender and Emancipation. The Paradox of Hanna Rydh', *in* M. Díaz-Andreu & M. L. S. Sørensen (eds.), *Excavating Women. An History of Women in European Archaeology*, Routledge, 1998, 155–174.

Arwill-Nordbladh 2008: E. Arwill-Nordbladh, 'Twelve Timely Tales: On Biographies of Pioneering Women Archaeologists', *in Reviews in Anthropology*, 37/2–3, 2008, 136–168.

Association Research Inc. 2005: Association Research Inc., *Salary Survey conducted for the Society for American Archaeology in cooperation with the Society for History Archaeology*, 2005, [online: https://documents.saa.org/container/docs/default-source/doc-careerpractice/salary_survey2005.pdf].

Association Musé·e·s 2022: Association Musé·e·s (ed.), *Guide pour un musée féministe: Quelle place pour le féminisme dans les musées français ?*, Association musé·e·s, 2022.

Atalay 2006: S. Atalay, 'Indigenous Archaeology as Decolonizing Practice', *in American Indian Quarterly* 30, n°3/4, 2006, 280–310.

Atalay 2008: S. Atalay, 'Multivocality and Indigenous Archaeologies', *in* J. Habu, C. Fawcett & J.M. Matsunaga (eds.), *Evaluating Multiple Narratives. Beyond Nationalist, Colonialist, Imperialist Archaeologies*, Springer, 2008, 29–44.

Atalay 2012: S. Atalay, *Community-based Archaeology*, University of California Press, 2012.

Atalay 2019: S. Atalay, 'Can Archaeology Help Decolonize the Way Institutions Think? How Community-Based Research Is Transforming the Archaeology Training Toolbox and Helping to Transform Institutions', *in Archaeologies* 15/3, 2019, 514–535.

Audouze 2006: F. Audouze, 'Compte-rendu: L. Owen, "Distorting the Past. Gender and the Division of Labor in the European Palaeolithic"', *in Bulletin de la Société préhistorique française* 103/2, 2006, 411–415.

Augereau 2019: A. Augereau, 'Change and Continuity: Gender and Flint Knapping Activities During the Neolithic in the Paris Basin', *in* J. K. Koch & W. Kirleis, *Gender Transformations in Prehistoric and Archaic Societies*, Sidestone Press, 2019, 435–458.

Augereau 2021: A. Augereau, *Femmes néolithiques. Le genre dans les premières sociétés agricoles*, CNRS Éditions, 2021.

Augereau & Darmangeat 2022: A. Augereau & C. Darmangeat, 'Le passé du genre et ses enjeux contemporains', *in* A. Augereau & C. Darmangeat (eds.), *Aux origines du genre. Enjeux, méthodes et controverses*, PUF, 2022, 9–41.

Ayeb & Pampanay 2021: L. Ayeb & É. Pampanay, 'Introduction. Les études sur le genre en archéologie, histoire et histoire de l'art', *in Frontière·s* 5, 2021, [Accessed 6 April 2023, URL: https://publications-prairial.fr/frontiere-s/index.php?id=885].

Bacus 2006: E. A. Bacus, 'Gender in East and Southeast Asian Archaeology', *in* S. M. Nelson, *Handbook of Gender in Archaeology*, Altamira Press, 2006, 633–666.

Balme & Beck 1995: J. Balme & W. Beck (eds.), *Gendered Archaeology. The Second Australian Women in Archaeology Conference*, ANH Publications, RSPAS, Australian National University, 1995.

Baquedano *et al.* 2017: I. Baquedano, M. Carrillo, L. Palop & E. Baquedano, 'Género, ciencia y arqueología. El Museo Arqueológico Regional ante el reto de construir una sociedad justa con las mujeres', *in* L. Prados Torreira & C. López Ruiz (eds.), *Museos arqueológicos y género. Educando en igualdad*, UAM Ediciones, 2017, 217–245.

Bard *et al.* 2019: C. Bard, M. Blais, F. Dupuis-Déri (dir.), *Antiféminismes et masculinismes d'hier à aujourd'hui*, Presses universitaires de France, 2019.

Bardolph 2014: D. N. Bardolph, 'A Critical Evaluation of Recent Gendered Publishing Trends in American Archaeology', *in American Antiquity* 79/3, 2014, 522–540.

Bardolph & Vanderwarker 2016: D. N. Bardolph & A. M. Vanderwarker, 'Sociopolitics in Southeastern Archaeology: The Role of Gender in Scholarly Authorship', *in Southeastern Archaeology* 35/3, 2016, 175–193.

Battle-Baptiste 2011: W. Battle-Baptiste, *Black Feminist Archaeology*, Routledge, 2011.

Baxter 2005: J. E. Baxter, 'Gendered Perceptions in Archaeology: A Perspective from the SAA Member Needs Assessment Survey', *in The SAA Archaeological Records*, 5–4, 2005, 7–9.

Bayard *et al.* 2019: A. Bayard, V. Bayard-Maret & G. Cordeiro, 'Vers une archéologie des crises alimentaires?', *in Mélanges de l'École française de Rome - Moyen Âge* 131/1, [Accessed 12 December 2020, URL: http://journals.openedition.org/mefrm/5303; DOI: https://doi.org/10.4000/mefrm.5303].

Beaudry 1994: M. C. Beaudry, 'Women Historical Archeologists: Who's Counting?', *in Archeological Papers of the American Anthropological Association* 5/1, 1994, 225–228.

Beaudry & White 1994: M. C. Beaudry & J. White, 'Cowgirls with the Blues? A Study of Women's Publication and the Citation of Women's Work in Historical Archaeology', *in* Ch. Claassen (ed.), *Women in Archaeology*, University of Pennsylvania Press, 1994, 138–158.

Beauvalet-Boutouyrie & Berthiaud 2015: S. Beauvalet-Boutouyrie & E. Berthiaud, *Le rose et le bleu. La fabrique du féminin et du masculin: Cinq siècles d'histoire*, Belin, 2015.

Beck 1994: W. Beck, 'Women in Archeology: Australia and the United States', *in Archeological Papers of the American Anthropological Association* 5/1, 1994, 99–104.

Beck & Head 1990: W. Beck & L. Head, 'Women in Australian Prehistory', *in Australian Feminist Studies* 11, 1990, 29–48.

Belard 2012: C. Belard, 'Les ceintures de l'âge du fer en Champagne: genre et archéologie', *in Clio. Histoire, femmes et société* 36, 2012, 183–190.

Belard 2015: C. Belard, 'La notion de genre ou comment problématiser l'archéologie funéraire', *in Les Nouvelles de l'Archéologie* 140, 2015, 23–27.

Belard 2017a: C. Belard, *Pour une archéologie du genre. Les femmes en Champagne à l'âge du fer*, Hermann, 2017.

Belard 2017b: C. Belard, 'Nouvelles approches et perspectives méthodologiques pour l'archéologie funéraire du genre', *in* J. Wilczek, A. Cannot, T. Le Cozanet, J. Remy, J. Macháček & J. Klápště, *Interdisciplinarité et nouvelles approches dans les recherches sur l'âge du Fer*, 2017b, 99–101.

Belard 2020: C. Belard, 'Genre, corps, sexe... et matérialité: quand les sciences sociales questionnent l'objet "féminin" ou "masculin" en archéologie', *in* I. Algrain (coord.), *Archéologie du genre. Construction sociale des identités et culture matérielle*, Université des femmes, 2020, 21–40.

Bender 1991: S. Bender, 'Towards a History of Women in Northeastern U. S. Archaeology', *in* D. Walde & N. Willows (eds.), *The Archaeology of Gender. Proceedings of the Twenty-Second Annual Conference of the Archaeological Association of the University of Calgary*, University of Calgary Archaeological Association, 1991, 211–216.

Bender 1992: S. Bender, 'Marian E. White: Pioneer in New York Archaeology', *in The Bulletin – Journal of the New-York State Archaeological Association* 104, 1992, 14–20.

Bennet 2015: J. Bennet, 'How Not to Be 'Manterrupted' in Meetings', *in The Times*, 14 janvier 2015, [online: https://time.com/3666135/sheryl-sandberg-talking-while-female-manterruptions/].

Bérard 2014: R.-M. Bérard, 'Le métal et la parure: identité ethnique et identité de genre dans les nécropoles de Grande Grèce et de Sicile', *in Dialogues d'histoire ancienne*, Supplément n°10, 2014, 145–169.

Bereni *et al.* 2020: L. Bereni, S. Chauvin, A. Jaunait & A. Revillard, *Introduction aux études sur le genre*, 3e édition, De Boeck Supérieur, 2020.

Berger *et al.* 2019: E. Berger, L. Yang & W. Ye, 'Foot Binding in a Ming Dynasty Cemetery near Xi'an, China', *in International Journal of Paleopathology* 24, 2019, 79–88.

Berggren & Hodder 2003: A. Berggren & I. Hodder, 'Social Practice, Method, and Some Problems of Field Archaeology', *in American Antiquity* 68/3, 2003, 421–434.

Bertelsen *et al.* 1987: R. Bertelsen, A. Lillehammer & J.-R. Naess, *Were They All Men? An Examination of Sex Roles in Prehistoric Society*, Arkeologisk museum i Stavanger, 1987.

Berseneva 2008: N. Berseneva, 'Women and Children in the Sargat Culture', *in* K. M. Linduff & K. S. Rubinson (ed.), *Are All Warriors Male? Gender Roles on the Ancient Eurasian Steppe*, AltaMira Press, 2008, 131–151.

Bessière 2003: C. Bessière, 'Race/classe/genre. Parcours dans l'historiographie américaine des femmes du Sud autour de la guerre de Sécession', *in Clio. Femmes, genre, histoire* 17, 2003.

Bessière & Gollac 2020: C. Bessière & S. Gollac, *Le genre du capital. Comment la famille reproduit les inégalités*, La Découverte, 2020.

Bilge & Hill Collins 2023: S. Bilge & P. Hill Collins, *Intersectionnalité. Une introduction*, Éditions Amsterdam, 2023.

Binford 1981: L.R. Binford, *Bones. Ancient Men and Modern Myths*, Academic Press, 1981.

Bird 1993: C. F. M. Bird, 'Woman the Toolmaker: Evidence for Women's Use and Manufacture of Flaked Stone Tools in Australia and New Guinea', *in* H. Du Cros & L. Smith (eds.), *Women in Archaeology: A Feminist Critique*, Department of Prehistory, Research School of Pacific Studies, Australian National University, 1993, 22–30.

Blackless *et al.* 2000: M. Blackless, A. Charuvastra, A. Derryck, A. Fausto-Sterling, K. Lauzanne & E. Lee, 'How Sexually Dimorphic Are We? Review and Synthesis', *in American Journal of Human Biology* 12/2, 2000, 151–166.

Blackmore 2011: C. Blackmore, 'How to Queer the Past Without Sex: Queer Theory, Feminisms and the Archaeology of Identity', *in Journal of the World Archaeological Congress* 7/1, 2011, 75–96.

Blackmore & Rutecki 2014: C. Blackmore & D.M. Rutecki, 'Introducing the Queer Archaeology Interest Group. Who We Are and Why We Need your Support', *in The SAA Archaeological Record* 14/5, 2014, 18–19.

Blackmore *et al.* 2016: Ch. Blackmore, L. Drane, R. Baldwin & D. Ellis, 'Queering Fieldwork. Difference and Identity in Archaeological Practice', *in The SAA Archaeological Record* 16/1, 2016, 18–23.

Blakey 2014: M. L. Blakey, 'L'*African Burial Ground* de New York: d'un secret national à un monument national', *in* André Delpuech & J. Jacob (eds.), *Archéologie de l'esclavage colonial*, La Découverte, 2014, 317–345.

Blakey 2020: M. L. Blakey, 'Archaeology under the Blinding Light of Race', *in Current Anthropology* 61, suppl. 22, 2020, 183–197.

Boardman 2001: J. Boardman, *The History of Greek Vases*, Thames & Hudson, 2001.

Bochnak 2010: T. Bochnak, 'L'armement dans les tombes féminines à l'âge du Fer en Pologne', *in Istros* 16, 2010, 13–36.

Bolger 2013: D. Bolger, 'Gender, Labor, and Pottery Production in Prehistory', *in* D. L. Bolger (ed.), *A Companion to Gender Prehistory*, Wiley-Blackwell, 2013, 161–179.

Borck & Sanger 2017: L. Borck & M. C. Sanger, 'An Introduction to Anarchism in Archaeology', *in The SAA Archaeological Record* 17/1, 2017, 9–16.

Boucherie *et al.* 2017: A. Boucherie, D. Castex, C. Polet & S. Kacki, 'Normal Growth, Altered Growth ? Study of the Relationship Between Harris Lines and Bone Form Within a Post-Medieval Plague Cemetery (Dendermonde, Belgium, 16th Century)', *in American Journal of Human Biology* 29, 2017, e22885, (https://doi.org/10.1002/ajhb.22885).

Boucherie 2020: A. Boucherie, 'Approche archéo-anthropologique d'ensembles funéraires: question de sexe biologique ou de genre ?', *in* I. Algrain (ed.), *Archéologie du genre. Construction sociale des identités et culture matérielle*, Université des femmes, 2020, 41–59.

Boucherie *et al.* 2021: A. Boucherie, C. Polet, P. Lefèvre & M. Vercauteren, 'Sexing the Bony Labyrinth: A Morphometric Investigation in a Subadult and Adult Belgian Identified Sample', *in Journal of Forensic Sciences* 66/3, 2021, 808–820.

Boutboul & Bredoux 2019: S. Boutboul & L. Bredoux, 'L'université Paris-1 secouée par deux affaires de viol', *in Médiapart*, 20 mai 2019, [online: https://www.mediapart.fr/journal/france/200519/l-universite-paris-1-secouee-par-deux-affaires-de-viol?onglet=full].

Bourdieu 1998: P. Bourdieu, *La domination masculine*, Seuil, 1998.

Boussahba *et al.* 2021: M. Boussahba, E. Delanoë & S. Bakshi, *Qu'est-ce que l'intersectionnalité ? Dominations plurielles : sexe, classe et race*, Éditions Payot et Rivages, 2021.

Brosius 1996: M. Brosius, *Women in Ancient Persia (559–331 BC)*, Clarendon Press, 1996.

Browman 2013: D. Browman, *Cultural Negotiations: The Role of Women in the Founding of Americanist Archaeology*, University of Nebraska Press, 2013.

Brown 2018: K. M. Brown, 'Gender, Race, and Mentorship: A Perspective from California Archaeology', *in California Archaeology* 10/2, 2018, 187–209.

Bruchac 2014: M. Bruchac, 'Decolonization in Archaeological Theory', *in* C. Smith (ed.), *Encyclopedia of Global Archaeology*, Springer, 2014, 2069–2077.

Brumfiel 2006: E.M. Brumfiel, 'Methods in Feminist and Gender Archaeology: A Feeling for Difference – and Likeness', *in* S. M. Nelson (ed.), *Handbook of Gender in Archaeology*, AltamiraPress, 2006, 31–58.

Brunache *et al.* 2021: P. Brunache, B.E. Dadzie, K. Goodlett, L. Hampden, A. Khreisheh, C.V. Ngonadi, D. Parikh & J.P. Sires, 'Contemporary Archaeology and Anti-Racism: a Manifesto from the European Society of Black and Allied Archaeologists', *in European Journal of Archaeology* 24/3, 2012, 294–298.

Bruzek 2002: J. Bruzek, 'A Method for Visual Determination of Sex, Using the Human Hip Bone', *in American Journal of Physical Anthropology* 117, 2002, 157–168.

Bruzek & Ferembach 1992: J. Bruzek & D. Ferembach, 'Fiabilité de la méthode visuelle de détermination du sexe à partir du bassin, proposée par le "Groupe de travail d'Anthropologues européens", Application à l'os coxal', *in Archivio per l'Antropologia e la Etnologia* 122, 1992, 145–161.

Brůžek *et al.* 2012: J. Brůžek, M. Lázničková-Galetová, P. Galeta & J. Maestracci, 'Les empreintes de mains dans l'art pariétal: possibilités et limites d'interprétations mises en relief par l'anthropologie médico-légale', *in* J. Clottes (dir.), *L'art pléistocène dans le monde / Pleistocene art of the world / Arte pleistoceno en el mundo. Actes du Congrès IFRAO, Tarascon-sur-Ariège, septembre 2010 – Symposium. 'Application des techniques forensiques aux recherches sur l'art pléistocène'*, Société préhistorique Ariège-Pyrénées, 2012, 1187–1206.

Butler 2005 (1990): J. Butler, *Trouble dans le genre*, La Découverte, 2005 (1990) = J. Butler, *Gender Trouble. Feminism and the Subversion of identity*, Routledge, 1990.

Cabrera Bonet 2016: P. Cabrera Bonet, 'Identidad y género, modelos y contramodelos. El nuevo discurso expositivo de grecia en el Museo Arqueológico Nacional', *in Revista ICOM CE Digital*, n°9, Museos, arqueología y género: relatos, recursos y experiencias, 2016, 102–114.

Caesar 1999: C. Caesar, 'The Construction of Masculinity – The Driving Force of History: A New Way of Understanding Change in the Past', *in Lund Archaeological Review* 5, 1999, 17–36.

Campetti 2015: C. Campetti, 'Out in the Field? Queer Archaeologists, Queer Archaeology and CRM', *in Annual meeting for the Society for American Archaeology, San Francisco, CA*, 2015, [online: https://core.tdar.org/document/395581/out-in-the-field-queer-archaeologists-queer-archaeology-and-crm].

Cappellin 2010: P. Cappellin, 'Plafond, parois de verre ou ciel de plomb ? De la persistance des inégalités', *in Cahiers du Genre* 48, 2010, 31–57.

Carrigan *et al.* 1985: T. Carrigan, B. Connell & J. Lee, 'Toward a New Sociology of Masculinity', *in Theory and Sociology* 14/5, 1985, 551–604.

Carruthers *et al.* 2021: W. Carruthers, J. C. Niala, S. Davis, B. Challis, P. A. Schiappacasse, S. Dixon, M. Milosavljevic, L. Moore, R. Nevell, A. Fitzpatrick, H. Abd el Gawad & A. Stevenson, 'Special Issue: Inequality and Race in the Histories of Archaeology', *in Bulletin of the History of Archaeology*, 2021.

Carter 2018: Ch. Carter, 'Racist Monuments Are Killing Us', *in Museum Anthropology* 41/2, 2018, 139–141.

Carter 2017: I. Carter, 'Pregnant in the Field: Have Trowel, Will Travel', *in The Guardian*, 1st July 2017 [online: https://www.theguardian.com/lifeandstyle/2017/jul/01/pregnant-in-the-field-blog-photography-have-trowel-will-travel].

Cartledge 1998: P. Cartledge, 'The *machismo* of the Athenian Empire – or the Reign of the *phaulus* ?', *in* L. Foxhall & J. Salmon (eds.), *When Men Were Men. Masculinity, Power and Identity in Classical Antiquity*, Routledge, 1998, 54–67.

Casella 2000: E. Casella, '"Doing trade": a Sexual Economy of Nineteenth-Century Australian Female Convict Prisons', *in World Archaeology* 32/2, 2000, 209–221.

Casey *et al.* 1998: M. Casey, D. Donlon, J. Hope & S. Wellfare (eds.), *Redefining Archaeology: Feminist Perspectives*, Australian National University Press, 1998.

Cervulle 2012: M. Cervulle, 'La conscience dominante. Rapports sociaux de race et subjectivation', *in Cahiers du Genre* 53, 2012/2, 37–54.

Challis 2015: D. Challis, 'Queering Display. LGBT History and the Ancient World', *in* K. Fisher, R. Langlands (eds.), *Sex, Knowledge, and Receptions of the Past*, Oxford University Press, 45–64.

Champion 1998: S. Champion, 'Women in British Archaeology', *in* M. Díaz-Andreu & M. L. S. Sørensen (eds.), *Excavating Women. An History of Women in European Archaeology*, Routledge, 1998, 175–197.

Chapoutot 2008: J. Chapoutot, *Le Nazisme et l'Antiquité*, Presses universitaires de France, 2008.

Chilton 1994: E. Chilton, 'In Search of Paleo-Women: Gender Implications of Remains From Paleoindian Sites in the Northeast', *in Bulletin of the Massachusetts Archeological Society* 55, 1994, 8–14.

Chirikure 2014: S. Chirikure, 'Indigenous Peoples, Working with and for', *in* C. Smith (ed.), *Encyclopedia of Global Archaeology*, Springer, 2014, 3834–3841.

Chirikure 2020: S. Chirikure, *Great Zimbabwe: Reclaiming a 'Confiscated' Past*, Routledge, 2020.

Cicalo 2015: A. Cicalo, "Those Stones Speak:' Black-Activist Engagement with Slavery Archaeology in Rio de Janeiro', *in Latin American and Caribbean Ethnic Studies* 10/3, 2015, 251–270.

Claassen 1993: Ch. Claassen, 'Black and White Women at Irene Mound', *in Southeastern Archaeology* 12/2, 1993, 137–147.

Claassen 1994: Ch. Claassen (ed.), *Women in Archaeology*, University of Pennsylvania Press, 1994.

Claassen 2000: Ch. Claassen, 'Homophobia and Women Archaeologists', *in World Archaeology* 32/2, 2000, 173–179.

Claassen *et al.* 1999: Ch. Claassen, M. O'Neal, T. Wilson, E. Arnold & B. Lansdell, 'Hearing and Reading Southeastern Archaeology: A Review of the Annual Meetings of SEAC from 1983 through 1995 and the Journal Southeastern Archaeology', *in Southeastern Archaeology* 18, 1999, 85–97.

Clancy *et al.* 2014: K. B. H. Clancy, R. G. Nelson, J. N. Rutherford & K. Hinde, 'Survey of Academic Field Experiences (SAFE): Trainees Report Harassment and Assault', *in PLoS One* 9/7, 2014, [online: https://doi.org/10.1371/journal.pone.0102172].

Clayton & Hoskin 2020: Z. Clayton & D. Hoskin, 'Activists on the Inside. The Victoria and Albert Museum LGBTQ Working Group', *in* J. G. Adair & A. K. Levin (eds.), *Museums, Sexuality, and Gender Activism*, Routledge, 57–68.

Cobb & Croucher 2016: H. Cobb, K. Croucher, 'Personal, Political, Pedagogic: Challenging the Binary Bind in Archaeological Teaching, Learning and Fieldwork', *in Journal of Archaeological Method Theory* 23, 2016, 949–969 [online: https://link.springer.com/article/10.1007/s10816–016–9292–0].

Cobb & Croucher 2020: H. Cobb & K. Croucher, *Assembling Archaeology: Teaching, Practice, and Research*, Oxford University Press, 2020.

Cocozza 2017: P. Cocozza, 'Does New DNA Evidence Prove That There Were Female Viking Warlords?', *in The Guardian*, 12 September 2017, [https://www.theguardian.com/science/shortcuts/2017/sep/12/does-new-dna-evidence-prove-that-there-were-female-viking-warlords].

Cohen 2016: C. Cohen, *Femmes de la Préhistoire*, Belin, 2016.

Cohen E.E. 2016: E.E. Cohen, 'The Athenian Businesswoman', *in* S.L. Budin & J. MacIntosh Turfa (eds.), *Women in Antiquity. Real Women Across the Ancient World*, Routledge, 2016, 714–725.

Colaninno *et al.* 2020: C. E. Colaninno, S. P. Lambert, E. L. Beahm & C. G. Drexler, 'Creating and Supporting a Harassment- and Assault-Free Field School', *in Advances in Archaeological Practice* 8/2, 2020, 111–122.

Colleter 2021: R. Colleter, 'Archéologie du handicap et inégalités sociales au couvent des Jacobins de Rennes (XIIIe-XVIIIe siècles)', *in Les Nouvelles de l'Archéologie* 165, 2021, [Accessed 20 March 2023, URL: http://journals.openedition.org/nda/13013].

Colleter *et al.* 2014: R. Colleter, N. Gryspeirt, D. Jouneau, N. Rolland & M. Guillon, 'Au cœur d'une communauté villageoise du premier Moyen Âge dans la vallée de l'Andelle: l'église Saint-Crespin de Romilly-sur-Andelle (Eure) et son cimetière (fin du VIe - milieu du XIe siècle)', dans L. Liogier *et al.*, *Journées archéologiques de Haute-Normandie. Rouen, 24–26 mai 2013*, Presses universitaires de Rouen et du Havre, 2014, 143–163.

Colomer *et al.* 1999: L. Colomer, P. González Marcén, S. Montón Subías & M. Picazo (eds.), *Arqueología y teoría feminista. Estudios sobre mujeres y cultura material en arqueología*, Icaria, 1999.

Coltofean-Arizancu *et al.* 2021: L. Coltofean-Arizancu, B. Gaydarska & U. Matić, *Gender Stereotypes in Archaeology. A Short Reflection in Image and Text*, Sidestone Press, 2021.

Coltofean-Arizancu *et al.* 2023: L. Coltofean-Arizancu, B. Gaydarska, S. Plutniak, L. Mary, M. Hlad, I. Algrain, B. Pasquini, S. Vandevelde, E. Stamataki, B. Wouters & A. Sengeløv, 'Harassment, assault, bullying and intimidation (HABI) in European archaeology', *in Antiquity* 97(393), 2023, 726–744, [doi:10.15184/aqy.2023.58].

Colwell-Chanthaphonh *et al.* 2010: C. Colwell-Chanthaphonh, T. J. Ferguson, D. Lippert, R. H. Mcguire, G. P. Nicholas, J. E. Watkins & L. J. Zimmerman, 'The Premise and Promise of Indigenous Archaeology', *in American Antiquity* 75/2, 2010, 228–238.

Connell 2014 (1995): R. Connell, *Masculinités. Enjeux sociaux de l'hégémonie*, Éditions Amsterdam, 2014 (1995) = R. Connell, *Masculinities*, University of California Press, 1995.

Covey 1998: H. C. Covey, *Social Perceptions of People with Disabilities in History*, Charles C. Thomas, 1998.

Conkey 2003: M. Conkey, 'Has Feminism Changed Archaeology?', *in Signs* 28/3, 2003, 867–888.

Conkey & Spector 1984: M. Conkey & J. Spector, 'Archaeology and the Study of Gender', *in Advances in Archaeological Method and Theory* 7, 1984, 1–38.

Cook 2019: K. Cook, 'EmboDIYing Disruption: Queer, Feminist and Inclusive Digital Archaeologies', *in European Journal of Archaeology* 22/3, 2019, 398–414.

Costin 2013: C. L. Costin, 'Gender and Textile Production in Prehistory', *in* D. L. Bolger (ed.), *A Companion to Gender Prehistory*, Wiley-Blackwell, 2013, 180–202.

Coto-Sarmiento *et al.* 2019: M. Coto-Sarmiento, A. L. Delgado, L. López Martínez, J. Martín Alonso, A. Pastor Pérez, A. Ruíz & M. Yubero Gómez, *Informe Acoso sexual en Arqueología*, 2019, [online: https://zenodo.org/record/3662763#.X8ThJs6g_Dc].

Coudart 1998: A. Coudart, 'Archaeology of French Women and French Women in Archaeology', *in* M. Díaz-Andreu & M. L. S. Sørensen (eds.), *Excavating Women. An History of Women in European Archaeology*, Routledge, 1998, 61–85.

Cousin 2015: L. Cousin, 'La dot et sa gestion par les femmes en Babylonie aux deuxième et premier millénaires av. J.-C.', *in Circé. Histoire, savoirs, sociétés* 6/1, 2015 [Accessed 13 February 2022, URL: http://www.revue-circe.uvsq.fr/la-dot-et-sa-gestion-par-les-femmes-en-babylonie-aux-deuxieme-et-premier-millenaires-av-j-c/].

Crass 2001: B. A. Crass, 'Gender and Mortuary Analysis: What Can Grave Goods Really Tell Us ?', *in* B. Arnold & N. L. Wicker (eds.), *Gender and the Archaeology of Death*, Altamira Press, 2001, 105–118.

Crenshaw 1989: K. Crenshaw, 'Demarginalizing the Intersection of Race and Sex: A Black Feminist Critique of Antidiscrimination Doctrine, Feminist Theory and Antiracist Politics', *in University of Chicago Legal Forum*, 1989, 139–168.

Crenshaw 1991: K. Crenshaw, 'Mapping the Margins: Intersectionality, Identity Politics, and Violence against Women of Color', *in Stanford Law Review*, vol. 43, n°6, juillet 1991, 1241–1299.

Cryle 2015: P. Cryle, 'Anachronistic Readings of Eighteenth-century Libertinage in Nineteenth- and Twentieth-century France', *in* K. Fisher & R. Langlands (eds.), *Sex, Knowledge, and Receptions of the Past*, Oxford University Press, 65–85.

Cuozzo 2008: M. Cuozzo, 'Interpretazione delle necropoli e questioni di genere nell'archeologia italiana: il caso di Pontecagnano', *in* L. Prados Torreira & C. Riuz López (eds.), *Arqueología del género. 1er Encuentro Internacional en la UAM*, UAM Ediciones, 2008, 105–138.

Curtoni & Politis 2006: R. P. Curtoni & G. G. Politis, 'Race and Racism in South American Archaeology', *in World Archaeology*, 38/1, 2006, 93–108.

Dahlberg 1983a: F. Dahlberg (ed.), *Woman the Gatherer*, Yale University Press, 1983.

Dahlberg 1983b: F. Dahlberg, 'Introduction', F. Dahlberg (ed.), *Woman the Gatherer*, Yale University Press, 1983, 1–33.

Danis 2016: A. Danis, 'Making a Place in the Field. A Report from the First Queer Archaeology Interest Group Forum', *in The SAA Archaeological Record*, 16/1, 2016, 37–39.

Darmangeat 2022: Ch. Darmangeat, *Le communisme primitif n'est plus ce qu'il était. Aux origines de l'oppression des femmes*, Smolny, 2022.

Darmangeat 2013: Ch. Darmangeat, *Conversation sur l'origine des inégalités*, Agone, 2013.

David 2010: R. David, 'Cardiovascular Disease and Diet in Ancient Egypt', *in* A. Woods, A. McFarlane & S. Binder (eds.), *Egyptian Culture and Society. Studies in Honour of Naguib Kanawati*, The American University in Cairo Press, 2010 (CASAE 38/1), 105–118.

Davis 1971: A. Davis 'Reflections on the Black Woman's Role in the Community of Slaves', *in The Black Scholar* 3/4, 1971, 2–15.

Davis 1982 (1981): A. Davis, *Femmes, race et classe*, Des Femmes, 1982 = A. Davis, *Women, Race & Class*, Women's Press, 1981.

De Beauvoir 1949: S. de Beauvoir, *Le deuxième sexe. Tome II: l'expérience vécue*, Gallimard (Poche), 1949.

De Leiuen 2018: C. De Leiuen, 'Gender, Feminist, and Queer Archaeologies: Australian Perspective', *in* C. Smith, *Encyclopedia of Global Archaeology*, Springer, 2018, 2961–2968.

Deetz 2015: K. Deetz, 'Don't Call it a Comeback, We've Been Here for Years: Reintroducing the African Diaspora Archaeology Newsletter', *in African Diaspora Archaeology Newsletter* 15/1, 2015, 1–11.

Delattre 2018: V. Delattre, *Handicap: Quand l'archéologie nous éclaire*, Le Pommier, 2018.

Delattre 2021: V. Delattre, 'Construire une archéologie éclairée des handicaps', *in Les nouvelles de l'archéologie* 165, Archéologies du handicap, 2021, 4–7.

Delphy 1998: C. Delphy, *L'ennemi principal 1. Économie politique du patriarcat*, Syllepse, 1998.

Delphy 2001: C. Delphy, *L'ennemi principal 2. Penser le genre*, Syllepse, 2001.

Delpuech & Jacob 2014: A. Delpuech & J. Jacob, *Archéologie de l'esclavage colonial,* La Découverte, 2014.

Demoule 2012: J.-P. Demoule, 'Pouvoirs, sexes et genres', *in Les Nouvelles de l'Archéologie* 127, 2012, 21–25 [online: http://journals.openedition.org/nda/1319].

Demoule 2020: J.-P. Demoule, *Aux origines, l'archéologie. Une science au cœur des grands débats de notre temps*, La Découverte, 2020.

Denis & Mary 2021: S. Denis & L. Mary, 'Compte-rendu de l'ouvrage d'Augereau Anne (2021) - Femmes néolithiques. Le genre dans les premières sociétés agricoles', *in Bulletin de la Société préhistorique française* 118, 2021, 585–588.

Díaz-Andreu 2005: M. Díaz-Andreu, 'Gender Identity', *in* M. Díaz-Andreu, S. Lucy, S. Babić & D. N. Edwards (eds.), *The Archaeology of Identity. Approaches to Gender, Age, Status Ethnicity and Religion*, Routledge, 2005, 13–42.

Díaz-Andreu & Sanz Gallego 1994: M. Díaz-Andreu & N. Sanz Gallego, 'Women in Spanish Archaeology', *in* M. C. Nelson, S. M. Nelson & A. Wylie (eds.), *Equity Issues for Women in Archeology*, American Anthropological Association, 1994, 121–130.

Díaz-Andreu & Sørensen 1998: M. Díaz-Andreu & M. L. S. Sørensen (eds.), *Excavating Women. An History of Women in European Archaeology*, Routledge, 1998.

Díaz-Andreu & Tortosa 1998: M. Díaz-Andreu & T. Tortosa, 'Gender, Symbolism and Power in Iberian Societies', in P.P. Funari, M. Hall & S. Jones (eds.), *Historical Archaeology. Back from the Edge*, Routledge, 1998, 99–121.

Díaz-Andreu & Montón Subías 2013: M. Díaz-Andreu & S. Montón Subías, 'Feminist and Gender Issues in Southwestern Europe: Spanish, Portuguese and French Prehistoric Archaeologies', *in* D. L. Bolger (ed.), *A Companion to Gender Prehistory*, Wiley-Blackwell, 2013, 438–457.

Díaz-Andreu & Pope 2024: M. Díaz-Andreu & R. Pope, 'The History of Gender Archaeology', *in* M. Díaz-Andreu & L. Coltofean (eds.), *The Oxford Handbook of the History of Archaeology*, Oxford University Press, 2024,

Dionísio Rechena 2016: A.M. Dionísio Rechena, 'As mulheres em museus arqueológicos ou o silêncio de Eva', *in Revista ICOM CE Digital*, n°9, Museos, arqueología y género: relatos, recursos y experiencias, 2016, 56–64.

Dommasnes 1992: L. H. Dommasnes, 'Two Decades of Women in Prehistory and in Archaeology in Norway. A Review', *in Norwegian Archaeological Review* 25/1, 1992, 1–14.

Dommasnes 2018: L. H. Dommasnes, 'Gender, Feminist, and Queer Archaeologies: European Perspective', *in* C. Smith (ed.), *Encyclopedia of Global Archaeology*, Springer, 2018, 2968–2980.

Dommasnes 2021: L. H. Dommasnes, 'The Beginnings of Gender Archaeology Networks in Europe: A Norwegian Perspective', *in* D. Gutsmiedl-Schümann, M. Helmbrecht & J. Kranzbühler (eds.), *Feministische Perspektiven auf Gender und Archäologie Beiträge der Tagung zum 25-jährigen Bestehen von FemArc – Netzwerk archäologisch arbeitender Frauen e.V.*, Waxmann, 2021, 69–90.

Dommasnes & Kleppe 1988: L. H. Dommasnes & E. Kleppe, 'Women in Archaeology in Norway', *in Archaeological Review from Cambridge* 7/2, 1988, 230–234.

Dommasnes *et al.* 1998: L. H. Dommasnes, E. J. Kleppe, G. Mandt & J.-R. Næss, 'Women Archaeologists in Retrospect. The Norwegian Case', *in* M. Díaz-Andreu & M. L. S. Sørensen (eds.), *Excavating Women. An History of Women in European Archaeology*, Routledge, 1998, 105–124.

Dommasnes & Montón-Subías 2012: L. H. Dommasnes & S. Montón-Subías, 'European Gender Archaeologies in Historical Perspective', *in European Journal of Archaeology* 15/3, 2012, 367–391.

Dommasnes & Wicker 2010: L. H. Dommasnes & N. L. Wicker, 'Situating Gender in European Archaeologies: Introduction', *in* L. H. Dommasnes, T. Hjorungdal, S. Montón-Subías, M. Sánchez Romero & N. Wicker (eds.), *Situating Gender in European Archaeologies*, Archaeolingua Alapitvany, 2010, 11–22.

Dorlin 2002: E. Dorlin, 'Autopsie du sexe', *in Les Temps Modernes*, 619, 2002, 115–143.

Dorlin 2006: E. Dorlin, *La matrice de la race. Généalogie sexuelle et coloniale de la Nation* française, La Découverte (coll. 'Sciences humaines et sociales', 312), 2006.

Dorlin 2008: E. Dorlin, *Sexe, genre et sexualités. Introduction à la théorie féministe*, PUF, 2008.

Dotte-Sarout 2021: É. Dotte-Sarout, 'Pacific Matildas: Finding the Women in the History of Pacific Archaeology', *in Bulletin of the History of Archaeology* 31/1, 2021, [online, https://archaeologybulletin.org/articles/10.5334/bha-656].

Dotte-Sarout *et al.* 2020: É. Dotte-Sarout, A. Di Piazza, F. Valentin & M. Spriggs, *Pour une histoire de la préhistoire océanienne. Approches historiographiques de l'archéologie francophone dans le Pacifique*, pacific-credo Publications, 2020.

Doucette 2001: D. L. Doucette, 'Decoding the Gender Bias: Inferences of Atlatls in Female Mortuary Contexts', *in* B. Arnold & N. L. Wicker (eds.), *Gender and the Archaeology of Death*, Altamira Press, 2001, 159–177.

Dowson 1998a: T. A. Dowson, *Sexual Difference and Epistemological Privilege in Archaeology*, paper presented to the Theoretical Archaeology Group conference, Birmingham, 1998.

Dowson 1998b: T. A. Dowson, 'Homosexualitat, teoria queer i arqueologia', *in Cota Zero* 14, 1998, 81–87.

Dowson 2000a: T. A. Dowson (ed.), *World Archaeology* 32/2 'Queer Archaeologies', 2000.

Dowson 2000b: T. A. Dowson, 'Why Queer Archaeology? An Introduction', *in World Archaeology* 32/2, 2000, 161–165.

Dowson 2006: T. A. Dowson, 'Why Queer Archaeology? An Introduction', *in* P. L. Geller & M. K. Stockett (eds.), *Feminist Anthropology. Past, Present, and Future*, University of Pennsylvania Press, 2006, 89–102.

Dowson 2009: T. A. Dowson, 'Queer Theory Meets Archaeology: Disrupting Epistemological Privilege and Heteronormativity in Constructing the Past', *in The Ashgate Research Companion to Queer Theory*, 2009, 277–294.

Du Cros & Smith 1993: H. du Cros & L. Smith (eds.), *Women in Archaeology: A Feminist Critique*, Department of Prehistory, Research School of Pacific Studies, Australian National University, 1993.

Dufrêne 2014: B. Dufrêne, 'La place des femmes dans le patrimoine', *in Revue française des sciences de l'information et de la communication* 4, 2014, [Accessed 27 April 2023, URL: http://journals.openedition.org/rfsic/977].

Dunand 2004: F. Dunand, 'Les enfants et la mort en Égypte', *in* V. Dasen (ed.), *Naissance et petite enfance dans l'Antiquité. Actes du colloque de Fribourg, 28 novembre - 1er décembre 2001* (Orbis Biblicus et Orientalis 203), Academic Press, 2004, 13–32.

Duncan 1995: C. Duncan, *Civilizing Rituals. Inside Public Art Museums*, Routledge, 1995.

Dupuis-Déri 2018: F. Dupuis-Déri, *La crise de la masculinité: autopsie d'un mythe tenace*, Éditions du Remue-Ménage, 2018.

Duru-Bellat 2017: M. Duru-Bellat, *La tyrannie du genre*, Presses de Sciences Po, 2017.

Dylla *et al.* 2016: E. Dylla, S. A. Ketchum & C. McDavid, 'Listening More and Talking Less. Being a Good Ally', *in The SAA Archaeological Record* 16/1, 2016, 31–35.

Eaverly 2013: M. A. Eaverly, *Tale Men / Pale Women. Color and Gender in Archaic Greece and Egypt. A Comparative Approach*, The University of Michigan Press, 2013.

Ebert & Patterson 2007: V. Ebert, T. C. Patterson, 'Gender in South American Archaeology', *in* S. M. Nelson, *Worlds of Gender. The Archaeology of Women's Lives around the Globe*, Altamira Press, 2007, 259–291.

Echo-Hawk & Zimmerman 2006: R. Echo-Hawk & L. J. Zimmerman, 'Beyond Racism: Some Opinions about Racialism and American Archaeology', *in American Indian Quarterly* 30, 3/4, 2006, 461–485.

Eddisford & Morgan 2018: D. Eddisford & C. Morgan, 'Single Context Archaeology as Anarchist Praxis', *in Journal of Contemporary Archaeology* 5/2, 2018, 245–254.

Eger 2007: A. A. Eger, 'Age and Male Sexuality: "Queer Space" in the Roman Bath-house. Age and Ageing in the Roman Empire', *in Journal of Roman Archaeology Supplementary Series* 65, 2007, 131–52.

Ehrenberg 1989: M. Ehrenberg, *Women in Prehistory*, British Museum Publications, 1989.

Engelstad *et al.* 1994: E. Engelstad, G. Mandt & J.-R. Naess, 'Equity Issues in Norwegian Archaeology', *in* M. Nelson, S. Nelson & A. Wylie (eds.), *Equity Issues for Women in Archaeology*, American Anthropological Association, 1994, 139–145.

Epperson 2004: T. W. Epperson, 'Critical Race Theory and the Archaeology of the African Diaspora', *in Historical Archaeology* 38/1, 2004, 101–108.

Eppler 2017: K. Eppler, 'Frau – Mann, Jung – Alt, Arm – Reich. Museale Darstellung und Visualisierung frühmittelalterlicher Gesellschafts- und Gender(re) konstruktionen im Landesmuseum Württemberg', *in* J.E. Fries, D. Gutsmiedl-Schümann, J.Z. Matias & U. Rambuscheck (eds.), *Images of the Past. Gender and its Representations*, Waxmann, 2017, 171–184.

Escobar García & Baquedano Pérez 2016: I. Escobar García & E. Baquedano Pérez, '¿Cómo nos (re)presentamos? Iconografías de género en las exposiciones y actividades del Museo arqueológico regional de la comunidad de Madrid', *in Revista ICOM CE Digital*, n°9, Museos, arqueología y género: relatos, recursos y experiencias, 2016, 128–141.

Esposito & Pollini 2021: A. Esposito & A. Pollini, 'Gender, Identities, and Material Culture in the Italic Peninsula: Burial Practices and Loom Weights in Perspective', *in Etruscan Studies* 24, 2021, 18–35, [https://doi.org/10.1515/etst-2020–0011].

Everill 2007: P. Everill, 'British Contract Archaeology: Antiquarians and Labourers; Developers and Diggers', *in* Y. Hamilakis & P. Duke (eds.), *Archaeology and Capitalism: From Ethics to Politics*, Routledge, 2007, 176–205.

Ezekiel 2002: J. Ezekiel, 'La "blanchité" du mouvement des femmes américain', communication au Colloque international *Ruptures, résistances et utopies*, Université de Toulouse II-Le Mirail, 20 septembre 2002.

Falk 2022: O. Falk, 'La hache de guerre d'Occam. Réflexions sur l'archéologie responsable inspirées par Bj 581', *in* A. Augereau & C. Darmangeat (eds.), *Aux origines du genre. Enjeux, méthodes et controverses*, PUF, 2022, 87–99.

Fassin 2004: E. Fassin, 'Le genre aux États-Unis', *in* C. Bard, C. Baudelot & J. Mossuz-Lavau (eds.), *Quand les femmes s'en mêlent. Genre et pouvoir*, Éditions de La Martinière, 2004, 23–43.

Fatás Monforte & Martínez Llano 2016: P. Fatás Monforte & A. Martínez Llano, 'Una reflexión sobre la presentación de la mujer paleolítica en el Museo de Altamira', *in Revista ICOM CE Digital*, n°9, Museos, arqueología y género: relatos, recursos y experiencias, 2016, 90–100.

Fausto-Sterling 2000: A. Fausto-Sterling, *Sexing the Body. Gender Politics and the Construction of Sexuality*, Basic Books, 2000.

Federici 2014 : S. Federici, *Caliban et la Sorcière. Femmes, corps et accumulation primitive*, Éditions Entremonde, 2014 = S. Federici, *Caliban and the Witch: Women, the Body and Primitive Accumulation*, Autonomedia, 2004.

Federici 2019 : S. Federici, *Le capitalisme patriarcal*, La Fabrique, 2019 = S. Federici, *Patriarchy of the Wage: Notes on Marx, Gender and Feminism*, PM Press, 2021.

Fernández 1999: M.A. Fernández, *Sexismo lingüístico. Análisis y propuestas ante la discriminación sexual en el lenguaje*, Narcea, 1999.

Fernández Poncela 2012: A.M. Fernández Poncela, *La violencia en el lenguaje o el lenguaje que violenta. Equidad de género y lenguaje*, UAMX, 2012.

Ferris 2003: N. Ferris, 'Between Colonial and Indigenous Archaeologies: Legal and Extra-legal Ownership of the Archaeological Past in North America', *in Canadian Journal of Archaeology* 27, 2003, 154–190.

Finlay 1999: N. Finlay (ed.), *Archaeological Review from Cambridge*, 15/2, 'Disability and Archaeology', 1999.

Finlay 2013: N. Finlay, 'Gender and Lithic Studies in Prehistoric Archaeology', *in* D. Bolger (ed.), *A Companion to Gender Prehistory*, Wiley-Blackwell, 2013, 142–160.

Fitzpatrick 2021: A. Fitzpatrick, 'Accountability in Action: How Can Archaeology Makes Amends?', *in* W. Carruthers *et al.* (eds.), *Bulletin of the History of Archaeology* 31/1, Special Issue: Inequality and Race in the Histories of Archaeology, 2021, 14–16.

Flewellen *et al.* 2021: A. O. Flewellen, J. P. Dunnavant, A. Odewale, A. Jones, T. Wolde-Michael, Z. Crossland & M. Franklin, 'The Future of Archaeology is Antiracist: Archaeology in the Time of Black Lives Matter', *in American Antiquity* 86/2, 2021, 224–243.

Flexner 2014: J. L. Flexner, 'The Historical Archaeology of States and Non-States: Anarchist Perspectives from Hawai'I and Vanuata', *in Journal of Pacific Archaeology* 5/2, 2014, 81–97.

Flexner & Gonzalez-Tennant 2018: J. L. Flexner & E. Gonzalez-Tennant, 'Anarchy and Archaeology. Introduction', *in Journal of Contemporary Archaeology* 5/2, 2018, 213–302.

Fonnesbeck-Sandberg *et al.* 1972: E. Fonnesbeck-Sandberg, B. Pauly Hansen, K. Jespersen, L. Bender Jørgensen, K. Løkkegård, T. Matz, U. Fraes Rasmussen, L. Slumstrup, I. Stoumann, F. Waagebech, T. Wanning, S. Wiell, L. Wienecke & S. Ørnager, 'Han, hun og arkæologien. "Arkæologiske studier"', *in Kontaktstencil* 4, 1972, 5–10.

Ford 1994: A. Ford, 'The Status of Women in Mesoamerican Archaeology: Why are the Best Men Winning?', *in* C. Claassen (ed.), *Women in Archaeology*, University of Pennsylvania Press, 1994, 159–172.

Fournier *et al.* 2015: T. Fournier, J. Jarty, N. Lapeyre & P. Touraille, 'L'alimentation, arme du genre', *in Journal des anthropologues* 140–141, 2015, [Accessed 24 March 2023, DOI: https://doi.org/10.4000/jda.6022].

Fox 2016: S.C. Fox, 'The Bioarchaeology of Women in Greek Antiquity', *in* S.L. Budin & J. MacIntosh Turfa (eds.), *Women in Antiquity. Real Women Across the Ancient World*, Routledge, 2016, 647–659.

Franklin 1997a: M. Franklin, '"Power to the People": Sociopolitics and the Archaeology of Black Americans', *in Historical Archaeology* 31/3, 1997, 36–50.

Franklin 1997b: M. Franklin, 'Why Are There So Few Black American Archaeologists?', *in Antiquity* 71, 1997, 799–801.

Franklin 2001a: M. Franklin, 'A Black Feminist-inspired Archaeology ?', *in Journal of Social Archaeology* 1/1, 2001, 108–125.

Franklin 2021: M. Franklin, '"The Future of Archaeology Is Antiracist": Archaeology in the Time of Black Lives', *in American Antiquity* 86/2, 2021, 224–243.

Franklin 2001b: M. Franklin, 'The Archaeological and Symbolic Dimensions of Soul Food: Race, Culture, and Afro-Virginian Identity', *in* C. E. Orser Jr. (ed.), *Race, Material Culture, and the Archaeology of Identity*, University of Utah Press, 2001, 88–107.

Franklin *et al.* 2020: M. Franklin, J. P. Dunnavant, A. O. Flewellen & A. Odewale, 'The Future is Now: Archaeology and the Eradication of Anti-Blackness', *in International Journal of Historical Archaeology* 24, 2020, 753–766.

Fraser 2006: M. Fraser, *Dis/Abling Exclusion, En/Abling Access: Identifying and Removing Barriers in Archaeological Practice for Persons with (Dis/) Abilities*, American University – Washington D.C., thèse de doctorat, 2006.

Friðriksdóttir 2020: J. K. Friðriksdóttir, *Les femmes vikings, des femmes puissantes*, Autrement, 2020 = J. K. Friðriksdóttir, *Valkyries: Women of the Viking World*, Bloomsbury, 2020.

Friedan 1963: B. Friedan, *The Feminine Mystique*, W.W. Norton, 1963.

Friedl 1975: E. Friedl, 'Part I: Hunting and Gathering Societies', *in* E. Friedl (ed.), *Women and Men: An Anthropologist's View*, Waveland Press, 1975, 12–45.

Fries & Gutsmiedl-Schümann 2013: J. E. Fries & D. Gutsmiedl-Schümann (eds.), *Ausgräberinnen, Forscherinnen, Pionierinnen. Ausgewählte Porträts früher Archäologinnen im Kontext ihrer Zeit*, Waxmann, 2013.

Froidevaux-Metterie 2021: C. Froidevaux-Metterie, *Un corps à soi*, Éditions du Seuil, 2021.

Fryer & Raczek 2020: T. C. Fryer & T. P. Raczek, 'Introduction: Toward an Engaged Feminist Heritage Praxis', *in Archaeological Papers of the American Anthropological Association* 31, 2020, 7–25.

Fulkerson & Tushingham 2019: T. J. Fulkerson & S. Tushingham, 'Who Dominates the Discourses of the Past? Gender, Occupational Affiliation, and Multivocality in North American Archaeology Publishing', *in American Antiquity* 84/3, 2019, 379–399.

GAEL 2022a: GAEL (Groupe Archéo en Lutte) Alsace & Notre Condition, 'Enquête au pays des démagogues', *in Notre Condition*, 20 January 2022, [online: https://

notrecondition.fr/2022/01/20/miseres-de-larcheologie-dossier-i/].

GAEL 2022b: GAEL (Groupe Archéo en Lutte), 'Nouvelle attaque gouvernementale contre l'archéologie (communiqué du 22 février 2022). Réponse de membres des Groupes Archéo en Lutte à la coupe des budgets des fouilles programmées', *in Notre Condition*, 22 February 2022, [online: https://notrecondition.fr/2022/02/22/nouvelle-attaque-gouvernementale-contre-larcheologie-communique-du-22-fevrier-2022/].

Galle & Young 2004: J. E. Galle & A. L. Young (eds.), *Engendering African American Archaeology: A Southern Perspective*, University of Tennessee Press, 2004.

Gamble *et al.* 2020: L. Gamble, D. Martin, J. Hendon, C. Santoro, S. Herr, Ch. Rieth, S. Van der Linde, Ch. Rodning, M. Hegmon & J. Birch, 'Statement and Commitments from SAA Editors to Change the Underrepresentation of Black, Indigenous, and Other Scholars from Diverse Backgrounds in Our Publications', *in Advances in Archaeological Practice* 8/3, 2020, p. v-vi.

Garofalo & Garvin 2020: E. M. Garofalo & H. M. Garvin, 'The Confusion Between Biological Sex and Gender and Potential Implications of Misinterpretations', *in* A. R. Klales (ed.), *Sex Estimation of the Human Skeleton*, Academic Press, 2020, p. 35–52.

Gautier & Zancarini-Fournel 2022: C. Gautier, M. Zancarini-Fournel, *De la défense des savoirs critiques. Quand le pouvoir s'en prend à l'autonomie de la recherche*, La Découverte, 2022.

Geller 2005: P. L. Geller, 'Skeletal Analysis and Theoretical Complications', *in World Archaeology* 37/4, 2005, 597–609.

Geller 2006: P. L. Geller, 'Altering Identities: Body Modification and the pre-Columbian Maya', *in* R. Gowland & C. Knüsel (eds.), *The Social Archaeology of Funerary Remains*, Oxbow Books, 2006, 279–291.

Geller 2008: P. L. Geller, 'Conceiving Sex. Fomenting a Feminist Bioarchaeology', *in Journal of Social Archaeology* 8/1, 2008, 113–138.

Geller 2009: P. L. Geller, 'Identity and Difference: Complicating Gender in Archaeology', *in Annual Review of Anthropology* 38, 2009, 65–81.

Geller 2016: P. L. Geller, 'This is not a Manifesto: Archaeology and Feminism', *in* M. Amoretti & N. Vassallo (eds.), *Meta-Philosophical Reflection on Feminist Philosophies of Science*, Springer (Boston Studies in the Philosophy and History of Science, vol. 317), 2016, 151–170.

Geller 2017a: P. L. Geller, 'Brave Old World. Ancient DNA and Sex Determination', *in* S. C. Agarwal & J. K. Wesp (eds.), *Exploring Sex and Gender in Bioarchaeology*, University of New Mexico Press, 2017, 71–98.

Geller 2017b: P. L. Geller, *The Bioarchaeology of Socio-Sexual Lives. Queering Common Sense About Sex, Gender, and Sexuality*, Springer, 2017.

Geller 2019: P. L. Geller, 'The Fallacy of the Transgender Skeleton', *in* J. E. Buikstra (ed.), *Bioarchaeologists Speak Out. Deep Time Perspectives on Contemporary Issues*, Springer, 2019, 231–242.

Georgeson-Usher 2020: C. Georgeson-Usher, 'All that Moves Us. Bodies in Land', *in* J. Adair & A. K. Levin (eds.), *Museums, Sexuality, and Gender Activism*, Routledge, 145–153.

Gero 1983: J. M. Gero, 'Gender Bias in Archaeology: A Cross-Cultural Perspective', *in* J. M. Gero, D. M. Lacy & M. L. Blakey (eds.), *The Socio-Politics of Archaeology*, University of Massachusetts, 1983, 51–57.

Gero 1985: J. M. Gero, 'Socio-Politics and the Woman-at-Home Ideology', *in American Antiquity* 50/2, 1985, 342–350.

Gero 1991: J. Gero, 'Genderlithics: Women's Role in Stone Tool Production', *in* J. Gero & M. Conkey (eds.), *Engendering Archaeology: Women and Prehistory*, Basil Blackwell, 1991, 163–193.

Gero 1994: J. M. Gero, 'Excavation Bias and the Woman at Home Ideology', *in Archeological Papers of the American Anthropological Association* 5/1, 1994, 37–42.

Gero 1996: J. M. Gero, 'Archaeological Practice and Gendered Encounters with Field Data', *in* R. P. Wright (ed.), *Gender and Archaeology*, University of Pennsylvania Press, 1996, 251–280.

Gero & Conkey 1991: J. Gero & M. Conkey (eds.), *Engendering Archaeology: Women and Prehistory*, Blackwell, 1991.

Gibson 2020: R. Gibson, *The Corseted Skeleton. A Bioarchaeology of Binding*, Palgrave Macmillan, 2020.

Gilchrist 1994: R. Gilchrist, *Gender and Material Culture. The Archaeology of Religious Women*, Routledge, 1994.

Gilchrist 1997: R. Gilchrist, 'Ambivalent Bodies: Gender and Medieval Archaeology', *in* J. Moore & E. Scott (eds.), *Invisible People and Processes. Writing Gender and Childhood into European Archaeology*, Leicester University Press, 1997, 42–58.

Gilchrist 1999: R. Gilchrist, *Gender and Archaeology. Contesting the Past*, Routledge, 1999.

Gilchrist 2000: R. Gilchrist, 'Unsexing the Body: the Interior Sexuality of Medieval Religious Women', *in* R. A. Schmidt & B. L. Voss (eds.), *Archaeologies of Sexuality*, Routledge, 2000, 89–103.

Gilchrist 2009: R. Gilchrist, 'Rethinking Later Medieval Masculinity: The Male Body in Death', *in* D. Sayer & H. Williams (eds.), *Mortuary Practices and Social Identities in the Middle Ages: Essays in Burial*

Archaeology in Honour of Heinrich Härke, University of Exeter Press, 2009, 236–252.

Gimbutas 1974: M. Gimbutas, *The Gods and Goddesses of Old Europe, 7000 to 3500 BC. Myths, Legends and Cult Images*, Thames & Hudson, 1974.

Glick & Fiske 1996: P. Glick & S. T. Fiske, 'The Ambivalent Sexism Inventory: Differentiating Hostile and Benevolent Sexism', *in Journal of Personality and Social Psychology* 70, 1996, 491–512.

Goffman 1975: E. Goffman, *Stigmate, les usages sociaux des handicaps*, Les éditions de minuit, 1975.

Gontijo & Schaan 2017: F. Gontijo & D. P. Schaan, 'Sexualidade e Teoria Queer', *in Revista de Arqueologia* 30/2, 2017, 51–70.

Gonzalez 2016: S. Gonzalez, 'Indigenous Values and Methods in Archaeological Practice: Low-Impact Archaeology Through the Kashaya Pomo Interpretive Trail Project', *in American Antiquity* 81/3, 2016, 533–549.

Gonzalez *et al.* 2006: S. Gonzalez, D. Modzelewski, L. M. Panich & T. D. Schneider, 'Archaeology for the Seventh Generation', *in American Indian Quarterly* 30, 3/4, 2006, 388–415.

Gonzalez-Tennant 2018: E. Gonzalez-Tennant, 'Anarchism, Decolonization, and Collaborative Archaeology', *in Journal of Contemporary Archaeology* 5/2, 2018, 238–244.

Gourevitch 2011: D. Gourevitch, *Pour une archéologie de la médecine romaine*, De Boccard, 2011.

Goutas *et al.* 2020: N. Goutas, F. Bocquentin, Ch. Bouchaud, M. Boudadi-Maligne, S. Costamagno, S. Ducasse, Y. A. Gómez Coutouly, Y. Maigrot, L. Mevel, O. Munoz, R. Rocca & C. Noûs, 'Chronique d'une mort annoncée ? Quand la Loi de programmation de la recherche sonne le glas de la recherche publique', *in Les Nouvelles de l'Archéologie* 161, 2020, [http://journals.openedition.org/nda/10216].

Graham 2001: S. Graham, 'Sulawesi's Fifth Gender', *in Inside Indonesia*, n°66, avril-juin 2001.

Gran-Aymerich & Gran-Aymerich 1991: E. Gran-Aymerich & J. Gran-Aymerich, *Jane Dieulafoy. Une vie d'homme*, Perrin, 1991.

Gräslund 2001: A.-S. Gräslund, 'The Position of Iron Age Scandinavian Women: Evidence from Graves and Rune Stones', *in* B. Arnold & N. L. Wicker (eds.), *Gender and the Archaeology of Death*, Altamira Press, 2001, 81–102.

Greenfield 2000: P. Greenfield, 'Children, Material Culture and Weaving. Historical Change and Developmental Change', *in* J. Sofaer Derevenski (ed.), *Children and Material Culture*, Routledge, 2000, 72–86.

Grimm 2000: L. Grimm, 'Apprentice Flintknapping. Relating Material Culture and Social Practice in the Upper Paleolithic', *in* J. Sofaer Derevenski (ed.), *Children and Material Culture*, Routledge, 2000, 53–71.

Guillaumin 1992: C. Guillaumin, *Sexe, race et pratique du pouvoir*, Côté-femmes, 1992.

Guillaumin 2002: C. Guillaumin, *L'idéologie raciste*, Gallimard, 2002.

Guliaev 2003: V. Guliaev, 'Amazons in the Scythia: New Finds at the Middle Don, Southern Russia', *in World Archaeology* 35/1, 2003, 112–125.

Guliaev *et al.* 2019: V.I. Guliaev, S.A. Volodin & A.A. Shevchenko, 'Donskaya arkheologicheskaya ekspeditsiya (Expédition archéologique dans la region du Don)', 2019, [Accessed 10 November 2020, https://www.archaeolog.ru/ru/expeditions/expeditions-2019/donskaya-arkheologicheskaya-ekspeditsiya].

Halcrow 2017: S. Halcrow, 'Having Babies as an Academic Archaeologist', 2017, [online: https://childhoodbioarchaeology.org/2017/02/21/having-babies-as-an-academic-archaeologist/].

Hamilakis 2012: Y. Hamilakis, 'Are We Postcolonial Yet? Tales from the Battlefield', *in Archaeologies: Journal of the World Archaeological Congress*, 2012, 67–76.

Hamilakis & Duke 2007: Y. Hamilakis & P. Duke, *Archaeology and Capitalism. From Ethics to Politic*, Walnut Creek, 2007.

Hamilton 2014: S. Hamilton, 'Under-Representation in Contemporary Archaeology', *in Papers from the Institute of Archaeology*, 24/1, 2014, 1–9 [online: http:// dx.doi.org/10.5334/pia.469].

Hanisch 1970: C. Hanisch, 'Reconsidering Warfare, Status, and Gender in the Eurasian Steppe Iron Age', *in* S. Firestone (ed.), *Notes from the Second Year: Women's Liberation. Major Writings of the Radical Feminists*, 1970, 76–77.

Hanks 2008: B. Hanks, 'Reconsidering Warfare, Status, and Gender in the Eurasian Steppe Iron Age', *in* K. M. Linduff & K. S. Rubinson, *Are All Warriors Male? Gender Roles on the Ancient Eurasian Steppe*, AltaMira Press, 2008, 15–34.

Hannestad 1984: L. Hannestad, 'Slaves and the Fountain House Theme', *in* H.A.G. Brijder (ed.), *Ancient Greek and Related Pottery: Proceedings of the International Vase Symposium in Amsterdam, 12–15 April, 1984*, A. Pierson Museum, 1984, 252–255.

Hanscam & Witcher 2022: E. Hanscam & R. Witcher, 'Women in *Antiquity*: An Analysis of Gender and Publishing in a Global Archaeology Journal', *in Journal of Field Archaeology* 48/2, 2022, 87–101.

Haraway 1984: D. Haraway, 'Teddy Bear Patriarchy: Taxidermy in the Garden of Eden, New York City, 1908–1936', *in Social Text* 11, Winter, 1984–1985, 20–64.

Harrell 2014: K. Harrell, 'Man/Woman, Warrior/Maiden: the Lefkandi Toumba female burial reconsidered', dans Y. Galanakis, T. Wilkinson & J. Bennet (eds.), *Athyrmata: Critical Essays on the Archaeology of the Eastern Mediterranean in Honour of E. Susan Sherratt*, Archaeopress, 2014, 99–104.

Hart 2020: S. M. Hart, 'Gender, Masculinity, and Professional–Avocational Heritage Collaborations', *in Archaeological Papers of the American Anthropological Association* 31, 2020, 54–65.

Hayeur-Smith *et al.* 2019: M. Hayeur-Smith, G. Lucas & Q. Mould, 'Men in Black: Performing Masculinity in 17th- and 18th-century Iceland', *in Journal of Social Archaeology* 19/2, 2019, 229–254.

Hays-Gilpin 2000: K. Hays-Gilpin, 'Feminist Scholarship in Archaeology', *in The Annals of the American Academy of Political and Social Science* 571, 2000, 89–106.

Heath-Stout 2019: L. Heath-Stout, *Diversity, Identity and Oppression. In the Production of Archaeological Knowledge*, PhD thesis from Boston University, 2019.

Heath-Stout 2020a: L. Heath-Stout, 'Who Writes about Archaeology? An Intersectional Study of Authorship in Archaeological Journals', *in American Antiquity* 85/3, 2020, 407–426.

Heath-Stout 2020b: L. Heath-Stout, 'Guest Editorial Introduction: Gender, Equity, and the Peer Review Process at the Journal of Field Archaeology', *in Journal of Field Archaeology* 45/3, 2020, 135–139.

Heath-Stout 2021: L. Heath-Stout, 'Pulled In or Pushed Out ? Diversity, Discrimination, and the Recruitment of the Next Generation of Archaeologists', in *SAA Presidential Forum 2021* [online: www.lauraheathstout.com/saa2021].

Heath-Stout 2022: L. Heath-Stout, 'The Invisibly Disabled Archaeologist', *in International Journal of Historical Archaeology*, 2022, [online: https://doi.org/10.1007/s10761–022–00653–8].

Heath-Stout & Hannigan 2020: L. Heath-Stout & E. M. Hannigan, 'Affording Archaeology: How Field School Costs Promote Exclusivity', *in Advances in Archaeological Practice* 8/2, 2020, 123–133.

Hedenstierna-Jonsson *et al.* 2017: C. Hedenstierna-Jonsson, A. Kjellström, T. Zachrisson, M. Krzewińska, V. Sobrado, N. Price, T. Günther, M. Jakobsson, A. Götherström & J. Storå, 'A Female Viking Warrior Confirmed by Genomics. Brief Communication', *in American Journal of Physical Anthropology*, vol. 164/4, 2017, 853–860.

Hendon 2006: J. A. Hendon, 'The Engendered Household', *in* S. M. Nelson (ed.), *Handbook of Gender in Archaeology*, Altamira Press, 2006, 171–198.

Héritier 1996: F. Héritier, *Masculin/Féminin I. La pensée de la différence*, Odile Jacob Poches, 1996.

Héritier 2000: F. Héritier, 'Famille', *in* M. Izard & P. Bonte (dir.), *Dictionnaire de l'ethnologie et de l'anthropologie*, 3rd edition, PUF, 2000, 273–275.

Hill 2016: K. Hill, *Women and Museums, 1850–1914. Modernity and the Gendering of Knowledge*, Manchester University Press, 2016.

Hinton 1986: P. Hinton, 'An Analysis of Burial Rites at Münsingen-Rain: An Approach to the Study of Iron Age Society', *in* A. Duval & J. Gomez de Soto (eds.), *Actes du VIIIe colloque sur les âges du Fer en France non méditerranéenne, Angoulême 18–20 mai 1984. Aquitania Suppl. 1*, 1986, 351–368.

Hitchcock & Nikolaidou 2013: L. Hitchcock & M. Nikolaidou, 'Gender in Greek and Aegean Prehistory', *in* D. Bolger (ed.), *A Companion to Gender Prehistory*, Wiley-Blackwell, 2013, 502–525.

Hjørungdal 1994: T. Hjørungdal, 'Poles Apart. Have There Been Any Male and Female Graves ?', *in Current Swedish Archaeology* 2, 1994, 141–148.

Hodder 1984: I. Hodder, 'Archaeology in 1984', *in Antiquity* 58, 1984, 25–32.

Hodgetts *et al.* 2020: L. Hodgetts, K. Supernant, N. Lyons & J. R. Welch, 'Broadening #MeToo: Tracking Dynamics in Canadian Archaeology Through a Survey on Experiences Within the Discipline', *in Canadian Journal of Archaeology/Journal Canadien d'Archéologie* 44, 2020, 20–47.

Hollimon 1997: S.E. Hollimon, 'The Third Gender in Native California: Two-Spirit Undertakers among the Chumash and Their Neighbors', *in* C. Claassen & R.A. Joyce (eds.), *Women in Prehistory: North America and Mesoamerica*, University of Pennsylvania Press, 1997, 173–188.

Hollimon 2000: S. E. Hollimon, 'Archaeology of the 'Aqi: Gender and Sexuality in Prehistoric Chumash Society', *in* R. A. Schmidt & B. L. Voss (eds.), *Archaeologies of Sexuality*, Routledge, 2000, 176–196.

Hollimon 2001: S. E. Hollimon, 'Warfare and Gender in the Northern Plains: Osteological Evidence of Trauma Reconsidered', *in* B. Arnold & N.L. Wicker (eds.), *Gender and the Archaeology of Death*, Altamira Press, 2001, 179–193.

Hollimon 2006: S. E. Hollimon, 'The Archaeology of Nonbinary Genders in Native North American Societies', *in* S. M. Nelson (ed.), *Handbook of Gender in Archaeology*, Altamira Press, 2006, 435–450.

Hollimon 2011: S. E. Hollimon, 'Sex and Gender in Bioarchaeological Research. Theory, Method, and Interpretation', *in* S. C. Agarwal & B. A. Glencross (eds.), *Social Bioarchaeology*, Wiley-Blackwell, 2011, 149–182.

Hollimon 2017: S. E. Hollimon, 'Bioarchaeological Approaches to Nonbinary Genders. Case Studies from Native North America', *in* S. C. Agarwal & J. K. Wesp (eds.), *Exploring Sex and Gender in Bioarchaeology*, University of New Mexico Press, 2017, 51–69.

Holm-Olsen & Mandt 1974: I. M. Holm-Olsen & G. Mandt, 'Kvinnens stilling i norsk arkeologi', *in Kontaktstencil* 6, 1974, 68–75.

Houby-Nielsen 2000: S. Houby-Nielsen, 'Child Burials in Ancient Athens', *in* J. Sofaer Derevenski (ed.), *Children and Material Culture*, Routledge, 2000, 151–166.

Howard 2019: J. J. Howard, 'An Ethnographic Approach to African Diaspora Archaeology: The Bocas Way', *in Transforming Anthropology* 27/2, 2019, 133–148.

Howard 2010: G. Howell, *Gertrude Bell. Queen of the Desert, Shaper of Nations*, Farrar, Straus and Giroux, 2010.

Hunt 2020: H. Hunt, 'Curating Gertrude Stein: Identity Politics in the Exhibition Catalogue', *in* J.G. Adair & A.K. Levin (eds.), *Museums, Sexuality, and Gender Activism*, Londres, Routledge, 2020, 231–238.

Husquin 2020: C. Husquin, *L'intégrité du corps en question: perceptions et représentations de l'atteinte physique dans la Rome antique*, Presses universitaires de Rennes (coll. 'Histoire'), 2020.

Hutson 2002: S. R. Hutson, 'Gendered Citation Practices in American Antiquity and Other Archaeology Journals', *in American Antiquity* 67/2, 2002, 331–342.

Iacono 2013: F. Iacono, 'Marxist Archaeologies', *in* A. Gardner & M. Lake, U. Sommer (eds.), *The Oxford Handbook of Archaeological Theory*, 2013 [DOI: https://doi.org/10.1093/oxfordhb/9780199567942.013.011].

ICOM 2013: ICOM, *Résolutions adoptées par la 28e Assemblée générale de l'ICOM*, Rio de Janeiro, [Accessed 16 July 2022: https://icom.museum/wp-content/uploads/2018/07/ICOMs-Resolutions_2013_Fr.pdf].

Initiative for Heritage Conservancy 2014: Initiative for Heritage Conservancy, *Discovering the Archaeologists of Greece 2012–14*, 2014, [online: http://e-archaeology.org/wp-content/uploads/2016/06/EL-DISCO-2014-Greece-national-report-english-.pdf].

Izquierdo Peraile 2016: I. Izquierdo Peraile, 'A vueltas con el género… Hablando de mujeres en los museos de arqueología', *in Revista ICOM CE Digital*, n°9, Museos, arqueología y género: relatos, recursos y experiencias, 2016, 14–26.

Izquierdo Peraile 2017: I. Izquierdo Peraile, 'Sobre musas, museos y mujeres… Apuntes, experiencias y retos en torno a la arqueología y la museología contemporáneas', *in* L. Prados Torreira & C. López Ruiz (eds.), *Museos arqueológicos y género. Educando en igualdad*, UAM Ediciones, 2017, 69–161.

Jácome & Furquim 2018: C. Jácome & L. Furquim, 'Gender and Feminism in Brazilian Archaeology', *in* C. Smith, *Encyclopedia of Global Archaeology*, Springer, 2018 [online: https://doi.org/10.1007/978-3-319-51726-1_3347-2].

Janik & Zawadzka 1998: L. Janik & H. Zawadzka, 'Gender Politics in Polish Archaeology', *in* M. Díaz-Andreu & M. L. S. Sørensen (eds.), *Excavating Women. An History of Women in European Archaeology*, Routledge, 1998, 86–104.

Jensen & Matić 2017: B. Jensen & U. Matić, *Archaeologies of Gender and Violence*, Oxbow Books, 2017.

Jesch 2017a: J. Jesch, 'Let's Debate Female Viking Warriors Yet Again', *in* Blog *Norse and Viking Ramblings*, 9 September 2017 [Accessed 20 February 2023: http://norseandviking.blogspot.com/2017/09/lets-debate-female-viking-warriors-yet.html].

Jesch 2017b: J. Jesch, 'Some Further Discussion of the Article on Bj 581', *in* Blog *Norse and Viking Ramblings*, 18 September 2017 [Accessed 20 February 2023: http://norseandviking.blogspot.com/2017/09/some-further-discussion-of-article-on.html].

Jogersen 1998: L. B. Jogersen, 'The State of Denmark. Lis Jacobsen and Other Women in and around archaeology', *in* M. Díaz-Andreu & M. L. S. Sørensen (eds.), *Excavating Women. An History of Women in European Archaeology*, Routledge, 1998, 214–234.

Johannsesson & Le Couteur 2020: Å. Johannsesson & C. Le Couteur, 'Nonbinary Difference: Dionysus, *Arianna*, and the Fictive Arts of Museum Photography', *in* J. G. Adair & A. K. Levin (eds.), *Museums, Sexuality, and Gender Activism*, Routledge, 167–179.

Jones-Bley 2008: K. Jones-Bley, '*Arma Feminamque Cano*: Warrior-Women in the Indo-European World', *in* K. M. Linduff & K. S. Rubinson, *Are All Warriors Male? Gender Roles on the Ancient Eurasian Steppe*, AltaMira Press, 2008, 35–50.

Jorgensen-Rideout 2017: S. Jorgensen-Rideout, 'Beyond Theory: Queer Theory in Practice', *in The Post Hole* 50, December 2017, 20–25, [https://www.theposthole.org/read/article/379].

Jouët *et al.* 2017: J. Jouët, K. Niemeyer & B. Pavard, 'Faire des vagues. Les mobilisations féministes online', *in Réseaux* 2017/1 (n°201), 21–57 [online, DOI: 10.3917/res.201.0019].

Joukowsky & Cohen 2004: M. Joukowsky & G. M. Cohen (eds.), *Breaking Ground. Pioneering Women Archaeologists*, University of Michigan Press, 2004.

Journet 2014: N. Journet, 'Les traditions du "Troisième sexe"', *in* M. Fournier (ed.), *Masculin-Féminin. Pluriel*, Éditions Sciences Humaines (Essais), 2014, 95–98 [online, DOI: 10.3917/sh.fourn.2014.01.0095].

Joyce 2000: R. A. Joyce, 'A Precolumbian Gaze: Male Sexuality among the Ancient Maya', *in* R. A. Schmidt & B. L. Voss (eds.), *Archaeologies of Sexuality*, Routledge, 2000, 263–283.

Joyce 2007: R. A. Joyce, 'Embodied Subjectivity: Gender, Femininity, Masculinity, Sexuality', *in* L. Meskell & R. W. Preucel, *A Companion to Social Archaeology*, Blackwell, 2007, 82–95.

Joyce 2008: R. A. Joyce, *Ancient Bodies, Ancient Lives. Sex, Gender, and Archaeology*, Thames & Hudson, 2008.

Kacki & Villotte 2006: S. Kacki & S. Villotte, 'Maladie hyperostosique et mode de vie: intérêt d'une démarche bio-archéologique. Exemple du cimetière du Couvent des Soeurs Grises de Beauvais (Oise), XVe - XVIIIe siècles', *in Bulletins et Mémoires de la Société d'Anthropologie de Paris* 18/1–2 (n.s.), 2006, p. 55–64.

Kacki *et al.* 2018: S. Kacki, P. Velemínský, Niels Lynnerup *et al.*, 'Rich Table but Short Life: Diffuse Idiopathic Skeletal Hyperostosis in Danish Astronomer Tycho Brahe (1546–1601) and its Possible Consequences', *in PLOS ONE* 13(4), e0195920, (https://doi.org/10.1371/journal.pone.0195920).

Kaiser 2014: A. Kaiser, *Archaeology, Sexism, and Scandal. The Long-Suppressed Story of One Woman's Discoveries and the Man Who Stole Credit for Them*, Rowman & Littlefield, 2014.

Karlin & Pigeot 1989: Cl. Karlin & N. Pigeot, 'Chasseurs-cueilleurs magdaléniens. L'apprentissage de la taille du silex', *in Le Courrier du CNRS* 73, sept. 1989, Dossiers scientifiques, CNRS, 10–12.

Kästner & Karlisch 1991: S. Kästner & S. M. Karlisch, *Feminismus und Archäologie ?*, Tübingen, 1991.

Kästner *et al.* 1998: S. Kästner, V. Maier & A. Schülke, 'From Pictures to Stories. Traces of female PhD graduates from the Department of Prehistoric Archaeology, University of Tübingen, Germany', *in* M. Díaz-Andreu & M. L. S. Sørensen (eds.), *Excavating Women. An History of Women in European Archaeology*, Routledge, 1998, 266–294.

Katz 2018: J. Katz, 'Queer Curating and Covert Censorship', *in On Curating*, n°37, p. 33–38.

Kehoe 1990: A. B. Kehoe, 'Points and Lines', *in* S. M. Nelson & A. B. Kehoe (eds.), *Powers of Observations. Alternative Views in Archaeology*, American Anthropological Association, 23–38.

Kelley & Hill 1994: J. H. Kelley & W. Hill, 'Relationships Between Graduate Training and Placement in Canadian Archaeology', dans M. Nelson, S. Nelson & A. Wylie (eds.), *Equity Issues for Women in Archaeology*, American Anthropological Association, 1994, 47–52.

Kelvin & Hodgetts 2020: L. Kelvin & L. Hodgetts, 'Unsettling Archaeology', *in Canadian Journal of Archaeology* 44, 2020, 1–19.

Kennedy 2014: R.F. Kennedy, *Immigrant Women in Athens. Gender, Ethnicity, and Citizenship in the Classical City*, Routledge, 2014.

Kent 1998: S. Kent, *Gender in African Prehistory*, Altamira Press, 1998.

Kenyon 1969: K.M. Kenyon, 'Women in Academic Life. The Galton Lecture 1969', *in Journal of Biosoc. Science*, Supplement 2, 1969, 107–118.

Kergoat 2000: D. Kergoat, 'Division sexuelle du travail et rapports sociaux de sexe', *in* H. Hirata, F. Laborie, H. Le Doaré & D. Senotier (dir.), *Dictionnaire critique du féminisme*, PUF, 2000.

Khudaverdyan *et al.* 2020: A.Y. Khudaverdyan, A.A. Yengibaryan, S.G. Hobosyan, A.A. Hovhanesyan & A.A. Saratikyan, 'An Early Armenian female warrior of the 8–6 century BC from Bover I site (Armenia)', *in International Journal of Osteoarchaeology* 30, 2020, 119–128.

Kimmel 1987: M. Kimmel (dir.), *Changing Men: New Directions in the Study of Men and Masculinity*, Sage Publications, 1987.

King 1998: H. King, *Hippocrates' Woman. Reading the Female Body in Ancient Greece*, Routledge, 1998.

Kirsch 1977: C. Kirsch, 'Forces productives, rapports de production et origine des inégalités entre hommes et femmes', *in Anthropologie et Sociétés* 1/3, 1977, 15–41.

Kleppe 1985: E. J. Kleppe, 'Arkæologistudiet og arbejdssituationen', *in K.A.N.* 1, 1985, 16–24.

Knapp 1998a: A. B. Knapp, 'Boys Will Be Boys: Maculinist Approaches to a Gendered Archaeology', *in* K. Hays-Gilpin & D. S. Withley (eds.), *Reader in Gender Archaeology*, 1998, 365–373.

Knapp 1998b: A. B. Knapp, 'Who's Come a Long Way Baby? Masculinist Approaches to a Gendered Archaeology', *in Archaeological Dialogues* 5/2, 1998, 91–106.

Koch & Mertens 2002: J. Koch & E.-M. Mertens (eds.), *Eine Dame zwischen 500 Herren. Johanna Mestorf – Werk und Wirkung*, Waxmann, 2002.

Kokkinidou & Nikolaidou 1993: D. Kokkinidou & M. Nikolaidou, *Η αρχαιολογία και η κοινωνική ταυτότητα του φύλου: προσεγγίσεις στην αιγαιακή προϊστορία*, Vanias, 1993.

Kokkinidou & Nikolaidou 2009: D. Kokkinidou & M. Nikolaidou, 'Feminism and Greek Archaeology: An Encounter Long Over-Due', *in* K. Kopaka (ed.), *FYLO: Engendering Prehistoric "Stratigraphies" in the Aegean and the Mediterranean*, Université de Liège, 2009, 25–37.

Kolhatkar *et al.* 2020: M. Kolhatkar, L. Trudel-Lopez, A. Loyer Rousselle, M. Johnson Gervais & J. Gagné, 'Le CNTAQ, 2017–2019: bilan de trois années de normalisation de la pratique archéologique québécoise et perspectives futures', *in Archéologiques*, 2020, 28–46.

Kramer & Stark 1988: C. Kramer, M. Stark, 'The Status of Women in Archeology', *in Anthropology News* 29/9, 1988, 1–12.

Kranzbühler 2019: J. Kranzbühler, 'Osteology Defines Sex and Archaeology Defines Gender? Insights from Physical Anthropology', *in* J. K. Koch & W. Kirleis (eds.), *Gender Transformations in Prehistoric and Archaic Societies*, Sidestone Press, 2019, 125–132.

Kraus 2000: C. Kraus, 'La bicatégorisation par sexe à l'"épreuve de la science". Le cas des recherches en biologie sur la détermination du sexe chez les Humains', *in* D. Gardey & I. Löwy (eds.), *L'invention du naturel. Les sciences et la fabrication du féminin et du masculin*, Éditions des archives contemporaines, 2000, 187–213.

Lafont 1994: B. Lafont, 'Normes, normativité, diversité dans le Proche-Orient ancien', *in Cahiers du Centre Gustave Glotz* 5, 1994, 1–25.

Lagrave 1990: R.-M. Lagrave, 'Recherches féministes ou recherches sur les femmes ?', *in Actes de la recherche en sciences sociales* 83, 1990, 27–39.

Laqueur 1992 (1990): T. Laqueur, *La fabrique du sexe. Essai sur le corps et le genre en Occident*, Gallimard (Poche), 1992 = T. Laqueur, Making Sex. Body and Gender, from the Greeks to Freud, Harvard University Press, 1990.

Laluk 2021: N. C. Laluk, 'Changing How Archaeology Is Done in Native American Contexts: An Ndee (Apache) Case Study', *in Journal of Social Archaeology* 21/1, 2021, 53–73.

Laroche & Blakey 1997: Ch. J. Laroche & M. L. Blakey, 'Seizing Intellectual Power: The Dialogue at the New York African Burial Ground', *in Historical Archaeology* 31/3, 1997, 84–106.

Laufer 2004: J. Laufer, 'Femmes et carrières: la question du plafond de verre', *in Revue française de gestion* 30 (151), 2004, 117–127.

Lauwaert 2020: F. Lauwaert, *'Quel dommage que tu ne sois pas un garçon !' Rencontres avec des femmes remarquables en Chine impériale*, Académie royale de Belgique, 2020.

Lazar *et al.* 2014: I. Lazar, T. Kompare, H. van Londen & T. Schenk, 'The Archaeologist of the Future is Likely to be a Woman: Age and Gender Patterns in European Archaeology, Archaeologies', *in Journal of the World Archaeological Congress*, 2014, 257–280 [DOI: 10.1007/s11759–014–9263–6].

Le Talec 2016: J.-Y. Le Talec, 'Des Men's Studies aux Masculinity Studies: du patriarcat à la pluralité des masculinités', *in SociologieS*, 2016, [online: http://journals.openedition.org/sociologies/5234].

Lecadet 2019: C. Lecadet, 'Le handicap, sport de combat', *in Vacarme* 3, 88, 2019, 38–47.

Lee 2009: M.M. Lee, 'Body-Modification in Classical Greece', *in* T. Fögen & M. M. Lee (eds.), *Bodies and Boundaries in Graeco-Roman Antiquity*, De Gruyter, 2009, 155–180.

Lee 2012: M. M. Lee, 'Dress and Adornment in Archaic and Classical Greece', *in* S. L. James & S. Dillon (eds.), *A Companion to Women in the Ancient World*, Wiley-Blackwell, 2012, 179–190.

Lee 2019: N. Lee, 'Boarding: Black Women in Nantucket Generating Income and Building Community', *in Transforming Anthropology* 27/2, 2019, 91–104.

Lee 2020: N. Lee, 'Here We Go Again. The Need to Contest and Refute Biological Determinism in Archaeology', *in Archaeological Dialogues* 27, 2020, 20–22.

Lee & DeVore 1968: R.B. Lee & I. DeVore (eds.), *Man the Hunter*, Routledge, 1969.

Lee & Scott 2019: N. Lee & J. N. Scott, 'Introduction: New Directions in Africa Diaspora Archaeology', *in Transforming Anthropology* 27/2, 2019, 85–90.

Lehoërff 2009: A. Lehoërff, 'L'enseignement de l'archéologie en licence dans les universités françaises', *in Les Nouvelles de l'Archéologie* 115, 2009, 57–64.

Leighton 2020: M. Leighton, 'Myths of Meritocracy, Friendship, and Fun Work: Class and Gender in North American Academic Communities', *in American Anthropologist* 122/3, 2020, 444–458.

Leone *et al.* 2005: M. P. Leone, Ch. J. Laroche & J. J. Babiarz, 'The Archaeology of Black Americans in Recent Times', *in Annual Review of Anthropology* 34, 2005, 575–598.

Levin 2010a: A.K. Levin, *Gender, Sexuality and Museums. A Routledge Reader*, Routledge, 2010.

Levin 2010b: A.K. Levin, 'Introduction', *in* A.K. Levin (ed.), *Gender, Sexuality and Museums. A Routledge Reader*, Routledge, 2010, 1–11.

Levin 2020: A.K. Levin, 'Introduction. Museums, Sexuality, and Gender Activism', *in* J.G. Adair & A.K. Levin (eds.), *Museums, Sexuality, and Gender Activism*, Routledge, 2020, 5–20.

Lewis 2002: S. Lewis, *The Athenian Woman: an Iconographic Handbook*, Routledge, 2002.

Lewis 2006: S. Lewis, 'Iconography and the Study of Gender', *in* S. Schroer (ed.), *Images and Gender. Contributions to the Hermeneutics of Reading Ancient Art*, Academic Press/Vandenhoeck & Ruprecht, 2006, 23–39.

Liibert *et al.* 2014: K. Liibert, M. Malińska, L. Wachowicz & A. Marciniak, *Discovering the Archaeologists of Poland 2012–14*, 2014, [online: http://e-archaeology.org/wp-content/uploads/2016/06/PL-DISCO-Poland-national-report-english.pdf].

Lillehammer 1988: G. Lillehammer, 'Kvinner i yrkessammenheng', *in K.A.N.* 6, 1988, 21–35.

Lima 1995: T. Lima, 'Pratos e mais pratos: louças domésticas, divisões culturais e limites sociais no Rio de Janeiro, século XIX', *in Anais do Museu Paulista: História e Cultura Material* 3/1, 1995, 129–191.

Lima 2003: T. Lima, 'Estudos de gênero na Arqueologia Brasileira. Por que não?', *in Habitus* 1/1, 2003, 129–139.

Linduff & Sun 2004: K. M. Linduff & Y. Sun, *Gender and Chinese Archaeology*, Altamira Press, 2004.

Lion 2021: B. Lion, 'Alimentation et société en Mésopotamie', *in* F. Quellier (dir.), *Histoire de l'alimentation. De la Préhistoire à nos jours*, Belin, 2021, 67–91.

Lippert 2006: D. Lippert, 'Building a Bridge to Cross a Thousand Years', *in American Indian Quarterly* 30, n°3/4, 2006, 431–440.

Lippert 2008: D. Lippert, 'The Rise of Indigenous Archaeology: How Repatriation Has Transformed Archaeological Ethics and Practice', *in Opening Archaeology: Repatriation's Impact on Contemporary Research and Practice*, 2008, 151–160.

Loraux 1981: N. Loraux, *Les enfants d'Athéna. Idées athéniennes sur la citoyenneté et la division des sexes*, F. Maspero, 1981.

Löwy 2003: I. Löwy, 'Intersexe et transsexualités: Les technologies de la médecine et la séparation du sexe biologique du sexe social', *in Cahiers du Genre* 34/1, 2003, 81–104.

Lozny 2011: L. Lozny, 'Polish Archaeology in retrospective', *in* L. Lozny (ed.), *Comparative Archaeologies. A Sociological View of the Science of the Past*, Springer, 2011, 195–220.

Lucy 2005: S. Lucy, 'The Archaeology of Age', *in* M. Díaz-Andreu, S. Lucy, S. Babić & D.N. Edwards (eds.), *The Archaeology of Identity. Approaches to Gender, Age, Status Ethnicity and Religion*, Routledge, 2005, 43–66.

Lugones 2007: M. Lugones, 'Heterosexualims and the Colonial/Modern Gender System', *in Hypatia* 22/1, 2007, 186–209.

Lydon & Rizvi 2016: J. Lydon & U. Z. Rizvi (eds.), *Handbook of Postcolonial Archaeology*, Routledge, 2016.

Lyons 2004: D. Lyons, 'Gender Research in African Archaeology', *in* S. M. Nelson (ed.), *Worlds of Gender. The Archaeology of Women's Lives around the Globe*, Altamira Press, 2004, 1–37.

Lyons 2006: D. Lyons, 'A Critical Appraisal of Gender Research in African Archaeology', *in* S. M. Nelson (ed.), *Handbook of Gender in Archaeology*, Altamira Press, 2006, 595–632.

MacEachern 1996: S. MacEachern, 'Foreign Countries: The Development of Ethnoarchaeology in Sub-Saharan Africa', *in Journal of World Prehistory* 10/3, 1996, 243–304.

Maceira-Ochoa 2017: L. Maceira-Ochoa, '¿Vestigios para un futuro igualitario? Pensar la educación en los museos arqueológicos desde una perspectiva feminista', *in* L. Prados Torreira & C. López Ruiz (eds.), *Museos arqueológicos y género. Educando en igualdad*, UAM Ediciones, 2017, 69–103.

Macinthosh *et al.* 2017: A. Macintosh, R. Pinhasi & J.T. Stock, 'Prehistoric Women's Manual Labor Exceeded That of Athletes Through the First 5500 Years of Farming in Central Europe', *in Science Advances* 3/11, 2017, [DOI: 10.1126/sciadv.aao3893].

MacKinnon 1979: C. MacKinnon, *Sexual Harassement of Working Women. A Case of Sex Discrimination*, Yale University Press, 1979.

Maillet 2020: C. Maillet, *Les genres fluides. De Jeanne d'Arc aux saintes trans*, Arkhê, 2020.

Manakidou 1992–1993: E. Manakidou, 'Athenerinnen in schwarzfigurigen Brunnenhausszenen', *in Hephaistos* 11/12, 1992–1993, 51–91.

Mandt 1976: G. Mandt, 'Konferanse om kvinneforskning', *in Kontaktstencil* 11, 1976, 47–59.

Mandt & Naess 1986: G. Mandt & J. R. Naess, 'Hvem skapte og gjenskaper vår fjerne fortid? Struktur og innhold i norsk arkeologi i perspektivet: 'Hvor mannliger vitenskapen?'', *in K.A.N.* 3, 1986, 3–28.

Manfrini-Aragno 1992: I. Manfrini-Aragno, 'Femmes à la fontaine: réalité et imaginaire', *in* C. Bron & E. Kassapoglou (eds.), *L'image en jeu. De l'Antiquité à Paul Klee*, Cabédita, 1992, 127–148.

Manias 2015: C. Manias, 'Scholarly Visions of Prehistoric Sexuality, 1859–1900', *in* K. Fisher & R. Langlands (eds.), Sex, Knowledge, and Receptions of the Past, Oxford University Press, 2015, 177–199.

Martin 1991: E. Martin, 'The Egg and the Sperm: How Science Has Constructed a Romance Based on Stereotypical Male- Female Roles', *in Signs: Journal of Women in Culture and Society* 16/3, 1991, 485–501.

Martinez 2014: D. R. Martinez, 'Indigenous Archaeologies', *in* C. Smith (ed.), *Encyclopedia of Global Archaeology*, Springer, 2014, 3772–3777.

Mary 2020a: L. Mary, 'Le féminisme et la question du genre en archéologie: de la théorie à la pratique', *in* I. Algrain (ed.), *Archéologie du genre. Construction sociale des identités et culture matérielle*, Université des femmes, 2020, 197–210.

Mary 2020b: L. Mary, 'Paye ta Truelle: la lutte féministe en archéologie', *Chronique Féministe* 125, 2020b, 39–41.

Mary 2021: L. Mary, 'Déstabiliser la binarité en archéologie: le cas des tombes 137 et 260 de la nécropole mérovingienne de Bossut-Gottechain', *in Frontière·s*

5/1, 2021, 17–25 (online: https://publications-prairial.fr/frontiere-s/index.php?id=819).

Mary *et al.* 2019: L. Mary, B. Pasquini & S. Vandevelde, 'Le sexisme en archéologie, ça n'existe pas !' / 'Sexism in Archaeology, It Doesn't Exist !', *in Canadian Journal of Bioethics* 2/2, 2019, 215–242.

Mary & Rocca 2021: L. Mary, R. Rocca, 'Compte-rendu de l'ouvrage de Patou-Mathis Marylène (2020) – L'homme préhistorique est aussi une femme: une histoire de l'invisibilité des femmes', *in Bulletin de la Société préhistorique française* 118, 2021, 168–170.

Masclans *et al.* 2019: A. Masclans, S. Duboscq, K. F. Achino, B. Morell & J. F. Gibaja, 'Looking for Sexual Differences During the Middle Neolithic in the Northeast of the Iberian Peninsula', *in Journal of Archaeological Science: Reports* 26, 2019, 101858, [https://doi.org/10.1016/j.jasrep.2019.05.023].

Mathieu 1973: N.-C. Mathieu, 'Homme-culture et femme-nature ?', *in L'Homme* 13/3, 1973, 101–113.

Mathieu 1991: N.-C. Mathieu, *L'anatomie politique. Catégorisations et idéologies du sexe*, Côté-femmes, 1991.

Mathieu 2010: A. Mathieu, *Approche du genre au travers du mobilier funéraire issu de cinq nécropoles danubiennes*, mémoire de master 2, Université de Provence, 2010.

Matić 2012: U. Matić, 'To Queer or Not to Queer? That is the Question: Sex/Gender, Prestige and Burial no. 10 on the Mokrin Necropolis', *in Dacia NS* 56, 2012, 169–185.

Matić 2016: U. Matić, '(De)queering Hatshepsut: Binary Bind in Archaeology of Egypt and Kingship beyond the Corporeal', *in Journal of Archaeological Method and Theory* 23/3, 2016, 810–831.

Matić 2017: U. Matić, '"Her Striking but Cold Beauty": Gender and Violence in Depictions of Queen Nefertiti smiting the enemies', *in* B. Jensen & U. Matić (eds.), *Archaeologies of Gender and Violence*, Oxbow Books, 2017, 103–121.

Matić 2020: U. Matić, *Ethnic Identities in the Land of the Pharaohs. Past and Present Approaches in Egyptology*, Cambridge University Press, 2020.

Matić 2021: U. Matić, *Violence and Gender in Ancient Egypt*, Routledge, 2021.

Mayor 2017: A. Mayor, *Les Amazones. Quand les femmes étaient les égales des hommes (VIIIe siècle av. J.-C. - Ier siècle apr. J.-C.)*, La Découverte, 2017 = A. Mayor, *The Amazons. Lives and Legends of Warrior Women across the Ancient World*, Princeton University Press, 2014.

Mazé 2020: C. Mazé, '"J'ai donné du pain à celui qui avait faim…". Manque de nourriture et inégalités alimentaires en Égypte ancienne (IIIe-II millénaires a.C.)', *in* E. Galbois & S. Rougier-Blanc (eds.), *Maigreur et minceur dans les sociétés anciennes. Grèce, Orient, Rome*, Ausonius, 2020 (coll. 'Scripta Antiqua', 132), p. 53–70.

Mazouz 2020: S. Mazouz, *Race*, Anamosa éditions, 2020.

McGuire 2008: R. McGuire, 'Marxism', *in* R. A. Bentley, H. D. G. Maschner & Ch. Chippindale (eds.), *Handbook of Archaeological Theories*, Altamira Press, 2008, 73–93.

McGuire 2018: R. McGuire, 'Capitalism in Archaeological Theory', *in* C. Smith (ed.), *Encyclopedia of Global Archaeology*, 2018, [online: https://doi.org/10.1007/978-3-319-51726-1_254-2].

McGuire & Reckner 2003: R. McGuire & P. Reckner, 'Building a Working-Class Archaeology: The Colorado Coal Field War Project', *in Industrial Archaeology Review*, 25/2, 2003, 83–95.

McGuire & Walker 1999: R. McGuire & M. Walker, 'Class Confrontations in Archaeology', *in Historical Archaeology* 33/1, 1999, 159–183.

Mckee 1999: L. Mckee, 'Food Supply and Plantation Social Order: An Archaeological Perspective', *in* T. A. Singleton (ed.), *"I, Too, Am America": Archaeological Studies of African-American Life*, University Press of Virginia, 1999, 218–239.

McLemore & Reynolds 1979: D. McLemore & L. Reynolds, 'Employment of Female Archaeologists in the U.S. Forest Service', *in National Women's Anthropology Newsletter* 4/1, 1979, 6–9.

Mead 1963: M. Mead, *Mœurs et sexualité en Océanie*, Plon, 1963.

Merriman 1999: N. Merriman, 'Introduction', *in* N. Merriman (ed.), *Making Early Histories in Museums*, Leicester University Press, 1999, 1–11.

Mertens & Koch 2005: E. M. Mertens & J. K. Koch, 'Jenseits von 'weiblichen Kammern und Särgen' Entwicklung der archäologischen geschlechterforschung in Deutschland', *in* J. E. Fries, J.K. Koch (eds.), *Ausgrabenzwischen Materialclustern und Zeitscheiben. Perspektiven zur archäologischen Geschlechterforschung. Frauen – Forschung – Archäologie* 6, Waxmann, 2005, 25–56.

Merton 1968: R. K. Merton, 'The Matthew Effect in Science', *in Science* 159, 1968, 56–63.

Meskell 1999: L. Meskell, *Archaeologies of Social Life, Age, Sex, Class et cetera in Ancient Egypt*, Blackwell, 1999.

Meyers *et al.* 2015: M. Meyers, T. Boudreaux, S. Carmody, V. Dekle, E. Horton & A. Wright, 'Preliminary Results of the SEAC Sexual Harassment Survey', *in The Newsletter of the Southeastern Archaeological Conference* 57/1, 2015, 19–35.

Meyers *et al.* 2018: M. Meyers, T. E. Horton, E. A. Boudreaux, S. B. Carmody, A. P. Wright & V. G.

Dekle, 'The Context and Consequences of Sexual Harassment in Southeastern Archaeology', *in Advances in Archaeological Practice* 6/4, 2018, 1–13.

Michel 2012: C. Michel. 'L'alimentation au Proche-Orient ancien : les sources et leur exploitation', dans *L'histoire de l'alimentation dans l'Antiquité. Bilan historiographique*, (Dialogues d'Histoire Ancienne, Supplément 7), 2012, 17–45.

Mickel 2021: A. Mickel, *Why Those Who Shovel Are Silent: A History of Local Archaeological Knowledge and Labor*, University Press of Colorado, 2021.

Milcent 2003: P.-Y. Milcent, 'Statut et fonctions d'un personnage féminin hors norme', in C. Rolley (dir.), *La tombe princière de Vix*, Picard, 2003, 312–366.

Miller *et al.* 2004: P. Miller, S. Parker & S. Gillinson, *Disablism: How to Tackle the Last Prejudice*, Demos, 2004.

Millett 1970: K. Millett, *Sexual Politics*, Doubleday, 1970.

Ministère de la Culture et de la Communication 2016: Ministère de la Culture et de la Communication, *Observatoire de l'égalité entre femmes et hommes dans la culture et la communication*, 2016 [online: https://www.culture.gouv.fr/content/download/136693/1466600/version/3/file/DEPS_Egalite%20HF_int%C3%A9rieur%2Bcouv.pdf].

Ministère de la Culture et de la Communication 2019: Ministère de la Culture et de la Communication, *Observatoire de l'égalité entre femmes et hommes dans la culture et la communication*, 2019, [online: https://www.culture.gouv.fr/Media/Thematiques/Etudes-et-statistiques/Files/Publications/Observatoire-egalite-H-F/Septieme-rapport-de-l-Observatoire-de-l-egalite-femmes-hommes-8mars-2019].

Ministère de la Culture 2021: Ministère de la Culture et de la Communication, *Observatoire de l'égalité entre femmes et hommes dans la culture et la communication*, 2021, [online: https://www.culture.gouv.fr/Thematiques/Etudes-et-statistiques/Publications/Collections-d-ouvrages/Observatoire-de-l-egalite-entre-femmes-et-hommes-dans-la-culture-et-la-communication/Observatoire-2021-de-l-egalite-entre-femmes-et-hommes-dans-la-culture-et-la-communication].

Minkoff & Morris 2016: M. F. Minkoff & A. E. Morris, 'Urban Archaeology Corps, A Civically Engaged Youth Employment Programme', *in Journal of Community Archaeology & Heritage* 3/3, 2016, 220–236.

Moen & Pedersen 2024: M. Moen & U. Pedersen, *The Routledge Handbook of Gender Archaeology*, Routledge, 2024.

Moilanen *et al.* 2022: U. Moilanen, T. Kirkinen, N. Saari, A. Rohrlach, J. Krause, P. Onkamo & E. Salmela, 'A Woman with a Sword? – Weapon Grave at Suontaka Vesitorninmäki, Finland', *in European Journal of Archaeology* 25/1, 2022, 42–60 [doi:10.1017/eaa.2021.30].

Monge & Selinsky 2016: J. Monge & P. Selinsky, 'Patterns of Violence Against Women in the Iron Age Town of Hasanlu, Solduz Valley, Iran', *in* S.L. Budin & J. MacIntosh Turfa (eds.), *Women in Antiquity. Real Women Across the Ancient World*, Routledge, 2016, 138–155.

Mónton-Subías 2018: S. Mónton-Subías, 'Gender, Feminist, and Queer Archaeologies: A Spanish Perspective', *in* C. Smith (ed.), *Encyclopedia of Global Archaeology*, Springer, 2018, 2980–2988.

Montón-Subías & Meyer 2014: S. Montón-Subías & W. Meyer, 'Engendered Archaeologies', *in Encyclopedia of Global Archaeology*, Springer, 2014, 2372–2381.

Moral 2016: E. Moral, 'Qu(e)erying Sex and Gender in Archaeology: A Critique of the "Third" and Other Sexual Categories', *in Journal of Archaeological Method and Theory* 23/3, 2016, 788–809.

Moraw 2021: S. Moraw, 'FemArc – Netzwerk archäologisch arbeitender Frauen e. V.: die ersten 25 Jahre', *in* D. Gutsmiedl-Schümann, M. Helmbrecht, J. Kranzbühler, *Feministische Perspektiven auf Gender und Archäologie Beiträge der Tagung zum 25-jährigen Bestehen von FemArc – Netzwerk archäologisch arbeitender Frauen e. V.*, Waxmann, 2021, 41–68.

Moreau 1898: F. Moreau, *Album Caranda*, 18 fasc., Saint-Quentin, 1898.

Morgan 2015: C. Morgan, 'Punk, DIY, and Anarchy in Archaeological Thought and Practice', *in Online Journal in Public Archaeology* 5, 2015, 123–146.

Morris 1992: E. L. Morris, 'Women in British Archaeology. Report Prepared for the Council of the Institute of Field Archaeologists', *in The Institute of Field Archaeologists, Occasional Paper* 4, 1992.

Morris 2017: A. Morris, 'Materialities of Homeplace', *in Historical Archaeology* 51, 2017, 28–42.

Moser 1996: S. Moser, 'Science, Stratigraphy and the Deep Sequence: Excavation vs Regional Survey and the Question of Gendered Practice in Archaeology', *in Antiquity* 70, 1996, 813–823.

Moser 1999: S. Moser, 'The Dilemma of Didactic Displays: Habitat Dioramas, Life-groups and Reconstructions of the Past', *in* N. Merriman (ed.), *Making Early Histories in Museums*, Leicester University Press, 1999, 95–116.

Moser 2007: S. Moser, 'On Disciplinary Culture: Archaeology as Fieldwork and Its Gendered Associations', *in Journal of Archaeological Method and Theory* 14, 2007, 235–263.

Muckle 2014: R. Muckle, 'On Sexual Harassment and Abuse in Archaeology', *in The SAA Archaeological Record*, 2014, 32–33.

Murail *et al.* 2005: P. Murail, J. Bruzek, F. Houët & E. Cunha, 'DSP: A Tool For Probabilistic Sex Diagnosis Using Worldwide Variability in Hip-Bone

Measurements', *in Bulletins et Mémoires de la Société d'Anthropologie de Paris* 17/3–4, 2005, 167–176.

Murray *et al.* 2020: S.C. Murrray, I. Chorghay & J. MacPherson, 'The Dipylon Mistress: Social and Economic Complexity, the Gendering of Craft Production, and Early Greek Ceramic Material Culture', *in American Journal of Archaeology* 124/2, 2020, 215–244.

Nakhai 2017: B.A. Nakhai, 'Keeping Archaeological Field Work Safe from Sexual Harassment and Physical Violence', 2017, [online: https://iaassyriology.com/field-work-safe].

Nakhai 2018: B.A. Nakhai, 'How to Avoid Gender-Based Hostility During Fieldwork', *in The Chronicle of Higher Education*, 15 juillet 2018 [online: https://www.chronicle.com/article/how-to-avoid-gender-based-hostility-during-fieldwork/].

NASEM 2018: NASEM - National Academies of Sciences, Engineering, and Medicine, *Sexual Harassment of Women: Climate, Culture, and Consequences in Academic Sciences, Engineering, and Medicine*, National Academies Press, 2018.

Ndlovu 2009: N. Ndlovu, 'Transformation Challenges in South African Archaeology', *in South African Archaeological Bulletin* 64, 2009, 91–93.

Neal 2008: L. A. Neal, 'Glass Ceiling Syndrome for Women in Archaeology', *in The SAA Archaeological Record* 8/4, 2008, 31–34.

Nelson *et al.* 1994: M. Nelson, S. M. Nelson & A. Wylie (eds.), *Equity Issues for Women in Archaeology*, American Anthropological Association, 1994.

Nelson & Nelson 1994: S. M. Nelson & M. Nelson, 'Conclusion', *in* M. Nelson, S. M. Nelson & A. Wylie (eds.), *Equity Issues for Women in Archaeology*, American Anthropological Association, 1994, 229–235.

Nelson 1991: S. M. Nelson, 'Women Archaeologists in Asia and the Pacific', *in* D. Walde & N. Willows (eds.), *The Archaeology of Gender. Proceedings of the Twenty-Second Annual Conference of the Archaeological Association of the University of Calgary*, University of Calgary Archaeological Association, 1991, 217–219.

Nelson 2006a: S. M. Nelson (ed.), *Handbook of Gender in Archaeology*, AltaMira Press, 2006.

Nelson 2006b: S. M. Nelson, 'Introduction. Archaeological Perspectives on Gender', *in* S. M. Nelson (ed.), *Handbook of Gender in Archaeology*, AltaMira Press, 2006, 1–27.

Nevett 1995: L.C. Nevett, 'Gender Relations in the Classical Greek Household: The Archaeological Evidence', *in The Annual of the British School at Athens* 90, 1995, p. 363–381.

Nevett 1999: L.C. Nevett, *House and Society in the Ancient Greek World*, Cambridge University Press, 1999.

Nicholas & Andrews 2008: G. P. Nicholas & T. Andrews, 'Indigenous Archaeology in a Post-Modern World', *in* G. Nicholas & T. Andrews (eds.), *At a Crossroads: Archaeology and First Peoples in Canada*, SFU Archaeology Press, 1997, 1–18.

Nicholas 2008: G. P. Nicholas, 'Native Peoples and Archaeology', *in* D. Pearsall, *Encyclopedia of Archaeology* 3, Academic Press, 2008, 1660–1669.

Nicholas 2009: G. Nicholas, 'Review: Handbook of Gender in Archaeology by Sarah Milledge Nelson', *in Canadian Journal of Archaeology / Journal Canadien d'Archéologie* 33, n°1, 2009, 150–153.

Nicholas 2016: G. P. Nicholas, *Being and Becoming Indigenous Archaeologists*, Routledge, 2016.

Nikolaidou & Kokkinidou 1998: M. Nikolaidou & D. Kokkinidou, 'Greek Women in Archaeology. An Untold Story', *in* M. Díaz-Andreu & M. L. S. Sørensen (eds.), *Excavating Women. An History of Women in European Archaeology*, Routledge, 1998, 266–294.

Nixon Chen 2013: K.T. Nixon Chen, 'The Disciplinary Power of Museums', *in International Journal of Social Science and Humanity* 3/4, juillet 2013, 407–410.

Nochlin 2021 (1971): L. Nochlin, *Pourquoi n'y a-t-il pas eu de grands artistes femmes ?*, Thames & Hudson, 2021 = L. Nochlin, 'Why Have There Been No Great Women Artists ?', *in ARTnews* 69/9, January 1971, 22–39.

Norton 2017: Norton H., 'How The Female Viking Warrior Was Written Out of History ', *in The Guardian*, 12 September 2017, [https://www.theguardian.com/science/2017/sep/15/how-the-female-viking-warrior-was-written-out-of-history].

Novak 2017: S. A. Novak, 'On the Stories of Men and the Substance of Women. Interrogating Gender through Violence', *in* S. C. Agarwal & J. K. Wesp (eds.), *Exploring Sex and Gender in Bioarchaeology*, University of New Mexico Press, 2017, 129–164.

Nutt 2017: A.E. Nutt, 'Wonder Woman Lived: Viking Warrior Skeleton Identified as Female, 128 Years After Its Discovery', *in The Washington Post*, 14 September 2017, [https://www.washingtonpost.com/news/speaking-of-science/wp/2017/09/14/wonder-woman-lives-viking-warrior-skeleton-identified-as-female-128-years-after-its-discovery/].

Oakley 1972: A. Oakley, *Sex, Gender and Society*, Temple Smith, 1972.

Odewale *et al.* 2018: A. Odewale, J. Dunnavant, A. Flewellen & A. Jones, 'Archaeology for the Next Generation', *in Anthropology News* 59/1, 2018, e210-e215 [doi:10.1111/AN.729].

Odewale & Slocum 2020: A. Odewale & K. Slocum, *The Rise, Destruction, and Rebuilding of Tulsa's Greenwood*

District. A Source List, 2020, [https://tulsasyllabus.web.unc.edu/].

Oland 2008: M. Oland, 'Motherhood and the Future of Women in Archaeology', *in The SAA Archaeological Record* 8/4, 2008, 22–24.

Oland 2020: M. H. Oland, 'Teaching Archaeology with Inclusive Pedagogy', *in Journal of Archaeology and Education* 4/1, 2020.

O'Mahony 2015: T. O'Mahony, *Enabled Archaeology Guide 41*, 2015, [online: http://www.bajr.org/BAJRGuides/41_Enabled_Archaeology/41EnabledArchaeology.pdf].

O'Mahony 2016: T. O'Mahony, 'Archaeology From a Disabled Enabled Perspective', *in London Archaeologist* 14/10, 2016, 265–269.

O'Mahony 2018: T. O'Mahony, 'Reflections in UK Archaeology – A Personal Journey in Academic Life', *in Journal of Community Archaeology & Heritage* 5/3, 2018, 216–218.

Ortner 1974: S.B. Ortner, 'Is Female to Male as Nature is to Culture ?', *in* M. Zimbalist Rosaldo & L. Lamphere (eds.), *Women, Culture and Society*, Stanford University Press, 67–87.

Ortner 1996: S.B. Ortner, *Making Gender. The Politics and Erotics of Culture*, Beacon, 1996.

Osborne 1998: R. Osborne, 'Sculpted Men of Athens: Masculinity and Power in the Field of Vision', *in* L. Foxhall & J. Salmon (eds.), *Thinking Men: Masculinity and its Self-Representation in the Classical Tradition*, Routledge, 1998, 23–42.

Oser 1998: Ch. Oser, 'The Archaeology of the African Diaspora', *in Annual Review of Anthropology* 27, 1998, 63–82.

Otto 2016: A. Otto, 'Professional Women and Women at Work in Mesopotamia and Syria (3rd and Early 2nd Millennia BC): The (Rare) Information from Visual Images', *in* B. Lion & C. Michel (eds.), *The Role of Women in Work and Society in the Ancient Near East*, De Gruyter, 2016, 112–148.

Oyewumi 1997: O. Oyewumi, *The Invention of Women. Making an African Sense of Western Gender Discourses*, University of Minnesota Press, 1997.

Oyewumi 1998: O. Oyewumi, 'De-Confounding Gender: Feminist Theorizing and Western Culture, a comment on Hawkesworth's "Confounding Gender"', *in Signs* 23/4, 1049–1062.

Palincas 2021: N. Palincas, 'Archaeology and Gender in Europe (AGE) – a Working Community of the EAA: The First Ten Years (2008–2018)', *in* D. Gutsmiedl-Schümann, M. Helmbrecht & J. Kranzbühler (eds.), *Feministische Perspektiven auf Gender und Archäologie Beiträge der Tagung zum 25-jährigen Bestehen von FemArc – Netzwerk archäologisch arbeitender Frauen e.V.*, Waxmann, 2021, 91–122.

Paoletti 2012: J.B. Paoletti, *Pink and Blue. Telling the Boys from the Girls in America*, Indiana University Press, 2012.

Parent 2017: L. Parent, 'Ableism/disablism, on dit ça comment en français?', *in Canadian Journal of Disability Studies* 6/2, 2017, 183–212.

Park & Nye 1991: K. Park & R. A. Nye, '"Destiny is Anatomy", Essay Review of Thomas Laqueur, Making Sex: Body and Gender from the Greeks to Freud (1990)', *in The New Republic*, 18 February 1991, 53–57.

Park *et al.* 2020: G. Park, L.-Y. Wang & B. Marwick, 'How do Archaeologists Write about Racism? Computational Text Analysis of 41 Years of Society of American Archaeology Annual Meeting Abstracts', *in OSF Prepints*, 2020, [online: https://osf.io/preprints/zm73f/].

Pastor Quiles & Mateo Corredor 2022: M. Pastor Quiles & D. Mateo Corredor, '(Still) a Man's World. Análisis de la evolución de la presencia de autoras en revistas científicas españolas de Arqueología (1970–2020)', *in Archivo Español de Arqueología* 95, 2022, [Accessed 1st April 2022, DOI: https://doi.org/10.3989/aespa.095.022.02].

Pateman 1983: C. Pateman, 'Feminist Critiques of the Public/Private Dichotomy', *in* S.I. Benn, G.F. Gaus, *Public and Private in Social Life*, St Martin's Press, 1983.

Patterson 2003: T. Patterson, *Marx's Ghost: Conversations with Archaeologists*, Routledge, 2003.

Pavard 2017: B. Pavard, 'Faire naître et mourir les vagues: comment s'écrit l'histoire des féminismes', *in Itinéraires* 2017/2, [Accessed 6 April 2022, http://journals.openedition.org/itineraires/3787].

Pavard *et al.* 2020: B. Pavard, F. Rochefort & M. Zancarini-Fournel, *Ne nous libérez pas, on s'en charge. Une histoire des féminismes de 1789 à nos jours*, La Découverte, 2020.

Peled 2016: I. Peled, 'Visualizing Masculinities: The Gala, Hegemony, and Mesopotamian Iconography', *in Near Eastern Archaeology* 79/3, Special Issue: Gender Archaeology, 2016, 158–165.

Péré-Nogues 2011: S. Péré-Nogues, 'Le genre au prisme de l'archéologie: quelques réflexions autour de la "dame de Vix"', *in Les Cahiers de Framespa* 7, 2011 [online: http://framespa.revues.org/660].

Perry & Joyce 2001: E. M. Perry & R. Joyce, 'Providing a Past for "Bodies That Matter": Judith Butler's Impact on the Archaeology of Gender', *in International*

Journal of Sexuality & Gender Studies 6/1, 2001, 63–76.

Persson 2015: H. Persson, *Shoes. Pleasure and Pain. [V&A exhibition, 13 June 2015 to 31 January 2016]*, V&A Publishing, 2015.

Pfefferkorn 2016: R. Pfefferkorn, *Genre et rapports sociaux de sexe*, 3rd edition, Syllepse, 2016.

Phillips & Creighton 2010: T. Phillips & J. Creighton, *Employing People with Disabilities: Good Practice Guidelines for Archaeologists*, Institute for Archaeologists (Institute for Archaeologists Professional Paper 9), 2010, [https://www.archaeologists.net/sites/default/files/Disabilitypaper.pdf].

Phillips & Gilchrist 2005: T. Phillips & R. Gilchrist, *Inclusive Accessible Archaeology Phase 1, Disability and Archaeological Fieldwork*, Higher Education Funding Council for England, University of Reading, 2005.

Phillips & Gilchrist 2012: T. Phillips & R. Gilchrist, 'Inclusive, Accessible, Archaeology', *in* R. Skeates, C. McDavid & J. Carman (eds.), *The Oxford Handbook of Public Archaeology*, 2012, 673–693 [online: https://doi.org/10.1093/oxfordhb/9780199237821.013.0035].

Picazo 1998: M. Picazo, 'The First Women Archaeologists in Crete', *in* M. Díaz-Andreu & M. L. S. Sørensen (eds.), *Excavating Women. An History of Women in European Archaeology*, Routledge, 1998, 198–213.

Pigeot 1990: N. Pigeot, 'Technical and social actors in Prehistory – Flintknapping specialists and apprentices at Magdalenian Étiolles', *in Archaeological Review from Cambridge* 9/1, Technology in the Humanities, Cambridge, 1990, 126–141.

Pollock 1988: G. Pollock, *Vision and Difference: Feminism, Feminity and the Histories of Art*, Routledge, 1988.

Pollock 1999: G. Pollock, *Differencing the Canon: Feminist Desire and the Writing of Art's Histories*, Routledge, 1999.

Pope 2021: R. Pope, 'Women in the Present, Women in the Past', *in* International conference *"Modern" Women of the Past? Unearthing Gender and Antiquity*, organised by the Chau Chak Wing Museum, Camperdown, University of Sydney, 2021, [https://youtu.be/hJe6388wmSY.s].

Pope & Davies 2023: R. Pope & M. H. Davies, 'Peggy Piggot: Women and British Archaeology (1930–1945)', *in Oxford Journal of Archaeology* 42/3, 2023, 256–279.

Pope & Davies 2025: R. Pope & M. H. Davies, 'Peggy Piggot and Post-war British Archaeology', *in European Journal of Archaeology* 28/1, 2025, 101–122.

Pope & Teather 2025: R. Pope & A. Teather, 'Documenting the profession: Recording historic access and retention issues for women in UK archaeology', *in Archaeological Dialogues*, Published online 2025, 1–25.

Potter 1994: P. Potter, *Public Archaeology in Annapolis: A Critical Approach to History in Maryland's Ancient City*, Smithsonian Institution Press, 1994.

Pottier 2018: J.-M. Pottier, 'Dans cette traduction de "L'Odyssée" par une femme, Ulysse et Pénélope comme vous ne les avez jamais vus', *in Slate*, 5 February 2018, [online: http://www.slate.fr/story/157033/odyssee-homere-traduction-femmes-etats-unis].

Power 2020: M. Power, 'Non-Binary and Intersex Visibility and Erasure in Roman Archaeology', *in Theoretical Roman Archaeology Journal* 3, 2020, 1–19.

Prados Torreira 2016: L. Prados Torreira 'Why Is It Necessary to Include the Gender Perspective in Archaeological Museums ? Some Examples from Spanish Museums', *in Museum Worlds: Advances in Research* 4, 18–32.

Prados Torreira 2017: L. Prados Torreira, '¿Abogan los museos arqueológicos del siglo XXI por una educación en igualdad?', *in* L. Prados Torreira & C. López Ruiz (eds.), *Museos arqueológicos y género. Educando en igualdad*, Madrid, UAM Ediciones, 2017, 23–49.

Prados Torreira & López Ruiz 2017: L. Prados Torreira & C. López Ruiz, 'Otro museo es possible: museos arqueológicos, museos integradores. Un largo camino por recorrer', *in* L. Prados Torreira & C. López Ruiz (eds.), *Museos arqueológicos y género. Educando en igualdad*, UAM Ediciones, 2017, 11–21.

Price 2017: M. Price, 'DNA Proves Fearsome Viking Warrior Was a Woman', *in Science*, 8 septembre 2017, [https://www.science.org/content/article/dna-proves-fearsome-viking-warrior-was-woman].

Price *et al.* 2019: N. Price, C. Hedenstierna-Jonson, T. Zachrisson, A. Kjellström, J. Storå, M. Krzewińska, T. Günther, V. Sobrado, M. Jakobsson & A. Götherström, 'Viking Warrior Women? Reassessing Birka Chamber Grave Bj 581', *in Antiquity* 93 (367), 181–198.

Procopiou 2019: H. Procopiou, 'Former les futurs archéologues à l'université: quels enjeux ?', *in Les Nouvelles de l'Archéologie* 157–158, 2019, [Accessed 18 December 2021 ; http://journals.openedition.org/nda/7456].

Quave *et al.* 2021: K. E. Quave, S. M. Fie, A. Qing Qing Greiff & D. A. Agnew, 'Centering the Margins. Knowledge Production in the Introductory Archaeology Course', *in Advances in Archaeological Practice* 9/2, 2021, 87–100.

Quellier 2021: F. Quellier, 'Introduction. Clio et les dons de Comus', *in* F. Quellier (dir.), *Histoire de l'alimentation. De la Préhistoire à nos jours*, Belin, 2021, p. 7–9.

Querol 2005: M.A. Querol, ''El origen del hombre' y la identidad femenina: mitos duraderos', *in* M. Sanchez Romero (ed.), *Arqueología y Género*, Universidad de Granada, 441–456.

Querol Fernández 2016: M.A. Querol, 'Mujeres del pasado, mujeres del presente: el mensaje sobre los roles femeninos en los modernos museos arqueológicos', *in Revista ICOM CE Digital*, n°9, Museos, arqueología y género: relatos, recursos y experiencias, p. 44–55.

Querol 2017: M.A. Querol, 'La desigualdad como norma: el papel de los museos arqueológicos en su superación', *in* L. Prados Torreira & C. López Ruiz (eds.), *Museos arqueológicos y género. Educando en igualdad*, UAM Ediciones, 2017, 51–67.

Radde 2018: H. Radde, 'Sexual Harassment Among California Archaeologists: Results of the Gender Equity and Sexual Harassment Survey', *in California Archaeology* 10/2, 2018, 231–255.

Rathbone 2013: S. Rathbone, *The four and a half inch pointing trowel ... and the damage done*, 2013, [online: http://rmchapple.blogspot.com/2013/09/the-four-and-half-inch-pointing-trowel.html].

Rathbone 2017: S. Rathbone, 'Anarchist Literature and the Development of Anarchist Counter-Archaeologies', *in World Archaeology* 47/3, 2017, 291–305.

Rathbun 1987: T.A. Rathbun, 'Health and Disease in a South Carolina Plantation: 1840–1870', *in American Journal of Physical Anthropology* 74, 1987, 239–353.

Rautman 2012: E. Rautman, 'Who Gets Published in American Antiquity ?', *in The SAA Archaeological Record* 12/2, 2012, 25–30.

Raynal 2021: A. Raynal, 'Las Tesis, ces chiliennes qui chantent et dansent contre le viol', *in La Déferlante* 1, 2021, 22–30.

Rebay-Salisbury *et al.* 2022: K. Rebay-Salisbury, P. Bortel, L. Janker, M. Bas, D. Pany-Kucera, R.B. Salisbury, C. Gerner & F. Kanz, 'Gendered burial practices of early Bronze Age children align with peptide-based sex identification: A case study from Franzhausen I, Austria', *in Journal of Archaeological Science* 139, 2022, 105549.

Reyman 1992: J. Reyman (ed.), *Rediscovering Our Past: Essays on the History of American Archaeology*, Aldershot, 1992.

Ribeiro 2017: L. Ribeiro, 'Crítica Feminista, Arqueologia e Descolonialidade: sobre resistir na ciência', *in Revista de Arqueologia* 30/1, 2017, 210–234.

Ribeiro *et al.* 2017: L. Ribeiro, B. S. R. Silva, S. K. S. Schimidt & L. P. Passos, 'No prelo. A Saia Justa da Arqueologia Brasileira: mulheres e feminismos em apuro bibliográfico', *in Estudos Feministas* 25, 2017, 1093–1110.

Rich 1980: A. Rich, 'Compulsory Heterosexuality and Lesbian Existence', *in Signs: Journal of Women in Culture and Society* 5, 1980, 631–660.

Ringrose 2003: K. M. Ringrose, *The Perfect Servant: Eunuchs and the Social Construction of Gender in Byzantium*, University of Chicago Press, 2003.

Rizvi 2008: U. Z. Rizvi, 'Looking Forward, Looking Back: A Special Issue of The SAA Archaeological Record from the Committee on the Status of Women in Archaeology (COSWA)', *in The SAA Archaeological Record* 8/4, 2008, p. 6–7.

Rizvi 2019: U. Z. Rizvi, 'Archaeological Encounters: The Role of the Speculative in Decolonial Archaeology', *in Journal of Contemporary Archaeology* 6/1, 2019, 154–167.

Rochefort 2018: F. Rochefort, *Histoire mondiale des féminismes*, Que sais-je, 2018.

Rocks-Macqueen 2014: D. Rocks-Macqueen, *Professional Archaeology- Disability Friendly ?*, 2014, [online: https://dougsarchaeology.wordpress.com/2014/08/11/professional-archaeology-disability-friendly/].

Rossiter 2003: M. W. Rossiter, 'L'effet Matthieu Mathilda en sciences', *in Les cahiers du CEDREF* 11, 2003, 21–39 [URL: http://journals.openedition.org/cedref/503] = Rossiter 1993: 'The Matthew Mathilda Effect in Science', *in Social Studies of Science* 23, 1993, 325–341.

Rostain 2011: S. Rostain, 'Amazonie: une archéologie en attente de décolonisation', *in Les Nouvelles de l'Archéologie* 126, 2011, 41–45.

Roubineau 2015: J.-M. Roubineau, *Les cités grecques, VIe-IIe siècles av. J.-C. Essai d'histoire sociale*, PUF, 2015.

Rovira Hortalà 2017: M.C. Rovira Hortalà, 'El universo femenino en la museografía del Museu d'Arqueologia de Catalunya', *in* L. Prados Torreira & C. López Ruiz (eds.), *Museos arqueológicos y género. Educando en igualdad*, UAM Ediciones, 2017, 187–199.

Rubin 1998 (1975): G. Rubin, 'L'économie politique du sexe: transactions sur les femmes et systems de sexe/genre', translated by N.-C. Mathieu, *Cahiers du CEDREF* 7, 1998 = G. Rubin, The Traffic in Women: Notes on the "Political Economy" of Sex, *in* R. R. Reiter (ed.), *Toward an Anthropology of Women*, Monthly Review Press, 1975, 157–210.

Rutecki & Blackmore 2016: D. M. Rutecki & C. Blackmore, 'Towards an Inclusive Queer Archaeology. An Overview and an Introduction', *in Special issue of The SAA Archaeological Record* 16/1, 2016, 9–11.

Sabetai 2009: V. Sabetai, 'The Poetics of Maidenhood: Visual Constructs of Womanhood in Vase-Painting', *in* S. Schmidt & J.H. Oakley (eds.), *Hermeneutik der Bilder. Beiträge zur Ikonographie und Interpretation griechischer Vasenmalerei*, C.H. Beck, 2009, 103–114.

Salas-Medellín 2021: R. Salas-Medellín, A. Jaramillo González, D. Mendoza León, Y. Ramírez Corredor, M.

E. Orejuela Mesa, D. P. Castro Montes, A. Gutiérrez Lara & M. Bran Pérez, 'Hilando en colectivo hacia una arqueología de género y feminista en Colombia: Colectivo GEFA (género, feminismo y arqueología)', *in Anales De Arqueología Y Etnología* 76/2, 2021, 97–123 [online: https://doi.org/10.48162/rev.46.004].

Sanahuja & Picazo 1989: M. E. Sanahuja & M. Picazo, 'Los estudios de las mujeres a lo largo de la Prehistoria y en la Antigüedad griega: estado de la cuestión', *in Arqueocrítica* 1, 1989, 32–37.

Sánchez Romero 2016: M. Sánchez Romero, 'El patrimonio prehistórico y la construcción de discursos igualitarios sobre nuestro pasado', *in Revista ICOM CE Digital*, n°9, Museos, arqueología y género: relatos, recursos y experiencias, 28–35.

Sand 2017: Ch. Sand, 'Des musées archéologiques en Océanie ?', *in Les Nouvelles de l'Archéologie* 147, 2017, 8–13.

Sand 2020: Ch. Sand, 'La question du "premier occupant" en Nouvelle-Calédonie (Mélanésie du sud): écrits archéologiques dans un contexte colonial et de décolonisation', *in* É. Dotte-Sarout, A. Di Piazza, F. Valentin & M. Spriggs (eds.), *Pour une histoire de la préhistoire océanienne. Approches historiographiques de l'archéologie francophone dans le Pacifique*, pacific-credo Publications, 2020, 269–298.

Sand *et al.* 2011: Ch. Sand, J. Bole & A.-J. Ouetcho, 'Évolutions du discours archéologique sur 150 ans d'histoire coloniale et postcoloniale en Nouvelle-Calédonie', *in Les Nouvelles de l'Archéologie* 126, 2011, 37–40.

Santana 2019: L. Q. Santana, 'Entre techos de cristal y nichos académicos: estado actual de las mujeres en la arqueología peruana', *in Desde el Sur* 11/2, 2019, 261–281.

Sanz 2017: N. Sanz, 'Museos, género y Cooperación Internacional', *in* L. Prados Torreira & C. López Ruiz (eds.), *Museos arqueológicos y género. Educando en igualdad*, UAM Ediciones, 2017, 105–129.

Saripanidi 2020: V. Saripanidi, 'Genre, statut social et pouvoir dans la Macédoine archaïque', *in* I. Algrain (ed.), *Archéologie du genre. Construction sociale des identités et culture matérielle*, Université des femmes, 2020, 73–109.

Sarlet & Dardenne 2012: M. Sarlet & B. Dardenne, 'Le sexisme bienveillant comme processus de maintien des inégalités sociales entre les genres', *in L'année psychologique* 112, 2012, 435–463.

Sassaman 1992: K. Sassaman, 'Lithic Technology and the Hunter-Gatherer Sexual Division of Labor', *in North American Archaeologist* 13, 1992, 249–262.

Schiebinger 1986: L. Schiebinger, 'Skeletons in the Closet: The First Illustrations of the Female Skeleton in Eighteenth-Century Anatomy', dans *Representations*, n°14, The Making of the Modern Body: Sexuality and Society in the Nineteenth Century, 1986, p. 42–82.

Schmidt & Voss 2000: R.A. Schmidt & B.L. Voss (eds.), *Archaeologies of Sexuality*, Routledge, 2000.

Schmitt Pantel 2009: P. Schmitt Pantel, *Aithra et Pandora. Femmes, genre et cité dans la Grèce classique*, L'Harmattan (coll. 'Bibliothèque du féminisme'), 2009.

Schumann 2019: R. Schumann, 'Overcoming the Silence: Race, Archaeology, and Memory', *in Journal of African Diaspora Archaeology and Heritage* 8/3, 2019, 252–272.

Schwarzer 2010: M. Schwarzer, 'Women in the Temple: Gender and Leadership in Museums', *in* A.K. Levin (ed.), *Gender, Sexuality and Museums. A Routledge Reader*, Routledge, 2010, 16–27.

Scott 1997: E. Scott, 'Introduction: on the incompleteness of archaeological narratives', *in* J. Moore & E. Scott (eds.), *Invisible People and Processes: Writing Gender and Childhood into European Archaeology*, Leicester University Press, 1997, 1–12.

Scott 1986: J.W. Scott, 'Gender: a Useful Category of Historical Analysis', *in American Historical Review* 91/5, 1986, 1053–1075 = 'Le genre: une catégorie utile de l'analyse historique', French translation by E. Varikas, *in Les Cahiers du Grif* 37–38, 1988, 125–155.

Scott 2010: J.W. Scott, 'Fantasmes du millénaire: le futur du "genre" au XXIe siècle', *in Clio. Histoire, femmes et sociétés* 32, 2010/2, 89–117.

Sebillote-Cuchet 2022: V. Sebillote-Cuchet, *Artémise. Une femme capitaine de vaisseaux en Grèce antique*, Fayard, 2022.

Sellberg 2015: K. Sellberg, 'Queer (Mis)Representations of Early Modern Sexual Monsters', *in* K. Fisher & R. Langlands (eds.), *Sex, Knowledge, and Receptions of the Past*, Oxford University Press, 243–264.

Sesma 2016: E. Sesma, 'Creating Mindful Heritage Narratives: Black Women in Slavery and Freedom', *in Journal of African Diaspora Archaeology and Heritage* 5, 2016, 38–61.

Shakespeare 1999: T. Shakespeare, 'Commentary: Observations on Disability and Archaeology', in *Archaeological Review from Cambridge* 15/2, 1999, 99–101.

Shanks 1992: M. Shanks, *Experiencing the Past: On the Character of Archaeology*, Routledge, 1992.

Shapiro 2003: H.A. Shapiro, 'Brief Encounters: Women and Men at the Fountain House', *in* B. Schmaltz & M. Söldner (eds.), *Griechische Keramik im kulturellen Kontext. Akten des Internationalen Vasen-Symposions in Kiel vom 24.-28.9.2001 veranstaltet durch das Archäologische Institut der Christian-Albrechts-Universität zu Kiel*, Scriptorum, 2003, 96–98.

Sheperd 2003: N. Sheperd, 'When the Hand That Hold the Trowel Is Black…', *in Journal of Social Archaeology* 3/3, 2003, 334–352.

Sheppard 2013: K. Sheppard, *The Life of Margaret Alice Murray: A Woman's Work in Archaeology,* Lexington Books, 2013.

Siapkas 2014: J. Siapkas, 'Ancient Ethnicity and Modern Identity', *in* J. McInerney (ed.), *A Companion to Ethnicity in the Ancient Mediterranean*, Berkeley, 2014, 66–81.

Sinopoli 2006: C. Sinopoli, 'Gender and Archaeology in South and Southwest Asia', *in* S. M. Nelson (ed.), *Handbook of Gender in Archaeology*, Altamira Press, 2006, 667–690.

Skogstrand 2010: L. Skogstrand, 'Is Androcentric Archaeology Really About Men?', *in Archaeologies* 7, 2010, 56–74.

Skogstrand 2016: L. Skogstrand, *Warriors and other Men: Notions of Masculinity from the Late Bronze Age to the Early Iron Age in Scandinavia*, Archaeopress Archaeology, 2016.

Skogstrand 2017: L. Skogstrand, 'The Role of Violence in the Construction of Prehistoric Masculinities', *in* U. Matić & B. Jensen (eds.), *Archaeologies of Gender and Violence*, Routledge, 2017, 77–102.

Slocum 1975: S. Slocum, 'Woman the Gatherer: Male Bias in Anthropology', *in* R. R. Reiter (ed.), *Toward an Anthropology of Women*. Monthly Review Press, 1975, 36–50.

Smith & Du Cros 1994: L. Smith & H. Du Cros, 'Equity and Gender in Australian Archeology: A Survey of the "Women in Archaeology" Conference, 1991', *in* M. Nelson, S. Nelson & A. Wylie (eds.), *Equity Issues for Women in Archaeology*, American Anthropological Association, 1994, 115–120.

Smith 2000: P. J. Smith, 'Dorothy Garrod as the First Woman Professor at Cambridge University', *in Antiquity* 74 (283), 2000, 131–136.

Smith *et al.* 2019: C. Smith, H. Burke & J. Ralph, 'Pursuing Social Justice Through Collaborative Archaeologies in Aboriginal Australia', *in Archaeologies: Journal of the World Archaeological Congress*, 2019, 536–569.

Smith & Burke 2006: C. Smith & H. Burke, 'Glass Ceilings, Glass Parasols and Australian Academic Archaeology', *in Australian Archaeology* 62/1, 2006, 13–25.

Smith & Jackson 2006: C. Smith & G. Jackson, 'Decolonizing Indigenous Archaeology: Developments from down Under', *in American Indian Quarterly* 30, 3/4, 2006, 311–349.

Smith & O'Donnell 2006: C. Smith & E. O'Donnell, 'Gender and the Disciplinary Culture of Australian Archaeology', *in* S. M. Nelson (ed.), *Handbook of Gender in Archaeology*, Altamira Press, 2006, 691–732.

Sneed 2021: D. Sneed, 'Disability and Infanticide in Ancient Greece', *in Hesperia* 90/4, 2021, 747–772.

Snow 2013: D.R. Snow, 'Sexual Dimorphism in European Upper Paleolithic Cave Art', *in American Antiquity* 78/4, 2013, 746–761.

Sofaer Derevenski 2000: J. Sofaer Derevenski, 'Material Culture Schock. Confronting Expectations in the Material Culture of Children', *in* J. Sofaer Derevenski (ed.), *Children and Material Culture*, Routledge, 2000, 3–16.

Sofaer 2006: J. Sofaer, *The Body as Material Culture. A Theoretical Osteoarchaeology*, Cambridge University Press (coll. 'Topics in Contemporary Archaeology'), 2006.

Sohn 2018: E. Sohn, 'A Guide to Juggling Fieldwork and Pregnancy', *in Nature* 554, 2018, 393–395.

Solnit 2012: R. Solnit, 'Men Still Explain Things to Me', *in The Nation*, 20 August 2012, [online: https://www.thenation.com/article/archive/men-still-explain-things-me/].

Sontag 1972: S. Sontag, 'The Double Standard of Aging', *in The Saturday Review*, 23 September 1972, 285–294.

Sørensen 1997: M. L. S. Sørensen, 'Reading Dress: The Construction of Social Categories and Identities in Bronze Age Europe', *in Journal of European Archaeology* 5/1, 1997, 93–114.

Sørensen 1998: M. L. S. Sørensen, 'Rescue and Recovery: On Historiographies of Female Archaeologists', *in* M. Díaz-Andreu & M. L. S. Sørensen (eds.), *Excavating Women. An History of Women in European Archaeology*, Routledge, 1998, 47–76.

Sørensen 2000: M.L.S. Sørensen, *Gender Archaeology*, Polity Press, 2000.

Sørensen 2013: M. L. S. Sørensen, 'The History of Gender Archaeology in Northern Europe', *in* D. Bolger, *A Companion to Gender Prehistory*, Wiley-Blackwell, 2013, 396–412.

Sourvinou-Inwood 1995: C. Sourvinou-Inwood, 'Male and Female, Public and Private, Ancient and Modern', *in* E. Reeder, *Pandora. Women in Classical Greece*, Walters Art Gallery, 1995, 111–120.

Spector 1983: J. Spector, 'Male/Female Task Differentiation among the Hidatsa: Toward the Development of an Archaeological Approach to the Study of Gender', *in* P. Albers & B. Medicine (eds.), *The Hidden Half*, University Press of America, 1983, 77–99.

Spector 1993: J. Spector, *What This Awl Means: Feminist Archaeology at a Wahpeton Dakota Village*, Minnesota Historical Society Press, 1993.

Spector 1998: J. Spector, 'What This Awl Means: Feminist Archaeology at a Wahpeton Dakota Village', *in* K. Hays-Gilpin, & D. S. Whitley, *Reader in Gender Archaeology*, Routledge, 1998, 359–364.

Spivak 2020 (1988): G.C. Spivak, *Les subalternes peuvent-elles parler ?*, translated by J. Vidal, Éditions Amsterdam, 2020 = G.C. Spivak, 'Can the Subaltern Speak', *in* C. Nelson & L. Grossberg (eds.), *Marxism and the Interpretation of Culture*, Macmillan Education, 1988, 271–313.

Spongberg *et al.* 2005: M. Spongberg, A. Curthoys & B. Caine, *Companion to Women's Historical Writing*, Palgrave MacMillan, 2005.

Spriggs 1984: M. Spriggs (ed.), *Marxist Perspectives in Archaeology*, Cambridge University Press, 1984.

Springate 2014: M. Springate, *Queer Forum: Queer Scholarship and Queer Experience*, annual meeting of the Society of Historical Archaeology, Québec, 2014.

Springate 2020: M. E. Springate, 'Intersectionality, Queer Archaeology, and Sexual Effects: Recent Advances in the Archaeology of Sexualities', *in* Ch. E. Oser, A. Zarankin, P. Funari, S. Lawrence et J. Symonds, *The Routledge Handbook of Global Historical Archaeology*, Routledge, 2020, 95–116.

Stark 1991: M. Stark, 'A Perspective on Women's Status in American Archaeology', *in* D. Walde & N.D. Willows (eds.), *The Archaeology of Gender. Proceedings of the Twenty-Second Annual Conference of the Archaeological Association of the University of Calgary*, University of Calgary Archaeological Association, 1991, 187–194.

Steeves 2015: P. Steeves, 'Academia, Archaeology, CRM, and Tribal Historic Preservation', *in Archaeologies: Journal of the World Archaeological Congress*, 2015, 121–141.

Stolpe 1889: H. Stolpe, 'Ett och annat på Björkö', *in Ny Illustrerad Tidning* 25, 1889, 4–16.

Stepan 1986: N. L. Stepan, 'Race and Gender: The Role of Analogy in Science', *in Isis* 77/2, 1986, 261–277.

Stephen 2002: L. Stephen, 'Sexualities and Gender in Zapotec Oaxaca', *in Latin American Perspectives* 29/2, 2002, 41–59.

Sterling 2015: K. Sterling, 'Black Feminist Theory in Prehistory', *in Archaeologies: Journal of the World Archaeological Congress*, 2015, 93–120.

Stewart 1977: J. C. Stewart, *Agencies and Archaeologists: Professional Women in Public Archaeology*, Society for American Archaeology, 1977.

Stocking 2015: G.W. Stocking, On the limits of presentism and historicism in the historiography of behavorial sciences, *in Journal of the History of Behavorial Sciences* 1/3, 1965, 211–218.

Ströbeck 2016: L. Ströbeck, 'Gender and Sexuality', *in* J. Lydon & U. Z. Rizvi, *Handbook of Postcolonial Archaeology*, Routledge, 2016, 327–350.

Tabet 1979: P. Tabet, 'Les mains, les outils, les armes', dans *L'Homme. Revue française d'anthropologie* 19, n°3–4, Dossier: Les catégories de sexe en anthropologie sociale, 1979, 5–61.

Tabet 2001: P. Tabet, 'La grande arnaque. L'expropriation de la sexualité des femmes', *in Actuel Marx* 30/2, 2001, 131–152.

Tavera 2019: C. M. Tavera, 'Una mirada feminista a la comunidad arqueológica peruana', *in Desde el Sur* 11/2, 2019, 239–260.

Tavera & Santana 2021: C. M. Tavera & L. Q. Santana, 'Desigualdades impresas: un primer paso para el estudio de la historia de las mujeres en la arqueología peruana', *in Chungará (Arica)* 53/1, 2021 [online: http://dx.doi.org/10.4067/S0717–73562021005000301].

Tavera & Santana 2022: C. M. Tavera & L. Q. Santana, *Mujeres del Pasado y del Presente. Una visión desde la arquelogía peruana*, Instituto Peruano de Estudios Arquelógicos, 2022.

Taylor 1998: T. Taylor, *The Prehistory of Sex: Four Million Years of Human Sexual Culture*, Random House, 1998.

Testart 1986: A. Testart, *Essai sur les fondements de la division sexuelle du travail chez les chasseurs-cueilleurs*, EHESS (coll. 'Cahiers de l'Homme'), 1986.

Thålin-Bergman 1975: L. Thålin-Bergman (ed.), *O forna tiders kvinnor*, Stockholm, Statens historiska museum, 1975.

Thébaud 2004: F. Thébaud, 'Le genre aux États-Unis', *in* C. Bard, C. Baudelot & J. Mossuz-Lavau (eds.), *Quand les femmes s'en mêlent. Genre et pouvoir*, Éditions de La Martinière, 2004, 44–63.

Thébaud 2007 (1998): F. Thébaud, *Écrire l'histoire des femmes et du genre*, 2nd edition, ENS éditions, 2007 (1998).

Thomas 2022: A. Thomas, 'Faire parler les morts: comportements des hommes et des femmes néolithiques', *in* A. Augereau & C. Darmangeat (eds.), *Aux origines du genre. Enjeux, méthodes et controverses*, PUF, 2022, 77–86.

Thompson 2022: E.L. Thompson, 'The MFA's complicated history with censoring queer desire pervades new exhibit', *GBH News*, 4 January 2022 [Accessed 16 June 2022, https://www.wgbh.org/news/commentary/2022/01/04/the-mfas-complicated-history-with-censoring-queer-desire-pervades-new-exhibit].

Tillier 2021: A. Tillier, 'Male gaze et Antiquité: Hélène de Troie au cinéma et à la télévision', *in* F. Bièvre-Perrin (ed.), *Antiquipop*, 20 December 2021 [online: https://antiquipop.hypotheses.org/10214].

Tjahjadi 2020: J. Tjahjadi, 'Beyond Adam and Eve. Supra-binary and Non-binary Representations and Bodies in the Mediterranean Neolithic Period', *in Young Anthropology–Undergraduate Student Journal of Anthropology* 2, 2020, 22–28.

Torres & Moncayo 2018: K. Torres & E. Moncayo, 'Imaginarios, oportunidades y desigualdad de género: de la academia a la práctica arqueológica', *in* M. Cordero (ed.), *De Arqueología Hablamos las Mujeres: Perspectiva Sobre el Pasado Ecuatoriano*, Ediciones Uleam, 2018, 163–173.

Torres-Rouff 2002: C. Torres-Rouff, 'Cranial Vault Modification and Ethnicity in Middle Horizon San Pedro de Atacama, Chile', *in Current Anthropology* 43/1, 2002, p. 163–171.

Touraille 2008: P. Touraille, *Hommes grands, femmes petites. Une évolution coûteuse. Les régimes de genre comme force sélective de l'adaptation biologique*, Éditions de la MSH, 2008.

Treherne 1995: P. Treherne, 'The warrior's beauty: the masculine body and self-identity in Bronze-Age Europe', *in Journal of European Archaeology* 3/1, 1995,105–144.

Trémeaud 2015a: C. Trémeaud, 'La richesse des femmes ou comment l'archéologie vient au genre', *in Les Nouvelles de l'Archéologie* 140, 2015a, 35–41.

Trémeaud 2015b: C. Trémeaud, 'Les données funéraires au prisme du genre dans le monde nord-alpin', *in* M. Nordez, L. Rousseau & M. Cervel, *Recherches sur l'âge du Bronze, Nouvelles approches et perspectives*, *Bulletin de l'APRAB*, suppl. n°1, Nantes, 2015b, 43–55.

Trémeaud 2015c: C. Trémeaud (ed.), *Les Nouvelles de l'Archéologie, Genre et archéologie*, 140, 2015c.

Trémeaud 2017: C. Trémeaud, 'Great Women ? The Emergence of Female in Elite's Graves in the Celtic World (Late Bronze Age – La Tène B)', *in* K. Winger & C. Keller (eds.), *Big Men or Women? Neue interdisziplinäre Ansätze der Frauenforschung für die Eisenzeits*, Universitätsforschungen zur Prähistorischen Archäologie, 2017, 41–56.

Trémeaud 2018: C. Trémeaud, *Genre et hiérarchisation dans le monde nord-alpin, aux âges du Bronze et du Fer*, BAR Publishing, 2018 (BAR International Series 2912).

Trémeaud 2019: C. Trémeaud, 'Tracing gender in Funerary Data: The Case Study of Elite Graves in the North-Alpine Complex (Late Bronze Age to La Tène B)', *in* J. K. Koch & W. Kirle (eds.), *Gender Transformations in Prehistoric and Archaic Societies*, Sidestone Press, 2019, 275–294.

Trémeaud 2020: C. Trémeaud, 'Enquête sur la précarité en archéologie préventive', *in Les Nouvelles de l'Archéologie* 159, 2020, [online: http://journals.openedition.org/nda/9786].

Trémeaud 2021: C. Trémeaud (ed.), *Les Nouvelles de l'Archéologie. Genre et mobilités en archéologie* 163, 2021.

Trigger 1989: B. Trigger, *A History of Archaeological Thought*, University of Cambridge Press, 1989.

Tuaillon 2019: V. Tuaillon, *Les couilles sur la table*, Binge Audio éditions, 2019.

Tufféry 2019: C. Tufféry, 'L'éthique du care en archéologie préventive: un retour d'expérience et quelques pistes de réflexion', *in Canadian Journal of Bioethics /Revue canadienne de bioéthique* 2/3, 2019, 128–137.

Turnbull 2012: S. Turnbull, *Samurai Women 1184–1877*, Bloomsbury Publishing, 2012.

Turner & Anderson 2003: G. Turner & T. Anderson, 'Marked Occupational Dental Abrasion from Medieval Kent', *in International Journal of Osteoarchaeology* 13, 2003, 168–172.

Tushingham *et al.* 2017: S. Tushingham, T. Fulkerson & K. Hill, 'The Peer Review Gap: A Longitudinal Case Study of Gendered Publishing and Occupational Patterns in a Female-Rich Discipline, Western North America (1974–2016)', *in PLoS ONE* 12/11, 2017, [online, https://doi.org/10.1371/journal.pone.0188403].

Tyburczy 2016: J. Tyburczy, *Sex Museums. The Politics and Performance of Display*, University of Chicago Press, 2016.

Ucko 1987: P. Ucko, *Academic Freedom and Apartheid: The Story of the World Archaeological Congress*, Duckworth, 1987.

Ulm *et al.* 2013: S. Ulm, G. Mate, C. Dalley & S. Nichols, 'A Working Profile: The Changing Face of Professional Archaeology in Australia', *in Australian Archaeology* 76, 2013, 34–43.

Van der Vaart-Verschoof 2019: S. van der Vaart-Verschoof, '#Metoo – a woman in academia & archeology ', 2019, [online: http://vandervaart-verschoof.com/metoo-a-woman-in-academia-archeology/].

VanDerwarker *et al.* 2018: A. M. VanDerwarker, K. M. Brown, T. Gonzalez & H. Radde, 'The UCSB Gender Equity Project: Taking Stock of Mentorship, Equity, and Harassment in California Archaeology Through Qualitative Survey Data', *in California Archaeology* 10/2, 2018, 131–158.

Vandevelde 2020: S. Vandevelde, 'Combattre les discriminations: résistance ou résilience ? Retour sur l'exposition Archéo-Sexisme et la charte Chantier-Éthique', *in Société Canadienne d'Anthropologie/ Canadian Anthropology Society* 14/2, 2020, [online: https://cascacultureblog.wordpress.com/2020/10/14/combattre-les-discriminations-resistance-ou-resilience-retour-sur-lexposition-archeo-sexisme-et-la-charte-chantier-ethique/].

Van Wees 1998: H. van Wees, 'A Brief History of Tears: Gender Differentiation in Archaic Greece', *in* L. Foxhall & J. Salmon (eds.), *When Men Were Men. Masculinity, Power and Identity in Classical Antiquity*, Routledge, 1998, 10–53.

Vergès 2017: F. Vergès, *Le Ventre des femmes. Capitalisme, racialisation, féminisme*, Albin Michel (coll. 'Bibliothèque Idées'), 2017.

Vermeule 1969: E. Vermeule, 'Some Erotica in Boston', *Antike Kunst*, 1969, 9–15.

Victor & Beaudry 1992: K. L. Victor & M. C. Beaudry, 'Women's Participation in American Prehistoric and Historical Archaeology: A Comparative Look at the Journals American Antiquity and Historical Archaeology', *in* Ch. Claassen (ed.), *Exploring Gender through Archaeology: Selected Papers from the 1991 Boone Conference*, Prehistory Press, U.S., 1992, 11–21.

Viennot 2014: É. Viennot, *Non le masculin ne l'emporte pas sur le féminin ! Petite histoire des résistances de la langue française*, Éditions iXe, 2014.

Villotte *et al.* 2010: S. Villotte, S. Churchill, O. Dutour & D. Henry-Gambier, 'Subsistence Activities and the Sexual Division of Labor in the European Upper Paleolithic and Mesolithic: Evidence from Upper Limb Enthesopathies', *in Journal of Human Evolution* 59/1, 2010, 35–43.

Vlachou 2012: V. Vlachou, 'Death and Burial in the Greek World. IV. Greek funerary rituals in their archaeological context', *in* A. Hermary & B. Jaeger (eds.), *ThesCRA VIII*, The J. Paul Getty Museum, 363–384.

Vlachou 2020: V. Vlachou, 'Les femmes et l'offrande d'étoffes dans les sanctuaires grecs. Une enquête sur la participation des femmes à la vie religieuse des cités archaïques et classiques', *in* I. Algrain (ed.), *Archéologie du genre. Construction sociale des identités et culture matérielle*, Université des femmes, 2020, 111–143.

Voss 2000a: B. L. Voss, 'Feminisms, Queer Theories, and the Archaeological Study of Past Sexualities', *in World Archaeology* 32/2, 2000, 180–192.

Voss 2000b: B. L. Voss, 'Colonial Sex: Archaeology, Structured Space, and Sexuality in Alta California's Spanish-colonial Missions', *in* R.A. Schmidt, B.L. Voss (eds.), *Archaeologies of Sexuality*, Routledge, 2000, 35–61.

Voss 2008: B. L. Voss, 'Sexuality Studies in Archaeology', *in Annual Review of Anthropology* 37, 2008, p. 317–336.

Voss 2021a: B. L. Voss, 'Disrupting Cultures of Harassment in Archaeology: Social-Environmental and Trauma-Informed Approaches to Disciplinary Transformation', *in American Antiquity* 86/3, 447–464, [online: https://doi.org/10.1017/aaq.2021.19].

Voss 2021b: B. L. Voss, 'Documenting Cultures of Harassment in Archaeology: A Review and Analysis of Quantitative and Qualitative Research Studies', *in American Antiquity* 86/2, 244–260, [online: https://doi.org/10.1017/aaq.2020.118].

Voss & Schmidt 2000: B.L. Voss & R.A. Schmidt, 'Archaeologies of Sexuality: an Introduction', *in* R.A. Schmidt & B.L. Voss (eds.), *Archaeologies of Sexuality*, Routledge, 2000, 1–32.

Wadley 1997: L. Wadley, *Our Gendered Past*, Witwatersrand University Press, 1997.

Walde & Willows 1991: D. Walde & N. D. Willows (eds.), *The Archaeology of Gender. Proceedings of the Twenty-Second Annual Conference of the Archaeological Association of the University of Calgary*, University of Calgary Archaeological Association, 1991.

Wallace 1995: S. Wallace, *Recognising Change in Systems of Prehistoric Ceramic Produc-tion: A Statistical Approach to Identifying Standardisation in Ceramic Attributes, Applied at Kissonerga-Mosphilia, Cyprus*, Undergraduate dissertation, University of Edinburgh, UK, 1995.

Walley 2018: M. Walley, 'Exploring Potential Archaeological Expressions of Nonbinary Gender in Pre-Contact Inuit Contexts', *in Études Inuit Studies* 42/1–2, 2018, 269–289.

Walley 2020: M. Walley, *Incorporating Nonbinary Gender into Inuit Archaeology. Oral Testimony and Material Inroads*, Routledge, 2020.

Walrath 2017: D. Walrath, 'Bones, Biases, and Birth. Excavating Contemporary Gender Norms from Reproductive Bodies of the Past', *in* S.C. Agarwal & J.K. Wesp (eds.), *Exploring Sex and Gender in Bioarchaeology*, University of New Mexico Press, 2017, 15–49.

Warner 1993: M. Warner, 'Introduction', *in* M. Warner (ed.), *Fear of a Queer Planet. Queer Politics and Social Theory*, The University of Minnesota, 1993, vii-xxxi.

Watkins 2000: J. Watkins, *Indigenous Archaeology: American Indian Values and Scientific Practice*, AltaMira Press, 2000.

Watson & Kennedy 1991: P.J. Watson, M.C. Kennedy, 'The Development of Horticulture in the Eastern Woodlands of North America: Women's Role', *in* J. Gero, M. Conkey (eds.), *Engendering Archaeology: Women and Prehistory*, Blackwell, 1991, 255–275.

Weber 1965: M. Weber, *Essais sur la théorie de la science*, Plon, 1965.

Weedman 2001: K. Weedman, 'Who's "That Girl": British, South African, and American Women as Africanist Archaeologists in Colonial Africa (1860s–1960s)', *in African Archaeological Review* 18/1, 2001, 1–47.

Weglian 2001: E. Weglian, 'Grave Goods Do Not a Gender Make: A Case Study from Singen am Hohentwiel, Germany', *in* B. Arnold & N.L. Wicker (eds.), *Gender and the Archaeology of Death*, Altamira Press, 2001, 137–155.

Weismantel 2013: M. Weismantel, 'Towards a Transgender Archaeology: A Queer Rampage Through Prehistory', *in* S. Stryker & A.Z. Aizura (eds.), *The Transgender Studies Reader* 2, Routledge, 2013, 319–334.

Wengrow & Graeber 2015: D. Wengrow & D. Graeber, 'Farewell to the "Childhood of Man": Ritual, Seasonality, and the Origins of Inequality', *in Journal of the Royal Anthropological Institute* 21/3, 2015, 597–619.

Wengrow & Graeber 2021: D. Wengrow & D. Graeber, *Au commencement était... Une nouvelle histoire de l'humanité*, Éditions Les liens qui libèrent, 2021 = D. Wengrow, D. Graeber, *The Dawn of Everything: A New History of Humanity*, Farrar, Straus and Giroux, 2021.

Wesp 2017: J. K. Wesp, 'Embodying Sex/Gender Systems in Bioarchaeological Research', *in* S.C. Agarwal & J.K. Wesp (eds.), *Exploring Sex and Gender in Bioarchaeology*, University of New Mexico Press, 2017, 99–126.

White 2005: C. D. White, 'Gendered Food Behaviour among the Maya: Time, Place, Status and Ritual', *in Journal of Social Archaeology* 5, 2005, 356–382.

White 2014: B. White, 'Who cares about the Supreme Court Ruling ? Archaeologists aren't allowed to have kids anyway', 2014, [online: http://www.succinctresearch.com/archaeologists-arent-allowed-to-have-kids-anyway/].

White & Draycott 2020: W. A. White & C. Draycott, 'Why the Whiteness of archaeology is a problem', *in Sapiens*, 2020, [https://www. sapiens.org/archaeology/archaeology-diversity/].

Whitehouse 1998: R. Whitehouse, *Gender and Italian Archaeology. Challenging the Stereotypes*, Routledge, 1998.

Whitehouse 2006: R. Whitehouse, 'Gender Archaeology in Europe', *in* S.M. Nelson (ed.), *Handbook of Gender in Archaeology*, Altamira Press, 2006, 733–785.

Whitehouse 2013: R. Whitehouse, 'Margaret Murray (1863–1963): Pioneer Egyptologist, Feminist and First Female Archaeology Lecturer', *in Archaeology International* 16, 2013, 120–127.

Wiels 2006: J. Wiels, 'La différence des sexes, une chimère persistante', *in* C. Vidal (dir.), *Féminin/Masculin. Mythes et idéologies*, Belin, 2006, 76–81.

Wildesen 1980: L. E. Wildesen, 'The Status of Women in Archeology: Results of a Preliminary Survey', *in Anthropology News* 21/5, 1980, 5–8.

Wilkie 2003: L. Wilkie, *The Archaeology of Mothering: An African-American Midwife's Tale*, Routledge, 2003.

Williams 1993: D. Williams, 'Women on Athenian Vases: Problems of Interpretation', *in* A. Cameron & A. Kuhrt (eds.), *Images of Women in Antiquity*, Taylor and Francis, 1993, 92–106.

Wilson 2017: E. Wilson, 'Translator's Note', *in* Homer, *The Odyssey*, translated by Emily Wilson, Norton, 2017, 81–91.

Wilson 2018: Ch. Wilson, 'Indigenous Archaeologies: Australian Perspective', *in* C. Smith (ed.), *Encyclopedia of Global Archaeology*, Springer, 2018, 3786–3793.

Wittig 2018a (1980): M. Wittig, 'La pensée straight', *in* M. Wittig, *La pensée straight*, ouvrage coordonné par Sam Bourcier, Éditions Amsterdam, 2018, 67–77 = M. Wittig, 'La pensée straight', *in Questions Féministes* 7, 1980, 45–53.

Wittig 2018b (1980): M. Wittig, 'On ne naît pas femme', *in* M. Wittig, *La pensée straight*, edited by Sam Bourcier, Éditions Amsterdam, 2018, 53–65.

Wobst 2005: H. M. Wobst, 'Power to the (Indigenous) Past and Present! Or: The Theory and Method Behind Archaeological Theory and Method', *in* C. Smith & H. M. Wobst (eds.), *Indigenous Archaeologies: Decolonizing Theory and Practice*, Routledge, 2005, 17–32.

Wood & Cotton 1999: B. Wood & J. Cotton, 'The Representation of Prehistory in Museums', *in* N. Merriman (ed.), *Making Early Histories in Museums*, Leicester University Press, 1999, 28–43.

Woodall & Perricone 1981: J. N. Woodall & P. J. Perricone, 'The Archaeologist as Cowboy: The Consequences of the Professional Stereotype', *in Journal of Field Archaeology* 8, 1981, 506–508.

Wragg Sykes 2014: B. Wragg Sykes, 'Maternity leaves archaeological-style: blogging and breastfeeding', *in Day of archaeology*, 2014, [online: https://www.dayofarchaeology.com/maternity-leave-archaeological-style-blogging-and-breastfeeding/].

Wright 1991: R.P. Gero, 'Women's Labor and Pottery Production in Prehistory', *in* J. Gero & M. Conkey (eds.), *Engendering Archaeology: Women and Prehistory*, Basil Blackwell, 1991, 194–223.

Wright 2000: R.P. Wright, 'Digging Women', *in The Women's Review of Books* 17/5, 2000, 18–19.

Wright 2002: R.P. Wright, 'COSWA Committee Article: Gender Equity, Sexual Harassment, and Professional Ethics', *in The SAA Archaeological Record* 2/4, 2002, 18–19.

Wright 2008: R.P. Wright, 'Sexual Harassment and Professional Ethics', *in The SAA Archaeological Record* 8/4, 2008, 27–30.

Wylie 1993: A. Wylie, 'Workplace Issues for Women in Archaeology: The Chilly Climate', *in* H. du Cros & L. Smith (eds.), *Women in Archaeology: A Feminist Critique*, Department of Prehistory, Research School of Pacific Studies, Australian National University, 1993, 245–258.

Wylie 1997: A. Wylie, 'The Engendering of Archaeology. Refiguring Feminist Science Studies', *in Osiris* 12, 1997, 80–99.

Wylie 2007: A. Wylie, 'Doing Archaeology as a Feminist: Introduction', *in Journal of Archaeological Method and Theory* 14, 2007, 209–216.

Yates 1993: T. Yates, 'Frameworks for an Archaeology of the Body', *in* C. Tilley (ed.), *Interpretative Archaeology*, Routledge, 1993, 31–72.

Yellen 1991: J. Yellen, 'Women, Archaeology, and the National Science Foundation: An Analysis of Fiscal Year 1989 Data', *in* D. Walde & N. Willows (eds.), *The Archaeology of Gender. Proceedings of the Twenty-Second Annual Conference of the Archaeological Association of the University of Calgary*, University of Calgary Archaeological Association, 1991, 201–210.

Zeder 1997: M. Zeder, *The American Archaeologist: A Profile*, AltaMira, 1997.

Zihlman 1978: A. Zihlman, 'Women in Evolution. Part II', *in Signs* 1, 1978, 4–20.

Zihlman 1983: A.L. Zihlman, 'Woman as Shapers of the Human Adaptation', F. Dahlberg (ed.), *Woman the Gatherer*, Yale University Press, 1983, 75–120.

Zihlman 2013: A. Zihlman, 'Engendering Human Evolution', *in* D. L. Bolger (ed.), *A Companion to Gender Prehistory*, Wiley-Blackwell, 2013, 23–44.

Zorzin 2015a: N. Zorzin, 'Archaeology and Capitalism: Successful Relationship or Economic and Ethical Alienation ?', *in* C. Gnecco & D. Lippert (eds.), *Ethics and Archaeological Praxis*, Springer, 2015, 115–139.

Zorzin 2015b: N. Zorzin, 'Dystopian Archaeologies: the Implementation of the Logic of Capital in Heritage Management', *in International Journal of Historical Archaeology* 19/4, 2015, 791–809.

Online resources

- Associations and collectives

Association Aparea: https://blogs.univ-tlse2.fr/aparea/

Association Archéo-Éthique: https://archeoethique.wixsite.com/association

Association Musé·e·s: https://associationmusees.wordpress.com

CifA - Equality and Diversity Group: https://www.archaeologists.net/equality-and-diversity-group

Enabled Archaeology Foundation: https://enabledarchaeologyfoundation.wordpress.com/

Every Dig Sexism: https://everydigsexism.wordpress.com/

Paye ta Truelle website: https://payetatruelle.wixsite.com/projet

Paye ta Truelle Tumblr: https://payetatruelle.tumblr.com/

Queer Archaeology: https://queerarchaeology.com/

Society of Black Archaeologists: https://www.societyofblackarchaeologists.com/

Sportula: https://thesportula.wordpress.com/

The Black Trowel Collective: https://blacktrowelcollective.wordpress.com/

Virtual Conference for Women Archaeologists and Paleontologists: https://womenpaleoarch.sciencesconf.org/

- Blogs and initiatives

Amelia the Archaeologist, website: www.ameliathearchaeologist.com

Antiquipop: https://antiquipop.hypotheses.org/

Archaeology Podcast Network, episode 33, Enabled Archaeology – Theresa O'Mahony: https://www.archaeologypodcastnetwork.com/anarchaeologist/33

The Black Trowel Collective, 'Foundations for an anarchist archaeology: A community manifesto', Savage Minds, 2016: https://savageminds.org/2016/10/31/foundations-of-an-anarchist-archaeology-a-community-manifesto/

Breaking Ground: Women in Old World Archaeology, https://www.brown.edu/Research/Breaking_Ground/

Blog *Archaeology Sucks: Reports from the Field*: https://archaeologysucks.tumblr.com/post/169701119390/im-a-disabled-student-i-went-into-archaeology

Inclusive Archaeology Project, website: https://inclusivearchaeology.wordpress.com/

Inclusive, Accessible, Archaeology: https://www.archaeologyuk.org/accessible/aboutiaaproject.php

RESPECT - Acting against Harassment in Archaeology: http://www.bajr.org/BAJRGuides/44.%20Harrasment/Sexual-Harassment-in-Archaeology.pdf

Seeing Red. Period and Menstrual Hygiene Equality Guide: https://mentorwomxn.org/wp-content/uploads/sites/4/2020/06/Seeing_Red_Guide_FinalV1.pdf

Interview of Faustine Boulay, founder of ALDHHAA, by Ch. Asselin on Digimind (21 May 2021): https://blog.digimind.com/fr/tendances/fake-news-histoire-art-archeologie

- History of archaeology

I. Algrain & L. Mary, *Les femmes archéologues au tournant du XXe siècle: petites mains ou 'Men-Women'?*, podcast produced for the symposium 'Le genre des célibats', 1st and 2nd October 2021: https://legenredescelibats.wordpress.com/2021/08/30/isabelle-algrain-laura-mary/

La Prof, YouTube video 'Gertrude Bell - Gentes Dames Badass #6', posted on 11 April 2018: https://www.youtube.com/watch?v=Gv6etRwpWMs

Pacific Matildas: Finding the women in the history of Pacific archaeolog project: https://www.uwa.edu.au/projects/pacific-matildas-finding-the-women-in-the-history-of-pacific-archaeology

Z. Rashid & J. Grieve, *Irene Mound: The two very different stories of women excavators*: https://trowelblazers.com/irene-mound/

Trowel Blazers: www.trowelblazers.com

G. Whalen, *The Women of The Irene Mound*, interview of John White: http://www.sip.armstrong.edu/Irene/oral.html

Glossary

Ableism: a system of norms and values that organizes life in society around the figure of the able-bodied person.

Androcentrism: the attitude of seeing the world solely or mainly from the male point of view.

Black Feminism: political and social movement, and also a field of study, that focuses on the multidimensional aspects of the oppression of Black women in the society.

Care: concept referring to the work and emotional labour involved in maintaining relationships and satisfying the needs of others.

Cisgender (adj.): refers to a person whose gender identity (feminine or masculine) corresponds to the sex assigned at birth.

Classism: refers to the discrimination suffered by a person or group of people at the hands of an individual or group of individuals belonging to a more privileged social class.

Colonialism: ideology justifying the political domination and economic exploitation of territories annexed by a state.

Commercial archaeology: or *archéologie préventive* in French. Archaeological survey and excavation carried out as part of the planning process in advance of construction or other land development.

Critical Race Theory: a method that analyses and questions the predominant role played by the law in the construction of racial differences and the perpetuation of racism in the United States.

Essentialism: the view that men and women are inherently different. Their feminine or masculine nature therefore determines not only their appearance, but also their thoughts and behaviour.

Ethnocentrism: the tendency to focus on the norms and values of one's own society when analysing other societies.

Excavations organised by university academics or researchers: or *archéologie programmée* in French. Archaeological excavations organised by professors mostly during the summer. The majority of excavators are students.

Gender fluid: refers to a person whose gender is fluid, oscillating between feminine and masculine.

Glass wall phenomenon: a mechanism favouring exclusion and differentiated opportunities.

Heteronormativity: all the norms that make heterosexuality appear natural and superior to other sexual orientations.

Heteropatriarchy: socio-political system based on the interweaving of patriarchy and heterosexuality. In this system, people who do not respect certain norms (masculine, cisgender, heterosexual) are discriminated against as 'abnormal', 'deviant', 'perverse' or 'dangerous'.

Imperialism: domination by one country over another country or countries. Imperialism is often justified by ethnocentric arguments. For example, 'superior' European countries have a duty to 'civilize' 'savage' and 'inferior' non-European populations.

Intersectionality: a concept defined by Kimberlé Crenshaw in 1989 that refers to the interconnected nature of social categories such as race, gender, age, class and sexuality, and how they interact to shape individual experiences.

Intersexuality: term used to designate a group of people whose sexual characteristics do not correspond to typical, binary male or female norms.

Leaky pipeline: refers to the fact that women become increasingly rare as you move up the hierarchy.

LGBT: or LGBTQIA+ in its full form, refers to lesbian, gay, bisexual, transgender, queer, intersex and asexual people.

Manterrupting: behaviour in which men cut women off during discussions.

Mansplaining: behaviour that consists, for men, in explaining to a woman something she already knows - or is even a recognized specialist in - with a potentially paternalistic or condescending tone.

Masculinism: a social and political movement focused on defending and promoting the rights and interests of men.

Masculinity(/ies): refers to the traits, behaviours and characteristics associated with men and being a man.

Matilda effect: systematic denial or minimization of women's contributions to science.

Matriarchy: a system in which power is exercised predominantly by women.

Neo-colonialism: term used to designate the political and economic control that a former colonial state continues to exercise over its former colonies.

Non-binary gender: refers to a person whose gender identity does not correspond to either feminine or masculine norms.

Patriarchy: a system in which power is exercised predominantly by men.

Queer: the term queer, both a political movement and a personal identification, refers to the deconstruction of dominant norms, notably of gender and sexuality, by minority identities.

Racisation: the process by which a dominant group defines a dominated group as a race.

Racialised (adj.): a racialised person is someone who is the victim of racist discrimination.

Sexage: a synonym for patriarchy in French feminist research.

Transgender (adj.): refers to a person whose gender identity does not correspond to the sex assigned at birth.

Transidentity: refers to the fact that a transgender person identifies with a gender other than that assigned at birth.

Non-exhaustive who's who

Agbe-Davies, Anna: American archaeologist. Her research focuses on colonial plantations in the southeastern United States and the Caribbean, as well as the African diaspora.

Alberti, Benjamin: American archaeologist. His work focuses on masculinities and the application of queer theory in archaeology.

Arwill-Nordbladh, Elisabeth: Professor emeritus at the University of Gothenburg (Sweden). She has worked on the Matilda effect in archaeology.

Atalay, Sonya: American archaeologist. She is a specialist in Indigenous archaeology. Her research focuses on the repatriation of human remains to Native American communities.

Augereau, Anne: French prehistoric archaeologist. She is a specialist in Neolithic gender issues.

Bardolph, Dana: American archaeologist. Her work focuses on raising awareness of gender and sexual violence in archaeology.

Battle-Baptiste, Whitney: American archaeologist and professor of anthropology at the University of Massachusetts. Her research focuses on the links between race, gender, class and sexuality, during slavery and after its abolition. She is the author of 'Black Feminist Archaeology' (2011).

Beaudry, Mary (1950 - 2020): American archaeologist and professor of archaeology at Boston University. Her research interests include gender and colonialism.

Belard, Chloé: French archaeologist. She is a specialist in gender issues in Champagne during the Iron Age, and one of the first two researchers to defend a thesis in gender archaeology in France.

Bell, Gertrude (1868 - 1926): British archaeologist, diplomat and spy. She took part in numerous excavations in Mesopotamia. She is best known for having founded the National Museum of Iraq.

bell hooks (1952 - 2001): bell hooks (not capitalized), or by her real name Gloria Jean Watkins. American feminist researcher and activist. Her research focuses on the interweaving of gender, race and class, and the perpetuation of systems of oppression based on these three categories.

Blackmore, Chelsea: American archaeologist. Her research focuses on the roles played by white supremacy and heteronormativity in archaeological interpretations of ancient Mesoamerican societies.

Bourcier, Sam: sociologist, lecturer at the University of Lille, trans-feminist and queer activist.

Bourdieu, Pierre (1930 - 2002): French sociologist. His extensive bibliography includes La domination masculine (1998), in which he analyses social relations between the sexes and seeks to explain what other researchers call 'patriarchy'.

Boyd Hawkes, Harriet (1871 - 1945): American archaeologist. She is best known for the excavations at Gournia (Crete), which she directed in the early 20th century.

Brumfiel, Elizabeth M. (1945 - 2012): American archaeologist. She was one of the first researchers to examine women's roles among the Aztec people.

Butler, Judith: American philosopher and professor at UC Berkeley. They theorize on the concept of 'gender performativity" and is the author of 'Gender Trouble. Feminism and the Subversion of Identity' (1993), a major work in the field of gender and queer studies.

Carruthers, William: American archaeologist. His research focuses on ethics in archaeology, with a particular emphasis on decolonization issues.

Caton Thompson, Gertrude (1888 - 1985): British archaeologist. She directed numerous excavations, notably in Mesopotamia, Egypt and Zimbabwe. She became the first president of the Prehistoric Society in 1940.

Claassen, Cheryl: American archaeologist. She is the author of an abundant bibliography on women in archaeology. She was the first researcher to focus on the discrimination faced by lesbians in the profession.

Conkey, Margaret: American prehistoric archaeologist. She was one of the first archaeologists to undertake research on gender in archaeology. She co-authored the seminal article 'Archaeology and the Study of Gender' (1984).

Connell, Raewyn: Australian sociologist. She introduced masculinities into the field of gender studies and theorized the concept of 'hegemonic masculinity'.

Crenshaw, Kimberlé: American law professor and Afrofeminist activist. She defines and popularizes the concept of 'intersectionality'.

de Beauvoir, Simone (1908 - 1986): French philosopher. She is the author of an extensive bibliography, including 'Le Deuxième Sexe' (1949), and is a major figure in feminist theory.

Delphy, Christine: French sociologist and feminist activist. She is a leading exponent of materialist feminism. Her research focuses on the gendered division of labour, particularly at home.

Devis, Angela: American philosophy professor and Afrofeminist activist. She is the author of the major work 'Women, Race and Class' (1981).

Dommasnes, Liv Helga: Professor of archaeology at the University of Bergen (Norway). She is one of the first researchers to take an interest in gender issues in archaeology, starting in the 1980s. She is also interested in queer archaeology. She is the author of an extensive bibliography on the impact of feminist thinking on the interpretation of archaeological data and on professionals in the discipline.

Dorlin, Elsa: French philosopher. Her research focuses on the intersection of gender, race and sexuality.

Dowson, Thomas: Archaeologist who trained in South-Africa and works in England. He was the first researcher to tackle the issue of discrimination against homosexual men in archaeology.

Epperson, Terrence: American archaeologist. His research focuses on the application of Critical Race Theory to archaeology and on the African diaspora.

Federici, Sylvia: social sciences professor and feminist activist. Her research focuses on the interweaving of feminism and capitalism.

Flewellen, Ayana Omilade: American archaeologist and activist. She is co-founder of the Society of Black Archaeologists.

Franklin, Maria: archaeologist and professor at the University of Texas. She is the author of the article 'Black feminist-inspired archaeology?' (2001), now considered the founding text of the Black feminist archaeology.

Fraser, Meredith: American archaeologist. In 2006, she defended the first doctoral thesis on the issue of disability within the profession.

Friedan, Betty (1921 - 2006): American journalist and essayist. In 1963, she published 'The Mystified Woman', often regarded as a catalyst for the second wave of American feminism.

Garrod, Dorothy (1892 - 1968): British prehistorian. She was the first woman to hold a professorship at Cambridge University.

Geller, Pamela: American archaeologist. Her research lies at the crossroads of bioarchaeology, gender studies and queer theory.

Gero, Joan (1944 - 2016): American archaeologist. She was one of the first to take an interest in the place of women in the profession. Her article 'Socio-Politics and the Woman at Home Ideology', published in 1985, paved the way for publications on the place of women and minorities within the profession.

Gibson, Rebecca: American archaeologist. Her research focuses on gender issues as applied to bioarchaeology. She is a corset specialist.

Gilchrist, Roberta: Canadian archaeologist who works in the United Kingdom. She specializes in the medieval period. She is the author of the reference work 'Gender and Archaeology: Contesting the Past' (1999).

Gimbutas, Marija (1921 - 1974): Lithuanian-born American prehistorian. Her controversial work The Civilization of the Goddess (1991) popularizes the existence of a matriarchal European society supplanted in the Bronze Age by a patriarchal one.

Guillaumin, Colette (1934 - 2017): French sociologist and feminist activist. She theorized the concept of 'sexage'.

Haraway, Donna: University of California professor emeritus and American feminist activist. Her research focuses on the subjectivity of science and the links between science and different systems of oppression.

Hays-Gilpin, Kelley: American archaeologist. She is a specialist in Native rock art in the Southwestern United States. She also fights for greater equality within the profession.

Heath-Stout, Laura: American archaeologist. Her research focuses on the various manifestations of sexism, racism, heterosexism, classism and validism in archaeology. She is the author of an extensive bibliography on these issues.

Héritier, Françoise (1933 - 2017): French anthropologist and feminist activist. In particular, she theorized the concept of 'valence différentielle des sexes'.

Hodder, Ian: British archaeologist. One of the pioneers of the post-processualist approach to archaeology.

Hollimon, Sandra: American archaeologist. Her research focuses on the non-binarity of sex and gender in archaeology, using the Indigenous populations of North America as a case study.

Laqueur, Thomas: American historian of medicine, sexuality and gender. Author of 'Making sex: body and gender' (1990).

Leighton, Mary: American anthropologist. She developed the concept of 'informal performativity' (2020) to describe the spirit of 'field culture' in archaeology.

Leroi-Gourhan, Arlette (1913 - 2005): French archaeologist. A pioneer of paleopalynology.

Lippert, Dorothy: American archaeologist and member of the Choctaw tribe. She specializes in the repatriation of material remains to Indigenous populations in archaeology.

Lorde, Audre: American essayist, poet and feminist activist. She is committed to the African-American civil rights movement.

Mathieu, Nicole-Claude (1937 - 2014): French anthropologist and feminist activist. She theorized the concept of 'rapports sociaux de sexe' (gender).

Matić, Uroš: archaeologist attached to the Austrian Archaeological Institute. He specializes in questions of violence, ethnicity and gender in ancient Egypt.

Mead, Margaret (1901 - 1978): American anthropologist. Her research focused on the sexual division of labour and sexuality in Oceanic and Southeast Asian cultures.

Montón Subías, Sandra: Spanish archaeologist. She specializes in gender issues and maintenance activities, both in the past and within the archaeological profession.

Moser, Stephanie: Professor of British archaeology. Her research focuses on masculinity and different forms of masculinity within the practice of the profession.

Murray, Margaret (1863 - 1963): British Egyptologist. One of the first female archaeologists to work at University College London, she directed a series of excavations and published numerous books on Egyptology.

Nelson, Sarah M. (1931 - 2020): American archaeologist and professor emeritus at the University of Denver. She is the author of an extensive bibliography on gender issues in archaeology. She is also a specialist in East Asian cultures.

O'Mahony, Theresa (deceased 2019): British archaeologist. She is a specialist in disability in archaeology and herself has a motor disability. Her master's thesis defended in 2014 but not published, 'Archaeology for All? An Examination of Attitudes Towards Disability Within Archaeology' led to a series of conferences in the UK, the publication of an article, the creation of an Enabled Archaeology guide, available for free access on the British Archaeological Jobs Resource website and the formation of the Enabled Archaeology Foundation collective.

Oland, Maxine: American archaeologist. She is the author of the first article to address the difficulties faced by pregnant women in archaeology.

Petrie, Hilda (1871 - 1956): British archaeologist. Wife of William Flinders Petrie, she took part in his excavations in Egypt, produced his drawings and edited his texts, but most of her work went unreported and her husband rarely mentioned her name in his publications.

Ross Ellingson, Mary (1906–1993): Canadian archaeologist. She worked on the Olynthus site in Greece during the 1930s. She was in charge of worker supervision and photography. She was also involved in the study of terracotta figurines, the subject of her master's thesis, which she later developed in her doctoral dissertation. Plagiarized by her thesis supervisor, she disappeared from archaeology after her marriage.

Rossiter, Margaret: American historian of science and professor. She theorizes the 'Matilda effect'.

Rydh, Hanna (1891 - 1964): Swedish prehistorian and feminist activist.

Sánchez Romero, Margarita: Spanish archaeologist. She is director of the University Institute of Women's and Gender Studies at the University of Granada. She is the author of numerous articles on the place of women in Spanish archaeology.

Scott, Joan: American historian. The French translation of her article 'Genre : une catégorie utile de l'analyse historique' popularized the concept of 'gender' within the French research community.

Skogstrand, Lisbeth: Norwegian archaeologist. She specializes in Bronze Age and Iron Age masculinities in Scandinavia.

Spector, Janet D. (1944 - 2011): American archaeologist. She is co-author of the seminal article on gender archaeology in the USA, 'Archaeology and the Study of Gender' (1984). She is also the author of *What This Awl Means: Feminist Archaeology at a Wahpeton Dakota Village* (1993). For 25 years, she was a professor of anthropology at the University of Minnesota, where she helped establish the university's gender studies department.

Sterling, Kathleen: American archaeologist. She was the first to apply Black feminist theory to European prehistory.

Stig Sørensen, Marie-Louise: Danish archaeologist, Emeritus Professor at the University of Cambridge. She is a specialist in the Bronze Age and gender issues in archaeology. She is the author of the reference work 'Gender Archaeology' (2000).

Tabet, Paola: Italian anthropologist. One of the leading figures in materialist feminism.

Touraille, Priscille: French anthropologist. She is a specialist in gender issues and nutrition.

Trémeaud, Caroline: French archaeologist. She is a specialist in gender issues in North Alpine Bronze Age contexts. She was one of the first two researchers in France to defend a thesis in gender archaeology.

Voss, Barbara: American archaeologist. She is a specialist in queer archaeology.

Walley, Meghan: American archaeologist. Her research focuses on oral culture and LGBT+ issues in archaeology, particularly the question of non-binarity in Inuit culture.

Watkins, Joe: American archaeologist. He is one of the most active researchers defending Indigenous rights in archaeology.

Wittig, Monique: French feminist philosopher, theorist and activist. She is a major figure in French and American materialist feminism. She is the author of 'The Straight Mind'.

Wright, Rita P.: American archaeologist and professor emeritus at New York University. She specializes in Indus civilization and gender roles in archaeology.

Wylie, Alison: philosopher of archaeology and feminist activist. She specializes in ethical issues and feminist archaeology.

www.ingramcontent.com/pod-product-compliance
Lightning Source LLC
LaVergne TN
LVHW070539140326
833932LV00064B/2545